M

THE UNQUIET AMERICAN

the UNQUIET AMERICAN

AMERICAN

RICHARD HOLBROOKE IN THE WORLD

DEREK CHOLLET
and
SAMANTHA POWER
Editors

PUBLICAFFAIRS
NEW YORK

Who is the happy Warrior? Who is he
Whom every Man in arms should wish to be?
—It is the generous Spirit, who, when brought
Among the tasks of real life, hath wrought
Upon the plan that pleased his childish thought:
Whose high endeavours are an inward light
That make the path before him always bright:
Who, with a natural instinct to discern
What knowledge can perform, is diligent to learn;
Abides by this resolve, and stops not there,
But makes his moral being his prime care; . . .

Who, not content that former worth stand fast,
Looks forward, persevering to the last,
From well to better, daily self-surpast:
Who, whether praise of him must walk the earth
For ever, and to noble deeds give birth,
Or He must go to dust without his fame,
And leave a dead unprofitable name,
Finds comfort in himself and in his cause;
And, while the mortal mist is gathering, draws
His breath in confidence of Heaven's applause;
This is the happy Warrior; this is He
Whom every Man in arms should wish to be.

—William Wordsworth
from "Character of the Happy Warrior"

Contents

Preface   *xi*
Derek Chollet and Samantha Power

Introduction   1
Kati Marton

ONE The Audacity of Determination   7

  Thinker, Doer, Mentor, Friend   8
  Strobe Talbott

  The Machine That Fails (Winter 1970–1971)   23
  Foreword to *Paris 1919:*
    Six Months That Changed the World (2003)   34
  The Paradox of George F. Kennan (March 21, 2005)   39
  Richard Holbrooke

TWO The Journalist   43

  Reporting Truth to Power   44
  E. Benjamin Skinner
  That Magnificent Hunger   58
  Jonathan Alter

  The Writing on the Wall (July 27, 1961)   62
  Washington Dateline:
    The New Battlelines (Winter 1973–1974)   65
  Jack Frost Nipping at the Years (March 5, 1975)   72
  Richard Holbrooke

THREE Vietnam 75

Richard Holbrooke and the Vietnam War:
  Past and Prologue 76
Gordon M. Goldstein

A Generation Conditioned by the
  Impact of Vietnam (December 20, 1969) 96
A Little Lying Goes a Long Way (September 10, 1971) 99
Pushing Sand (May 3, 1975) 101
Our Second Civil War (August 28, 2004) 106
Why Vietnam Matters (2008) 109
Richard Holbrooke

FOUR Asia in the Carter Years 115

Restoring America's Role in Asia 116
Richard Bernstein

Escaping the Domino Trap (September 7, 1975) 132
Conscience and Catastrophe (July 30, 1984) 146
Much Too Tough to Be Cute (March 3, 1997) 157
The Day the Door to China
  Opened Wide (December 15, 2008) 159
Richard Holbrooke

FIVE Europe in the Clinton Years 163

Holbrooke, a European Power 164
Roger Cohen

America, a European Power (March/April 1995) 176
Hungarian History in the Making
  (December 1999) 190
Berlin's Unquiet Ghosts (September 10, 2001) 194
Richard Holbrooke

SIX Bosnia and Dayton 197

Ending a War 198
Derek Chollet

Bosnia: The "Cleansing" Goes On (August 16, 1992) 209
With Broken Glass (April 25, 1993) 212
Why Are We in Bosnia? (May 18, 1998) 214
Foreword to *The Road to the Dayton Accords* (2006) 225
The Face of Evil (July 23, 2008) 235
Richard Holbrooke

SEVEN The United Nations 239

Holbrooke in Turtle Bay 240
James Traub

The United Nations:
 Flawed But Indispensable (November 2, 1999) 251
Last Best Hope (September 28, 2003) 257
Richard Holbrooke

EIGHT Fighting HIV/AIDS 263

The Global HIV/AIDS Crisis 264
John Tedstrom

AIDS: The Strategy Is Wrong (November 29, 2005) 274
Sorry, But AIDS Testing Is Critical (January 4, 2006)
278
Richard Holbrooke

NINE Afghanistan and Pakistan 281

The Last Mission 282
David Rohde

Rebuilding Nations (April 1, 2002) 296
Afghanistan: The Long Road Ahead (April 2, 2006) 300
Still Wrong in Afghanistan (January 23, 2008) 303
Hope in Pakistan; The Problems Are Real,
 But So Is the Progress (March 21, 2008) 306
Richard Holbrooke

TEN Mentor and Friend 309

All That's Left 310
Samantha Power

A Sense of Drift, a Time for Calm (Summer 1976) 319
The Next President: Mastering a
 Daunting Agenda (September/October 2008) 333
Richard Holbrooke

Notes 355
About the Contributors 359
Index 363

Preface

DEREK CHOLLET AND SAMANTHA POWER

Richard Holbrooke loved history. He had a keen sense of the past and how it helps define contemporary choices. So in the days after he passed away so suddenly in December 2010, and his friends and colleagues tried to make sense of the loss, we shared tales of all the ways in which Holbrooke had shaped history and changed lives. "Holbrooke stories" flew back and forth over email; they populated websites; and they dominated dinner conversations and hallway run-ins. Lacking the ability to talk or write *to* Holbrooke, we consoled ourselves by talking and writing *about* Holbrooke. Some stories portrayed him as a once-in-a-lifetime Great Man of History, some recalled his imperious side, but virtually all offered novel details on his trailblazing diplomacy, showing the large dent he made in the world around him.

This book is an effort to capture Richard Holbrooke's contributions to that world, a world he altered and devoured. Our aim was to produce more than a memorial or celebration of his life; it was to assemble a book that offered fresh insight into the man whose presence is sorely missed and whose contributions are known in silhouette but—with the lone exception of his role in ending the war in Bosnia—in surprisingly sparse detail. The contributors to this book each had a special relationship with Holbrooke. They include journalists who reported on him, friends who worked with him, mentees who were shepherded by him, and even a two-time hostage whose release he tried to negotiate. The contributors delve into the most important phases of his career. They offer colorful portraits of the man and new reporting on events that he rarely discussed.

Holbrooke was someone who elicited strong and diverse opinions, and each essay offers a unique window into his life story.*

The contributors offer perspectives on the history that Holbrooke witnessed, chronicled, participated in, and ultimately shaped. In taking readers on a journey through Holbrooke's life, the book also offers an up-close look at statecraft, journalism, politics, public service, and America's role in the world. Here, we take our cue from Holbrooke himself, who in the opening chapter of his memoir, *To End a War*, quotes the British historian Eric Hobsbawm: "For all of us there is a twilight zone between history and memory; between the past as a generalized record which is open to relatively dispassionate inspection and the past as a remembered part of, or background to, one's own life." Holbrooke was never a dispassionate inspector of anything, and nor, we are pleased to report, are the contributors to this book, as Holbrooke's "own life" is both background to—and window into—some of the most significant events in American and world history of the past fifty years.

This book follows Holbrooke's career chronologically, from his days as a budding journalist at Brown University, to Vietnam, Bosnia, the United Nations, and Afghanistan. We see in every mission what we know motivated him from the very start—as he wrote and underlined six times in his diary as a young man: "PURPOSE."

Every one of these chapters testifies to the tremendous energy he put into pursuing concrete goals, and his achievements speak for themselves: authoring a volume of the Pentagon Papers at the age of twenty-seven; editing *Foreign Policy* magazine; handling the normalization of relations with China; negotiating the Dayton peace for Bosnia; pushing for NATO expansion eastward; creating the American Academy in Berlin; masterminding a historic deal to pay back nearly $1 billion in U.S. arrears to the UN; promoting the global recognition of AIDS as a national security threat, and enlisting more than two hundred companies in the effort to provide antiretroviral treatment to HIV-positive workers; and orchestrating the civilian "surge" in Afghanistan. In all of these missions, he married huge ambition with a gift for improvisation. He wanted to be at the center of things and, from the White House job he

---

* As in any edited volume, each author in this book only speaks for himself or herself. And even though these essays cover nearly a half century of American diplomatic history, the views and opinions expressed here do not necessarily reflect the views of the U.S. government.

Holbrooke and Marton during an eleven-country tour of Africa when he was UN Ambassador. Holbrooke spent a large part of his life on airplanes—and he treated them like an extension of his office. (Courtesy of Kati Marton)

held at age twenty-six to his last mission as President Obama's Special Representative to Afghanistan and Pakistan, he constantly found a way to place himself there.

Notable though his achievements are on their face, his impact comes to seem all the more remarkable when one gets a behind-the-scenes feel in these chapters for the personal risks Holbrooke took, the bureaucratic fights he waged, and the people he crossed, in order to get results. Whether you were or weren't a fan of Richard Holbrooke, you will see in this book two simple truths. First, he made more of an impact in more places and on more issues than almost anybody appreciated and, arguably, more than anyone else. His reach and his range were staggering. And second, nothing about his achievements was foreordained; indeed most of his endeavors started with low odds of success. Without Holbrooke's dreaming, his bullying, his irrepressible activism, and his chronic longing for impact, the history of the last half century could in fact look quite different. As James Traub writes in his essay, for Holbrooke, "If it's worth doing, it's worth overdoing." That "overdoing" of his did not always win him friends, but it indisputably won him results.

Because writing was such a huge part of Holbrooke's life— as columnist, author, ghostwriter, and editor—this book also includes selections from his own pen—a small sample of the hundreds of articles he wrote over his career. In these writings, one hears the same distinct voice that has lodged permanently in our heads from conversation— opinionated, authoritative, unrelenting, and attentive to the small details that grab an audience's attention and offer ballast to the larger argument. As a writer of articles out of government, or as a writer of memos inside government, Holbrooke's purpose was the same: His readers should agree with him and do what he advised so as to make America more secure or some part of the world more peaceful.

EACH OF THE CONTRIBUTORS TO THIS BOOK HAS A DEMANDING DAY JOB, and yet none hesitated even a second when asked to contribute. All threw themselves into the writing task, conducting fresh interviews, poring over old diaries, letters, and primary source material, and regaling us with previously untold tales of Holbrooke in action. On reflection, it was probably hard for any of us to complain about the hazards of multitasking when our assignment was to write about perhaps the world's greatest multitasker—a man whose favorite word was "urgent" and who turned his double-fisted cell phone use into the stuff of legend. Nonetheless, we are enormously thankful to our fellow contributors, whose enthusiasm for Richard Holbrooke made it possible to meet our aims, which were threefold: to produce a book that would satisfy Holbrooke's own high editorial standards; to capture his voice and his ambition such that it read like he was sitting across the dinner table; and to inspire would-be public servants to see the enormous good a single individual can do in a life crammed with activity and driven by purpose.

We must single out a few individuals for special thanks. Strobe Talbott helped us conceptualize this book, which began as an ill-formed idea just days after Holbrooke's death. Ben Skinner was a full partner in this enterprise—mining the archives for Holbrooke's previously published articles, pitching in on editing, engaging with the contributors, and writing a terrific essay of his own. Amanda Urban helped us get the book off the ground, pairing us with PublicAffairs, and Alison Schwartz helped manage the production process with multiple authors. And the incredible team at PublicAffairs, especially Peter Osnos and Clive Priddle, contributed wise counsel and sound judgment (as well as near-infinite patience), taking on more oversight than they likely expected, and sharing our determination to produce a book befitting of its subject. We also thank Peter—who was a friend of Holbrooke's since the early 1970s and worked with him closely on many projects, including Clark Clifford's memoirs—for the inspired idea of including Holbrooke's own writings in the book. Mark Corsey and his fine copyediting team were indispensable in improving our essays and in transcribing Holbrooke's writings, as was Melissa Raymond in ensuring an elegant and bold design.

Finally, and most importantly, we are grateful to our friend, Kati Marton, for her encouragement and her constant willingness to engage on a project that brought the "big guy" back to life on the page. Amid all the pain of the last year, we hope that this book captures some of the same wit, wisdom, and spirit that she and Richard have provided so many for so long. Richard Holbrooke may never have been a quiet man, but he was the first to say that, in love, he was a very lucky one.

*Wedding day in Budapest,
May 28, 1995.
(Courtesy of Kati Marton)*

*With Nelson Mandela and
Kati, during Holbrooke's
December 1999 trip to
Africa as U.S. Ambassador
to the UN. (Courtesy of
Kati Marton)*

Introduction

Kati Marton

This book brings my husband so vividly to life that while reading it I half expected Richard to walk through the front door and call out my name. *The Unquiet American* is the work of a group of writers who either knew Richard intimately or had followed and observed his remarkable career for decades. It is clearly a labor of love, though it is full of sharp observations and critical probing, some of which I find myself wanting to argue with just as Richard would have. In these pages they paint Richard Holbrooke in the full colors of his passions and achievements, his "magnificent hunger," in Jonathan Alter's words, for life and all it had to offer. "Let's go, let's go!" he would pull me toward the front door, even as jet lag from the Kabul flight home told on his face. There was a movie, a play, a game, a friend—life!—waiting outside.

This book is about more than one man's life. I hope it will serve as a very human and rather unorthodox manual for future diplomats, and a source of renewed inspiration for those who might have lost their faith in public service. My husband never lost his early excitement in living a large, public life. He believed ambition was a good thing, as long as it was married to purpose. Yes, he was unquiet—but generally unquiet on behalf of those who otherwise would not have been heard. What a shame it would be if we had a government entirely composed of quiet, careful men and women.

The Unquiet American captures Richard's diplomatic style and his phenomenal energy. It was his special brand of diplomacy that earned him his place in history. For him, diplomacy was engagement, one person at a time, an entirely human enterprise. He was a careful student of the human psyche. He read his interlocutors' motives and vulnerabilities almost immediately.

For all the stories of his explosive personality, many of his most famous eruptions were staged to achieve a defined end. He was all the while paying very close attention to the man across the table, playing to his weaknesses, quickly rewarding his good behavior, attuned to him even as he pounded the table to get his attention.

The history of the Balkan wars and the peace talks that ended them is a personal story for me. The year 1995, when the war became too murderous for the world to ignore any longer, was the year I married Richard Holbrooke. The war shadowed every single day of our first year of marriage. In retrospect, I would not trade a single day of that turbulent year and the chance to observe history from such close range.

Richard did not believe that war—any war—was inevitable. At the opening dinner of the peace talks held in an enormous hangar in Dayton, Ohio's Wright-Patterson Air Force Base, my husband seated me between the two mortal foes, Serbian President Slobodan Milošević and Bosnian President Alija Izetbegović, and instructed me to make them talk to each other. Since Richard believed in using all available tools, he seated Milošević directly under a giant B-2 bomber, a dramatic symbol of American power—a message that was not lost on Milošević. For much of the evening, Milošević and Izetbegović avoided direct conversation with each other. But when, in despair, I asked them how the two of them first met, Milošević finally turned to Izetbegović and said, "Alija, I remember calling on you in your office in Sarajevo. You were seated on a green sofa—Moslem green." Izetbegović nodded and said he remembered the meeting. "You were very brave, Alija." "How did the war start?" I asked them. "Did you know your initial disagreement would lead to this terrible conflict?" "I did not think the fighting would be so serious," Izetbegović answered. Milošević nodded in agreement. It was amazing to hear these two protagonists sound genuinely surprised at the war they had unleashed. When, later that evening, I related this conversation to Richard, he just shook his head, appalled but not surprised.

He was a master tactician. When the talks seemed to have cratered out, he gathered his exhausted team and announced the talks were over. Pack your bags, he instructed them. Bags soon appeared outside the

American negotiators' doors. This was partly theater: a demonstration that Richard Holbrooke meant business. The Americans were leaving. At that point, I spotted Milošević standing outside our barracks in the snow. He said he wanted to speak with Richard. I ran inside to get my husband. Milošević told him he did not want to lose a peace that was within their grasp. The Serb offered to give up extra land to salvage it. Finally, the deal was done. The peace has held. No shot has been fired in anger in Bosnia since November 1995.

This book cites other examples of Richard's diplomatic prowess, including how, as U.S. ambassador to the UN, Richard persuaded right-wing Republicans on Capitol Hill to pay our $925 million back dues to the world body. "If we can't afford to lose," Richard told Jim Traub, "we might as well throw ourselves body and soul into the effort, like a skier in a downhill race just going flat out—you're either going to fall or win." He preferred to win, of course. "No cabinet member in any administration since the dawn of time," his aide Robert Orr recalled, "visited as many congressmen as Richard Holbrooke." In a now-legendary diplomatic stroke, he invited North Carolina's feared and reviled UN critic, Republican Senator Jesse Helms, to address the Security Council. By the end of his visit to New York, following the lavish dinner we hosted in Senator Helms's honor, the right-wing curmudgeon was sporting a UN baseball cap and the United States soon paid its UN dues.

Using the same combination of energy, determination, and a sense that some battles are worth putting all you have on the line, Richard succeeded in getting the Security Council to make AIDS part of its agenda—the first health issue ever to earn that place. His next campaign was to make testing for AIDS widely available. Again he was told to back off, that issues of privacy trumped the danger of the disease's spread. But Richard saw that millions of lives were at risk, which trumped other concerns. He went into high gear. Often, when we traveled in Africa, he would very publicly take an AIDS test, and persuade local leaders to do the same, to set an example and break through the wall of fear and ignorance.

This book gives glimpses of his diplomatic prowess, while also showing his diplomatic setbacks. But above all the book makes clear how much more than a diplomat he was. He was a voracious consumer of new sights and sounds. There was no continent, no culture nor tribe that left him unmoved. He had a magnetic attraction to all things new:

people, art, movies (how he loved the movies!), and countries. When we spoke of life after government service, we talked of travel, but not of the nostalgic kind. Richard wanted to reach those places where he had not yet been. The Outer Islands of Indonesia were on top of our list. Whether in Bhutan or Zambia, he always found something to admire, and some problem he might help fix. Above all things, he was a problem solver. Richard was never a tourist on this planet.

His energy has become the subject of countless anecdotes. I think he was the youngest middle-aged person I have ever known. He was passionately engaged in causes as various as Tibet, the battle against AIDS, the Asia Society, and the American Academy in Berlin and in the lives and careers of literally thousands of friends and protégés on every continent. And with all that, he managed to be a good and caring husband. How, I keep asking myself, did he manage all that? The answer in part is that he wasted no time. Any chance encounter at our local diner or fruit and vegetable market in Long Island with someone who could do something to advance one of his many causes would turn into a bilateral summit. Time was short. Richard had so much work to do.

But it wasn't just that he wasted no time; it was also that he spent every bit of himself. If something was worth the effort, he gave himself entirely to the task. Richard was his own best creation and the child was truly the father to the man. Here is the very young diplomat, as seen by his boss, Undersecretary of State Nicholas Katzenbach. "His ebullience," Katzenbach wrote of the twenty-three-year-old Richard, "is like a breath of fresh air in a world in which too few of us have retained the same excitement and earnestness which we once enjoyed." The same words capture Richard at the end of his life as at the beginning of his career.

Some weeks after his death, I was having lunch at the White House with Samantha Power, who introduced me to staffers who had worked with my husband. Most were young enough to be Richard's children. "Did you feel that he was of another generation?" I asked them. "No!" I was emphatically told. "He always seemed like the most energetic person in the room. And the most fully present." There were battles he lost, of course, but he always kept going. I have never met a more resilient or tenacious person in my life.

What this book cannot capture, and what I myself cannot fully convey, is Richard as a husband and best friend. The seventeen years we spent together were years of great personal and professional fulfillment.

Life for each of us was easier—and its inevitable blows less harsh—with a full partner to share them. From the year of our marriage—1995, the deadliest year of the Balkan wars and the year of Richard's greatest triumph—until his final mission to Afghanistan-Pakistan, we discussed everything, because everything interested him.

I also saw up close the ways he loved his country, and not in any chest-thumping way. He felt that America had a big role in and a big responsibility for the rest of the world. The lesson he learned during his very first diplomatic post, Vietnam, was that power must be exercised very carefully. The reckless adventurism of the Bush years pained him deeply. He longed to be back in the arena, to try to set things right again, to restore America's image as a place built on a set of values, not might alone.

The way he saw America imbued me with a deeper sense of what my adoptive country was really about. For Richard, our country is still the last best hope of mankind, a place of unlimited opportunities for refugees such as his parents and my family. In his eulogy, President Obama spoke of how Richard choked up during their first meeting after the 2008 presidential election. He was simply overcome by the fact that after African Americans had suffered slavery, segregation, and pernicious discrimination, there stood before him an African American for whom tens of millions of Americans had cast their vote. For my husband, a young man during the civil rights movement, it was a powerful moment, an affirmation of our great country.

In working toward peace in Afghanistan and Pakistan, he wanted desperately to help the United States find its better angels. I have never admired him more than when observing him during his final two years working on such a challenging beat. Facing breathtaking layers of adversity, he just kept on moving. Even if the progress he made in that most intractable region was incremental, he was engaged in the most complex and dangerous issue of the day. And that was precisely where he felt he belonged. His courage was contagious, as was his fascination with the impossible. Just ask the thousands of young people who either worked for him or met him in the field and were transformed by the experience. Who takes such time or cares so much about so many?

Fortunately most of us stored up enough Holbrookeisms—advice he dispensed generously on pretty much every subject—to draw on for years to come. Get to the point, I hear him whispering in my ear, when

I launch into a long anecdote. What do you hope to achieve, he is still asking me, when I walk into any meeting.

I think often these days of something Lady Bird Johnson said when I interviewed her for my book on presidential marriages. "Lyndon stretched me," the former first lady noted. Richard stretched everyone around him. I sometimes ask myself the question one of his aides asked, the night Richard died, "Now who will get the best from me?"

What we miss is the big man himself. We miss the man who exploded into a room with a thousand ideas and observations and turned life into a Technicolor movie.

He considered himself a fortunate man and a happy one. Two hours before he was fatally stricken, we laughed and joked as we made plans for a Christmas getaway. "It's only five days," Richard said, "but you and I know how to squeeze a lot into five days." I have never known a man who squeezed so much living into a single life.

CHAPTER ONE

The Audacity of Determination

One of Holbrooke's favorite quotes was from Herman Melville's Moby Dick*: "I am tormented with an everlasting itch for things remote. I love to sail forbidden seas, and land on barbarous coasts." (Courtesy of Kati Marton)*

Thinker, Doer, Mentor, Friend

STROBE TALBOTT

R ichard Holbrooke came as a package. To know the man in full was
to appreciate the most important contents. His was a unique combination of talent, intellect, energy, courage, conviction, gumption,
panache, and compassion. Many of those who "got" Richard were confident that he would, someday, receive proper credit for the contributions
he made to his country and the world. However, few of us anticipated
how quickly that would happen once he was gone. It certainly came
as a surprise to me, and it would have been considerable consolation
to him, especially since his last mission—as President Obama's and
Secretary Clinton's special representative on Afghanistan and Pakistan—
had been as thankless as it was grueling.

The State Department's announcement of his death early in the
evening of December 13, 2010, triggered an outpouring of testimonials
from around the world and from the various realms in which he had
been a seismic presence: from heads of state and international luminaries;
from representatives of humanitarian organizations, especially those that

fought for the rights of refugees and battled against HIV/AIDS, tuberculosis, and malaria; and from journalists and columnists who not only wrote about him, used him as a source, and let him use them to advance his many causes, but who also saw him as a master of their trade.

In everything he did, Richard cared most about getting results. Anything or anyone in his way he would push aside or run over. He had a low tolerance for form, politesse, and process for its own sake. He valued deference only when he was on the receiving end. He liked to think of himself as an irresistible force eager to meet an immovable object and then move it.

Such a figure is bound to be controversial, and Richard was willfully so. Many of the official panegyrics came from people who were glad they would never have to deal with him again. Obituaries listed various nicknames he had earned over the decades—Hurricane Holbrooke, the Bulldozer, and Raging Bull—and adjectives favored by his critics: brash, aggressive, feisty, unyielding, and, of course, undiplomatic.

Richard had heard all that—and it rankled. His skin was a lot thinner than he let on. Even when acknowledging many of the properties that others found objectionable, he would make the case that they were, in fact, assets for his life's work, which was "making a difference." I heard him use that phrase countless times. It was his motto.

Add to his rap sheet words like effective, pragmatic, imaginative, indefatigable, and idealistic, and the result is redolent of our national character: not the Ugly American, certainly not the Quiet American, but the Can-Do, Must-Do American—a personification of Thomas Paine's exhortation, "Lead, follow, or get out of the way!" The British statesman Mark Malloch-Brown put it piquantly: "He could not have been a European or Soviet diplomat. Only an American could have got away with it."

The best single tag I heard for the Holbrooke phenomenon came from Larry Summers. Richard, he said, embodied "the audacity of determination." Obama liked that one too, although it was the worst-kept secret in Washington that he never acquired a taste for Richard's operating style. That wasn't surprising, given Obama's signature preference for "no drama." Life with Richard was nothing if not dramatic. Yet, to his credit, Obama did more than just show up at a memorial service on January 14, 2011, laud Richard as the leading diplomat of his generation, and announce the creation of an annual award in his honor—he stayed for over two hours.

The extravaganza rivaled if not exceeded those that have attended the passing of U.S. presidents. It was directed by the mastermind behind the Kennedy Center Honors, George Stevens. Renée Fleming and the U.S. Army Chorus provided the music (Verdi's *Ave Maria* and *America the Beautiful*, respectively). Live C-SPAN coverage began half an hour early, as more than a thousand invited guests, among them numerous foreign dignitaries and Washington glitterati, filed into the Kennedy Center Opera House: Joe Biden, Colin Powell, Madeleine Albright, the presidents of Pakistan and Georgia, twenty foreign ministers, and sports and show business celebrities associated with Richard's charitable activities. (The TV cameras doted on the retired, seven-foot-two-inch NBA star Dikembe Mutombo, who had collaborated with Richard on education and poverty alleviation in his native Congo.)

Approximately seventy seats were reserved for the team of experts who had worked directly for Richard in the post he held when he died. They included officers from all around government—the departments of State, Treasury, Defense, and Agriculture, the intelligence, development, and law-enforcement communities—as well as from academe and the private sector. Richard got a kick out of assembling the band, and the more motley the better. It included an eccentric and iconoclastic professor, hard-as-nails military officers, hyphenated Americans with roots in Iran, India, and Pakistan; seasoned diplomats and successful lawyers who gave up easier, better paying, and more prestigious jobs to help him push a very large boulder up a very steep hill.

Diverse as they were, they constituted one of the most tightly knit, collegial, and dedicated "interagency" task forces ever. Above all, they were as devoted to Richard as he was to them. There was more barely controlled emotion in that section than anywhere else in the hall.

Meanwhile, Richard's wife Kati Marton, his two sons, David and Anthony, and his stepdaughter Lizzie Jennings were backstage with the other eulogists. In addition to Obama, they included both Clintons, Kofi Annan, Mike Mullen, the chairman of the Joint Chiefs of Staff, and David Rubenstein, the head of the Kennedy Center board, along with five of us who had dubbed ourselves "the mere friends": Jim Johnson, Les Gelb, Frank Wisner, Samantha Power, and myself.

As we were milling around commiserating, the idea arose that perhaps the Voice of God announcement that the program was about to begin should ask the people in the audience to turn their cell phones *on*, just in case the man whose life we were celebrating found a way of calling in. Such was the scope of his network of friends and his reputation for staying in touch, no matter where they were—or where he was.

That network had been abuzz for a month, since the day Richard's heart failed him during a meeting in Secretary Clinton's office and he had to be rushed to George Washington University Hospital. For the next three days, friends and colleagues kept a round-the-clock vigil in the hospital lobby. There were sometimes scores of people, including those who had braved a nasty winter storm to come from out of town. Some had known him since his precocious youth: as a junior foreign service officer in Vietnam, as an aide to Averell Harriman at the Paris Peace Talks on Vietnam, as director of the Peace Corps in Morocco, and as editor of *Foreign Policy*—all before he turned thirty-two.

There were hugs and tears. A number of people recalled how quick Richard was to come to their aid and comfort in times of distress, whether it was an illness or death in their families or setbacks in their professional lives. Several commented that if it were any of us upstairs in an operating room, Richard would be there in the lobby, rallying the troops, ambushing doctors for the latest information, and working the phones to get the best help in the world, wherever it was, whatever it took.

There were also plenty of laughs. Holbrooke lore often had a quality of screwball comedy. Secretary Clinton, who visited the hospital several times while Richard was in surgery and spent two hours with the pod of family and close friends immediately after his death, recounted an incident when he was so intent on getting her to change her mind on some issue she considered closed that he followed her into a ladies' room—in Pakistan, no less. (She told the story again during the memorial service, bringing down the house.)

As those days of anxiety gave way to weeks of mourning, my mind kept going back two decades, to a crisp Sunday morning in the spring of 1991, near the end of Richard's long interlude on Wall Street when Republicans controlled the White House. My wife Brooke and I were spending a weekend at a home with a tennis court and pool that Richard owned in one of the plummier exurban communities of central Connecticut. After a vigorous set of Canadian doubles and a swim, we went to a brunch at a neighbor's house. Richard's eyes lit up when he saw that their recreational facilities included a trampoline on the far side of a manicured lawn. After hastily paying respects to our hosts, he excused himself, went back outside, pulled off his shoes, rolled up the cuffs of his slacks, and clambered onto the canvas. He insisted that I join him. The result was an exceedingly amateurish blend of gymnastic duet and duel—sometimes semicoordinated, sometimes dangerously competitive, and constantly accompanied by talk, most of it coming from Richard.

The subject, naturally, was world affairs. Yugoslavia and the Soviet Union were coming apart at the seams. Richard was overflowing with observations, historical analogies, and, above all, strong opinions about how the U.S. government was responding. He was scathing about the George H. W. Bush administration's passivity toward the upheaval in the Balkans, which was careening into genocidal mayhem, but he gave the president high marks for supporting Mikhail Gorbachev's reforms that would soon lead to the largely peaceful disintegration of the USSR.

The incident was an antic example of Richard's knack for combining serious business with exuberant pleasure. His business *was* his pleasure; and, whatever his day job, the only business he really cared about was foreign policy. The work he so desperately wanted to do all his life was fun, even when it was exhausting. Partly for that reason, being his friend was also fun—and, often, also exhausting. That may be why it didn't seem entirely zany to us to be discussing the meltdown of European communism while bouncing into the air, sweating profusely, risking bodily harm, and caring not a whit about what the other guests, peering out the window, thought about the spectacle.

Richard brought the same playful spirit to more conventional and sedentary get-togethers. Breakfasts at the Candy Kitchen in Bridgehampton, dinners at La Chaumière in Georgetown, or—when we were together in the State Department in the nineties—late-afternoon catch-up sessions in each other's offices featured a mix of gossip, mordant commentary, and reciprocal teasing (I once got a rise out of him by calling him "solipsistic" and "unmodulated," and he reminded me for years afterward that I had shown my true colors by trafficking in such "obnoxiously WASP-Hotchkiss-Yale vocabulary").

But Topic A was always whatever Richard saw as the immediate test of American leadership in the world. He could connect pretty much anything to foreign policy: the plot twist in a movie he'd seen, the come-from-behind victory in a pro football game he'd watched over the weekend, or, most commonly—since he was a voracious and eclectic reader—the book he'd just finished.

We were both John le Carré fans, so the end of the Cold War gave us an excuse to reread *Tinker, Tailor, Soldier, Spy* and the other novels starring George Smiley. I remember Richard musing about how le Carré would adjust to the transformation of geopolitics. Perhaps, now that the Berlin Wall was rubble and the KGB had changed its name, Smiley would have to retire for good, making way for a new cast of characters who would be caught up in the disarray on the periphery of the defunct Soviet empire. Richard could imagine deliciously tangled plots to be hatched in the Caucasus, not least because the ethnic turmoil there had much in common with what he'd sensed brewing during trips he had made to the USSR as a private citizen in its dying days. (Le Carré did indeed find material in the Caucasus for several books in the nineties; one of the last novels Richard read, in 2010, was *Our Kind of Traitor*, about a Russian oligarch who tries to defect to Britain.)

Much as Richard enjoyed fiction, his first love was history, especially diplomatic history and, most of all, biographies of statesmen and studies of pivotal events, like the Treaty of Versailles or the origins of the Truman Doctrine and the Marshall Plan. He seemed to have read everything and, frighteningly, remembered everything. When he was appointed ambassador to Germany in 1993, he devoured every book on the subject he could get his hands on and virtually kidnapped Fritz Stern, a German-born historian of great distinction, to be his resident tutor in Bonn.

Books buttressed his view that history itself is not shaped by laws of nature or, as Tolstoy thought, by vast inscrutable "forces that move nations." Rather, Richard was on the side of "the Great Man" theory, which holds that history is an artifact of human agency. His driving desire to understand how the world works was coupled with his certitude that people in power could make it work better and an unrelenting, undisguised resolve to be in that category himself.

To many admirers and critics alike, ambition was Richard's most conspicuous quality. Less appreciated was the distinction he made between achievement of goals and the attainment of position, which he saw as a means to that end, not the end in itself.

Moreover, he believed that the combination of skill and will that he prized in himself could change the course of events only if it was part of a team effort. No question he wanted, if at all possible, to be the captain;

if not that, then the star player; if not that, then at least on the field; and if not that, then a forceful independent voice, exhorting from the sidelines; but never, *ever* a passive spectator.

Richard loved forensic combat. His strategy was, first, to establish the cosmic importance of whatever was most on his mind and, second, to make equally clear that his was the best, if not the only, sensible course of action. This take-no-prisoners style often aroused resistance and resentment—or, in the case of Henry Kissinger (who is no pushover), a backhanded compliment: "If Richard calls and asks you for something, just say yes. If you say no, you'll eventually get to yes, but the journey will be very painful."

In my own experience, I found, far more often than not, that Richard was in command of the facts, rigorous in his logic, and compelling in the essence of his position. Sure, he tended to overstate the extent to which the fate of the earth, or civilization, or at least the supreme national interest was at stake. But any sensible target of his browbeating should have the good sense to discount the hyperbole and pay attention to the nub of his argument.

At the same time, while he was a dazzlingly, sometimes excessively good talker, he was a good listener as well. If the thrust-and-parry of debate exposed a weakness in his position, he would adjust his analysis, modify his recommendation, then return to the offensive.

Richard was never bashful about enlisting history on his side—or, for that matter, anticipating what future historians would say. In the 1990s, during high-stress moments in the Situation Room, the Cabinet Room, or the Oval Office, he would lecture those around the table, including the president, on how future generations would not forgive us if we didn't take decisive action to stop the latest outrage in the former Yugoslavia, in Africa, or in Southeast Asia. Eyes might roll, but the net effect was the galvanizing of a consensus, led by Bill Clinton. Talk would then turn to action—an alchemy of which Richard was a wizard.

Eulogizing Richard in January 2011, President Clinton recalled, "He never was in a meeting in his life when he wasn't thinking, 'Okay, what are we going to *do?*' He loved the doers." He added that Richard was the ultimate doer himself. "I loved the guy," he said. "Doing in diplomacy saves lives."

The same is true of NGOs like Refugees International, which was founded in 1979 in response to the Indochina refugee crisis. Richard

In and out of government, Holbrooke appeared frequently before Congressional committees. Here, he listens as a Member of Congress makes a point. (AP Photo/Dennis Cook, December 19, 1995)

championed that cause from the State Department in the seventies, then chaired the board of the organization in the late nineties.

Richard was, at core, a happy warrior (the Wordsworth poem by that title, written after Lord Nelson's death at the Battle of Trafalgar, was a favorite of his). He had a preternatural self-confidence and a Joe Palooka resilience that enabled him to rebound from body blows.

In the nearly forty years I knew him, only once, in early January 1997, did I see him give in to anything more than fleeting discouragement. His triumph at Dayton behind him, he was back on Wall Street, making piles of money, bored stiff, and itching to get back into action. A game of musical chairs had been underway for months in Washington as the Clinton administration geared up for its second term. It looked as though he would be left standing when the music stopped. I was in New York for a meeting at the United Nations and went to see him at the apartment he and Kati had on the West Side late at night. He slumped listlessly on a couch—the metaphorical opposite of frolicking on a trampoline. It was one of the rare occasions I found him with no desire to talk about the issues of the day. "For the first time in my life," he said, "I feel old."

I never heard him say that or anything like it again, even though it wasn't until 1999 that he would return to government, as U.S. permanent representative to the UN.

Despondency and self-pity were simply not in Richard's nature. Ambitious as he was, he was also realistic about the capriciousness of fate, especially in his line of work. He'd had good luck when Harriman took him to Paris for the Vietnam Peace Talks and, again, nearly a decade later, when Jimmy Carter and Cyrus Vance made him, at thirty-six, assistant secretary of state for East Asia.

Yet the brass ring he most wanted eluded his grasp, repeatedly and narrowly. He was runner-up for secretary of state when Bill Clinton chose Madeleine Albright; he would very likely have been Al Gore's pick in 2000 if it weren't for the Florida recount and the Supreme Court's decision in Bush v. Gore, and John Kerry's if the 2004 election had gone the other way. Hillary Clinton might well have chosen Richard to be her secretary of state if the 2008 presidential race had turned out the way she hoped.

I suspect that these serial disappointments had a lot to do with Richard's notoriety among his Washington friends for bad-mouthing their city. He was scathing about the capital's rules, rituals, and rivalries. "You people must be crazy," he would say to me and others. "How can you stand this dreadful town?"

It wasn't quite a love-hate relationship (for all his ferocity of conviction and judgment, *hate* just wasn't in his vocabulary; Richard didn't go in much for unproductive passions). Rather, his version of Potomac fever was, by his own telling, a combination of allergy to what he saw as the pettiness of the politics, both personal and bureaucratic, as practiced in Washington and addiction to the concentration there of the kind of power he most wanted to exercise.

During his stints in the Clinton and Obama administrations, he shuttled down to Reagan National from LaGuardia at the beginning of the week, then flew home to New York at the weekend (he was too impatient for the Acela, not to mention for the Quiet Car, which most of his friends, myself included, preferred).

Yet he was always ready for the trip back to "the dreadful town." He loved the action there more than anything. He wanted to be in the thick of it and as close to the top as he could get. I suspect that if he had ever made it to the very top, he would have not regarded Washington as quite so dreadful, although he would still have relished flouting convention and raising the hackles of the establishment.

Since he died, I've found myself wondering what kind of secretary of state he would have made. A good one, I'll bet—a *very* good one. Had he occupied the post he'd so long hoped for, I can easily imagine that his inexhaustible and often frustrated capacity for striving would have been targeted on achieving as much as possible while he had maximum clout and the freedom to exercise it.

This was, however, not a topic of conversation between us. In the many intense private talks we had over the years, he didn't waste much time agonizing or fantasizing over what might have been. Instead, he concentrated on how best to play whatever hand he was dealt and beat the house.

That acceptance of adversity as a fact of life combined with a refusal to let it get him down and a gritty confidence that he could make his own luck carried over into his attitude toward the opportunities and challenges facing the U.S. His was a purpose-driven, utilitarian view of policy-making and diplomacy: Figure out what will advance American interests and defend American values; make a hard-headed calculation about the risks and costs, enlist key allies, find the best means of sub-duing your adversaries, and then get the job done.

A corollary of his belief in human agency was a deep interest in the psychology of those he was trying to persuade or pressure. During the Bosnia peace talks in the mid-nineties, he spent what sometimes seemed an inordinate amount of time on tactics and even seating charts. During a visit I made to Dayton early in the negotiations, I asked him what the principal issues were. "Never mind the substance," he said. "The whole point at this stage is to get these guys in a frame of mind where they want an agreement. The substance will fall into place later."

My wife Brooke was with me on that trip. Knowing that she and I had lived in Belgrade for two years in the early seventies, Richard seated her next to Slobodan Milošević during a surreal dinner at the Dayton Racquet Club for the assembled peacemakers (not yet successful) and war criminals (not yet indicted). Richard coached her on how to play to the Serbian dictator's vanity in nudging him toward concessions on several unresolved issues. She made some headway in getting him to ease an embargo of energy supplies to Bosnia. "Way to go, Brookie," said Richard afterward. "It's the little stuff that makes the big stuff possible."

On another occasion, I asked him how our exertions in the Balkans fit into the larger goals of American foreign policy. Again, he was dismissive of the premise. "Forget the sweep-of-history crap," he said. "Our goal is to end a war." Those last four words became the title of his 1998 book on the peace he, more than anyone, made in Bosnia.

In much the same spirit, Richard refused to associate himself with any of the competing schools in academe or opposing camps among the policy wonks. He cared only about the practice of foreign policy. To him, theory was, almost by definition, suspect. Not that he was averse to bold ideas—he just didn't want to clutter up the discussion of the present and future with anything that smacked of library stacks or, worse, ideological dogma.

I once made the mistake of invoking Immanuel Kant in support of the enlargement of NATO and the European Union—a big and controversial idea that Richard had long favored, but not because it would have pleased a professor in Königsberg who had been dead for nearly two hundred years. "Save that guy for some seminar in New Haven," he snapped. (Since my attachment to Yale was something of an obsession with him, I reminded him from time to time that his own alma mater, Brown, was also in the Ivy League.)

He found most doctrines too neat to be useful in the real world. Worse, disputes over them tended to stoke the polarization of the political environment, undercutting bipartisan support for the necessary degree of consistency in foreign policy from one administration to the next.

He took issue with politicians and pundits who sloppily invoked the legacies of presidents from an earlier era to support their side in quarrels over the U.S. role in the world in the late twentieth and early twenty-first centuries.

He had particular aversion to comparisons between Theodore Roosevelt and Woodrow Wilson that were invidious to Wilson: the Rough Rider who used the big stick to drive Spain out of the Western Hemisphere versus the one-worlder with the rosy dream that turned to a nightmare with the failure of the League of Nations and the rise of Hitler. In Richard's view, however much Roosevelt and Wilson may have disliked each other, they actually had similar views about the utility of international law *and* the importance of maintaining the primacy of American military force; both believed in making peace with treaties *and*, if confident of victory, in making war against those who threatened the peace or who committed what would come to be known as crimes against humanity.

That was Richard's belief too, and it was one of several themes to which he returned in his writing. He loved writing, and it showed. Along with his speeches, interviews, and testimonies before Congress, his op-eds and other articles were crucial to influencing policy, or at least the policy debate, when he was outside government and honing his intellectual resources for when he returned to government.

His long paper trail of muscular, lucid prose is rich in active verbs and notably free of words that end in *ism*.* To his ear, the suffix connoted abstract concepts that provoked pointless bickering and posed policy options in terms of false dichotomies. For him, pragmatism and idealism, exceptionalism and universalism, patriotism and internationalism were not either/or choices. He believed in all six, but also in the need to reconcile them insofar as possible or to apply them in different ratios, depending on the situation at hand.

The same went for *Realpolitik* and its putative antonym, *Moralpolitik*, as manifest in humanitarian intervention, notably in the Balkans. Richard saw hard and soft power as the yin and yang of the American brand. He believed that the U.S. had enough of both kinds of power to defend the weak around the world.

He was also wary of grand strategy—*any* grand strategy. "Diplomacy is not like chess," he once told Michael Ignatieff. "It's more like jazz—a constant improvisation on a theme." As both a student and practitioner of statecraft, he saw master plans as tending to blinker policy makers, causing them to miss or misread indications that their theory of the case is faulty or that circumstances have changed in ways that call for new assumptions, goals, and responses.

Richard's career was bookended by two cautionary tales about precisely that danger. In 1962, the year he entered the Foreign Service, the Kennedy administration had already made containing Soviet and Chinese expansion into Indochina an objective vital to the national interest. As a result, there were already more than 3,000 U.S. military personnel

---

* Between 1992 and 2008, Richard wrote thirty-nine op-ed columns for the *Washington Post*, totaling about 40,000 words. Aside from *terrorism* (which is a misnomer, since it applies to a tactic, not a political goal or ideology), only two *ism*'s—*realism* and *Wilsonianism*—appear in those columns and each only one time.

in South Vietnam. The consequence was to propel the U.S. into a quagmire, which led to the downfall of JFK's successor, Lyndon Johnson.

Almost forty years later, with the Cold War over, no hostile superpower to contain, and 9/11 confronting the U.S. with a new enemy, George W. Bush declared an open-ended "global war on terror." It began with the deceptively easy eviction of the Taliban regime in Kabul. Seven years and eight hundred U.S. and coalition casualties later, Richard, as a private citizen, wrote in his column for the *Washington Post* that the conflict in Afghanistan was likely to exceed the Vietnam misadventure as the longest war in American history.*

Once he joined the Obama administration, he kept his sense of déjà vu to himself, even as he worked tirelessly to avert a Vietnam-like debacle. He kept pushing for what he saw as a better balance between military might and robust diplomacy. In his view, there was no military solution to this conflict—as he said, "no unconditional surrender, not even total clarity on who the enemy is." Rather, it was a war that, by its prolonged and inconclusive nature, threatened to become a loser for the U.S. The military goal, in his view, was to create the favorable conditions for diplomacy. As U.S. and coalition forces made inroads against al-Qaeda and the more militant Taliban, it would be easier to secure political deals in Afghanistan, reinforced by a regional diplomatic settlement, thereby making possible the steady, responsible withdrawal of American forces.

Richard knew that "AfPak" would be his last government assignment. It was also his most frustrating one, although he didn't put it that way. Instead, he occasionally commented on the curious trajectory his public service had followed and the paradoxical way it was coming to an end. He'd held posts at the State Department twice before, both times as an assistant secretary. He'd presided in the seventies over East Asia and in the nineties over Europe out of well-appointed suites on the sixth floor, which, in that building, is considered close to heaven since it's just below the Secretary's office.

Here he was, back again in Foggy Bottom, but this time on the first floor, in cramped and inelegant quarters near the cafeteria. He took

---

* If the Vietnam War is dated from the Gulf of Tonkin resolution, then Afghanistan has already achieved that unwelcome distinction. However, Richard believed that the Vietnam War should be dated from 1961 since that was when the first American casualties were suffered. Measured in that way, Afghanistan will not become the longest U.S. war until after 2013.

wry pleasure in showing off what he called his "hovel." It gave him a chance to laugh at the ironies that attended the drama—and occasional melodrama—of his life. It was also the final manifestation of a distinctive feature of his career: his prominence and impact derived from the force of his personality and the prodigious vigor he brought to whatever job he had, never mind the rank or title that came with it. As ambassador to Bonn in the early nineties, he gave new meaning to the phrase "extraordinary and plenipotentiary" (for example, by creating a new institution to strengthen U.S.-German relations: the American Academy in Berlin). As an assistant secretary under Cyrus Vance and Warren Christopher, he spent a lot more time on the seventh floor—and at the White House—than others of comparable status.

The highest job he held was at the United Nations, from 1999 to the beginning of 2001, a post that came with a seat at the cabinet table in Washington. In that relatively short period of time, Richard promoted a more effective response to the plight of internally displaced persons while defending the world body against charges that it failed to stop eruptions of violence ("Blaming the UN for Rwanda is like blaming Madison Square Garden when the Knicks play badly"). Through prolonged efforts with foreign governments and the U.S. Congress, then controlled by the Republicans, he secured a bargain whereby the UN undertook reforms and the U.S. paid its back dues.

For these and other reasons, Richard was immensely proud. That pride could be—and, in his last years, frequently was—wounded. Yet there was ample room in his character for pride in his colleagues, especially the younger ones. Mentoring, for Richard, often meant pushing his protégés to higher positions often on higher floors of the building. That was one reason for the affection, admiration, and loyalty he engendered within his extended interagency team.

In addition to those who worked for him directly, Richard also convened a weekly meeting of about a hundred officials and experts from around government. He dubbed this body the *Shura*, an Arabic word for tribal counsel of the sort that Afghans used to govern themselves. I sat in on its meetings twice, once when Richard was leading the discussion, and again shortly after he died.

The collegiality and sense of common purpose within the *Shura* were in marked contrast to tensions within the government as a whole over AfPak, especially between Richard and some at the White House.

In the spring of 2010, the president's national security advisor, General Jim Jones, tried to maneuver him toward the exit. Secretary Clinton went straight to Obama and insisted that nobody except either of them could fire Richard. Jones backed down and was gone seven months later.

The showdown with Jones came to a head in April, shortly before Richard's sixty-ninth birthday—or, as I remember him saying, "the beginning of my seventh decade on this *extremely* messed-up planet" (you could almost hear the italics when Richard was in full voice). His body was sending him warning signals. He heeded them only to the point of sometimes imagining, a bit wistfully, a saner existence, with time for reading, writing a memoir, and fun with his family.

A number of his friends—including three who would later eulogize him at the Kennedy Center: Jim Johnson, Les Gelb, and Frank Wisner—formed a loose and benevolent cabal to persuade him to get out at a time of his own choosing, and the sooner the better, rather than letting himself be pushed out or, as we all feared, worked to death. Worried as I was about his health, I had trouble imagining him content to be back on the sidelines. As for Richard himself, he was determined not to give ammunition to his detractors by signaling that he was ready to quit. Still, he dropped a few hints that he might leave sometime after his seventieth birthday, perhaps in the summer or fall of 2011, assuming conditions in Afghanistan permitted the beginning of a drawdown of American forces.

Two months before he died, Richard ran into Larry Summers in the White House lobby. Larry introduced him to his fourteen-year-old stepdaughter, Maya, who had been having lunch with him in the White House Mess. She mentioned that she had some sense of what he was doing because she had read *The Kite Runner*, Khaled Hosseini's novel set in Kabul. Richard, who had, of course, read the book and could quote whole passages, fixed his eyes on her and engaged her in lively conversation for twenty minutes. Never mind if he was late to his next meeting; he had found someone who understood what was at stake in his last mission—someone whose world will be the better for all the difference he had made in those many missions that came before.

The Machine That Fails

RICHARD HOLBROOKE
Foreign Policy, No. 1, WINTER 1970–1971

> *This article ran in the inaugural issue of* Foreign Policy, *an upstart magazine that Holbrooke would join as managing editor after he left government for the first time, in 1972. In this article, Holbrooke, who had paid his first visit to the State Department during spring break from Brown in 1961, describes the department's crushing bureaucracy, which he would seek to reform, energize, or at times subvert throughout his career. After Holbrooke's death,* Foreign Policy *posted this article on its website, and it was passed around the State Department and admired for its accuracy after forty years.*

In the realm of policy some changes have been made, others promised. But the massive foreign affairs machine built up during the postwar era rumbles on, as ornate and unwieldy as ever. If meaning is attached to the President's promise of a new foreign policy for the seventies, then the shape of our massive bureaucracies must be changed, and those changes must be substantial.

"If we were to establish a new foreign policy for the era to come," Mr. Nixon went on to declare, "we had to begin with a basic restructuring of the process by which policy is made." But the restructuring has not yet met the problem—the accumulation of more than two decades of institutions, procedures and personnel, existing unchanged in a changing situation. Can we create an apparatus which will, in fact, "respond to the requirements of leadership in the 1970's"?

As a member of the bureaucracy myself, I feel its shortcomings with a special keenness. It is hard to decide whether to play the drama as tragedy, comedy, or simply theater of the absurd.

After several years' absence in private life, an elder statesman is recalled by the President to temporary duty in the State Department. He notices that there are twice as many Assistant Secretaries and "deputies" as he had remembered from his last stint of public service a decade before. "I have three people on my staff," he says, "who spend all their time attending meetings so they can come back and 'brief' me about what was said at the meetings. The funny thing is," he adds, "I don't give a damn what's said at any of those meetings."

Size—sheer, unmanageable size—is the root problem in Washington and overseas today. Most studies and recommendations discuss in detail valid but secondary issues: reorganizing, personnel policy, more managerial skill, the need for youth and new ideas, and so on. All these are important factors, but they are primarily unrecognized spin-offs of the central and dominant problem—*size.* There are two distinct but related ways that the apparatus is too big—in numbers of people (or, as we bureaucrats say, "warm bodies") and the multiplicity of chains of command. Of the two, the latter is by far the more serious:

An officer arrives at a consulate in an area where a minor guerrilla war has been going on for years. The United States is officially uninvolved, but the officer discovers that another agency of the U.S. government is giving limited covert assistance to the guerrilla movement. Rather than send a coded message (the code clerks work for the CIA), he dispatches a letter via the diplomatic pouch to his Ambassador and the Washington desk officer to ask how this was authorized and why. Neither man, it turns out, knew what was going on. After some interagency wrangling, the policy is changed—to the best of the officer's knowledge.

In order to appreciate how fragile and jerry-built the foreign affairs machine really is, with its five major engines and countless minor ones, it is only necessary to remember how it was built. The present structure was the result of compromises made in time of emergency, as America reacted after World War II to the newly perceived threat of the Cold War. Senior officials often disagreed over the need for new agencies even while agreeing that the function needed to be performed. Dean Acheson, for example, opposed the formation of a separate Central Intelligence Agency (CIA) in 1946. But for reasons which Presidents Truman and Eisenhower felt were valid, as each new front in the Cold War was perceived in Washington, a new agency or organization was formed to fight it: for "the battle for men's minds," the United States Information Agency (USIA); for technical assistance and economic development, a series of foreign aid agencies leading up to the present Agency for International Development (AID); for covert operations, as well as independent analysis, the CIA; for the building up of armed forces of friends and allies, a massive military assistance and advisory effort in more than 80 countries, under the control of the Pentagon; and, of course, a large U.S. military presence deployed around the globe.

To pull everything back in Washington, a National Security Council (NSC) was created in 1947. It has gradually acquired a staff of more than 100 officials and grown to its present position of pre-eminence within the foreign affairs establishment. Other new agencies have also been created, among the Peace Corps and the Arms Control and Disarmament Agency, while existing departments including Commerce, Labor and Agriculture, sent specialists overseas.

Despite the NSC, Washington's foreign policy apparatus has remained extremely cumbersome. Critics have usually focused on the State Department as the culprit, charging that it has failed to be the strong "coordinator" which several Presidents, most notably Kennedy and Johnson, expected. Richard Neustadt, for example, testifying before Senator Jackson's subcommittee in 1963 observed: "The State Department has not yet found means to take the *proffered role* and play it vigorously across the board" (emphasis added). Other critics have been harsher, and the strongest attacks have come from former high-ranking officials of State and the White House staff, people who were in an unusually good position to observe the problem.

They have accused the State Department of being overly cautious, unimaginative, filled with career officers thinking only of their own promotions, incapable of producing coherent recommendations or carrying out policy once the President has decided what the policy should be. In book after book of memoirs and analysis, the career Foreign Service has been found incapable and unwilling to serve the President, regardless of party, with the effectiveness, brilliance, and courage which is expected of it. In particular, State has been taxed of failing to "take charge" in 1966 when President Johnson set up a Senior Interdepartmental Group (SIG) under the Undersecretary of State.

The critics generally suggest that if the State Department had the right sort of creative, courageous, and effective people (whatever that means), then everything would be fine, and State would assume its rightful place at the center of American foreign policy, or as

Arthur Schlesinger put it in *A Thousand Days*, as the "Presidential 'agent' of coordination."

All these criticisms have validity. But the critics of the Department, in understandable frustration and bafflement, have nonetheless been blaming the Foreign Service for a situation which has long been out of its—or anyone's—control. They have repeatedly suggested remedies which are beyond the power of the Foreign Service and the State Department to administer. The critics fail to see the significance of the fact that every other agency involved in foreign affairs jealously guards its prerogatives and fights back whenever State makes the slightest movement to broaden its role; that Presidential exceptions frequently have weakened the theoretical hegemony of the American ambassador over all other official Americans; that several other major agencies have their own independent and private channels of communication back to their own headquarters in Washington; that the funds available to several other agencies for their overseas operations exceed those available to the State; that the White House has not always given State the necessary support. Those who hold high hopes for a resurgent State Department are, in short, victims of wishful thinking. They have failed to recognize how unlikely it is that any other agency will ever voluntarily relinquish its policy-making prerogatives, or release its grip on the levers that really matter—personnel assignments, promotions, recruitment, and the budget.

A desk officer in State has recently calculated that while in theory he is the focal point of all Washington efforts concerning "his" country, in fact there are 16 people working on the country in Washington, in different chains of command. They are receiving information directly from the Americans in the country through up to nine different channels. No one sees all the communications in every channel. Through great effort the desk officer has come to know all the other officers, but, he points out, they change regularly (himself included); someone is always out of town or sick; and most importantly, each one has his own boss, who can determine his future career; each one has his own set of priority projects and problems. "All I can do is try to stay on top of the really important problems," he says.

In fact, at its present size and with its present structure, the foreign affairs community cannot be pulled together under any central agency—not even the White House. Larger coordinating staffs are always possible, and perhaps inevitable; within the last year alone both State and the NSC have added or enlarged offices designed to fill a central coordinating role. But coordinating levels of government do not solve the problem, nor do large bureaucracies. In time, as former Secretary of State Dean Rusk once pointed out, most new levels become additional layers and only slow down further the movement of policy recommendations or action through the machine. Thus, many "routine" matters—problems of importance not necessarily requiring close attention from Presidential appointees—become immobilized by the requirement for "interagency coordination." Inertia takes over. Someone whose signature is required is off on a trip or too busy with something else; papers sit in in-boxes; no one ever says no but action is somehow not taken. The process has been brilliantly and precisely described by Professor Parkinson, and his Law seems to govern with inexorable force.

A junior member of the White House staff gets involved in a subject not normally of interest at the White House—routine training programs for overseas assignments. He finds that each agency runs its own training programs, emphasizing different points of view and in effect training its personnel for the bureaucratic battles ahead. Hearing this, a high Presidential assistant now decides to support a unification of the training programs for Vietnam. Every agency gives lip service to this concept. Everyone says it is necessary—but every agency offers technical reasons why it must continue its own separate training programs. Finally—and only because of high-level White House intervention—a unified training program for Vietnam is set up. The unusual White House involvement has resulted in a temporary combined training program, but there is little chance that it will be duplicated—as it should be— for other areas of the world.

Over time, each agency has acquired certain "pet projects" which its senior officials promote. These are often carried out by one agency despite concern and even mid-level opposition from others, as part of a tacit trade-off: "We'll let you do your thing, and you let us do ours." Such deals, or "non-aggression treaties," are almost never explicit but are nonetheless well understood by the participants. The results from such arrangements obviously vary. Sometimes programs are in direct conflict. Waste and duplication are frequent; lack of information about what one's colleagues are doing is common. These are all direct costs of the multi-agency system, which is too large and scattered to come under one driver.

A new Under Secretary of State discovers that a routine cable—the kind that Under Secretaries are not supposed to see—on the Food for Peace Program has received 27 clearances before being sent out. No one is able to convince him that 27 different people needed to agree to the dispatch of such a message.

The size of each of the five major agencies leads to additional problems. The distance and number of layers through which information must travel creates difficulties and misunderstandings. From the Secretary of State (to say nothing of the White House) to his country directors and desk officers is a long way. For many officers charged with responsibility for a specific country, the route to the *four* top policy-makers of the State Department may include the "alternate" country director, the country directors, a deputy assistant secretary of state, and the executive secretariat. And on the way up, any policy recommendation must receive clearance with all concerned horizontal layers. Sixteen bureau chiefs of assistant-secretary rank, with 2,500 personnel below them, report to the Secretary of State on policy matters. (On routine business, or during the Secretary's absence, they may report to one of his three top deputies or 336 staff members.) A separate set of officials in State, with more than 3,000 employees beneath them, handle "administration."

In producing a draft for the President's "State of the World" message, every State Department country desk was asked to submit a paragraph or two on its area. These paragraphs wended their way upward, were collected and sent to the White House along with a covering summary in a "huge bundle." "They didn't use a word of it—not a word," recalls an official who worked on the message.

On matters of an immediate and pressing nature, the President and his senior aides can usually decide, after the normal give-and-take, on a policy. If it involves few enough agencies and few enough people, the government can even carry it out with precision. But the number of issues that can be handled in this personalized way is very small, and is necessarily restricted to those matters of the greatest importance, and usually the greatest immediacy. If the press knows about a problem, big or small, that problem is far more likely to receive the personal attention of senior policy-makers than if it remains a well-kept secret. A former official of State puts it this way: "The amount of high-level interest in an issue varies with potential press interest."

On matters of long-range concern, the President and his senior aides can and do try to lay out a rational "long-range policy." But between the generalities of a vague policy document and its implementation by hundreds of people—*most of whom will never have read the policy document*—lie many places for miscalculation or derailment. With each agency deciding for itself what a policy means in terms of specific programs, there is more than enough room for disaster or, at the very least, confusion. Stalemate is one danger of the structure: the possibility that routine matters will not be dealt with until they become well-publicized problems.

A modest corollary to Parkinson's Law: The chances of catastrophe grow as organizations grow in number and in size, and as internal communications become more time-consuming and less intelligible.

Can the new era of shrinking commitments be one in which our huge bureaucracies also shrink in size? The odds, as every serious student of Professor Parkinson knows, are against it. Bureaucracies cling to their office space, their secretaries, their official cars, and their every allocated dollar and personnel position with a tenacity that drowning men might well envy. (The analogy may be apt in more ways than one.)

The person who has the most to gain from a massive reform of the foreign affairs machine—besides the American taxpayer—is the President himself. If a manageable and responsive apparatus is a true Presidential priority, then he personally must order major changes. Each President must decide whether or not he will attempt major changes, or instead choose to build small, personally loyal, bypass mechanisms with which to carry out policy on those matters of overwhelming high-level interest. Increasingly in recent years, the White House has chosen the latter route.

Since it would cut personnel and budget levels, major reform should be a popular move politically. Who except the bureaucratic losers themselves would voice serious opposition? Except for the military, the bureaucracies do not have much congressional support to fall back on. But the President must want reform and make it his personal priority if it is to succeed. For a man with far greater worries facing him daily, it is tempting to defer action on such an issue. In the absence of White House pressure, minor reforms and reorganization can always take place, but they are unlikely to be more than small adjustments, part of the self-protective coloration in which bureaucracies wrap themselves.

The test is not yet at hand. The plans, the discussions, the criticism of recent years do not go far enough. The White House—regardless of its occupant—will not be measurably better served in the future than it has been in the past unless major changes take place in every agency—unless, in fact, some agencies disappear. Fundamental questions, long submerged under the imperatives of the "postwar era," must be examined by people who are neither indebted nor subservient to the bureaucracies.

This is not a plea for the hegemony of the Foreign Service or the State Department as we know it today. It is clear to most people who have worked in Washington that State is presently unequipped to run U.S. foreign policy. Indeed, *no one* is equipped to run the foreign affairs machine today—a machine that fails. It requires a complete remodeling by people who are not predisposed in advance to one particular solution, but who are committed in advance to the search for a model which can be driven by the only man in it elected by the people—the President.

Such remodeling requires study. We have been surfeited with task forces in recent years, but—with the notable exception of the 1949 Hoover Commission Report—the studies have had their vision restricted, their mandate limited. If there is another task force, it must be able to deal with the entire foreign affairs/nation security apparatus. But how the President gets his answers—whether from a task force or from an individual who has his confidence—is not important. It is important that the President be personally committed to action. If he is not, then the bureaucracies, sensing indecision and ambivalence, will evade, and avoid, and survive.

Hard questions must be asked. Some of them have been raised in the press and in Congress. But they are rarely asked within the executive branch. Samples of such questions:

The United States Information Agency: Should we still maintain a worldwide information service with its own personnel, priorities, problems, programs, and promotion system? Do we need it?

The foreign aid program: Should AID remain in its present confused status? The Peterson Report of last February made some thoughtful recommendations, looking to the abolition of AID. But it also suggested a proliferation of new agencies. Could these proposals be reworked to fit the broader needs of a coherent foreign policy?

The Pentagon: Privately, almost every senior official of the past two administrations has lamented the power and bureaucratic strength of the Armed Forces. The recent Fitzhugh Report made some intriguing suggestions for cutting this power down. But, again, can Pentagon reforms be folded into a more inclusive scheme which encompasses *all* foreign affairs bureaucracies? And—in this case—will there be sufficient political strength to overcome the military and its allies?

The State Department: How can anyone reduce the layers between the "experts" and the policy-makers? How can the Department play its proper role of adviser to the Secretary of State and the President?

The Foreign Service: Should the FSO spend almost half his career in Washington, where he seems so ill-suited to the requirements? Should the Foreign Service continue to insist on a "well-rounded" officer, which results in men who know little about any specific area or functional field—but who are experts on surviving bureaucracies? How can the Foreign Service attract specialists—or, if it cannot, how can the State Department attract them from outside the Foreign Service? What is wrong with our professional diplomacy? ("Kennedy was angry because he thought the Foreign Service was too conservative. Nixon thinks they are too liberal," says a man who worked in both Administrations. "They are both wrong. The Foreign Service is just the Foreign Service.")

The Central Intelligence Agency: Is the CIA out of control, an "invisible government"? Why do so many ambassadors claim little or no knowledge of covert CIA operations in their countries? Should the CIA be allowed to conduct its business with little State Department involvement? Should State desk officers know exactly what the CIA is doing?

Career vs. Political: How can we reconcile the legitimate need for a professional career structure in foreign affairs—a corps of professionals—and the overriding need for more Presidential control?

Who is in charge: Who, finally, is to be put in charge of running the foreign affairs machine? Who will see that the policy, once decided, is carried out? Will it be the State Department, with its faults glaring at us from the pages of every memoir and almost every memo? Or the NSC structure, growing stronger every day? Or the Pentagon, finally taking charge through sheer bureaucratic strength and longer hours of work and better briefing charts than anyone else? Or will we continue the inefficient system that now exists—with bureaucratic stalemates and compromises, with Presidential decisions carried out (sometimes) but lesser matters usually deferred, with agencies either going their own way or becoming stalemated by "inter-agency coordination"?

I do not pretend to have the definitive answers. But my own conclusion is that a major reduction in the number of organizations and chains of command must take place, or else the bureaucratic chaos will get worse, and more bypass mechanisms will be created, and more layers will spring up, and . . .

If this vital premise is accepted, then institutional change could follow one of several possible paths. Ideally, the organization that is called the State Department could become the central point of the foreign affairs administrative structure. The balance of powers in our government is such that it would be a mistake to put central coordinating power into the hands of the NSC staff, which is immune to the legitimate and constitutional desire of Congress to play a role in policy through the appropriations process and through the confirmation of Presidential appointees, and hearings on policy. And much evidence piled up over the last decade shows that overreliance on a White House staff isolates the President from the great departments of government and leads to costly mistakes.

But only an *ideal* State Department, not today's State Department, could play the central role. Only a reformed organization, residing perhaps on the same physical shell but altogether different in internal structure, can do what must be done. Here, indeed, is where the greatest reforms, the most drastic surgery, must occur. More political appointees are surely needed, men on whom the President and the Secretary can rely; fewer FSO's on short Washington tours; a larger number of permanent Washington-based officials who understand both the Washington bureaucratic game and their regional specialty; much closer relationships between the other agencies (in whatever form they survive) and State; more authority to the desk officers and country directors, who should be aware of *everything* affecting U.S. relations with their country; and fewer layers between the desk officer and the Secretary of State.

During one recent discussion of this endless subject, an academic observer who is a devout student of bureaucracies scoffed at the chances of ever seeing the kinds of major reform which are proposed above: "Why even the Russian Revolution never produced anything that revolutionary."

Maybe he is right. Certainly there are many people in the government who do not believe that it is too big, or too cumbersome. In some recent studies, expansion of the foreign affairs apparatus has been advocated. But if a President wishes to get the machine under his control, he can—provided he is willing to upset a few established applecarts along the way. The price would not be as high as many people think, and the return, to the President and to the people, would be substantial. Only the bureaucracies would be the losers.

It's a famous story, but it bears retelling. Ellis Briggs, diplomat of much experience, was Ambassador in Prague in the late 1940's when the Czechs expelled all but 12 members of the swollen U.S. mission. If the Communists thought they were hurting the United States, Briggs recounts, they could not have been more wrong. They had, in fact, accomplished what Briggs had always wanted to do: to reduce the size of the U.S. mission in Czechoslovakia. "It was probably the most efficient embassy I ever headed," Briggs says.

Foreword to *Paris 1919:*
Six Months That Changed The World

RICHARD HOLBROOKE
FROM *Paris 1919*, BY MARGARET MACMILLAN

Holbrooke will forever be known as an energetic peace negotiator, and throughout his career he decried the tremendous miscalculations made in Paris in 1919. These would be particularly evident in many parts of the world where he would go to work, including the Balkans, Turkey, and even Vietnam: In 1919, President Wilson had unceremoniously brushed away a precocious, clean-shaven young Indochinese kitchen assistant at Versailles; a half century later the followers of that kitchen assistant, Ho Chi Minh, would hold the upper hand during Holbrooke's first crack at peace negotiations, in Paris in 1968. The 1919 failure is described in MacMillan's award-winning book, for which Holbrooke wrote this foreword.

In diplomacy, as in life itself, one often learns more from failures than from successes. Triumphs will seem, in retrospect, to be foreordained, a series of brilliant actions and decisions that may in fact have been lucky or inadvertent, whereas failures illuminate paths and pitfalls to be avoided—in the parlance of modern bureaucrats, lessons learned. With this in mind, it is time to look again at what happened in Paris in 1919. Margaret MacMillan's engrossing account of that seminal event contains some success stories, to be sure, but measured against the judgment of history and consequences, it is a study of flawed decisions with terrible consequences, many of which haunt us to this day.

In the headline version of history, the road from the Hall of Mirrors to the German invasion of Poland only twenty years later is usually presented as a straight line. But as MacMillan forcefully demonstrates, this widely accepted view of history distorts the nature of the decisions made in Paris and minimizes the importance of actions taken in the intervening years.

The manner in which the war ended—with an "armistice" and no fighting on German soil—played a significant role in subsequent events. "Things might have been different," MacMillan writes, "if Germany had been more thoroughly defeated." Most Germans outside the High Command did not realize that Germany was finished militarily, and therefore did not regard November 11, 1918, as a day of surrender. Hitler would capitalize on this; his promise to undo the Treaty of Versailles was a potent and popular theme during his rise to power. But MacMillan corrects the widely held view that the reparations payments imposed by the victors were so onerous as to have caused the wreck of the German economy that paved the way for Hitler.

By any standard, the cast of characters that assembled in Paris in 1919 was remarkable, from Lawrence of Arabia to a small Vietnamese kitchen hand later known as Ho Chi Minh. And for the first time in history, an American stood at the center of a great world drama. Woodrow Wilson inspired tens of millions who never met him, and frustrated those who worked with him. He was idealistic and remote, naive and rigid, noble and conflicted. His strengths and weaknesses, his health, even the influence of his overbearing and ignorant wife, were all critical factors in events of historic importance.

In the eighty years since he left office, Wilson's reputation has risen and fallen regularly—but he remains as fascinating and central to an understanding of modern American foreign policy as ever. His many supporters, from Herbert Hoover to Robert McNamara, have argued that his enemies in both Paris and the United States Senate were responsible for the undoing of one of history's noblest dreams. Others, including Senator Jesse Helms, have viewed Wilson's determined adversary, Senator Henry Cabot Lodge, as a principled protector of American sovereignty and charged Wilson with seeking to undermine the American Constitution. Another school of thought, especially prevalent in the latter years of the Cold War, criticized Wilson for unrealistic, overly moralistic goals; among its best-known practitioners are George F. Kennan and Henry Kissinger, who accused Wilson of "extraordinary conceit," even while conceding that he "originated what would become the dominant intellectual school of American foreign policy." (To Kissinger's horror, *his* president, Richard Nixon, placed Wilson's portrait in the place of honor in the Cabinet Room.)

THROUGH THE FOG OF THIS NEVER-ENDING DEBATE, ONE THING is clear: as Wilson arrived in France in December 1918, he ignited great hopes throughout the world with his stirring Fourteen Points— especially the groundbreaking concept of "self-determination." Yet Wilson, often ill-informed or badly prepared for detailed negotiations, seemed vague as to what his own phrase actually meant. "When I gave utterance to those words," he admitted later, "I said them without the knowledge that nationalities existed, which are coming to us day after day."

Even at the time it was recognized that the concept of self-determination was, as MacMillan puts it, "controversial and opaque."

"When the President talks of 'self-determination,'" Secretary of State Robert Lansing asked, "what unit has he in mind? Does he mean a race, a territorial area, or a community? . . . It will raise hopes which can never be realized. It will, I fear, cost thousands of lives. In the end it is bound to be discredited, to be called the dream of an idealist who failed to realize the danger until it was too late."

Lansing was one of the first to recognize a dilemma that lies at the core of many of today's bitterest disputes. Still, it was not Wilson's dreams but his decision to compromise them (by letting Japan take the Shantung peninsula in China, for example) that cost the world so dearly. Ironically, when Wilson returned home, he made the opposite mistake: by refusing to make relatively minor compromises with Senate moderates, he lost his chance to get the treaty (and American member- ship in the League of Nations) ratified.

Some of the most intractable problems of the modern world have roots in decisions made right after the end of the Great War. Among them one could list the four Balkan wars between 1991 and 1999; the crisis over Iraq (whose present borders resulted from Franco-British rivalries and casual mapmaking); the continuing quest of the Kurds for self-determination; disputes between Greece and Turkey; and the end- less struggle between Arabs and Jews over land that each thought had been promised them.

As the peacemakers met in Paris, new nations emerged and great empires died. Excessively ambitious, the Big Four set out to do nothing less than fix the world, from Europe to the far Pacific. But facing domestic pressures, events they could not control, and conflicting claims they could not reconcile, the negotiators were, in the end, simply overwhelmed—and made deals and compromises that would echo down through history.

Even then, they sensed that they were laying the seeds for future problems. "I cannot say for how many years, perhaps I should say for how many centuries, the crisis which has begun will continue," predicted Georges Clemenceau, whose own behavior contributed to the failure. "Yes, this treaty will bring us burdens, troubles, miseries, difficulties, and that will continue for long years."

MacMillan brings back to life some great dramas: the Italian walk-out after the failure of their effort to gain control of much of the Yugoslav coast; the Japanese grab of the Shantung peninsula, which launched the May Fourth Movement in China and started the path to war and revolution in Asia; the dismemberment of Hungary, which left millions of Hungarians permanently outside their own country's borders; the inability of the Big Four to deal with the new Soviet government, other than by sending a feckless expeditionary force into the Russian civil war; the dissolution of the Ottoman empire and the rise of one of the twentieth century's most remarkable leaders, Kemal Atatürk; and last but not least, the creation of Yugoslavia (originally, the Kingdom of the Serbs, Croats, and Slovenes) out of the disparate peoples of the south Balkans.

This state would survive under Marshal Tito's communist dictator-ship for decades, but when the patchwork put together in 1919 fell apart in the early 1990s, four wars followed—first Slovenia, then Croatia, then Bosnia-Herzegovina, and finally Kosovo. (A fifth, in Macedonia, was barely averted.)

As our American negotiating team shuttled around the Balkans in the fall of 1995 trying to end the war in Bosnia, the Versailles treaty was not far from my mind. Reading excerpts from Harold Nicolson's *Peacemaking 1919*, we joked that our goal was to undo Woodrow Wilson's legacy. When we forced the leaders of Bosnia, Croatia, and the Federal Republic of Yugoslavia to come together in Dayton, Ohio, in November 1995 and negotiate the end of the war, we were, in effect, burying another part of Versailles. In the spring of 2002, the last two parts of the Versailles creation still linked as "Yugoslavia" took another step, moving to the brink of a full and final divorce by agreeing to rename their country "Serbia and Montenegro"—probably a way station on the path to full separation.

Of course, at Dayton we were working on only one small part of the puzzle; in Paris they worked on the world. Margaret MacMillan's brilliant portrait of the men of Paris, what they tried to do, where they succeeded, and why they failed, is especially timely now. This story illuminates, as only great history can, not only the past but also the present. It could help guide us in the future. I only regret that it was not available a decade ago. But here it is: an irresistible voyage through history.

The Paradox of George F. Kennan

Richard Holbrooke
Washington Post, March 21, 2005

> *Holbrooke, who had begun writing a monthly* Washington Post
> *column after the 2004 election, differed on many issues from
> George Kennan. Not the least of these were the role of human rights
> in American foreign policy and NATO enlargement. But as he
> shows in this eulogy, Holbrooke never wavered in his deep and
> abiding respect for Kennan, who he considered an icon of his craft.*

George F. Kennan, who died last week at 101, was a unique figure in American history. I greatly admired him but disagreed with him profoundly on many critical issues, and, in the 35 years I knew him, I often reflected on this strange paradox.

His extraordinary memoirs had made the idea of a life in the Foreign Service seem both exciting and intellectually stimulating to me. He had watched Joseph Stalin at close hand, and sent Washington an analysis of Russia that became the most famous telegram in U.S. diplomatic history. This was followed closely by the most influential article ever written on American foreign policy, the "X" article in *Foreign Affairs*, which offered an easily understood, single-word description for a policy ("containment") that our nation was to pursue for 40 years—with ultimate success.

To a young, aspiring diplomat, Kennan's career suggested that good writing and the study of history—both in short supply in the government—could really matter. No one in government ever wrote better than

Kennan, and this was a critical component of his success; the same ideas expressed less cogently by others did not have the same impact. But Kennan was deeply ambivalent about the writings that had catapulted him to world fame. He felt lonely, conflicted and even anguished over his famous works, which, in retrospect, he felt were simplistic and had been misused by people he deplored. Yet his work inspired the hard-headed power politics that shaped the Cold War.

As editor of *Foreign Policy*, I once edited Kennan, an experience not easily forgotten. On the 25th anniversary of the X article, I asked him for an interview. He refused because of what he felt was the imprecision of the spoken word, but he offered to answer questions in writing. It was a generous gesture toward a tiny, unknown journal then challenging the prestigious quarterly that had made him famous. But editing Kennan was beyond difficult. He agonized over every comma and every adjective and revised regularly as the deadline approached. Having written in his memoirs that his 1946 "Long Telegram" read in retrospect "exactly like one of those primers put out by alarmed congressional committees," and that his X article was riddled with "serious deficiencies" that "inadvertently loosened a large boulder from the top of a cliff," Kennan did not want to be misunderstood—or misused—again.

Dean Acheson once told a Yale student named Bob Woodward, who was writing a thesis, that Kennan reminded him of his father's old horse who, when crossing wooden bridges, would make a lot of noise, then stop, alarmed by the racket he had caused. I printed this wonderful description alongside the Kennan interview in *Foreign Policy*. (Wonder whatever happened to young Woodward.)

When Stalin's daughter, Svetlana, defected, she went briefly to Princeton, and I arranged to bring Kennan's old Moscow boss, Averell Harriman, to Kennan's house for dinner. We sat, transfixed, as she told us bitterly that she had longed to meet the two great Americans (and their daughters) in wartime Moscow but was forbidden to by her tyrannical father. It was a small footnote to history, but Harriman, Kennan and Stalin's daughter meeting for the first time, 30 years after Stalin had prevented it, gave new layers to the human dimensions of history.

In 1996 Kennan went to Columbia University to hear a speech by Pamela Harriman, Averell's widow and, at that time, ambassador to France. A distinguished group, including Strobe Talbott, deputy secretary of state and one of Kennan's greatest admirers, gathered for dinner afterward in the home of Columbia's president. After dessert we asked Kennan to speak, giving him no advance warning. The 92-year-old legend rose slowly, and in a weak, high-pitched voice, delivered a flawlessly constructed and fairly brutal attack on one of the pillars of the Clinton administration policies Talbott and I were most closely associated with, the expansion of NATO to include Poland, Hungary and the Czech Republic.

Kennan's warning that enlarging NATO would destabilize Europe—"an enormous and historic strategic error"—carried the dinner audience with its eloquence and sense of history. Events, of course, proved Bill Clinton right, and Kennan—and the bulk of the liberal intellectual community—wrong. But in a sense, Kennan that evening was fulfilling his true role in American foreign policy: not the brilliant architect of containment but an eloquent skeptic, forcing people in power to make sure their easy justifications stood up before his polite but ferocious criticism. In today's Washington, with its emphasis on orthodox thinking, such a person could never rise inside the government, and even in 1947 it was almost an accident. This is a great loss, because, as the life of George F. Kennan shows, individual, original thinking by one lonely person can sometimes illuminate and guide us better than all the high-level panels and commissions and interagency meetings.

We disagreed on many issues: his belief in the need for a "council of elders"—really a plea for the power of elites—to contain the excesses of democracy; his 19th-century attitude toward Africa; his view that the promotion of human rights and democracy was a terrible, morally arrogant mistake; and his advocacy of a deal with Moscow over American troops in Europe. He had accurately predicted, at the end of the Cold War, the outbreak of ethnic violence in Yugoslavia, but he did not understand the need for American involvement in the problem, let alone the use of military force to end the Balkan wars. "Why should we try to stop ancient ethnic hatreds?" he asked me one day in the dark-paneled library of his house in Princeton. He shook his head as I tried to explain. He had been ambassador to Yugoslavia, and I wanted him to understand—to agree with me—as a sort of stamp of approval from one generation to another in the Balkans. But, though, as always, he was polite and gracious—and he loved the intellectual combat—he was firm in his disagreement. He was our greatest diplomat, and I admired him for his intellectual courage, but there was no bridging the gap.

CHAPTER TWO

The Journalist

Sharing a laugh with Christiane Amanpour, one of Holbrooke's favorite journalists. (Courtesy of Kati Marton)

Reporting Truth to Power

E. Benjamin Skinner

On a summer day in 2010, Richard Holbrooke called out to the writer Gay Talese as he walked near the Metropolitan Museum of Art on Manhattan's Upper East Side. Holbrooke was then a year into his final assignment at the State Department. But at the forefront of his mind was not the impending parliamentary election in Afghanistan; it was Talese's 2009 interview with *The Paris Review*.

"Here's a guy who was focused on the awful problems of the world, Afghanistan, terrorism, that awful regime in Pakistan," said Talese. But all he wanted to do was to talk about the art of nonfiction writing.

Throughout his career, critics gleefully caricatured Holbrooke's relationship with the media as self-promoting and manipulative. Unquestionably, he knew how to play the game. Early on, he had acknowledged "the odd, love-hate relationship between journalists and officials. They use each other: it is as simple, as brutal, as self-serving as that."[1] Holbrooke publicly adored reporters when they advanced his bureaucratic agenda; discreetly yet vigorously, he would also defend himself against bad press.

But his relationship with the media was far more than a marriage of convenience. From Vietnam through Afghanistan, when Holbrooke served in government, he would accost correspondents, often those with little fame but reams of clips with no bylines, and drill *them* for the real stories. Many suspected that he wanted to be one of them. At times, he *was* one of them.

Over his career, he would publish over 250 articles, chapters, forewords, monographs—including a study on pacification for the Pentagon Papers— as well as two *New York Times* best-sellers. Holbrooke delighted in the craft of writing. His early dispatches from Europe for the *Brown Daily Herald* read like travelogue, and he called his later articles for *Travel + Leisure* "my cotton candy." As a reporter, he had an eye for the symbolic. A Marine general pushing sand on the ground in Da Nang to show young Holbrooke how troops would advance across Vietnam became a metaphor for the impossibly particulate task of rolling back the Vietcong.

Holbrooke the journalist did more than write. His career spanned an era when Americans moved from newspapers to television and the Internet as their primary news sources, and Holbrooke kept pace. He mastered sound bites, but he didn't relish them. Near the end of his life, Holbrooke would decry "the assault of the 24-hour cycle and endless stream of mostly unprocessed data and rumor and commentary, all mixed into one messy stew."[2]

Holbrooke the writer was a throwback, and a fertile talent; Holbrooke the historian was more than a recorder of the times. He was a vibrant observer, a narrative thinker, keen on placing his hallmark, thrilled early at his role as first drafter of world affairs that he would later shape. Through it all, Holbrooke, the ethnic Jew, drew from at least one mandate of the Quaker meeting that, as a child, he attended with his mother: "Speak truth to power."

TO HIS FATHER, A RUSSIAN ÉMIGRÉ AND A PHYSICIAN, INTELLECTUAL curiosity was a catalyst for greatness, and Holbrooke's boyhood idols were Albert Einstein and Enrico Fermi. At high school in Scarsdale, New York, he peered beyond science, became sports editor of the school paper, and wrestled with his editor in chief and best friend David Rusk over subheads and word counts.

By sophomore year at Brown University, when he changed his major from physics to history, the *New York Times*'s Scotty Reston and Abe Rosenthal were atop his pantheon. From then on, while he excelled in those subjects he enjoyed—Holbrooke would summarize ninety-minute history lectures with three cogent words in his notes—he did not let his courses interfere with his education. "I spent a lot more time here than I did in my classes," Holbrooke recalled when visiting the *Brown Daily Herald* offices in fall 2007.[3]

The *Herald* was a way to satisfy what Matthew Arnold, in Holbrooke's favorite poem, called the "longing to inquire."[4] It gave him an excuse to interview those who had been eyewitnesses to history, and those who were making it.

Some encounters were sublime. In June 1959, Holbrooke, then eighteen and visiting San Francisco between his first two years at Brown, rode a train to Palo Alto to interview Alexander Kerensky. For 110 days in 1917, Kerensky had been the leader of Russia, before fleeing into exile after the October Revolution. Holbrooke, whose father had also fled Lenin, struck an immediate rapport, and soon the seventy-eight-year-old opened up broadly about his daring escape from the Bolsheviks, at one point breaking into song in the student café where they chatted.[5]

Other encounters were ridiculous. On Thursday evening, November 17, 1960, Holbrooke covered a rambling, incoherent talk by Norman Mailer at Brown's Carmichael Auditorium. The writer veered between Irish and English accents for no apparent reason, slurred out random poetry, and announced his candidacy for mayor of New York. A court-appointed medical examiner would later describe his state as "an acute paranoid breakdown with delusional thinking." But to Holbrooke, it was just a window into "the strange world of Norman Mailer."[6] Less than forty-eight hours after the talk, Mailer repeatedly stabbed his second wife at a party, narrowly missing her heart with his penknife.[7]

After the *Herald*'s managing board elected Holbrooke editor in chief in December 1960, he began to reshape the ninety-person, $35,000-a-year paper. At the time, Brown was the smallest university to publish a daily, but Holbrooke made the most of it. He expanded and reshuffled the board and, notably, addressed a writer shortage by breaking a long-standing gender barrier and assigning articles to female students. Editorially, Holbrooke, who lambasted soft, myopic, local news stories as "worth next-to-nothing," courted controversy with hard-charging commentary.[8] Unruffled by the fact that administration funds floated the paper, he would frequently editorialize against University Hall policies.

These were the simmering days of the civil rights movement, and the editor plunged into the debate. He ran a special series examining charges of discrimination at the university. The day after Kennedy's election in 1960, Holbrooke and the university welcomed Martin Luther King, Jr., who called the young senator's win "a great victory for tolerance in the nation."[9] To cover a more discordant racial note, Holbrooke assigned a coed, Larrine Sullivan, to interview Brown's most infamous alumnus, George Lincoln Rockwell, the founder of the American Nazi Party. Sullivan and Holbrooke had then started dating. They married in 1964 and divorced eight years later. "He was always looking for stories," she recalled. On his first trip to meet her parents in her segregated hometown in southern Maryland, he insisted on interviewing the superintendent of the black school system.

Most controversially, Holbrooke brought Malcolm X to campus at the height of his most divisive rhetoric. One of Holbrooke's reporters, Kitty Pierce, had profiled the Black Muslims after their February 1961 UN Security Council invasion to protest Patrice Lumumba's killing. After meeting with the minister in his office, Holbrooke walked with him, along with his looming bodyguards, to Sayles Hall, where Pierce introduced Malcolm X to an audience of 750. The school's administration had grave reservations about the *Herald*'s invitation to the black nationalist. But Holbrooke's vindication came when, at the end of a fiery talk, the minister suggested a discussion with Martin Luther King, Jr., with Brown's campus as the venue.

Shortly after he took over the paper, Holbrooke made his first visit to the Department of State. While Holbrooke had great access, he forwent a story, possibly because he was too close to be objective: Two months earlier, his best friend's father, Dean Rusk, had been sworn in as Kennedy's secretary of state.

Independently, Holbrooke threw himself into foreign affairs while at the *Herald*, never more so than during one remarkable assignment that he undertook at the end of his sophomore year.

"WHETHER YOU GO INTO JOURNALISM OR THE FOREIGN SERVICE AS A career," Scotty Reston told the gangly nineteen-year-old in May 1960, "you will always be able to say, 'I started my career at *the worst* diplomatic fiasco ever held.'"[10]

Three weeks earlier, on Tuesday, May 3, Holbrooke had flown from New York's Idlewild Airport to Amsterdam's Schiphol. In April, he had convinced the *Herald* editors that he spoke fluent French, and the paper's managing board, along with the university administration, had funded him to cover the Four Power Summit in Paris where Charles de Gaulle would host Dwight Eisenhower, Nikita Khrushchev, and U.K. Prime Minister Harold Macmillan, in an effort to forge some resolution to bitterly divided Berlin. The planning for the meeting had lasted months, and to many, this seemed like a chance, perhaps the last chance, to keep the Cold War from turning hot.

As Holbrooke packed for Europe, a CIA contractor named Francis Gary Powers boarded a U-2 spy plane in Peshawar, Pakistan. After the Soviets downed Powers over their territory, Khrushchev faced a critical decision. He could reveal the episode, demand an apology from Eisenhower, and thus scuttle the talks, or he could conceal or soft-pedal it until after Paris. Either way, as Khrushchev later acknowledged, the incident augured his loss of power, as it emboldened hard-liners in the Kremlin who claimed that Washington sought an empire.

Though he didn't know about the U-2 downing when he filed his first dispatch from Amsterdam, Holbrooke unconsciously predicted Khrushchev's initial response to it. The talks reflected the Soviet leader's "tremendous desire for personal prestige, for acceptance, for the right to sit in council with other established leaders of the world," Holbrooke wrote.[11] Khrushchev indeed at first acted to save the talks, giving Eisenhower cover for the U-2 incident by blaming the aerial espionage only on "imperialist circles and militarists" in the Pentagon. In the *Herald*, Holbrooke's insights ran directly below an announcement for cheerleading tryouts.

That Thursday night, stopping in London on his way to Paris, Holbrooke wandered until dawn through jubilant central London crowds under streetlights festooned with flowers and banners bearing the initials "MA." Princess Margaret was to marry Anthony Armstrong-Jones on Friday, in what would be the first televised royal wedding. Holbrooke reported, with thinly veiled disdain, that the British public and media were far more focused on the nuptials than they were on the impending talks. Parenthetically and sarcastically, he added: "One of the evening newspapers had a small story about the Russians shooting down an American plane and how Khrushchev thought this was no way to prepare for the Summit, but that isn't very important now is it?"[12]

After the wedding crowds dispersed, the young reporter walked to London's highest point, near St. Paul's Cathedral, where he found a plaque marking Old Chance Street, which had stood there for 647 years, until German bombers destroyed it in the Battle of Britain. To Holbrooke, the place represented British mettle, a toughness that once again would be tested if Paris failed and Berlin sparked war.[13]

On Monday, May 9, Holbrooke finally arrived in Paris, and the next day he traveled west to the suburb of Rocquencourt, near Versailles. There he visited the Supreme Headquarters Allied Powers Europe, housed in row upon row of prefab military buildings in Camp Voluceau. Impressed by the massive effort to contain the Soviets, Holbrooke enjoyed a briefing from commanders of an organization that, some thirty-five years later, he would be pivotal in expanding: NATO.

Later that week, he checked in at the summit's cavernous, peeling media headquarters at the Palais de Chaillot, across the Seine from the Eiffel Tower. The main hall, three hundred feet long but subdivided for the visiting press delegations, was largely empty, save for technical staff working in advance of the TV and radio correspondents. They and Holbrooke chatted up fourteen young female guides, provided by the French government. Holbrooke peered into Office E-3. It was empty. But soon, it would be filled with his *New York Times* idols.[14]

The following evening, he seized the chance to meet one of those idols when he introduced himself to Clifton Daniel, the *Times*'s dapper assistant managing editor. Daniel was there to head the paper's eleven-man team in Paris, and most of his writers, including Abe Rosenthal, who had won a Pulitzer Prize two weeks earlier, had just arrived. The *Times* was then trying to appeal to a younger demographic, but in Daniel, Holbrooke found a fellow critic of modern attempts to soften hard news.

Within minutes, Holbrooke's energy and poise had so impressed Daniel that the editor asked the college reporter if he would like to join the *Times* staff for the duration of the summit. For $10 per day, Holbrooke was to make occasional phone calls to foreign ministry officials and, most critically, fetch beers and hold seven conference room seats for the *Times* correspondents.[15]

Holbrooke got to work on the morning of Monday, May 16, excited to watch history being made. At 11 a.m., he arrived at the Palais to find the press corps buzzing with speculation about Khrushchev's intentions. Unbeknownst to them, several blocks to the east in the Élysée Palace, Khrushchev was smashing the summit on the ground in front of Macmillan, de Gaulle, and Eisenhower. The American president had forced Khrushchev's hand by acknowledging that he had authorized the espionage. An AP correspondent first broke the news to Holbrooke: According to French and British foreign ministry officials, Khrushchev would stall the summit until Eisenhower apologized for the U-2.

At 2:08 that afternoon, the Big Four finally emerged from the Élysée. The *Times* staff huddled and speculated on whether or not the summit would continue. At 2:45 p.m., over the PA system, organizers asked all reporters to come to Salle D to receive news from the Soviet officials. Fifteen minutes later, correspondents filled the room and spilled into the hallway. Soviet press secretary Mikhail Kharlamov read a statement that Khrushchev had delivered to the Western leaders a few hours earlier, decrying the U-2 overflights as "unprecedented actions directed against the sovereignty of the Soviet State." In lieu of an American apology, the summit, said Khrushchev through Kharlamov, would be "a useless waste of time."[16]

Holbrooke was stunned. His hard-won correspondent job was slipping away. "Well, I guess we'll be going home soon," said one reporter. As they walked out of the Palais that evening, Reston was downcast. "I've never seen such a mess," he said.

At eight that evening, Holbrooke joined Daniel at the U.S. embassy for a briefing on background. For Holbrooke, it was a window into the way high-level journalism was done. Daniel explained that they, and about eighty other hand-screened journalists, would have access to a White House source. They could print the information but could not identify the source. Regardless, Holbrooke later identified the source as Eisenhower's haggard press secretary James Hagerty, who, to the student reporter, seemed "totally out of his element in the world of international diplomacy."[17]

On Wednesday, Holbrooke arrived at the Palais and, after clearing tightened security, went to the fourth floor. The thousand assembled journalists quickly trebled as a rumor spread that Khrushchev himself might appear. The crowd soon swelled to the largest press conference ever, and Holbrooke, unlike many copyboys who had been sent down to the third floor for sandwiches, Carlsberg beer, and Pschitt orangeade, was in the thick of it. The first five rows of the conference hall were roped off for the Soviet claque. A harried Holbrooke managed to save four seats in the seventh row and three more a bit farther away for the *Times* reporters.

Shortly after 2 p.m., Khrushchev's car pulled up. When he appeared at the podium, the journalists, some of whom had waited in sweltering heat for hours, hissed and booed.[18] True to form, Khrushchev, assuming the catcallers were West Germans, railed against "those fascist bastards we didn't finish off at Stalingrad. We hit them so hard that we put them ten feet underground right away. If you boo us and attack us again, *look out!* We will hit you so hard there won't be a squeal out of you."[19] When a power failure silenced his microphone, Khrushchev jumped on his chair. "You see what happens in capitalist countries?" he shouted. The diatribe lasted two and a half hours.[20] The next day, the summit formally ended. Three months later, the French tore down the Palais.

After the fiasco, Holbrooke spent the summer hitchhiking across Europe with a friend. They soon arrived in a city that captured the teenager's imagination, as it seemed like the Berlin of a bygone era, a tinderbox where a world war had been sparked. He stepped into the cement footprints where Gavrilo Princip had stood when he shot Archduke Franz Ferdinand. It was his first visit to Sarajevo.

THE FOLLOWING SUMMER, HOLBROOKE'S LAST BEFORE GRADUATION, temperatures topped ninety degrees in New York City. But in the hallway of the tiny, first-floor, one-bedroom Greenwich Village flat that he shared with a friend, the temperature sometimes reached a hundred. On the platform of the West 4th Street subway, where Holbrooke would wait each evening for the Eighth Avenue line to take him to the old *Times* building on Broadway and 43rd, the heat was almost unbearable.

High temperatures and long hours were small prices to pay as Holbrooke pursued his dream and worked the night shift as a *New York Times* news clerk in the summer of 1961. Each morning he trekked past the Village hipsters in his crumpled oxford shirt and horn-rimmed spectacles, and turned onto the block that would be immortalized two years later when Bob Dylan, a month younger than Holbrooke and then living around the corner with his girlfriend, was photographed for the cover of "The Freewheelin' Bob Dylan." Holbrooke's casement window at 14 Jones Street looked out onto that spot, and the twenty-year-old would sit by that window after he returned home and read all of the day's New York papers.

The job itself was not glamorous: Each night, Holbrooke would get coffee and sandwiches for editors, and as cables came in to the radio room from foreign bureaus, Holbrooke would copy and distribute them. But he was in the thick of things, and, critically, he was meeting his heroes.

That summer, the star reporter at the *Times* was Gay Talese, and Holbrooke scored a small coup when he convinced Talese, whose writing he adored, to hang out early one evening with him in Washington Square Park. For the teetotaler Holbrooke, the counterculture was merely an academic interest, and while Talese famously partook in it with relish, that evening both teacher and student watched as a bongo musician played a cat-and-mouse game with the police in defiance of a local ordinance banning performances in the park.

The counterculture was also the inspiration for Holbrooke's greatest accomplishment that summer, his first published piece in the *Times*, a "Topics" editorial column on graffiti that ran in the July 27 edition. In it, Holbrooke compared the "repetitive and unfortunate obscenities" that dominated New York with the politically charged, historically infused markings found on the buildings he had visited the previous summer in Europe. The story ran without a byline, but Holbrooke worked hard on it and proudly gave copies to friends.[21]

A year later, when Holbrooke again sought a job at the *Times*, his rejection was a turning point. He had written Reston, then the *Times*'s Washington bureau chief, and when Reston turned him down, explaining that he only hired writers with five or six years of field experience, Holbrooke took the Foreign Service exam. As the exam was then based on the previous year's reporting in the *Times*, Holbrooke was well read on the questions.[22]

The birth of Holbrooke the diplomat did not mean the death of Holbrooke the journalist. When he arrived for his first assignment in Vietnam in 1962, he brandished a letter of introduction from Clifton Daniel; his connection to Dean Rusk, whose early praise of the Foreign Service had prompted him to apply, he rarely advertised.[23]

In Vietnam, Holbrooke drew even closer to the press corps, although he was no longer formally a part of it. When, at twenty-two, he arrived in Saigon, he believed the official U.S. line on the war. But his time in the Mekong Delta undermined that belief. He watched closely as Lieutenant Colonel John Paul Vann—whom he would later call "the most remarkable American that I saw in action"—pushed the truth, which he couldn't get the chairman of the Joint Chiefs of Staff to absorb, to David Halberstam, Neil Sheehan, Johnny Apple, and other correspondents. The Vietnam hands who were portraying the war most accurately, Holbrooke realized, were those journalists in their dispatches, not the American officials in their memoranda and cables. So he made them *his* sources, as much as he was theirs. Many would become lifelong friends.[24]

In the summer of 1966, Holbrooke returned to the States with his wife and newborn son and bought a small house off of MacArthur Boulevard in Washington. There, Polly Fritchey, the recently widowed mother of Frank Wisner, his close friend from Vietnam, took Holbrooke under her wing, introducing him to Georgetown society. Through her, he met many of the biggest names in the D.C. press corps. To the Washington correspondents, Holbrooke was the bright young thing who was more than a bureaucrat, because he had actually spent three years in the country that dominated foreign policy discussions that decade. The diplomat saw a chance to inform those who could influence policy from without, and he seized the opportunity. It was here, and during his time as the junior member of the U.S. delegation to the 1968 Paris Peace Talks, that he learned the power, and danger, of strategic leaks.

Despite his constant proximity to the media, and the close friends he had among the press, Holbrooke was disciplined with sensitive information. After a year at Princeton, he became Peace Corps director in Morocco in 1970. Shortly after arriving, Dan Ellsberg visited Casablanca with his new wife. Holbrooke, like Ellsberg, had contributed to the Pentagon Papers, and the RAND analyst knew that Holbrooke's views on the war were identical to his own. Having failed to convince Senators Fulbright and McGovern to release the papers to the public, Ellsberg was reaching out to see if he would support his intended leak. Holbrooke resisted.

When he returned to the States and left the Foreign Service after a decade in government, he took what would be his last full-time job in journalism. Two years earlier, Harvard professor Samuel Huntington and investment banker Warren Manshell, two friends cleaved apart by Vietnam, had founded a quarterly magazine called *Foreign Policy* as a forum for constructive debate. It was an upstart, going after the forty-eight-year-old *Foreign Affairs*, which had recused itself from any discussion of the war, and which then best embodied Christopher Hitchens's epithet: "the establishment house organ."[25] Even *Foreign Policy*'s 4" x 11" shape proclaimed its difference.

After the tragic death of the magazine's first editor, John Campbell, Holbrooke, who had entered the Foreign Service with Campbell, eulogized the thirty-one-year-old. At the funeral, Huntington, who knew Holbrooke from his time at Princeton, convinced him to helm the magazine.

For the first time in a decade, Holbrooke was an outsider looking in. But now his analysis of President Ford's foreign policy team conveyed an authority beyond his years. The journal quickly won praise for fluid, jargon-free prose and provocative articles. He took on media and political elites, and though he published works by giants like Paul Nitze and George Kennan, Holbrooke railed against his "pygmy generation" that had no principled great minds like that of Acheson or Harriman or Murrow.[26] Kissinger, a frequent target, scorned the publication. But he read it. And classified documents that he leaked found their way into Holbrooke's hands and onto the pages of his quarterly.

He pushed back at "the so-called 'neoconservative' school," which blamed the media for the country's drift and malaise: "This argument strikes me as a refuge for people who are no longer willing to present their case openly," Holbrooke wrote.[27] But with television now dominant, he worried that journalism risked devolving to entertainment and argued that "the press can no longer hide behind its traditional shield as a mere observer—it has become a participant."[28]

At the end of his life, Holbrooke would call his time at *Foreign Policy* "among the most important in my life and my career."[29] But, as President Obama eulogized just a month and a half after Holbrooke said that, "he belonged in the Arena." And the 1976 election gave him a chance to return to it.

That January, during a lively, four-hour dinner in Washington, Holbrooke and other elite Washington journalists met Jimmy Carter, whom Holbrooke later described as surprisingly calm and intellectually curious. Shortly thereafter, Holbrooke took a leave of absence from the magazine to join the Carter campaign.[30] He would write a few more bimonthly columns for *Newsweek International*—Stanley Karnow, his friend from Vietnam days, had enlisted his help—and he would later pen regular pieces in the *Asian Wall Street Journal* during the Reagan years and a monthly column in the *Washington Post* during the presidency of George W. Bush. But once he boarded the bus with Carter, his days as a full-time journalist were done. And once back in government—Carter made him the youngest-ever assistant secretary of state for East Asian and Pacific affairs—Holbrooke leveraged his years as part of the Washington press corps to advance his policy agenda. Sometimes Holbrooke leveraged them just to survive.

While his epic feud with Carter's National Security Advisor Zbigniew Brzezinski has long been the stuff of foreign policy legend, his use of the press for self-defense is less well known. During the last week of October 1978, while Holbrooke was on a trip to Southeast Asia, "Brzezinski tried to end my career," he later said. At Holbrooke's first stop in Vientiane, the American chargé held a reception for him and invited the Vietnamese ambassador to Laos. Though Holbrooke greeted him coolly, a week later, when he was out of telephone contact, far north along the Burma Road, Brzezinski triumphantly walked into the Oval Office with a report from the Foreign Broadcast Information Service, translating a Vietnamese News Agency (VNA) fabrication that Holbrooke had greeted the Vietnamese ambassador *chaudement*—warmly. Making matters worse, the Thai press had erred and claimed that, on a stopover between Laos and Burma, Holbrooke had told the Thai government that the U.S. was prepared to normalize relations with Vietnam within two months.

Brzezinski told Carter that such insubordination meant that he must fire Holbrooke. The president called Secretary of State Cy Vance, a loyal Holbrooke ally, who refused to believe the story. With Holbrooke just outside of Mandalay, Vance radioed him an order to return to Rangoon immediately. Holbrooke did just that and, after explaining his side to his comrades at State, he assumed that the crisis was averted. But Brzezinski, unrelenting, tried to leak the story to the press. Holbrooke beat Brzezinski at his own game. He commissioned a CIA study on the VNA story, which he leaked to conservative columnists Evans and Novak, who ran a story making Brzezinski look like a dupe of the North Vietnamese. While Brzezinski would have felt no more warmly to Holbrooke after the episode, he had to respect Holbrooke as a capable combatant in media wars.

After Holbrooke left government in 1981, Abe Rosenthal, his role model while at college, offered him a job at the *New York Times*. Shocked at the low pay, which raging inflation had made even worse since Holbrooke had last been a journalist, he instead tried his hand at business.[31]

But his love affair with journalism only grew over the last thirty years of his life. In the 1980s, Holbrooke became a regular talking head on the networks, often appearing on *Face The Nation*, *Nightline*, or *Meet the Press*. He perfected the delicate art of the exiled statesman, offering advice on how to remove Marcos from the Philippines and avoid a coup in South Korea.

His love for journalists themselves also grew over his final decades. After dating Diane Sawyer for seven years in the 1980s, Holbrooke met a journalist who would become the love of his life. Kati Marton was an NPR correspondent and the Bonn bureau chief for ABC, whose parents had been the last independent journalists reporting from Hungary after the communist takeover, until their arrests on false charges in 1955. Shortly after he proposed, Marton became the chair of the Committee to Protect Journalists. When Bosnian Serbs held *Christian Science Monitor* correspondent David Rohde in October 1995, she joined her husband in pressuring Serbian president Slobodan Milošević and won his release.

He had near-religious regard for war correspondents, and he felt the loss of the good ones keenly. In May 2000, when rebels gunned down the prolific Reuters journalist Kurt Schork in Sierra Leone, Holbrooke, then serving as U.S. ambassador to the United Nations, eulogized him as "perhaps the finest war correspondent of his generation."[32] During his life, Schork had rarely written under a byline. So Holbrooke had taken the time to make sure the world knew his name.

I MET HOLBROOKE FOR THE FIRST TIME IN AUGUST 2001. HE HAD READ my cowritten review of President Clinton's foreign policy for the *Foreign Service Journal*, an alumni magazine of sorts for foreign service officers, and he held me to task for underrating the president's efforts and, I suspect, for ignoring his. At twenty-five, I was dry-mouthed. But he took me seriously, and at the end of the conversation, he offered me a job. Over the next decade, as I worked and grew as a writer and a journalist, he was first my boss, then my mentor, and ultimately, my friend.

In late October 2009, as Secretary of State Hillary Clinton prepared for her first visit to Pakistan, I asked Holbrooke for a comment, as I approached deadline on a *Time* story about an unfolding, yet then buried, crisis in Sindh province. There, some 170 farmworkers had won their freedom from debt bondage through a district magistrate. But when they returned to the farms to claim their few possessions, their former masters held them at gunpoint, killing one of the plaintiffs and threatening to kill the others unless they returned to work to pay off fictional debts that averaged around $12.

High-level discussions with the Pakistani government were at a critical juncture, and I imagined that mine was the last call Holbrooke wanted to field. What should he care about a couple of hundred landless peasants, when the United States was spending nearly $200 million a day and U.S. casualties were nearing a thousand in neighboring Afghanistan? But a year earlier, Holbrooke had contributed a foreword to my book on modern-day slavery, and I thought, just possibly, I could move him to make a statement. U.S. Ambassador to Pakistan Anne Patterson gave me a quote. But Holbrooke was atypically mum.

It turns out that what he did was much more important than giving me a sound bite. When two officials in State's human trafficking office ran into him outside of the department cafeteria, he invited them into his office to talk about the situation. Before they could finish, instead of wasting time calling me back, he picked up the phone to call Husain Haqqani, Pakistan's ambassador in Washington. Fix the problem before the secretary touches down, Holbrooke told Haqqani in no uncertain terms. A week later, Sindh officials freed the hostages. To my knowledge, Holbrooke never spoke publicly about his actions to save their lives.

Until the end, Holbrooke spoke truth to power. Sometimes, he shouted it, as Milošević knew well. But today, some 170 men, women, and children are free because he understood that, just occasionally, a well-placed stage whisper works best.

That Magnificent Hunger

JONATHAN ALTER

When he traveled across the United States as a young man, Richard Holbrooke kept a notebook. Inside he had scrawled the word PURPOSE and underlined it six times. Having decided to lead a purposeful life, he needed journalists as chroniclers and companions. How could a person leave a mark on history without someone there to notice it? The question answered itself.

By temperament, he was much more swashbuckling journalist than cautious diplomat, and at first it seemed he was headed for the news business. But after editing the *Brown Daily Herald* in 1961–1962, he was turned down for a job on the *New York Times*, an early career setback he rarely failed to rub in the faces of anyone associated with the paper. He could have had a career like Leslie Gelb or Richard Burt—moving seamlessly (or in Richard's transparent case, with the seams showing) between the *Times* and government—but he succeeded in the State Department at such a young age that it was never practical. Instead, he used his considerable editorial skills to help assemble the Pentagon

Papers in the 1960s, serve as editor of *Foreign Policy* magazine in the 1970s, pen a monthly column for the *Washington Post* in the 1980s, and write scores of op-ed pieces on complex international issues throughout his career, most of them examples of clarity and liveliness in a genre known for neither.

At the time of his death, Richard was talking to his agent, Mort Janklow, about his memoirs, which he insisted would take two volumes. He had written Clark Clifford's memoirs in the early 1990s—they include one of the best accounts anywhere of the U.S. recognition of Israel in 1948—and his own highly regarded book, *To End a War*, about Bosnia and the Dayton Peace Accords. Out of friendship and a commitment to the integrity of the historical record, he rarely turned down requests to write forewords, blurbs, and exuberant reviews that ensured that important books weren't neglected. Words mattered to him. In any posting, he made sure his staff read George Orwell's essay, "Politics and the English Language."

He was a familiar fixture in newsrooms. For years when he was dating Diane Sawyer, he accompanied her to the studio at 5:00 a.m., full of suggestions for her morning news broadcasts. Years later, more than one MSNBC anchor complained that he always tried to write the questions he would be asked on camera. He could be scathing with print reporters. But even when he bellowed, "That's the stupidest question I ever heard!" it was often said with at least a touch of endearment. One *Times* man recalls showing up to a party at the Waldorf Astoria (where he mixed journalists with diplomats at lavish dinner salons while ambassador to the UN) only to have the host say at the door: "Who invited you?"

More often he employed flattery, which didn't fool hardened reporters and editors but worked nonetheless. Jonathan Randal of the *Washington Post* remembered attending a Holbrooke lecture at Harvard: "He told the crowd, 'There's a very important person in this room. Jon Randal is here.' If he'd seen someone more important than me, he would have recognized him, of course, but it warmed the cockles of my heart."

From his earliest years in Vietnam (when he counted David Halberstam, Neil Sheehan, and Johnny Apple as friends) to the day he collapsed at the State Department from a ruptured aorta (shortly before he was scheduled to have lunch with me at the Hay-Adams Hotel), Richard was a generous friend-source (or source-friend) to dozens of members of the press. These relationships can be both useful and a little hazardous for reporters. "He was as good at seducing journalists as he was at bullying dictators like Milošević," remembered Ray Bonner, formerly of the *Times*, who avoided seduction and clashed with Holbrooke over his handling of Far Eastern affairs in the Carter administration but later told him he was robbed of a Nobel Peace Prize for Bosnia.

"This was a delicate negotiation—who was the user and who the used, and why," recalled Christiane Amanpour, who first knew him in Bosnia. "We understood that when Holbrooke told us stuff, he was often spinning madly—as though the sheer force and quantity of words, said loudly and often enough, would change things on the ground or around the bargaining table. It was our job to get beyond the spin. But there were times when America's goals seemed so obviously right that our professional relationship with Holbrooke, or at least my own, was nothing to trouble our journalistic conscience. He was a very clever man, but in his work he also never lost sight of the moral dimension."

He won the affection of the reporters he chose to befriend because he was funny, larger than life, and honest in his off-the-record assessments of people—a sharp contrast to the buttoned-down bureaucrats who populate most of the government. Even when allowing himself to be profiled harmed him with colleagues and superiors, he didn't much care. From a young age, he knew that being accessible was a form of protection; reporters, once fed, don't burn their sources. And the benefits of being an oft-quoted public persona (higher status for jobs in and out of government) were worth ticking off a few jealous rivals.

Contrary to reputation, he was not a big leaker; when many in Washington suspected him as the source of a leaked 2009 memo from Karl Eikenberry, the U.S. ambassador to Afghanistan, they were almost certainly wrong. Instead of providing documents or scoops, he offered context and color—one-stop shopping for a busy reporter trying to get a sophisticated read on a complex foreign story. "He would have been a terrific editor of a newspaper because he always knew exactly what the news was," remembered Steven Weisman of the *Times*. "He was great not because he leaked but because he clarified."

Karen DeYoung of the *Post* noticed that "unlike a lot of public servants, he wasn't afraid of us. If you were bringing something to the table, he'd always talk and he was willing to make you a friend despite the adversarial relationship. He was confident enough and manipulative enough to make those relationships work for both parties."

DeYoung fondly recalled him in refugee camps in Pakistan walking into tents, sitting down on the dirt floor, and asking questions like he was a reporter—about the furthest thing imaginable from the usual dog and pony show for visiting U.S. officials. But his relentlessness in peddling a story could be grating. At a cavernous filing center one day, DeYoung was on deadline and turned away from Holbrooke, pretending to be on the phone. From the other side of the hall, he called her cell phone: "You can't get away from me!"

HIS FRIENDSHIPS WITH REPORTERS HARDLY GRANTED HIM IMMUNITY from scrutiny. I learned this in 1995 when *Newsweek*, then edited by Maynard Parker, Holbrooke's old friend from Vietnam, ran a story critical of his legendary ego. Not long after, I was with Richard the night he got off the plane in New York City from Dayton. This was the greatest American diplomatic triumph in years and Holbrooke was practically carried into an International Rescue Committee banquet on a litter. Huzzahs all around.

I wanted to know the secret of the breakthrough. He explained to me in the car over to *Nightline* how, after the talks broke down, he instructed the U.S. delegates to leave their luggage curbside so that the Serbs, Muslims, and Croats would think the U.S. was departing. That would have meant a humiliating defeat for all sides. The brilliant bluff worked and the parties returned to the table.

But instead of savoring his Nobel-worthy triumph, Richard was berating me for the negative article, which he knew I had nothing to do with. The histrionics continued as he got out of the car, went into makeup, and sat down to talk to Ted Koppel. "You tell Maynard I'm mad as hell!" he shouted to me only seconds before the red light went on, and he said evenly into the camera "Good evening, Ted. Yes, it was an historic day in Dayton. . . ."

The last reporter he saw before he collapsed was Susan Glasser, editor of a revived *Foreign Policy*. At the end of his life, Glasser recalled, he was delighted to be reconnecting to a publication that was important to him early in his career. At that last lunch in the State Department cafeteria, he was doing what had come naturally over fifty years: chewing over the world, suggesting story ideas, embodying a life of purpose, which meant advancing not just national and humanitarian interests but those of readers and viewers who shared at least a little of his magnificent hunger.

The Writing on the Wall

RICHARD HOLBROOKE
New York Times, JULY 27, 1961

> *Holbrooke published his first piece in a major publication at age*
> *twenty, while working as a copyboy/clerk at the* New York Times
> *between his junior and senior years at Brown University. In it, he*
> *compares the political expression in European graffiti, which he had*
> *observed while hitchhiking the previous summer, with the more*
> *crass street art of his hometown of New York City.*

For as long as man has had the means to do so, the writing or scratching of inscriptions on walls seems to have been a basic, or near-basic, human activity. These graffiti, as they are called, have been found on the walls of Pompeii; on the ancient Greek monuments and temples (where one of the more famous is the name "Byron" etched deep into a column of the ruins of the temple at Cape Sunion, some 140 years ago, during the Greek War of Independence); and they confront the citizens of New York continually as they go about their daily affairs.

The urge to mar the walls and sidewalks of the city with inscriptions of various kinds may well be lurking within all of us, but comparatively few people actually do so. Their handiwork, however, is seen by everyone. It falls into three general categories: the scrawled insults and messages of children, just learning some of the infinite uses of the alphabet; the repetitive and unfortunate obscenities or names and initials of visitors found on so many public monuments; and, finally, political slogans and messages, so much more common in Europe than in the United States.

THE TOURIST DOES HIS BIT

People constantly try to immortalize themselves by leaving their name indelibly connected to some famous monument or building; thus some of Europe's most renowned sites are the location of tourism's worst displays of vandalism: layer covers layer of initials, names, dates and home towns on the walls of many of France's great chateaux, Roman and Greek ruins, and even some ancient wall frescoes. The penalty for such destruction may be great, but generally police and guards are inadequate to the task of watching the scores of tourists (the Acropolis in Athens is a notable exception), and a few persons are ever carving something into a blank space on a famous wall.

KILROY ISN'T HERE ANY MORE

In the United States, graffiti have usually been confined, except perhaps during election campaigns, to the nonpolitical groups mentioned above. In contrast, Europe seems to be a Continent where graffiti are predominantly a weapon of the political wars; "Yankee Go Home" has lost most of the punch it had during the early Nineteen Fifties, but it is still in evidence in parts of Europe. But partisans of both the extreme Left and the extreme Right, who do most of the wall-politicking in Europe today, have largely abandoned this type of slogan, perhaps the most famous ever inscribed on the walls of the world. (Its unforgettable wartime predecessor, and perhaps its partial cause, "Kilroy was here," is long dead.)

For the French Left, the single word "Paix" (Peace) or the phrase "Paix en Algerie" have been a dominant theme for some years now. During General de Gaulle's years of political self-exile, from 1946 until May 1958, his name, or more often his symbol, the Cross of Lorraine, was seen frequently. It still is, but more and more now, his die-hard opponents on both the Left and the Right, finding themselves sandwiched between de Gaulle's tremendous power and prestige and their own discredit with the great mass of Frenchmen, have taken to writing the single word, "Non," denoting total disapproval of the Gaullist regime, on the walls and streets of France. Of course, it is impossible to tell whether an individual "Non" comes from the political Left or Right, but that does not seem to disturb partisans of both causes.

"WILL YOUR CHILDREN BE RADIOACTIVE?"

Why political graffiti are not as much a part of the American political scene as they are a part of Europe's is not clear. Perhaps it reflects the smaller membership of extremist groups in this country. Perhaps it is a function of a large apathy on the part of the public.

But recently the passions aroused by political events and issues, particularly the Cuban regime of Fidel Castro and the general problem of nuclear-bomb testing, have moved some persons into employing the walls of building and subway entrances to make their point. For the entire month of June a series of signs confronted the passerby in the West Fourth Street subway exit: "Ban the Bomb," "Peace by 1970—With or Without People," and so on. Finally, the slogans were scratched out—whether by the Transit Authority or by an advocate of nuclear testing is not known. Two days later they were back: "Will your children be active or radioactive?" one of them asked. This time it took only a few days for them to be removed, but no one really expects the walls to stay clean, or the wall-cleaners to give up, in the never-ending battle between those who write and those who remove graffiti.

Washington Dateline: The New Battlelines

RICHARD HOLBROOKE
Foreign Policy, No. 13, WINTER, 1973–1974

> *Holbrooke was always an astute observer of the players in Washington's foreign policy drama. Here he takes on one of his favorite targets during the 1970s, Henry Kissinger, who was a global figure as President Nixon's National Security Advisor and added a second hat as Secretary of State in September 1973. Holbrooke had first met Kissinger in Saigon, and while the 1970s saw them shouting across an ideological divide, they would eventually form a warm friendship and come to find much common cause.*

The fall of 1973 saw surprising new friendships and alliances within the foreign policy community. Battlelines formed during the Vietnam war, which looked for a long time like they might be fairly permanent alignments, have been breached and reformed in strange ways.

Until the end of this summer, Washington and the nation had been divided essentially along hawk-versus-dove lines. Vietnam had hung over the city like an oppressive cloud since the mid-1960's. One's position on that issue seemed to define where one stood on most other issues. Prior to that, there were other periods in which a fundamental division in foreign policy occasioned a great debate. Now we may be seeing the early outlines of another. It is too early to tell for certain, and the extraordinary political crisis that grips Washington obscures the question, but things look different today than a few months ago.

It was the rush of events that forced the rapid shifting of positions in Washington. Questions about the detente with the Soviet Union would not go away. Andrei Sakharov became an effective spokesman against it. The Russians' treatment of Jews gained attention. And evidence that the Russians knew about the Mideast war in advance, and did nothing to prevent it, raised more doubts.

As the new battlelines began to form, they became a special problem for the new Secretary of State. Would he be a beneficiary or a victim of them? Some old supporters were now turning against him, and help was coming from strange quarters. It was clear that Kissinger would be in his usual position in the middle, though sometimes jumping from one side to another, trying to blur issues and embrace opponents, trying to keep himself and his policies from being wrecked in the debate.

HENRY KISSINGER, SUPERSTAR

The summer ended with little warning of the storms that were about to break over Washington. The dominant event, of course, was the nomination of Henry Kissinger as Secretary of State. Suddenly the capital was awash in tidbits and rumors. Henry was everywhere, wearing an air of innocent helplessness, earnestly asking advice from almost everyone: "How should I run the Department? Can I really get control of it? Who are the best Foreign Service Officers? Should I keep emphasis on my National Security Council hat?"

There was about this performance the impression that it was just that—a performance. Kissinger had frequently proclaimed his contempt for some of those he was now consulting, many of whom had fought him over the war and wiretapping. His attacks had been subtle and often indirect; Kissinger often defused his critics by praising or embracing them, as he did so masterfully at his confirmation hearings. (When asked, for example, about certain people whose telephones had been tapped while they worked for him, with his prior knowledge, he replied with extravagant praise for his victims; and the issue—which deserved to receive a full airing—seemed to melt away.)

There were those in Washington who treated Kissinger's elaborate and semipublic round of consultations with derision and called it a charade—but they tended to be partially discredited by the fact that they were the people not consulted. Those consulted found themselves in a traditional Washington dilemma: even if you suspect that you are being used as an ornament and that your advice is not really valued for its substance, how can you refuse when the Secretary of State asks for advice?

The people Kissinger approached did in fact take his request with the utmost seriousness—probably more than Kissinger himself. As Kissinger undoubtedly knew, each man summoned would consult with his friends, and thus a large number of members of the foreign policy communities would feel that they had played a part in The Education Of The Secretary. Kissinger hoped this would "help build a broad bipartisan base for foreign policy"; he wanted to create a personal and policy base which could survive regardless of Nixon, Watergate, and Agnew, and he thus moved directly to defuse his critics.

This effort was partially effective. Major figures from the 1960's, like Cyrus Vance, Averell Harriman, Benjamin Read, William Bundy, Nicholas Katzenbach, Richard Neustadt, McGeorge Bundy, all made the visit to Kissinger's office (although neither Clark Clifford nor his law partner Paul Warnke got the call; perhaps they had gone too far in their opposition to Kissinger's policies). He took great pains and scored an impressive success in convincing the very people he had previously denigrated—the Senate Foreign Relations Committee—that he would henceforth consult with them regularly.

He used the same approach with two other special constituencies— the press and the State Department. He spoke at length to Washington's most powerful reporters, editors, and publishers, seeking ways to improve relations with them. He made the astute move of bringing our Ambassador to Cyprus, Robert McCloskey, back to assist him during the first few weeks. McCloskey, who had served as press spokesman for the State Department for eight years until early 1973, is universally respected and liked by journalists and fellow Department officials. He was an inspired choice, and did a great deal to get the Secretary off to a good start.

To the Department of State, Kissinger's appointment was the cause for great excitement. A few people—those who had risen with William Rogers—may have lamented the change and looked at it as the replacement of the hunted by the hunter. But for most, Kissinger offered a hope that the Department would finally assume its place as the focal point of policy formulation and implementation. Everyone knew that there would be major shifts in senior positions, and in time these shifts would trickle down to produce new power centers and new faces. There was some fear that Kissinger would undercut or bypass the Foreign Service, but it was pointed out that in fact he used Foreign Service Officers extensively at the National Security Council. There was a guessing game over names, and some concern that his style would not work at Foggy Bottom.

Coming into the Department with Kissinger were some familiar "insiders" in Washington—men whose names are rarely in newspapers but who carry great influence. These include Winston Lord, who had just left the White House but returned to take over State's Planning and Coordination Staff, and Larry Eagleburger, an FSO who moved back particularly to influence scheduling and personnel. Other key men who were with Kissinger at the White House may remain there; it was apparent that Kissinger would retain and extensively use the power that resided in his NSC position.

New names will emerge at State. George Vest (previously a hidden power within the Department on the European Security Conference) took over as the official press spokesman. Vest, who is widely respected, could become a major force in State. Some new men moved into key positions: among them, early attention focused on William H. Donaldson, a New York investment banker who replaced Curtis Tarr as an Undersecretary, with an expanded portfolio which theoretically includes energy matters. But Kissinger emphasized that many major appointments remain to be made, and the Department is still filled with rumors and maneuverings.

Although the usual complaints, bureaucratic sniping, and guerrilla warfare have not abated at State, there is a sense that the boss has real power, and that if they work hard, State will get a piece of the action.

The "co-opting" technique that Kissinger has developed seems almost institutionalized. When he went to the United Nations to deliver his maiden speech, it was predictable that he would cheer up the dispirited advocates of a strong U.N. simply by saying the things that he knew they wanted to hear—whether or not he really meant them. His past behavior had hurt the world organization; now he could score points easily, and at no cost, just by showing up and being polite. And when he added a call for a world food conference, reversing the position of the Department of Agriculture, he showed how easily he could gain new friends by taking an interest in nonstrategic issues.

In fact, he had been getting strong advice from various people that he pay more attention to economic affairs. In his speech at the Pacem in Terris conference in October, former Secretary of Commerce Peter Peterson—a man with close personal and professional ties to Kissinger—

spoke of how Kissinger has "moved from his familiar, metaphysical terrain of the MIRV and [been] forced to discover the megatonnage of the soybean."

AN UNPUBLISHED CRITIQUE

A direct attack on Kissinger's comprehension of the importance of economic issues to foreign policy and his ability to deal effectively in that area came from one of the most respected international economists in Washington. C. Fred Bergsten of The Brookings Institution (who from January 1969 until May 1971 was Kissinger's Assistant for International Economic Affairs) wrote a critique of Kissinger at the request of a national magazine. Although it was not published, it circulated privately in Washington. "Kissinger's record on economics is dismal," he wrote. "On most issues, he has totally abstained. This is true even on those major international monetary and trade policy decisions which led directly to the collapse of the postwar economic system in late 1971. . . . Where Kissinger did reluctantly get involved in economic issues, he usually bungled: on several occasions botching the textile negotiations with Japan, which have badly distorted both U.S.-Japan relations and overall U.S. foreign economic policy; contributing to the giveaway of wheat to the Soviet Union in the pell-mell rush to reach concrete agreements at the Moscow summit; ignoring the central economic issues in his call for a 'new Atlantic charter.'"

Bergsten asked why Kissinger has performed so poorly on this "central issue where foreign policy concerns must share equal responsibility with concerns about our domestic economy." Dismissing ignorance of the subject as "no excuse," Bergsten concluded that the "problem goes deeper into the Kissinger style. Kissinger is reluctant to engage actively in issues with lots of bureaucratic adversaries by whom he is not recognized as the leading authority in town, especially when he is not in control of the bureaucratic decision-making machinery. . . . Economic issues cannot be handled by superstar solos. They require both political and bureaucratic consensus at home and messy negotiations with a variety of leaders abroad. . . . Kissinger has yet to demonstrate the ability to develop a domestic consensus on any issue, with the possible exception of China policy, let alone those of economics where vested interests clash sharply." Bergsten also noted, however, that Kissinger has "a far greater opportunity to engage in economic issues from his new post at State. Haldeman, et al., are gone . . . and the President needs Kissinger now more than vice-versa anyway."

Kissinger told the Senate Foreign Relations Committee that he had "learned by experience the intricate connection between the solution of economic issues and political ones." Noting this, Bergsten concluded that if Kissinger truly grasped "the substantive importance of international economic issues" and "altered his personal style to handle them effectively" he could become one of the "great Secretaries of State." If he did not, however, he could become an "anachronism."

Applause and recognition surrounded Kissinger as the fall progressed. He seemed to stand even taller in an Administration peopled by pygmies and crooks. But as the issues became more pressing, attention turned.

First came the emergence of the "human rights" issue as a theme for the opposition. It had originally been almost the exclusive property of Senator Jackson. Jackson's position, and his famous Jackson Amendment to deny "most-favored nation" status to the Soviet Union if they continued to restrict the immigration of Jews to Israel, began to pick up significant supporters among liberals who had always considered Jackson a dangerous hawk. The poor treatment of Russian Jews found sympathetic listeners in Congress, where by mid-October an astonishing 75 senators had cosponsored the Jackson Amendment. Andrei Sakharov began to emerge as a part-time campaigner for Jackson, and his impact on American liberals, as they began to recover from the Vietnam obsession, was telling indeed. The "most-favored nation" legislation so urgently sought by the Administration was probably doomed for this year before the war began, but the outbreak of fighting on October 6 sharpened the issue and raised more doubts. Were the Russians taking us for a ride? What was detente really worth? Was there any connection at all between liberalized trade and human rights and relaxation of political military tensions? These questions had no clear answers, but they would be the focal points of a new debate within the government and the foreign policy community.

The debate, as Larry Stern deftly pointed out in *The Washington Post*, had "made political bedfellows of Henry Kissinger and Senator Fulbright, the National Association of Manufacturers, George Kennan, and Leonid Brezhnev," and had created a "consensus of sorts between

Senator Jackson and Professors Morgenthau and Arthur Schlesinger, Jr., between Human Events and Americans for Democratic Action, between Tom Wicker and Bill Buckley."

Washington had been talking about the Mideast before October 6, but not in terms of war in 1973. There had been a growing belief that the Arab strategy for the next few years would revolve around using oil as a major new card against the United States, and thus against Israel. People in Washington who had never considered such issues before were talking learnedly about "the energy crisis." As Peterson said, "It's now a status symbol to be able to drop such lines as the 'posted price of crude in the Gulf.'"

The war and the strange cease-fire that followed it left both the supporters of detente and its critics with new ammunition.

To its critics, detente has been revealed as a sharply limited arrangement which cannot head off a serious confrontation. They point out that the Russians violated the agreement Brezhnev and Nixon signed only months ago to consult with each other if either had knowledge of a third party threat to peace.

To its defenders, detente has been tested, but in the end it stopped the fighting. The U.S. and the Soviet Union had jointly sponsored a U.N. resolution for the first time since 1956, and Kissinger and the Russians had been able to limit the scope of the war.

Who was right? The available evidence was not conclusive, and the debate had only begun. The old battlelines were gone; new ones were forming. Will these set the framework for the foreign policy debate in the 1970s?

Jack Frost Nipping at the Years

Richard Holbrooke
New York Times, March 5, 1975

> *Whenever Holbrooke was out of government, he left Washington*
> *for his native Manhattan, which was always home for him. Here*
> *he reflects on his city and his father, who died in 1957 when*
> *Holbrooke was fifteen.*

The plane came down into New York through a heavy snowstorm, an hour late, and was diverted from La Guardia to Kennedy. Appointments of Great Importance were being jeopardized or canceled as our taxi crept slowly into Manhattan. Snow was falling steadily, the roads were slippery and everything was a mess. New York seemed at its most difficult, and the logistics of surviving through a two-city work day seemed hopeless and impossible.

Tempers were frayed. Tension was rising. The taxi driver was pleasant, but I kept urging him on, to go faster, which was clearly impossible.

Thoughts of the vulnerability of the great city to a snowstorm, of the patent unfairness of all this happening to me on such an important day: Why hadn't I taken the plane the night before? What a catastrophe if I'm late?

After the meeting, I came out into a heavy snowstorm on Ninth Avenue. There were no taxis and everyone looked cold and miserable. For a few minutes, I was, too.

I looked up into the tall buildings lost in the snow, and saw the absence of traffic. And suddenly, I felt for a moment that I was back in my Manhattan childhood. The city was a magic kingdom again. I remembered for the first time in years how wonderful it had been to be a child in New York in a snowstorm.

In 1947 we had an epic blizzard and the schools closed down. We sledded and skied in Central Park, walked down the middle of great avenues, and watched people abandon their cars in the middle of main streets. The paralysis that left adults tired and frustrated elevated us to joyous heights.

The parks were different, there was a feeling of true magic in the air. My father took me sledding down what seemed like mountain slopes in Central Park. People moved slowly through heavy snow drifts, their normal routines shattered. Maybe that upset them, but to us the change was an adventure. When we grew up we would speak of how the city can't handle the snow and complain about all the inconveniences that came with the storm. But when we were children—the world looked so different.

By mid-afternoon every adult in the city seemed to have abandoned his work plans and set about getting home, through difficult traffic and slush and ice.

As I stood on a street corner with a friend waiting for a ride, like two forlorn hitchhikers, the schools let out and we were almost knocked over by happy children sliding through the snow. Things hadn't changed, only we had.

The *New York Times* the next day had a front-page headline that read "6-Inch Snowfall Cripples Travel and Trade in the City." But the previous afternoon, as the sun set, I saw a man on cross-country skis going down Fifth Avenue.

CHAPTER THREE

Vietnam

Holbrooke in Vietnam.
(Courtesy of Kati Marton)

Richard Holbrooke and the Vietnam War: Past and Prologue

Gordon M. Goldstein

In September 2010, Richard Holbrooke spoke publicly for the last time about the legacy of the Vietnam War, a chapter of American history that consumed and defined the first seven years of his diplomatic career. The occasion was a conference sponsored by the State Department Historian's Office commemorating the publication of the final volume of papers in the official government history of the conflict, the longest in the annals of U.S. foreign policy. Holbrooke took the podium to address an audience of scholars, historians, and policy makers, many of whom had been subsumed by the Vietnam experience and had remained close in subsequent years.

His first boss in the outer provinces of the Mekong Delta, Rufus Phillips, was there; so were several of Holbrooke's friends from the press corps in Saigon—Morley Safer, Marvin Kalb, and his brother Bernard Kalb. Presidential counselor Harry McPherson, with whom Holbrooke worked in Lyndon Johnson's White House, was in attendance. Henry Kissinger, who had been a young Harvard professor when Holbrooke met him in 1965 in Vietnam, also addressed the conference. John Negroponte, Holbrooke's colleague in the Saigon embassy and his successor as ambassador to the United Nations, was another speaker. David Rusk—Holbrooke's oldest friend from growing up in Scarsdale, New York, and son of Dean Rusk, secretary of state to Kennedy and Johnson—sat in the second row. Holbrooke had been sure to invite all of these old friends for what became a kind of reunion. He wore a grey suit and a crisp red tie and seemed to choose his words with very deliberate care.

"The distance from today to my arrival in Vietnam in 1963 is greater from that day to the U.S. entry into World War I," he observed. "And I thought that if I met somebody who remembered World War I when I was in Vietnam, I thought I was talking to someone from another world." Holbrooke added: "Yet Vietnam will not go away, and I don't just mean these documents. The Vietnam War Memorial just a few blocks from here . . . is the most visited monument in Washington." Vietnam, he said, "divided the government, it divided the city, it divided the nation, it divided individual families." In political life, he noted, Vietnam "is still used as a metaphor by both the left and the right to justify wholly different situations." Holbrooke made it clear to the audience that for him, Vietnam remained living history, an indelible paradigm of historical, intellectual, and personal consequence. "As I leaf through the thousands of pages of documents and cables in these remarkable and important books," he said with evident emotion, "memories are triggered, many voices I haven't heard in years, some still forever, leap off the page and forgotten arguments briefly come back to life. A question still hangs over us, never quite answered: What did it all mean?"

SWORN INTO THE FOREIGN SERVICE IN 1962 FOLLOWING HIS GRADUATION from Brown University, where he was a history major, Holbrooke's initial expectations for a career in diplomacy were largely inchoate. "At the beginning I did not know where Vietnam was, except that it was someplace in Southeast Asia," he wrote in an unpublished memorandum, composed in 1969. But he soon learned that the country was fighting a communist insurgency. "I liked that," Holbrooke recalled, "the opportunity to find out what war was really like, without too much risk."[1]

Holbrooke was to be dispatched to an exotic and distant land, a new recruit to the diplomatic corps then presided over by Secretary of State Dean Rusk. Before arriving in South Vietnam, however, there would be a four-month training program in Berkeley, California. "The course was unspeakably bad," Holbrooke remembered, "and remains with me today as a singular horror, the worst part of which was a four-week, part-time group dynamics, or group psychotherapy, session." He tried to distract himself by bantering with his new friend, Vladimir Lehovich, also in the training program. Holbrooke scoured the campus, reading anything he could lay his hands on about Vietnam. And throughout he maintained a posture of "generally ignoring the work assigned to us by the teachers."[2]

His disdain for the proscribed course of study earned Holbrooke the enmity of his instructor, who sent a blistering report to Washington predicting that "I would not be an outstanding member of the American team in Vietnam" and regretting "the fact my negative influence during the course has lowered the performance of Mr. Lehovich, who seemed to have somewhat more potential."[3]

Despite his miserable indoctrination to the Foreign Service, Holbrooke was cleared for deployment to Vietnam. Before departing, he attended an official briefing delivered by an unidentified "young Golden Boy of the Vietnam Task Force" who was so sanguine about the prospects of crushing the insurgency that Holbrooke thought "we had better hurry to Saigon so as to get there before the war was over." He traveled to Asia by way of the Philippines and Tokyo. In an airport lounge, Holbrooke vividly recalled seeing an arresting photograph on the front page of the newspaper. It was a picture of an elderly monk named Thich Quang Duc who, on June 11, 1963, sat down at the center of a busy intersection in Saigon, drenched his body with gasoline with the help of three other monks, and then set himself ablaze while remaining serenely fixed in the lotus position as flames engulfed him. The monk had immolated himself as an act of political protest against the corrupt rule of South Vietnamese president Ngo Dinh Diem. "It was a dramatic event whose consequences were not foreseen at the time by the U.S. government," Holbrooke remarked. "Nor by us."[4]

Holbrooke and Lehovich landed at Tan Son Nhut airport in Saigon on June 26, 1963, shortly after 10:00 p.m. "The air was hot and muggy," he remembered, "the rainy season was just beginning." They were met at the airport by Tony Lake, another young foreign service officer who had arrived in Vietnam two months earlier, and by Ralph Boynton, an administrative officer of the rural affairs division of the United States

Operations Mission, known as USOM, which represented the civilian and foreign aid divisions of the U.S. government in Vietnam. Boynton gave the new recruits a directive. "I will always remember him telling us," wrote Holbrooke, "as we stood in our nice new suits in the heat of the tropical night waiting for our bags to come off the plane, 'When you come into work tomorrow, remember: we're a shirtsleeves outfit.'" Holbrooke would soon appropriate the new dress code for his role. Mastery of the local language would take longer. "I never did learn how to speak Vietnamese at better than the idiot level, although I did not know how bad I would be that first night in Saigon," he recalled. The young men left the airport and drove through the deserted streets of Saigon, which captivated Holbrooke, reminding him of Paris. His adventure had begun.

Holbrooke reported for his first day at USOM, housed in a capacious administrative building situated next to the Xa Loi Pagoda, the most significant Buddhist temple in Saigon. After work, he observed a stream of Vietnamese flowing in and out of the shrine. Intrigued, he followed the crowds and wandered inside. There he saw a small jar sitting on the altar holding "a blackened and dried-up substance that looked like overcooked liver." It was actually "the heart of Thich Quang Duc, the bonze [monk] who had burnt himself to death, miraculously preserved. And by worshipping the heart, the people were finding a way to express a forbidden political opinion, for the bonze had burned himself in protest against the government of Ngo Dinh Diem—although again I did not understand this, nor did the Embassy—forces were at work in Vietnam which would cause historic changes."[5]

Holbrooke was immediately dispatched to the field, assigned to work for George Melvin, the rural affairs chief for ten provinces north, east, and west of Saigon. In each province, rural affairs would have a dedicated representative, a position that the twenty-two-year-old Holbrooke would be appointed to after a brief apprenticeship. "The civilian provincial representatives were supposed to give the kind of advice on counterinsurgency which . . . could not come from the military," Holbrooke explained. It would be the beginning of his lifelong immersion in the analysis and implementation of counterinsurgency strategy, the multifaceted effort to provide security to vulnerable rural populations, while concurrently winning their allegiance through economic, political, and social development programs.[6]

One of the principal architects of America's counterinsurgency strategy in Vietnam in 1963 was Rufus Phillips, who would become a mentor to Holbrooke and a lifelong friend. Phillips was a young graduate of Yale, trained first as a CIA operative and then inducted into the army, which assigned him in 1954 to Vietnam, one of the first Americans on the scene in what would become a focal point of the Cold War. Holbrooke was fascinated by Phillips. "He was smart . . . quick and deeply committed to a victory of communism through the techniques known as counterinsurgency," Holbrooke wrote.[7] "He was a disciple of Major General Edward Lansdale, a legendary figure," who in 1963 was a "sworn enemy of General Maxwell Taylor, then the Chairman of the Joint Chiefs of Staff, later Ambassador in Saigon," who Holbrooke himself would eventually work for in the U.S. embassy. "Phillips was heading a team dedicated to their boss in exile, with many of the old hands reassembled," Holbrooke recorded in his memorandum. "I did not know any of this as I drove out into the South Vietnamese countryside for the first time."

Holbrooke and Melvin clambered into a sedan and traveled out of the city on Route 13, heading north of Saigon. It was known as "Bloody 13" because several Americans had already been killed by insurgents positioned along the road as it veered into contested territory. "Everything was new to me that day," Holbrooke remembered. "Melvin told me that while I worked for him I would hear things and do things that must not be discussed with anyone else. The ever-present sense of danger affects different people in different ways. For me, it made everything more intense and vivid; it made life itself a special sort of adventure. . . . For a long time, until the war became so ugly and so hopeless and so divisive at home, I loved being in Vietnam."[8]

Reporting to Melvin and Phillips, Holbrooke was assigned to a dangerous province in the southern portion of the Mekong Delta, where he lived alone in an apartment above a shop and spent his days dedicated to expanding the so-called "strategic hamlet" program, designed to win the allegiance of the population and protect it at its most constituent level of organization, driving down from the province to the district, from the district to the village, and from the village to the hamlet. Holbrooke helped to organize self-defense militias, create agriculture and health programs, encourage elected governing councils, and build schools. In a memorandum Holbrooke sent Melvin about six months after his arrival, he described a schoolhouse constructed in concert with the Army's 21st Division Engineering Battalion on a dirt road leading to the coast of the South China Sea. It served two hundred children on the same spot where the Vietcong twelve months earlier had destroyed the hamlet's only school. "Nothing could more perfectly express the common goals and aspirations of the people and the Army," Holbrooke proudly asserted in his report to Melvin. "The blow to the Viet Cong in this 'war for the minds and hearts of the people' was as potent as many a military operation." It was clear, Holbrooke concluded, that there was "an unlimited potential for civic action projects in Vietnam."[9]

Holbrooke's industry and zeal won plaudits from both senior American and Vietnamese officials. "Holbrooke is doing a terrific job," gushed David Bell, director of the Agency for International Development, in a memorandum to Secretary of State Rusk. "He is the only civilian stationed in Ba Xuyen, a province where the VC controls 94 percent of the area and 70 percent of the people." Bell told Rusk that the young man the secretary had known growing up in Scarsdale was adapting well to life in the town of Soc Trang. "He is in a very rough spot, and one that involves considerable personal risk," Bell explained. "He was, however, cheerful and plainly very dedicated to the fight against the Viet Cong. When I asked him if he needed anything he said only two things . . . decentralize administrative and financial flexibility to the provincial level."[10] The Vietnamese province chief of Ba Xuyen wrote his counterpart in the American rural affairs program praising Holbrooke's "outstanding service" and requesting that Holbrooke not be reassigned. "He has the command of the situation in the area concerning people and pacification," the province chief concluded.

The counterinsurgency effort was not performing at a sufficient level of effectiveness, in Holbrooke's view, despite the optimistic assessments that U.S. military advisers in the provinces were sending to the American embassy in Saigon. Holbrooke's skepticism was on display at a September 1963 meeting of roughly forty provincial representatives convened to evaluate the progress of the strategic hamlet program. Phillips, the U.S. pacification czar for the provinces, recalls the pessimism expressed about the program's gains in the Mekong Delta region, where Holbrooke was stationed. Some of the hamlets were systemically compromised by an infrastructure of the Viet Minh insurgency that had been established in the mid-1950s, when communist cadres created a secret organization throughout the south of the country following Vietnam's negotiated division in 1954. Many of the hamlets were secure during the day but then preyed on at night by insurgent forces.[11] The pattern became evident in Holbrooke's subsequent weekly dispatches to Phillips, one of which noted that the province chief of one hamlet had a brother who was a known Vietcong leader. "Recent incidents—kidnappings, and the refusal of certain militia to continue to bear arms—may indicate a new VC propaganda offensive in the area," Holbrooke reported. "In Ke Sach and Thuan Hoa districts, they have recruited over 100 youths recently, and reports indicate they may have been taken to the island of Vinh Binh for training."[12]

The perils and demands of life in Ba Xuyen province prompted Holbrooke to seek opportunities to visit with friends in Saigon, which was comparatively untouched by the simmering rural insurgency. On Friday, November 1, 1963, Holbrooke went to the airport at Soc Trang, planning to fly to Saigon to spend the weekend with Tony Lake and his wife. The flight was canceled and an announcement was issued that "all Americans were restricted to quarters." Holbrooke reached Lake by telephone at his home three blocks from the presidential palace. "He was calm but said that he was trapped in the house by small arms fire," Holbrooke recalled in a letter to his fiancée, Larrine "Litty" Sullivan. No explanation for the fighting was provided, and Holbrooke was advised to stay off the roads. "But I was damn mad, and wanted to get out of Soc Trang," he wrote.

Holbrooke decided he would make his way to Saigon via the city of Can Tho, where his friend Talbott Huey was stationed. Flanking an army truck as an escort, Holbrooke drove to Can Tho with a loaded .45 caliber pistol on the passenger seat next to him. When he arrived, Holbrooke took the clip out of the gun: "I had cocked the gun earlier, and now when I routinely went to clear the barrel, the goddamn thing went off." The roar from the gun was enormous, and the recoil jolted him backward. A shocked Holbrooke, expecting that any minute the police would swoop down, fled the car in a panic. He recalled running nowhere in particular. Five minutes later, he returned to inspect the damage. "By the greatest of luck the bullet—and .45s are very powerful things—had passed through the floor between the clutch and the four-wheel drive shaft. One inch to either side and it would have demolished one of the two mechanisms," he recounted in a letter to Litty. "So I got away with this disgraceful misuse of a weapon and hope to never do such a thing again." He spent the night with his friend Huey. "Can Tho was quiet, deadly quiet."

The evening lingered on with a sense of uncertainty. Eventually, an intelligence agent arrived and explained that American personnel were operating under a "Yellow alert, the last step before Red alert and immediate evacuation from Can Tho to the ships of the Seventh Fleet standing off the coast of Vietnam." Holbrooke noted that the operative delivering this news "was slightly drunk, and his warning seemed strange somehow."

Holbrooke called Lake again, who abruptly hung up the phone. Lake and his wife, Holbrooke wrote, had remained hidden inside a closet for seventeen hours as gunfire and shelling erupted and air attacks commenced. Lake's house was next to the barracks of the presidential guard, where Diem's troops were fighting for survival. "Bullets and bombs fell everywhere," houses were smashed and cars were burned. "I am really sorry I missed all of this," Holbrooke lamented in his letter, without a trace of irony.

The next day Holbrooke flew to Saigon, "sharing the plane with General Cao, the notorious commander of IV Corps, who was Diem's closest supporter. . . . He is finished, as are so many other people in this country." Holbrooke expressed his hope that his Vietnamese counterpart, the ineffectual province chief of Ba Xuyen, would now be swept aside: "I would assume that Colonel Chieu is through, and I hope so, I devoutly hope so; but there is always the chance he will escape."

Saigon, Holbrooke discovered, was jubilant over Diem's overthrow: "Rufus and others who have been here for years say that not even in the days when independence was in the air, was there so much visible joy in the city." Holbrooke made his way to Lake's house, where he slept on the floor. Vlad Lehovich, who was also a weekend guest, "picked up an unexploded shell from a 68 mm mortar and brought it into my room . . . which scared the hell out of me. . . . He finally gave it to some soldiers."[13]

With a seemingly preternatural ability to insinuate himself into the center of any situation or dynamic he encountered, Holbrooke would not take long to migrate from the outer provinces of Vietnam to the capital, the locus of American power. In early 1965, he was assigned to the American embassy in Saigon, where over a two-year period he would serve as an aide to Ambassador Maxwell Taylor and Ambassador Henry Cabot Lodge. Holbrooke's tenure in the capital would also include a unique assignment as a special assistant to Deputy Ambassador William J. Porter, with responsibility for civilian military affairs in support of American counterinsurgency operations. "In the midst of it all I am having a fascinating time working for Porter on other matters, like the non-war effort," he told Litty, now his wife. "This is really a challenging tightrope kind of job, but I am so far surviving and enjoying it."[14] Speaking of his third year of immersion in the Vietnam crisis, Holbrooke conceded: "It is too compelling a problem, and I do not regret having been involved in it, even if we have fouled up here something awful."[15]

Holbrooke's candor with his wife was also recapitulated frequently to members of the Saigon press pool, who would reach out to the young foreign service officer as a source to balance the spin of the "Five O'clock Follies," the official embassy briefings issued by the public affairs officer, Barry Zorthian. The great reporters of the Vietnam era—David Halberstam, Neil Sheehan, Morley Safer, Stanley Karnow, and others—would all become Holbrooke's lifelong friends. None of the other junior men in the embassy matched the breadth and depth of Holbrooke's relationships with the media, a skill he cultivated throughout his career.[16]

Holbrooke's transfer to Saigon would afford him a front-row seat to the Americanization of the Vietnam War. On the evening of February 6, 1965, Holbrooke dined at the home of Ambassador Porter and a distinguished guest, McGeorge Bundy, the White House national security adviser and former dean of the faculty at Harvard University. One of the iconic figures of the postwar U.S. foreign policy establishment, Bundy had a richly earned reputation for both a dominating intellect and imperiousness. "Bundy quizzed us in his quick, detached style for several hours, not once betraying emotion," Holbrooke later recalled. "There was no question he was brilliant, but his detachment from the realities of Vietnam disturbed me. In Ambassador Porter's dining room that night were people far less intelligent than Bundy, but they lived in Vietnam, and they knew things he did not. Yet if they could not present their views in a quick and clever way, Bundy either cut them off or ignored them."[17]

In the early hours of the next morning, Vietcong forces attacked the U.S. air base outside the central highlands town of Pleiku, killing 9 American soldiers and wounding 137 others. Bundy, inspecting the carnage firsthand, observed how the force of the attack had dismembered its victims, scattering limbs and body parts. The national security adviser recommended an immediate reprisal air attack to be followed by a perpetual bombing campaign against North Vietnam that Bundy characterized as a program of "graduated and sustained reprisal." The logic behind the strategy was the expectation that the United States could break the will of the insurgency through the application of incrementally greater levels of coercive force and destruction. President Johnson adopted Bundy's recommendation, which General Westmoreland, the Vietnamese theater commander, in turn swiftly appropriated as a pretext to push for the deployment of ground combat forces to defend the massive U.S. air base in Da Nang. That recommendation was also approved, prompting the arrival of the first 3,500 Marines in early March, soon to be followed by tens of thousands of additional troops operating under increasingly elastic rules of engagement. Thus in the winter of 1965, Vietnam became, suddenly and irrevocably, an American war.

For Holbrooke, the heightened military tensions in Saigon meant that his wife and all other American dependents would be forced to evacuate the city. Litty left for Bangkok and Holbrooke was once more living alone in a comfortable house not far from the embassy. One night, there was a knock at the door. Holbrooke greeted an agitated and breathless John Negroponte, another twenty-something diplomat from the U.S. embassy, who had dashed over in a panic. Returning to his apartment, Negroponte discovered a pair of drunken U.S. soldiers—one of whom was about six-foot-eight—who had broken in and were sitting at the dining room table swilling his liquor. The startled giant had lurched toward Negroponte, who fled.

"Do you mind if I spend the night?" Negroponte asked Holbrooke.

"Why don't you move in?" Holbrooke offered, noting that he now had ample space following Litty's forced departure.

Negroponte agreed and the two men became roommates. They played tennis frequently. Holbrooke tortured Negroponte by playing the same Beatles album with maniacal repetitiveness on the stereo. And along with their peers from the embassy—young talents like Peter Tarnoff, Frank Wisner Jr., and Tony Lake—after work they would frequent the American restaurants and bars of Saigon or in Cholon, the Chinese section of the city. And every night, it was the same, a ceaseless, energized, and increasingly obsessive discourse on the ends and means of the American war in Vietnam.[18] If he hungered for distraction, Holbrooke would choose occasionally to accompany Lake after hours on his late-night rounds in Saigon, doing the work of a junior diplomat, which included coaxing a drunk American to leave a bar quietly before getting tossed in a Vietnamese jail or counseling "love-struck" young soldiers, invariably from rural America, "that the girl they wanted to wed could not be granted an American visa because she had a police record as a prostitute," as Holbrooke recounted.[19]

Despite living and working in Vietnam's capital, Holbrooke continued to monitor the progress of the war in the rural territories, where along with his counterinsurgency mentor, Rufus Phillips, he believed the contest would ultimately be determined. "One day in early 1966, I travelled across the sand dunes and paddies south of Da Nang with a Vietnamese district chief and his American Adviser," Holbrooke recorded in an unpublished memorandum. "The area was then marked as a national Pacification Priority Area, and from Saigon and indeed Washington the word had come that no effort was to be spared in securing the area . . . and denying it to the VC." The territory was perceived to be strategically important. Located south of the massive U.S. air complex in Da Nang, it contained nine villages, twenty-eight hamlets, and roughly 30,000 people. "When the US marines had waded ashore in March of 1965 to spearhead the troop buildup, they had confidently planned for a gradual march southward," linking the key vectors of the population in an expanded zone of security. "But one painful year later," wrote Holbrooke, "the Marines found themselves bogged down in a strange new kind of war."[20]

While U.S. forces could roam freely through the territory by day and even at night if they moved in sufficient numbers, Holbrooke noted, "they found that they could not 'cleanse' the area of Viet Cong, no matter how they concentrated troops there." The American strategy was not generating the intended outcome. "The Marines had encountered the guerilla war head on, and despite the hours and days of instruction they had in 'counterinsurgency,' despite all the briefings which emphasized the political nature of the war, they could not understand what was going on or how to deal with it. And it appeared unlikely to me that they could ever learn." Using the imagery popular in counterinsurgency doctrine, Holbrooke observed that the objective of the Marines' mission was to link a so-called "oil spot"—a radius of security in a pacified area—with other pacified territories, expanding continuously outward: "It sounded simple, but after the Marines had been there a year they were still being mined and booby-trapped and ambushed from the rear throughout the area." The Marines struggling to connect the "oil spots" were beginning to realize, "slowly and expensively," Holbrooke remarked, that the political mobilization of populations "living under communist control" was extremely difficult to achieve, "and they were not going to switch sides in return for some free soap."[21]

In another reflection on the inherent difficulty of providing sustainable security to a widely dispersed rural population—the counterinsurgency imperative to "clear and hold" contested territory—Holbrooke recalled an exchange with Lewis Walt, the commander of the Marine Amphibious Force. "He was pushing sand in front of his hand in a wide semicircle, and explaining that the Marines would push the Viet Cong out in the same way," Holbrooke wrote. "All around us curious children watched this giant of a man pushing sand around, and chattered in Vietnamese. 'But the VC will just move in behind you,' I offered; having lived in Vietnam for several years, it was not hard to see the flaw in the concept. But Walt persisted in his belief, and went right on pushing sand, literally and figuratively, for the remainder of his command."

Holbrooke had started out at the periphery of power in the provinces of Vietnam. His appointment to the Saigon embassy brought him closer to the core of decision making. He would now migrate even further to the center of power, to the White House, where at the age of twenty-six, he was appointed as special assistant to the deputy national security adviser, Robert W. Komer. Once again, his precocious expertise in the civilian dimensions of counterinsurgency yielded a unique opportunity.

In 1966, President Johnson decided to create a separate office for the coordination of military and nonmilitary operations in Vietnam. Johnson chose to manage the process out of the White House. Pacification operations were first put under the authority of an entity called the Office of Civilian Operations, which morphed into the program exotically called Civil Operations and Revolutionary Development Support. In both of its incarnations, the pacification strategy sought to provide security to the rural population, degrade the insurgency's infrastructure, and win the allegiance and support of the villagers for the South Vietnamese government and its American benefactor.

By appointing Komer to spearhead the effort, Johnson had designated a senior official with a legendary reputation for personal intensity and a results-oriented expectation for all facets of performance. Komer's nickname was "the blowtorch." Holbrooke, in turn, came to be known as the blowtorch to the blowtorch. The two men had a synergistic energy and a shared determination to mobilize the sluggish machinery of the pacification effort. "They were in some respects two of a kind," recalled Peter Rosenblatt, who worked with Holbrooke on the small White House team. Holbrooke, who had already burnished a veritable brand identity in Vietnam for wild industriousness and great operational acumen, extended that aura further with all of the powers a White House staff position could provide. "It was extraordinary," said Rosenblatt. "Dick was only in his twenties but he already knew everyone throughout the entire government."[22] "He had a strategic mind coupled with an extraordinary operational capability," said Wisner, who engaged with Holbrooke constantly on Vietnam. "He could identify the pressure points and move them by whatever means necessary, including coercion and bullying."

Despite his amplified influence in the White House, Holbrooke remained systemically frustrated with the execution of the pacification strategy. "Returning to Vietnam after an absence of five months, I was struck by how little progress" was evident, Holbrooke wrote in a trip report in December 1966. "Sitting in on discussions within the Mission and hearing the same tired old arguments, visiting the Delta and listening to the same recital of difficulties and shortcomings, getting a constant refrain from each part of the Vietnam mosaic produced as if by rote—all emphasized the glacial pace at which real events happen in Vietnam." Holbrooke observed a government largely devoid of strong leaders and a "political structure still so fragmented and weak that division commanders can choose those orders that they intend to obey, and Ministries can follow their own paths regardless of the desires of the Prime Minister." The American presence in Vietnam, Holbrooke argued, was an unalloyed proposition, alternately "a beneficial catalyst and an oppressive burden." The United States mission, however, was clearly a mess. "In the almost four years I have worked on Vietnam and served in the Mission, I have never seen the Americans in such disarray."[23]

Continuing to believe that an effective pacification strategy was the only hope for the United States, Holbrooke was quick to reach out to Senator Jacob Javits of New York, who in the fall of 1966 made a speech arguing the same proposition. Holbrooke showed up unannounced at the senator's office and demanded an appointment. Politely rebuffed by the receptionist, Holbrooke would not desist. He launched a sufficiently angry tirade that one of the secretaries hurriedly looked for Leslie Gelb, author of the speech and the senator's foreign policy adviser. "He's going to be a problem," Gelb was told. "Would you see him?"

Gelb introduced himself to Holbrooke. Seeking to extract the obstreperous presence from the senator's waiting room, Gelb suggested they take a walk together. The two men wandered around Capitol Hill for two hours, talking about pacification and the political and military problems in Vietnam. It was the beginning of a forty-five-year friendship. "At the time, Dick's concern was not to get out of Vietnam, those words never passed his lips," said Gelb. "It was about doing pacification better."

By 1967, Gelb had moved on to the Department of Defense, where he was an international security specialist in the office of the secretary of defense, Robert S. McNamara. Gelb was tasked with a top-secret assignment to identify the most talented minds in the military and diplomatic apparatus of the U.S. government to prepare, on an anonymous basis, a comprehensive analytical history of the United States engagement in Vietnam. That study would become known as the Pentagon Papers.

A number of the authors were combat commanders in Vietnam who would ascend to two- or three-star generals. But to write a history and critique of the American pacification program, Gelb reached out to Holbrooke. "The authors were trying to preserve a piece of history," Gelb explained. And Holbrooke's analysis proved to be "far and away the most idiosyncratic volume of the whole study."

At the time he worked on the Pentagon Papers, Holbrooke had been recruited to serve as the principal Vietnam policy adviser to the undersecretary of state, Nicholas Katzenbach, the department's second most influential voice on Vietnam after Dean Rusk. Splitting his time between working for Katzenbach and preparing his history of American counterinsurgency programs in Vietnam, Holbrooke would spend hours at a stretch in a secure room in the Pentagon filled with more than fifty file cabinets of classified documents. The authors would gather throughout the day, poring over the voluminous archive and debating its contents.

"The process by which the American government came to increase its support for pacification is disorderly and haphazard," Holbrooke concluded in his extensive and scathing analysis. Proponents of the strategy "were often in such violent disagreement as to what pacification meant that they quarreled publicly among themselves and overlooked their common interests. At other times, people who disagreed strongly on major issues found themselves temporary allies with a common objective."[24]

According to Holbrooke, General William Westmoreland, the supreme United States commander in Vietnam, was highly ineffectual at implementing the strategy. "Although Westmoreland judged it repeatedly as a partial success, it appears now to have been a faultily conceived and clumsily executed program. It was conceptually unsound, lacked the support of the Vietnamese, created disagreements within the U.S. mission that were never resolved, and then faded away."[25]

Ambassador Henry Cabot Lodge, who Holbrooke had worked for in Saigon, was also singled out for his shortcomings. Given a mandate by President Johnson "to take charge of the American effort in South Vietnam" in July 1965, Lodge allowed diverse factions to argue the tactics and strategy of counterinsurgency, descending, as Holbrooke noted, into "debating minor points like medieval monks but also disagreeing on rather basic points—such as whether the object was to gain the population's support or to control them by force. (A popular Marine saying, which tried to bridge the gap, went: 'Get the people by the balls, and their hearts and minds will follow.') But each group found something that appealed to Lodge, and each in turn gained encouragement from him."[26]

Holbrooke also drilled down on one of the military's most acute misjudgments in Vietnam, reflected in a report produced by the army chief of staff: "Proceeding from the unstated assumption that our commitment in Vietnam had no implicit time limits, it proposed a strategy which it admitted would take years . . . to carry out. It did not examine alternative strategies that might be derived from a shorter time limit on the war. In fact, the report made no mention of one of the most crucial variables in the Vietnam equation—U.S. public support for the administration."[27]

Holbrooke's responsibilities as Katzenbach's Vietnam adviser from September 1967 to June 1968 required him to manage interagency coordination among the Defense Department, the Joint Chiefs of Staff, the Central Intelligence Agency, and the White House. More deeply, Holbrooke had to serve as a counselor to one of the administration's most subtle intellects, a University of Chicago law professor who was progressively losing faith in the American mission in Vietnam. In the aftermath of the Tet Offensive, when claims of American progress in reversing the course of the war imploded, General Westmoreland requested an additional 200,000 troops, potentially raising the American commitment in Vietnam to 750,000 men. "This is crazy and shouldn't happen," Holbrooke told Negroponte at the time. Katzenbach shared his young adviser's reservations and allowed him to work behind the scenes with others to scuttle Westmoreland's proposal, as did Clark Clifford, who succeeded McNamara as secretary of defense. President Johnson rejected Westmoreland's recommendation and initiated what would prove to be a torturous negotiating track with North Vietnam.

"I have immense respect for the quality of Holbrooke's political judgments and insights about Vietnam and about the domestic US context (political as well as bureaucratic) of our decisions regarding Vietnam," Katzenbach wrote in a State Department performance review. "He combines thorough familiarity with the facts with unusual maturity of view and is not afraid to press vigorously for actions that he thinks necessary. It is this respect for his judgment about both foreign and domestic political considerations which explains his ready access to the top-level officials who make the crucial recommendations to the President on Vietnam policy."

Katzenbach acknowledged that his twenty-seven-year-old adviser took great satisfaction in engaging with the chairman of the Joint Chiefs of Staff, the director of the CIA, and other senior officials. "I would not mark Holbrooke down because of his youthful, irrepressible enthusiasm (or even his neckties) and the pleasure with which he has reacted to the heady company he keeps," Katzenbach wryly observed. "I have never discouraged—in fact I suspect I have encouraged—his ebullience; it is like a breath of fresh air in a world in which too few of us have retained the same feeling of excitement and earnestness which we once enjoyed." Katzenbach concluded: "He should have, and I trust will have, a brilliant future before him."

There would be one last assignment in Holbrooke's extraordinary portfolio of Vietnam responsibilities. He would be the youngest member of the American delegation to the Paris Peace Talks led by Averell Harriman, a veteran of the Kennedy administration and the former governor of New York. Philip Habib, a highly respected diplomat who worked with Holbrooke in Saigon, was eager to carve out a place for him on the negotiating team but struggled to define an appropriate title. Finally, Habib simply designated Holbrooke as an "expert." The title had its advantages, Holbrooke told his wife. "Phil's theory, in listing me as an expert, is to confuse and perhaps upset" the North Vietnamese. "Who the hell is this expert? And what is he expert in? What are those crazy Americans up to?"[28]

On the night before their first meeting with the North Vietnamese in Paris, Holbrooke dined with Cyrus Vance, a future secretary of state, and other members of the negotiating team. When he returned to the Hotel de Crillon, he jotted off a quick letter to his family. "Tomorrow I meet the atheist godless communists for the first time in my new role as 'expert,'" Holbrooke noted. "I really have never worked so hard."[29]

The talks, which commenced in May 1968, accomplished nothing during the remaining months of Johnson's presidency, yielding no more consequential achievement than an agreement on the shape of the negotiating table. For Holbrooke, the collapse of any remaining hope may have been foreshadowed on June 6, when Senator Robert F. Kennedy was assassinated in Los Angeles following his victory in the California Democratic primary. Holbrooke sent Kennedy's widow, Ethel, a condolence letter. In it he recalled his decision to join the Foreign Service in 1962. "I was one of those people —there were many others— who were at just the critical moment of decision about their future when John F. Kennedy was President," explained Holbrooke. "It sounds corny, but I really did enter the government because of him. There was hope, and then it was gone—and then it returned, and now it seems gone again. I hope it isn't gone again forever, somehow."[30] The following autumn, Richard Nixon was elected president. Within months, Holbrooke resigned from the State Department.

"NO ONE CAN KNOW THE FULL STORY OF SOMETHING AS VAST AND complicated and as full of deceit as the war in Vietnam," Holbrooke wrote in one of his unpublished memoranda. "The historians will not know it. . . . But the historians will need to reinterpret Vietnam in light of their own times, as historians have always done. And the question of what happened will sometimes never be knowable. Vietnam will recede, and the details blur anyway . . . ."[31] The policy makers and scholars of the war remained central to Holbrooke's life in the decades that followed. And to a remarkable degree, Holbrooke's circle of intimate colleagues from that chapter would go on to shape the U.S. foreign policy establishment in the post-Vietnam era. Peter Tarnoff, supported by Holbrooke's vigorous and assiduous lobbying, would become the president of the Council on Foreign Relations and the undersecretary of state in the Clinton administration. Les Gelb would become a senior Defense Department official in the Carter administration, a *New York Times* foreign affairs columnist, and, also with Holbrooke's vigorous support, Tarnoff's successor as president of the Council on Foreign Relations. Frank Wisner would become ambassador to Egypt, India, and undersecretary of defense. Tony Lake would become national security adviser to President Bill Clinton. John Negroponte, in addition to serving as Holbrooke's successor as UN ambassador, would become ambassador to Honduras, Mexico, the Philippines, and Iraq, as well as deputy secretary of state and director of national intelligence. And Henry Kissinger, who Holbrooke had first met in Vietnam and later consulted in the Paris peace negotiations, would go on to negotiate America's withdrawal from Vietnam as Nixon's national security advisor and secretary of state.

Each member of the unique fraternity of young men who came of age through the crucible of Vietnam would interpret the lessons of the war differently. For Holbrooke, the searing experience of the United States faltering in its first foreign conflict taught a rigor and discipline in evaluating the limits of American power. He would revisit that history repeatedly in the decades that followed, propagating his insights in an endless stream of essays, journal articles, newspaper columns, book reviews, and a major work of narrative history, *Counsel to the President*, the memoir he coauthored with Clark Clifford, Johnson's secretary of defense, who as a private counselor to the president opposed the escalation of the war in 1965 and struggled to disentangle the United States from Vietnam when he replaced McNamara in the Pentagon in 1968.

As Holbrooke retrospectively analyzed the disaster of Vietnam, he dismissed the proposition that Saigon could have ever prevailed in the contest with Hanoi. "Three times in the 1960s the North Vietnamese had come south in great numbers," he wrote. "Three times they had been beaten back only with massive American muscle. In 1965, it took American ground troops and the air strikes in the north to stem the tide. In 1968, the Tet Offensive came within inches of success; a half a million men and more air strikes saved the day. In 1972, it took the heaviest air attacks in the history of warfare to stop Hanoi. What, then, was the basis for the hope that the next time the South Vietnamese could do it without us?"[32]

Holbrooke rejected the thesis that Hanoi would ever capitulate to higher levels of coercive force. To buttress his argument Holbrooke revisited the French colonial experience in Indochina. Recalling the efforts of French envoy Jean Sainteny in 1946 to negotiate with Ho Chi Minh to avoid a war directed against France's continuing occupation, Ho was reported to say: "If we go to war, you will kill ten Vietnamese for every Frenchman who dies. But we will pay that price and you will not be able to." "Ho is dead, but his words are still true," observed Holbrooke. "When we replaced the French, we inherited the most determined and toughest enemy we have ever faced. This is not intended to turn the North Vietnamese into heroes, simply an attempt to recognize their refusal to quit—and our inability to make them quit."[33]

For Holbrooke, Vietnam became a cautionary narrative of the risks of strategic overextension. In a way, the war haunted him, and it certainly followed him through the different chapters of his career, from his efforts to bring peace to the Balkans in the 1990s to his final tour of duty in government as the State Department's senior official tasked with coordinating the diplomatic and civilian dimensions of U.S. policy in Afghanistan and Pakistan.

At the State Department conference less than three months before he died, Holbrooke was exceedingly careful when asked to compare the parallels between Vietnam and Afghanistan. "There are many structural similarities between the two situations, but there is a funda- mental strategic difference," he explained, straining to calibrate his position. "In Afghanistan we . . . entered the war because we were attacked in the most serious attack on American soil in history, and the nation unanimously and on a bipartisan basis, without any significant dissent, myself certainly included, felt that we had to go into Afghanistan because the people who were in charge of the country had sheltered Osama bin Laden and Al Qaeda and could not remain there."

"But structurally there are obvious similarities," Holbrooke continued. He had privately explained to a handful of people he was close to that the three common dynamics shared by the conflicts in Vietnam and Afghanistan that troubled him the most were the existence of an indefensible border harboring enemy sanctuaries; American reliance on a corrupt partner government; and, most critically, the embrace of counterinsurgency doctrine, which he had learned through painful experience was an exceedingly difficult military and civilian strategy to execute. Holbrooke alluded to these similarities but did not state them. "And leafing through these books here, they leap out at you," he said of the 1960s archival papers. "Many of the programs that are being followed, many of the basic doctrines are the same ones that we were trying to apply in Vietnam. And I believe in history," Holbrooke said. "I think history is continuous."

A Generation Conditioned
by the Impact of Vietnam

Richard Holbrooke
Washington Post, December 20, 1969

> *During his mid-career fellowship at Princeton University's*
> *Woodrow Wilson School—at a moment when college campuses*
> *were exploding in protest over Vietnam—Holbrooke, then*
> *twenty-eight, reflected on the very large historical blind spot*
> *of the late-sixties college generation, lamenting how many*
> *were turning away from public service.*

Many efforts have been made to explain Youth to the rest of us, but to a person who graduated from college less than eight years ago and is now spending a year on campus, the most striking fact about "the kids" is when they were born. It seems an obvious point, perhaps, but it does make it easier to understand why they look at the world so differently from their parents or even their older siblings.

Today's 19-year-old college sophomore, for example, was born in 1950, which is to say long after the war that saved Europe from Hitler, after the Berlin blockade and the heroic airlift, after the Marshall Plan, after the fall of China. He was born the year the North Koreans struck across the 38th parallel. In that same year the other Senator McCarthy, Joe, made his famous speech in Wheeling, W. Va. Remember?

The kids don't, through no fault of their own. They were about 6 when Russian tanks moved into Budapest and crushed the Freedom Fighters; 10 when John F. Kennedy was inaugurated; 11 when the Berlin Wall went up; and 12 when the presence of Soviet missiles in Cuba led to history's first thermonuclear confrontation. They are too young to be children of the Kennedy administration. They don't remember the call to public service that JFK issued on Inauguration Day 1961. But they do remember the assassination; for many of them, it is their first political memory. While one can lament these facts, nothing will change them.

THESE YOUNG AMERICANS HAVE GROWN UP WITH VIETNAM. THE WAR has been with them at the dinner table, flickering on the TV, as they grew up. Vietnam is to a large extent all they know about their country in the outside world.

If a student was born in 1950, he was 12 when the advisory build-up began; 15 when the bombing of North Vietnam and our troop buildup started. Ask him about McCarthy, Hungary, Berlin, Cuba, and his answers are vague and incomplete. If it happened before 1965, it is ancient history.

Ultimately a country's self-image, its self-respect, are crucial to how it faces the future and how it conceives of its own role. The young—especially the privileged young—are growing up with a grim picture of their country, not at all like the picture that nurtured their parents, or even their older siblings.

Only eight years ago, when I graduated, a student saw a different world. Racial equality seemed more attainable than it does today; the free world stood united against a monolothic communist opponent who had ruthlessly stamped out hopes for freedom in Hungary (the different reaction to Czechoslovakia in 1968 is fascinating). Then there was a young President telling Americans—particularly young Americans—that they should ask what they could do for their country. Heeding his call, many of us went into the government, into politics, into other forms of public service.

Today, most of the best of the high school and college students would not consider government service. In recent talks with students, I have heard almost every conceivable accusation levied against the government: the students are certain their phones would be tapped, that their minds would be "controlled," that their private movements would be watched, and that nothing they do, say or think would have any effect on the great immovable monster of government. They tend to greet any evidence to the contrary with disbelief, and reject the proposition that while far from perfect, the government is not inherently evil.

Certainly it is true that not every student has decided that everything is rotten. And it is also true that in time some of the students may change their views. But it is disturbing that so many of the best students, those to whom public service would have looked honorable only a few years ago, have decided that the American political system is hopeless. And, as the war continues, this readiness to believe the worst about Washington will undoubtedly increase.

THERE ARE NO EASY SOLUTIONS TO THE GROWING ALIENATION OF YOUNG Americans. Telling the students that they don't know enough relatively recent history—while true enough—solves nothing; it is not the kids' fault that they have no first-hand feel for the times of Owen Lattimore or Imre Nagy. They did not live through the 1950s and they were not taught about them. Each generation is conditioned by those events it has lived through, and for the next generation of Americans that means Vietnam.

And this conditioning will outlast the war. The end of the fighting will not bring with it the end of attitudes which by then will be deeply embedded in the minds of most young, college-educated Americans. The *way* that the war finally ends may have a powerful influence over the way our nation sees itself. But in the meantime, the growing estrangement of many of today's young from their past and their nation will continue—and it will cost America a great deal.

The young have inherited a new tradition from their older siblings—public protest and "participatory politics." To many of the best, there appear to be huge differences between the rhetorical ideals of America and what they see of America. Much of what they see they sincerely believe to be wrong. Combining cynicism and idealism, and having been exposed through television more directly to America's shortcomings than any previous generation, they are less ready to accept these shortcomings.

The great hope is that these young students, unwilling to accept what they view as inequality or injustice, will find ways to do what, for the most part, they still want to do—improve the world they live in and will inherit. The great danger is that, growing frustrated and obsessed with Vietnam, and increasingly remote from the historical experiences of the 1950s and 1960s, the students will conclude that the very worst is in fact true about the American political structure and about American society.

A Little Lying Goes a Long Way

RICHARD HOLBROOKE
New York Times, SEPTEMBER 10, 1971

> *While directing the Peace Corps in Morocco, Holbrooke penned this*
> *remarkable op-ed, which seemed to boil out of years of frustration.*
> *He had drafted a study on pacification as part of the Pentagon*
> *Papers, and earlier that year Daniel Ellsberg had visited Holbrooke*
> *to try to convince him to go along with his famous leak, which*
> *the* New York Times *began publishing that summer (Holbrooke*
> *declined). Two months after this op-ed, Holbrooke submitted his*
> *resignation from the Peace Corps, and he left government service*
> *the following year.*

Why is there so much resistance among people who work in the Government to the seemingly obvious fact that, in our democracy, if the Government lies it will eventually get caught; that lying on the outside, furthermore, breeds and actually promotes lying on the inside?

The result of pushing an official line with the American public turns out to be that even in the privacy of the classified briefing rooms the public misrepresentation relentlessly triumphs. It becomes harder and harder for anyone to say, even in private, that the emperor does not, in fact, have any clothes.

Vietnam alone can provide enough examples of this syndrome to fill a library, and it is important to recognize that Vietnam was not an aberration but the result of systems and structures and pressures of the postwar foreign policy machine. If under maximum stress and in time of maximum danger, the system could not arrive at intellectually honest assessments even in private, then the system and the structure must be judged at least partial failures.

Many people will be able to recall meetings in which a publicly taken position affected internal debate. There was the senior general who early in the war dictated that his intelligence chief would find no more repeat no more than 25,000 Vietcong in his overall enemy order of battle. (Those were the early, early optimistic days.)

There were the high-level meetings in Washington and Saigon in which attempts to put forward assessments less positive than the official line were cut off, and the suggestion even made that there was something less than loyal about these assessments. Everyone who was there should be able to match these sad memories.

People began to distrust each other, and increasingly withhold personal opinions, if they differ from official positions, when they participate in "policy" meetings. After a meeting in which a senior official has provided his colleagues and subordinates with precisely the same interpretation of the latest captured documents that he has recently given the press, other people in the room tend to wander out, in somewhat of a stupor, having suppressed their own opinions. In this situation one is left with a growing sense of futility: if this is what passes for discussion within the Government, then maybe the Government is not actually engaged in deliberate lying (as almost everyone now seems to believe). Perhaps the Government is deceiving itself, as well as the public.

Obviously, this is not always the case. Some lies are deliberate and knowingly perpetrated on the public. But it would surprise most outside observers to learn how often the "lie" is believed on the inside. In these cases historians tend to call the "lie" a misassessment.

As long as the Government insists on misrepresenting the facts publicly, for whatever policy reasons, it will pay many hidden—and I believe unacceptable—costs. But let us not overlook the growth of cynicism and self-deceit among the bureaucrats, the natural selection process that drives candor out of the conference rooms and memoranda. In the long run, that cost may prove to be the highest of all.

In the present era of self-deception, younger officers in both military and foreign service are apt to either adapt themselves to the system or drop out in disgust. Unfortunately, most will adapt.

Pushing Sand

RICHARD HOLBROOKE
The New Republic, MAY 3, 1975

> *In Vietnam, Holbrooke saw up close the limits of programs meant*
> *to pacify populations by winning "hearts and minds." In this*
> *searing piece, published in* The New Republic *three days after*
> *Saigon fell and reprinted a week later in the* Washington Post,
> *he describes how a difficult reality confounded General Lew Walt's*
> *Combined Action Program: his troops were, literally and*
> *figuratively, pushing sand.*

For at least eight years it seemed reasonable to me to assume that sooner or later, no matter what we did in Vietnam, things would end badly for us. This feeling was not based on any desire to see us humiliated, or any feeling that the other side represented the forces of goodness and light; it just seemed that the only way stave off an eventual Communist victory was with an open-ended, and therefore endless, application of American firepower in support of the South Vietnamese regime. No matter how much force we were willing to use, this would not end the war, only prevent Saigon's defeat. And the human suffering would be bottomless. The war would go on until the North Vietnamese achieved their objectives. As Ho Chi Minh tried to tell the French 30 years ago, his forces would outlast everyone else—by one day.

The end was inevitable, and our efforts to avoid or delay it were wrongheaded and against everyone's interests—political, strategic, humanitarian, even (to use a phrase so rarely invoked in Washington) moral.

But even believing that, as many other people also did, I was almost totally unprepared for the dimensions and speed of the tragedy that began unfolding in Indochina a few weeks ago. It seemed reasonable to expect the offensive in South Vietnam to come in 1976, timed to coincide with the presidential elections here, as had the last two great offensives, in 1968 and 1972. It also seemed reasonable to suppose that there would be some intelligence warning that it was coming.

"You can't believe how bad things are around here," a friend working in the administration told me on the day Pnom Penh fell. "We are simply and totally without leadership, and the situation in Indochina is so horrible . . ." His voice trailed off, and I said, "I know." "No, you don't," he replied. "It's worse than you think."

There are a large number of things that need to be said about the present drama in Indochina. Some of them must await the end; others require time and a little distance. We must, for example, begin to look beyond Indochina, and toward the question of the proper role of the United States in Asia and in the rest of the world: Reports of the imminent demise of American influence around the world, many of them emanating curiously from high administration officials, are clearly very premature. So too is the effort to portray the Democratic Congress as a group of crazy isolationists who are thwarting Henry Kissinger's grand design for a generation of peace. Many Democratic "doves" are deeply concerned lest recent events be misunderstood and stand ready to clarify to the world what our real national interests should be. But in the current debate one can hear clearly the opening salvos of a presidential campaign in which, for the first time since 1948, "the role of Congress" will be a major issue. And with that as background noise, it is not surprising that the present relationship between administration loyalists and Congress will be dyed through and through with distrust and hostility.

But these are issues to discuss some other day. These are days for those who lived in Indochina to be jarred anew each morning as they pick up their newspapers, to be shaken each night as they watch television. For each of those obscure place names means something to some American, and it is worth remembering what we tried to do out there, and how we tried, and how we failed.

My own images, three years after I last visited Vietnam, six years after I last worked on the area in the government, nine years after I last lived there, are mostly of the wild, weird contrast between the people of

Vietnam and the Americans who had come to help them. The distance between them seemed immense, unbridgeable, with all the goodwill in the world. The other day, as I went up an escalator in the Pentagon, I ran smack into a huge photograph on the wall of an army officer standing in a rice paddy, in combat fatigues, hand on hip, M-16 on his shoulder, looking squarely and confidently into the camera. Behind him strung out across the paddy, slightly out of focus, were South Vietnamese soldiers, presumably the ones in the unit he was advising. The plaque under the photograph said "Vietnam 1964." The look of confidence on that man's face somehow went through me and brought back other rice paddies, other false hopes.

I remember a trip with the Ninth Marine Regiment through the area south of Da Nang in 1965, about eight months after the marines had landed. Their original plans had called for the establishment of a beachhead in the Da Nang area, then the gradual sweep outward into the surrounding countryside, westward and southward, pacifying the area, that is, cleansing it of Vietcong. Then the South Vietnamese would take over behind them as they moved forward.

That was the plan, and kneeling in some sand in a tiny hamlet south of Da Nang, Gen. Lewis Walt, the commander of the Marine Amphibious Force, showed me how it would work. Walt was a powerful and unforgettable figure, a man who looked the way you would want a marine to look. He was one of the true heroes of the marine corps' fight through the South Pacific in World War II, and he was impossible to dislike. He was also the wrong man for the job, and besides, it was the wrong job. He was pushing the sand in front of his hand in a wide semicircle, and explaining that the marines would push the Vietcong out in the same way. All around us curious children watched this giant of a man pushing sand around, and chattered in Vietnamese. "But the VC will just move in behind you," I offered; having lived in Vietnam for several years, it was not hard to see the flaw in the concept. But Walt persisted in his belief, and went right on pushing sand, literally and figuratively, for the remainder of his command.

The Ninth Marine Regiment carried with it its battle flags from past wars, and while I do not remember them in detail I do remember that the impression they made on me was profoundly moving. Guadalcanal, Iwo Jima—the names seemed so historic—and here they were somewhere between Da Nang and Hoi An; even they didn't know where. We walked to a hamlet where the marines had helped build a schoolhouse for the children, and as we approached, the regimental commander proudly told me how there had been no school here before the marines came, but now they had a schoolhouse and a teacher. This was the way the marines would win the hearts and minds (the phrase was actually used, it must be remembered) of the people.

When we got to the schoolhouse it was burned down. A young marine captain, company commander, explained to his superior that one of the children—they didn't know which one—had burned it to the ground a few hours earlier. The marines puzzled over that a while, but couldn't understand it. Why would anyone want to burn down the school?

We went on to another hamlet, where the marines had already been for several months. They knew all the people in the hamlet and were obviously very popular with them. Everyone came out and waved and spoke a few words of English. I was told by the marines that they would be leaving this hamlet soon to go on, but that this was still a secret. A few minutes later a Vietnamese girl came up to me and said, in half-English, half-Vietnamese, "Why the 3/9 [the actual battalion designation for that unit in that hamlet] go? We want them stay."

The marines interpreted that as a sign of their success, but it was really a sign of their trap. They would be either liked and therefore trapped because the people would not like the South Vietnamese troops who would replace them; or they would be hated and the schools they built burned down. Or, in fact, they would be both at once—liked for their strange generosity and naiveness, for the money that came with them; and hated for their heavy-handed ways, for their lack of under-standing, for their use of the women (who of course invited it in many cases), for simply not belonging in South Vietnam at all.

These stories are about the marines, but they could have been about any Americans. Only a very few understood where they were, and they could not, no matter how well placed they were, influence the behavior and policies of a 500,000-man expeditionary force.

Our behavior in Vietnam can be judged on many levels. In historic and global terms, it stands under examination as a part of a worldwide policy, and will be judged on that basis. In domestic terms it will be judged for what it did to our national soul, to our self-image, which will not be the same again. In Vietnam itself, which is what concerns me here, it was the most curious mixture of high idealism and stupidity, of deceit and self-deceit, of moving heroism and inexcusable cruelty. For a long time I tried to separate out these contradictory strains, to under-stand why some things seemed right and some others seemed wrong, to see also if there was any way that some good could come out of the whole mess. But then finally it all seemed to come down to one simple, horrible truth: we didn't belong there, we had no business doing what we were doing, even the good parts of it.

Our Second Civil War

Richard Holbrooke
Washington Post, August 28, 2004

> *On the eve of the 2004 Republican National Convention,*
> *Holbrooke wrote this reflection on the recent attacks against the*
> *Democratic candidate for president, Senator John Kerry, to whom*
> *he was a close adviser. Swift Boat Veterans for Truth, a right-wing*
> *anti-Kerry group, was attacking Kerry's war record in Vietnam*
> *and, as Holbrooke wrote, was stirring up old wounds.*

Americans under 40 can be excused if they think that the presidential campaign went a bit nuts recently. After all, why has campaign coverage been dominated by a war that ended 29 years ago, even as a dozen Americans were dying and more than 130,000 fighting in Iraq?

Well, kids, welcome to an encore presentation of our Second Civil War. The anger and viciousness of the Swift boat debate provide just a brief reminder of how Vietnam divided our nation for a decade. One of my best friends in high school wrote me a furious letter in 1966, saying that since I was then in Vietnam, I must be a war criminal, and he would never speak to me again. And he never did.

Since most of the media covering the election remember the Vietnam era, it fascinates them still, and thus they tend to overdo it. For Americans of a certain age, Vietnam is the war that will not die—until they do. On one side are those who believe that Vietnam was a war we could have won if not for the congressional doves, the left-wing press and the long-haired antiwar demonstrators. On the other are those who turned against the war in the mid- and late-1960s and never forgot the drama of those days.

"Vietnam cleaves us still," President Bush said so eloquently in his inaugural address. Of course, that was George Herbert Walker Bush, in 1989. He worked with men such as John McCain and John Kerry to try to end the divisions Vietnam had caused in our society. Not so for the Swift boat veterans—the group that the current President Bush refuses to repudiate—who have revived the sort of charges that were such a bitter part of the Vietnam era itself.

Anyone who was in Vietnam knows that "the fog of war" was more than a cliché. I remember visiting destroyed hamlets in the lower Mekong Delta in the mid-1960s, sometimes only hours after the fighting had stopped, and hearing different versions of what had just transpired from survivors who had been right next to each other during the attack. Is it any wonder that memories would differ on details of events 33 years ago? But the timing of the attack by the anti-Kerry Swift boat veterans is rooted in politics and personal vendettas; on examination their charges are sloppy and self-contradictory.

I did not know John Kerry in Vietnam, but I knew the area he was in, having served in the same area as a civilian. I've talked to him often about Vietnam in recent years, and there is no question in my mind that it was the defining experience of his adult years, just as it was for me and hundreds of thousands of other Americans, including those now attacking him.

His personal saga embodies the American experience in Vietnam. First he was a good hero in a bad war—a man who volunteered for duty in the Navy and then asked for an assignment on the boats that were to ply the dangerous rivers of Vietnam—when most of his college-educated contemporaries (including George W. Bush and Dick Cheney and Bill Clinton)—found easy ways to avoid Vietnam. Then, carrying shrapnel in his thigh, he became an eloquent but moderate member of the antiwar movement.

John Kerry introduced his Vietnam record into his campaign because it is a central part of who he is. But stirring up the embers of our Second Civil War was not his intention. Younger people I have talked to tell me that this past week it seemed to them nothing more than a silly, irrelevant argument about a distant war; to a certain extent, I agree. All those who served in Vietnam put their lives at risk, and at this distance from the war they all deserve respect. Those of us who survived should show younger Americans that we learned something from the war; John Kerry clearly did, but the same cannot be said of his Swift boat critics. To have a sterile debate about the minutiae of his service, when the basic facts of his heroism are undeniable—and while Americans are again in a war that seems to have no exit—is particularly grotesque.

Watching this debate over Vietnam while a new generation of Americans are risking their lives in Iraq, I had a sudden vision: a television talk show in April of 2025, on the 50th anniversary of the end of the war in Vietnam. After being pushed into the studio in wheelchairs, the ancient veterans suddenly come to life with still another round of name-calling. How long before the lessons from Vietnam can be absorbed into our national life without resurrecting a civil war that cleaves us still?

Why Vietnam Matters

RICHARD HOLBROOKE

FROM *Why Vietnam Matters*, BY RUFUS PHILLIPS

> *Always deeply loyal to old mentors, Holbrooke wrote this foreword to* Why Vietnam Matters, *a history of the conflict written in 2008 by Rufus Phillips. Phillips, as head of a USAID pacification program, was Holbrooke's first boss when the newly minted diplomat arrived in rural Vietnam. This essay provides a personal retrospective of Holbrooke's years in Vietnam and an homage to Phillips—who despite being in his 80s, just a few years later would volunteer to travel to Afghanistan to help with Holbrooke's efforts there.*

In 1951, at the height of the Cold War, the CIA spotted a talented young man at its favorite recruiting grounds, Yale University. Thus began the saga of Rufus Phillips, one of the most remarkable figures of America's tortured involvement in Vietnam. Rufus got to Saigon in August 1954, shortly after the French defeat in Indochina. It was a critical time for the region. The United States was replacing the French as the major outside power, and the Viet Minh (the Vietnamese Communists, led by Ho Chi Minh), who already controlled the northern half of the nation, were soon to begin a twenty-year drive to unify Vietnam under their control. Working under the legendary and controversial Edward Lansdale (the model for the character of Colonel Hillandale in the bestselling book, *The Ugly American*), Rufus rose rapidly. He was intelligent, energetic, and charismatic.

Eight years later, he was back in Vietnam, running a groundbreaking division of the United States foreign aid mission called the Office of Rural Affairs, dedicated to what would be called today "nation-building." (In those days it was usually referred to as "pacifi-cation"—a word no longer politically correct.) And one year after that, Rufus Phillips became my first boss.

I had joined the Foreign Service in 1962, drawn to it by President John F. Kennedy's stirring calls to public service. Others in my genera-tion went into the Peace Corps, or rode Freedom buses south to fight segregation. For me, in part because my best friend in high school had been David Rusk, whose father, the future secretary of state, had talked to our senior class about something called the Foreign Service, I took and passed the Foreign Service exam when I was a senior in college. I entered the Foreign Service one month after graduating. Less than a year later, after language training and area studies, I was sent to Vietnam along with several other young diplomats, including Vladimir Lehovich, to whom I owe many things, including years of friendship and his advice and assistance for this Foreword.

Unknown to Vlad and me, the undersecretary of state for political affairs, U. Alexis Johnson, wanted to try a small experiment, and give a few young FSOs field experience, outside embassies. Almost by chance, partly because we were bachelors, Vlad and I were the first selected. There were about 10,000 to 12,000 American military personnel, mostly as advisers to the Vietnamese Armed Forces, in Vietnam when we arrived. American deaths in Vietnam had reached about 50. Both numbers seemed enormous to us. As I recall, we were not in the slightest bit concerned about our own safety. We were young, and indestructible. Bad things hap-pened to other people. Soon we would be joined by some of the best young diplomats of our generation, many of whom went on to stellar careers: Frank Wisner, Tony Lake (who joined the Foreign Service with Vlad and me), Peter Tarnoff, John Negroponte (with whom I would eventually share a house), and Les Aspin (then an Air Force captain who never wore a uniform), were among the tight group of junior officials who came to Viet-nam and became, in many cases, lifelong friends. Not everyone survived intact. One of our group, Doug Ramsey, was captured by the Viet Cong and spent years in hellish conditions before coming home in the early 1970s with other prisoners. There were others who died, at least one by his own hand. Tony Lake and a colleague, Edie Smith, barely survived a bomb attack just outside their offices in the U.S. Embassy.

For Vlad and me, Rufus was at the center of this exciting time in our lives. There was about him something slightly mysterious. He was young enough to be our older brother, but he was respected by everyone including the ambassador. He was close to senior Vietnamese officials. His past was the subject of whispers, but he was said to be a personal protégé of the great Lansdale. He had briefed Kennedy personally!

All of this turned out to be true. But what I remember most was his inspirational style of leadership, his endless energy, his boundless optimism about his mission and its importance to the nation. He believed, as did other members of his generation, that America could accomplish almost anything, if we did it right. In the early sixties, especially right after John F. Kennedy's extraordinary achievement in the Cuban Missile Crisis, our slightly younger group believed the same thing. Rufus gave this belief shape and substance.

Why Vietnam Matters is a major contribution to the history of Vietnam. It contains important lessons for the wars America is currently fighting in Iraq and Afghanistan. So much of what the current generation of military and civilian officials claim are new doctrines and ideas are identical to programs and strategies that were virtually all tried in Vietnam. General David Petraeus' much-praised counter-insurgency handbook, for example, bears a strong (and not accidental) resemblance to the manuals we studied in the Vietnam era.

VLAD REMINDS ME THAT, WITH THE CREATION OF THE RURAL AFFAIRS, Rufus Phillips "turned the traditional U.S. aid effort on its head." The aid mission was, he recalls, "a headquarters-focused, capital-oriented organization that helped ministries in Saigon and had no presence in the countryside. Suddenly Rufe grafted onto that bureaucratic mission a group of creative, problem-solving, often strikingly young and highly motivated Americans, most not career-AID, who went into the country's provinces to work with Vietnamese on vital local needs like schools, wells, refugees, and rice and pig culture, as well as more basic issues of physical security and representative local government."

The reader may well ask what possible qualifications two young men from New York City, educated at Ivy League colleges, had for such work. The truth is that we had none. This was not, of course, true of most of our colleagues, who were not FSOs and did know a thing or two about pigs and wells. Anyway, Rufus understood our limitations, and assigned us at first to work under other people. But when he thought we were ready (of course we were not), he sent us into two neighboring provinces in the Mekong Delta to oversee the distribution of American aid funds and supplies, and assist the local government. Our work has distinct echoes of today's Provincial Reconstruction Teams in Afghanistan, although we had none of the heavy security structure that surrounds Americans in today's even more dangerous war zones. When I visited the PRT in the province of Khost, in eastern Afghanistan, in April 2008, and watched Kael Weston, a career diplomat working closely with local tribal leaders, mullahs, and police officials, I felt I was watching someone who could have stepped right out of Rural Affairs/Vietnam.

The Rural Affairs philosophy was not always pleasing to the Saigon government or other American officials. It cut bureaucratic corners and reduced corruption. What Rufus cared about most was defeating the Viet Cong, and he sometimes broke crockery to do the job.

In late 1963, Rufus left Vietnam for family reasons. To him Rural Affairs was "the most dedicated bunch I had ever seen in government or elsewhere"—a comment that still resonates with me over forty years later. "Everyone was treated as an equal," Rufus said. "We were all on a first-name basis." In 2007, Lang Ha, one of Rural Affairs' first local employees, who was forced to stay behind in Vietnam for 17 years after North Vietnam's victory in 1975, remembered:

"We were different. Yes, we were not only colleagues—we were brothers and sisters in the big family of Rural Affairs. . . . We worked together, we were happy when there was success, unhappy when we met failure, but we were all the time together. I remember when our staff could come back from the field the main office in Saigon was like a bee-hive. With Rural Affairs, the interaction between American staff and local employees also changed completely, and for the better."

Rufus was the best informed American about the situation in rural Vietnam, but not until this book has it been understood that for several crucial years in the 1960s he was probably the best informed American on events in the country as a whole, and perhaps the American most trusted and listened to by the Vietnamese. In this book, he brings new detail to the such well-studied subjects as the 1963 coup against President Diem, and the work of General Lansdale.

Why Vietnam Matters will probably be the last insider book written by an important participant in that now-distant war. When Rufus started it years ago, every publisher and agent told him that no one wanted another Vietnam memoir. In this case they were wrong; this is an important book. The reader may not agree with everything in this book, especially some of its conclusions. But for those of us who served under him, and for whom Vietnam was a seminal and shaping experience, that is not the point. We are heartened to know that, after all these years, Rufus Phillips has not lost his fire, his conviction, his belief in the possibility of American greatness and leadership. In that sense, he remains our leader.

CHAPTER FOUR

Asia in the Carter Years

As the assistant secretary of state for East Asian affairs, Holbrooke greets Vietnam's deputy foreign minister for talks in 1977. (Associated Press)

Restoring America's Role in Asia

RICHARD BERNSTEIN

The scene has an almost Conradian quality, perhaps a bit of Graham Greene or Somerset Maugham. Whatever the literary reference, there is Richard Holbrooke, photographed in 1979 or 1980 on an embankment near the Thai-Cambodian border. He was Jimmy Carter's assistant secretary of state for East Asia and Pacific affairs. His hair is disheveled; he wears an open-necked cotton shirt rather than his usual dark suit and tie. Surrounding him among the jacaranda trees, Cambodians, refugees from a real-life heart of darkness, are picking up relief rice, sent at Holbrooke's insistence to avoid what would otherwise have been a terrible famine in western Cambodia, a consequence of the brutal utopianism of the Khmer Rouge regime.

The picture, taken by Lionel Rosenblatt, the foreign service officer whom Holbrooke had dispatched to Thailand to oversee the refugee and emergency aid effort, depicts Holbrooke in what had become a familiar activity. He went to Thailand frequently during his years as assistant secretary, and whenever he did, he visited the camps on the borders of

Laos and Cambodia where tens of thousands of desperately needy and hungry people, attacked by pirates and unwanted by neighboring countries, were turning up, escaping political repression in the newly Communist countries of Indochina or simply trying to find a place where there was something to eat.

Many people were important in the effort to provide sanctuary for the Indochinese refugees, more than 1.5 million of whom poured out of Vietnam, Cambodia, and Laos following the Communist takeovers in those countries. Stephen J. Solarz, Democrat of Brooklyn, was the first congressman to pay serious attention to the issue, holding hearings at the House Subcommittee on Asian Affairs and urging his colleagues to issue visas to tens of thousands of refugees and to appropriate funds. The American ambassador in Thailand, Morton Abramowitz, devoted the lion's share of his efforts to the program. President Carter himself, alerted by the eyewitness account of his wife, Rosalynn, whom Holbrooke escorted to two camps in 1978, raised the quotas so that eventually more than half a million Indochinese refugees were resettled in the United States. But people involved in the program, including Abramowitz and Rosenblatt, credit Holbrooke with an indispensable role.

"We were just about down on our knees when Holbrooke became assistant secretary," Rosenblatt said, recalling that in the previous administration, some 11,000 refugees were resettled, but the program to help others had become an orphan even as every month tens of thousands of desperate people were arriving in countries less and less willing to take them even temporarily. "He could easily have said I'm not interested and sent it down to a lower level," Rosenblatt said. "But he made it a priority."

Holbrooke, whose early years as a young foreign service officer were spent in Vietnam, understood that, to make it successful, what Rosenblatt called a "polyvalent approach" was essential. Congress had to be persuaded to appropriate money. A staff had to be recruited, both in Washington and on the ground where the refugees were arriving. Most important, it wasn't enough to provide food and shelter to refugees in places like Thailand, Malaysia, and the Philippines where the majority of them were showing up. It was also necessary to persuade more distant countries to accept them as immigrants.

"Whether it was journalists, legislators, financial experts, diplomats from other countries, he'd get that Rolodex going," Rosenblatt said.

"He'd start thinking of the people we needed to contact for help. It was a pleasure to watch him operate. When we'd go to the camps, he'd ask a barrage of questions en route, and when he was there, all he wanted was to be left alone, talking and learning by himself, and then he'd formulate his thoughts on the way back. He was totally focused. On the way back, he'd talk about how we could move this forward. He'd think about a journalist we could approach. He'd know who was in the country whose support we could enlist."

All his life Holbrooke suffered from his reputation as an almost brutally ambitious figure whose purpose in being assistant secretary of state under Carter was to become secretary of state in some future administration. But whatever element of truth there was to that common image, Holbrooke's tireless and effective campaigning on behalf of refugees demonstrated the other side of the man, the humanitarian who took great pleasure in helping others, even when there was no career advantage in it for himself. His modus operandi with any task was to take total possession of it, and his work for the refugees was no exception. He ordered Rosenblatt to escort any congressmen or congresswomen who came to Thailand to the camps to see for themselves the desperation and misery. He testified on the Hill, including before Solarz's committee. He arranged the first lady's visit, knowing full well that it was a sure way to get the refugees' plight on all the evening news programs simultaneously. As it happened, Mrs. Carter witnessed a child dying in front of her eyes. He buttonholed journalists and persuaded them to cover the refugee story, among them Mike Wallace, whose *60 Minutes* broadcast from the Laotian border helped enormously to bring the refugees' plight to public attention. He worked the corridors at the G7 meeting in Tokyo in 1978 to persuade other countries to give permanent homes to thousands of refugees.

"There was a lot of ambivalence in the administration about what our refugee policy could and should be," Frank Wisner, a colleague and friend of Holbrooke from the Vietnam days recalled. "Holbrooke was unbelievably decisive. He plunged in and said, 'There is no choice but the U.S. taking the lead in this latest diffusion. We must provide haven for them, short-term camp facilities, and take action to get governments to stop pirates killing and maiming them on high seas. But if we don't have a place to put the refugees long term, we don't have a policy at all.' Holbrooke used the G7 Summit to bring that decision to a conclusion, and there are thousands of Southeast Asians living in the U.S. today. It was because of Richard Holbrooke. There's no doubt about that."

THE ISSUE OF THE INDOCHINESE REFUGEES WAS ONLY ONE THAT CAME up in Holbrooke's tenure as assistant secretary and certainly it was one of the least anticipated, but it also emblemized the eventful and even dramatic four years when for the first time, Holbrooke occupied a key policy-making position. There's no question that his tenure as assistant secretary established him as a key player in American foreign affairs, the guy to turn to when something really needed to get done. This is not to say that Holbrooke's four years on the sixth floor of the State Department were always happy. He had his enemies and was dealt his share of bureaucratic defeats and frustrations. But he also showed what would later be an almost unprecedented combination of skills and aptitudes— his ability to mobilize influential people, to cajole and persuade, to pay relentless attention to detail, to build a staff of enormously talented people, to attract the attention of the press, and to do it all with a sort of controlled fury tempered by the facts that, one, it was for a good cause, and two, he never (or almost never) lost his sense of humor.

Holbrooke had initially backed Sargent Shriver for president as the 1976 presidential campaign got underway. But he switched to the then little-known governor from Georgia named Jimmy Carter, eventually becoming Carter's foreign policy coordinator. Holbrooke was thirty-five. The biggest thing he'd run up to that point in his life was the Peace Corps in Morocco, but he was well connected, conspicuously intelligent, indefatigable, and, true, unabashedly ambitious. He had served in Vietnam in the 1960s and had been a member of the American delegation to the Paris Peace Talks with Vietnam, led by Averell Harriman, who became a mentor. Holbrooke was also the editor of *Foreign Policy*, which was widely read in Washington, New York, and other outposts of the foreign policy establishment. He would like to have been named national security advisor, the job that went to Zbigniew Brzezinski. But when he was offered the position of assistant secretary for East Asia and the Pacific, he took it unhesitatingly. Harriman had once held that post. So had Dean Rusk, who had risen to be secretary of state under John F. Kennedy. It was a visible post with plenty of upside potential, dealing with an area that had been and promised to be at the center of American interests.

This was, of course, because of the two situations that developed before the new administration came into power. One was the humiliating loss of Indochina that had taken place barely a year and a half earlier, a loss that, in Henry Kissinger's words, reflected an "enfeeblement" of American power and prestige in Asia. The other, somewhat compensating event, had been the famous opening of China engineered by Kissinger that resulted in President Richard M. Nixon's breakthrough visit to Beijing in 1972. The big geo-strategic question that Holbrooke asked in an article in the *New York Times Magazine*, published just six months after the Vietnam debacle, was what, in this new situation, was the proper role for the United States?

Holbrooke came up with several recommendations, all aimed at restoring American prestige and influence in a region where it had suffered its greatest losses—first in China after World War II, then in Vietnam, Laos, and Cambodia in 1975. One was to recognize that the "demicolonial role" that the United States had played in Asia ever since the end of World War II, openly or secretly involving itself in the affairs of almost every country in the region, was irrevocably over. And, Holbrooke wrote, while some might bemoan the end of that time and experience a nostalgic yearning for its restoration, the end of that kind of preeminence was actually a good thing because it would allow the United States to maintain and even enjoy a degree of detachment, to have the luxury of not concerning itself with every political development in every country.

In other words, Holbrooke felt we could do more by doing less. The first priority was to build on Nixon's opening with China, most obviously by moving to full diplomatic relations as quickly as possible. At the same time, we needed to make Japan the cornerstone of our Asian-Pacific policy, taking advantage of the fact that for the first time in decades, China, Japan, and the United States all had good relations with one another. We were still the dominant outside power in East Asia, and we would continue to be. But besides that, we needed to heed the lesson of Vietnam, which was to avoid getting "trapped in a small and secondary country to which we must remain committed," a country like Korea. Indeed, Holbrooke argued, it would be a good thing if we could withdraw the 40,000 American troops that had been stationed in that country since the end of the Korean War, though, he admitted, a withdrawal anytime soon was a long shot. Above all, in relinquishing our demicolonial status and in capitalizing on the new relationship with China, the United States could, in the words of the headline to Holbrooke's article, "escape the domino trap" and move to a new era in its relations with our Pacific neighbors.

DURING HIS YEARS AS ASSISTANT SECRETARY, HOLBROOKE ADHERED pretty closely to the blueprint he laid out in that article, though his term was marked less by detachment and more by a series of crises in South Korea, the Philippines, East Timor, and, as I've noted, along the Thai border with Laos and Cambodia. The greatest strategic achievement of the Carter years was no doubt the normalization with China, which initiated an enormous expansion of Chinese-American relations involving elements that would have been unthinkable a few years earlier—military contacts, intelligence sharing, and student exchanges among them. The truth is that Holbrooke was kept at arm's length from the normalization negotiation, which was the sort of front-burner, page-one worthy issue that more senior officials wanted to handle. But he was deeply involved in the less visible expansion of relations, which enabled him to say at the end of his term that the Carter administration had engineered "the basic legal and institutional framework within which economic, cultural, scientific, and technological relationships between the Chinese and American people can develop their full potential."[1]

At the same time, Holbrooke actively promoted U.S.-Japanese relations. He led the unsuccessful effort to pursue normalization negotiations with Vietnam, even as similar negotiations were taking place with China, part of an effort to put the domino trap to rest. Holbrooke, in speeches and later in articles, liked to say that during the Carter years, the United States, so far from being enfeebled in the wake of the crushing defeat in Indochina, possessed greater prestige and influence in Asia than at any time in the recent past, and it was a prestige and influence enjoyed without serious conflicts or tensions with any of the region's major powers. "The arc from Korean through Taiwan and the Philippines, at the very center of great power rivalry and instability for much of this century, is less subject to these strains today than at any time in well over forty years," Holbrooke said in a speech in the summer of 1980. The statement seems entirely justified. Indeed, in light of current-day tensions with China, the years when Holbrooke was assistant secretary of state for East Asia acquire a retrospective glow.

BUT IT WASN'T EASY, ESPECIALLY AT THE BEGINNING. "THE FIRST SIX months were very tough," recalled Abramowitz, who became Holbrooke's counterpart in the Defense Department as the Carter team took office, and there were several reasons for that. Holbrooke was a leading member of what William Safire (just starting his career in punditry at the *New York Times*) called "the new boy network," the group of young men (and they were mostly men), including Tony Lake, director of policy planning at State; Leslie Gelb, assistant secretary for political-military affairs; Peter Tarnoff, effectively Secretary of State Cyrus Vance's chief of staff; and Richard Moose, assistant secretary of state for Africa, most of whom had first met each other in Vietnam when they were even younger men and were now moving into positions of real power and authority. "He represents a component of the incoming administration," the *New York Times* reported on Holbrooke's appointment as assistant secretary, "young and outspoken, and having served in staff jobs to senior figures but with little actual experience in policy making."[2]

To greater or lesser degrees, all of the members of the new-boy network were critics of the Indochina Wars—Lake and Moose more outspoken in this regard than Holbrooke, Tarnoff, or Gelb. Influenced by their times, they tended toward a kind of breezy informality, especially in contrast to the more buttoned-down followers of Nixon and Kissinger whom they were replacing. They wanted to do things more transparently, with less factional infighting and compartmentalized secrecy than had existed in the outgoing administration. Even before taking office, Holbrooke was buttonholing other bright, young foreign service officers, recruiting them to his team, and ending up with a cast of deputy secretaries who went on to distinguished careers. Among them: John Negroponte, later ambassador at the UN; Robert Oakley, who became director of the State Department office for combating terrorism; and William Gleysteen, a China-born career diplomat who was subsequently appointed ambassador to Korea.

But Holbrooke also arrived with what an old friend, Nicholas Platt, who was later ambassador to Pakistan and the Philippines, called "a mixed reputation for brilliance and brashness," which was the reputation that Holbrooke was to carry with him for the rest of his life. The *New York Times* wrote of "the arrogant self-confidence of some of the newcomers," and this was a mixed blessing. As an outsider, Holbrooke was already regarded with suspicion by many of the career officers in his bureau at the State Department, and his manner didn't help.

"It was his style," Gelb recalled. "It unnerved them—Dick in his office in his socks, his shirt half out. The whole scene was calculated not to endear him to these guys, but I'd say that by the end of the first year, they began to see his smarts and his willingness to do tough things, and that won them over. Not that they didn't see what they considered his faults, but they had respect for him." Some important foreign allies were also put off. "The Japanese had a very low opinion of Dick because he was so young," said Platt, who was the head of the Japan desk at State. Platt remembered when Japanese Prime Minister Takeo Fukuda came for a state visit in the early months of the new administration: "Holbrooke went to Andrews Air Force Base to meet him, and Blythe was dressed in jeans and a mink coat." (Blythe was Blythe Babyak, an aspiring television reporter who was briefly Holbrooke's second wife.) "The Japanese never really forgave him," Platt said. "They never actually said anything, but it was obvious from their body language."

More generally, the more hawkish members of the American foreign policy establishment, who were still divided between Cold War–era hawks and doves, tended to see Carter himself as soft on foreign policy, an image that was fostered by the antiwar reputations of the new-boy network like Holbrooke, Lake, and Moose whom he had brought into visible positions in Washington. In fact, there was a wide variety of opinions even among the new boys, with Holbrooke and Gelb more hard-line than probably Carter himself, but that didn't make much of a difference. "If you were generally critical of what Nixon and Kissinger were doing, then you were just considered a crazy dove who wanted to get out, and that was the reputation all of us carried into the State Department with us," Gelb said. The impression was intensified by the fact that during the campaign, Carter had called for withdrawing American troops from South Korea, where some 40,000 of them had been stationed since the end of the Korean War in 1952, and that was one of the main reasons Holbrooke's first six months proved so tough. Indeed, it was an issue that took three years of sometimes nerve-racking work to resolve.

IN THAT SEPTEMBER 1975 NEW YORK TIMES MAGAZINE ARTICLE, Holbrooke rather unambiguously called for a withdrawal of troops, and many in the administration assumed that Carter had gotten the idea from his assistant secretary for East Asia, though Holbrooke himself always denied that. In his *Times* piece, Holbrooke had certainly portrayed a troop withdrawal as a good thing, if also unlikely to be carried out soon. But, in any early confrontation of his theoretical idealism and practical reality, he soon changed his mind and joined what became almost a conspiracy among the leading members of the administration's foreign policy team to get the president to back off the idea. Holbrooke, according to the *Washington Post* reporter Don Oberdorfer, termed this "a full-scale rebellion against the president."

"Holbrooke worked hard to get Carter to take [the troop withdrawal idea] back," said Peter Tarnoff. "He knew it was the wrong policy. The real question was how to handle the president."

To coordinate that and other efforts, Holbrooke spearheaded the creation of an interagency Asian group that met once a week to talk things over. Its other members included Abramowitz at the Defense Department, Michael Armacost, an Asia expert on the National Security Council, and others. Inside the meeting rooms of the Carter administration, all of them began to argue that, as Abramowitz put it years later, "our position in Asia was dwindling and it would erode even further at a time when we were trying to preserve our position in the Pacific and with the Chinese after the Vietnam debacle."

In the end, Carter did back off the idea, though very reluctantly and not until 1979 when, accompanied by Holbrooke, Platt, Vance, Brzezinski, and Gleysteen, he met with South Korean leader Park Chung Hee. As Platt remembered it, Carter and Park held a tense meeting at which Park, nervously snapping his fingers, told the American president that a troop withdrawal would play into the hands of the North Koreans, would weaken the United States in Asia, and would strengthen the Chinese—all arguments that the rest of the American delegation supported. But Carter was in a rage as the autocratic South Korean leader lectured him on the best thing to do with American forces. Sitting in his limousine after the meeting with Park, the still-smoldering Carter listened as Gleysteen, then the American ambassador in Seoul, laid out the negative consequences of pulling out. The key element in the argument was a Central Intelligence Agency finding that North Korea had substantially more troops facing the South than had previously been known.

"I guess the meeting on Korea that we've been trying to arrange all this time is finally taking place," Holbrooke quipped as he, Platt, and the others followed in another limousine. He was referring to the failure of the members of the "rebellion" to make their case on Korea directly to the president.

As a result of Gleysteen's briefing, Carter, still in the limousine, agreed to reconsider his position on the condition that Park add to the South Korean defense budget and release some political prisoners. With that, as Platt put it, "Holbrooke sallied forth to repair the damage," meaning he contacted his South Korean counterparts to get their consent to Carter's conditions. They did, and in their next meeting, Carter told Park that he would put American troop withdrawals on hold.

THE POINT IS THAT NO ONE IN THE NEW-BOY NETWORK, AND ESPECIALLY not Holbrooke, was "soft" on foreign policy. Indeed, if there is a single theme running through Holbrooke's years as assistant secretary, it would be his effort to hold a kind of realistic middle ground between competing tendencies inside the administration. His two great rivals demonstrate this. On the one hand, Holbrooke had frequent arguments with Patricia Derian, Carter's assistant secretary of state for human rights and the person charged by the president with carrying out his highly publicized demand that human rights be at the center of American foreign policy. The issue that most divided Holbrooke and Derian was how to deal with Philippine president Ferdinand Marcos, who had declared martial law; put his main political rival, Benigno Aquino, and other dissidents in prison; and clamped down on protest. But Holbrooke was charged with negotiating treaty extensions for the two large American military installations in the Philippines, Clark Air Base and the Subic Bay Naval Base, and that negotiation required good relations with the Philippine president.

"Pat Derian was on his case, because there's no question that Dick was not tough on human rights with Marcos," Gelb remembered. "Derian would jab him in open meetings at the department, and she'd complain to [Deputy Secretary of State Warren] Christopher."

The argument over Marcos came to a head in the spring of 1978 when Vice President Walter Mondale was planning a trip to the Philippines, with Holbrooke accompanying him. The trip came in the wake of elections for a new National Assembly tarnished by numerous credible allegations of vote fraud and the arrests of some six hundred protestors. To proceed in a business-as-usual way, Derian argued, would make Carter's human rights policy seem meaningless and the Mondale trip should be either canceled or postponed. "There was a huge argument between Holbrooke and Derian on this issue, and Dick adopted the harder view, which was that the bases were exceedingly important," Abramowitz remembered. A Solomonic solution was devised whereby the vice president went to the Philippines as planned, but he raised the issue of human rights abuses in what Marcos himself called a "lively exchange" and met with a few of Marcos's local critics, not including the imprisoned Aquino.

HOLBROOKE'S OTHER BÊTE NOIR IN THE CARTER ADMINISTRATION WAS Brzezinski, who, as Holbrooke's friends put it, treated Holbrooke with something close to disdain, especially when it came to the normalization of relations with China. This was something that Holbrooke had to endure, even as he fought to play a role. Some of this was simple bureaucratic rivalry, a collateral effect of Brzezinski's ongoing struggle with Secretary of State Vance to control China policy and thus to indirectly control policy toward the Soviet Union. But there was a difference, if not exactly of ideology, then of temperament as well, with Vance generally more cautious on China normalization, not wanting a deal with Beijing to disrupt such priorities as arms control negotiations with the Soviet Union. "Vance understood the importance of China," Tarnoff recalled, "but he came from a period and a generation for which U.S.-Soviet relations were paramount, and he was not willing to compromise those relations over China."

The debate was about timing, but it was also about how to overcome the main stumbling block in the normalization negotiations, which was the American wish to ensure Taiwan's long-term future, satisfying the demands both of public opinion and of key figures in Congress. When Carter took office, the United States still formally recognized Taiwan, otherwise known as the Republic of China, and had only a liaison office with Beijing. In the ideal world, the offices would have been switched, the embassy going to Beijing, the lower-ranking liaison office to Taipei. Beijing made it clear that it would not tolerate any official state-to-state relationship with Taiwan. It would also never formally agree to two other American preferences, namely, that it relinquish force in dealing with Taiwan and that it recognize an American right to sell arms to Taiwan. Holbrooke was intimately familiar with these problems, and generally he agreed with Brzezinski that the pace of normalization with China should be faster rather than slower. But he fought, or tried to fight, the bureaucratic battle on behalf of his boss, Vance. In the end, it was Brzezinski—and, to a lesser extent, the future American ambassador to China, the labor leader Leonard Woodcock—who controlled China policy, outmaneuvering Vance and the State Department.

In what was surely the most painful aspect of his time as assistant secretary, Holbrooke was more than bureaucratically sidelined by Brzezinski. He was systematically excluded, kept out of the loop. Brzezinski genuinely disliked Holbrooke, apparently believing, as Gelb put it, that he and his group were "left-wing nuts." Brzezinski also accused Holbrooke of leaking to the press, an accusation that had some truth to it. In any case, matters came to a head in late 1977 and 1978 as Brzezinski planned to travel to China for talks with paramount leader Deng Xiaoping. In *A Great Wall*, his history of Sino-American relations, the journalist Patrick Tyler writes that Brzezinski had Holbrooke cut from the group that would attend the central meeting of the trip, the one with Deng. Holbrooke got both Woodcock and Gleysteen to remonstrate on his behalf, arguing that to exclude the assistant secretary for Asia in that fashion would be to "destroy the processes of government," but this was to no avail.[3] It got so bad that when Holbrooke found his car last in the official motorcades, Tyler reports, he would jump out of his limousine and ask Woodcock if he could ride in his.[4]

"I was present as deputy executive secretary watching these wars take place," Wisner remembered. "Holbrooke fought back by every bureaucratic ruse known to man, being there with the ideas, pushing Vance to fight, preparing back channel notes to the president, every way you do these things."

Still, it was a battle that Vance and therefore Holbrooke lost, and that loss was perhaps Holbrooke's first major, bitter experience in the nastiness of bureaucratic warfare, prefiguring the troubles he was to have thirty years later when, as President Barack Obama's special emissary for Afghanistan and Pakistan, he felt excluded from the president's inner circle. But as he did later, Holbrooke soldiered on under Carter, including on the China issue. After the delicate issue of Taiwan had been finessed—mainly by the United States reserving the right to sell arms to Taiwan and China not openly objecting—normalization was announced on December 15, 1978. From that point on, Holbrooke was a frequent visitor to Beijing.

I accompanied him once on a private tour he made to the homes of several unofficial artists in Beijing, young people who were expressing moderately dissenting views inside China and who had even demonstrated for the right to show their work. We went, for example, to the home and studio of Wang Keping, who worked in a tiny, drab, concrete apartment. Using the simplest of tools, he made powerful political statements from odd pieces of wood he was able to find—the head of a man, for example, with a plug inserted into his mouth and a bas-relief of Chairman Mao as a figure on a totem pole. Holbrooke, clearly moved by what he saw, commented that these guys, laboring away in primitive circumstances with primitive tools, nurtured what seemed to him the spark of freedom. He wasn't inclined to put human rights at the center of the agenda with China or, for that matter, with any other country, but as his later championship of rights for Tibetans and his meeting with the Dalai Lama would clearly indicate, the question of human dignity was never far from his mind.

"He had a very strong humanitarian streak, not a human rights streak but a humanitarian streak," Abramowitz said. He was referring to Holbrooke's powerful and skillful championship of the Indochinese refugees, but he could have been speaking more generally as well. Moreover, while he always remained a secondary player on China, he proved to be a powerful and influential assistant secretary. From early on, by recruiting figures like Oakley, Armacost, Negroponte, and others, Holbrooke placed a cadre of highly talented foreign policy officials into key positions, and it was a group that understood Holbrooke and worked well with him. It was also an early instance of something that Holbrooke would do repeatedly in his career: build a team of talented, dedicated men and women who would take on Holbrooke's mission as their own.

"He didn't hire shrinking violets," Negroponte said. "He liked to have people who he felt were intellectual peers that he could argue things out with. It was collegial atmosphere, and also stimulating, not one where everybody sat there and listened to the word according to Richard Holbrooke."

THERE WERE OTHER THINGS ABOUT HOLBROOKE'S MODUS OPERANDI that would reappear in his later incarnations in government, not least his extraordinary skill as a networker and his ability to know just about everybody who counted, whether the foreign leaders whom he met on his travels as assistant secretary, the congressmen he needed to open the United States to Indochinese refugees, or the journalists who would give publicity to the issues he felt were important.

"He knew these guys better than anybody in Washington," Gelb said of Holbrooke's connections with Asian leaders. "And he did the same thing in Washington. He knew all the senators. And don't leave out the press, with which he had more contact than all the assistant secretaries put together. Mind you, he enjoyed it, but it was also power."

There's no question that a lot of Holbrooke's fantastic energy corresponded to the dimensions of his ambition. He wanted to be secretary of state. But, as his intense and polyvalent activity on behalf of refugees demonstrated, he also wanted to do good. Even though he fought constantly with Derian over what he saw as her unrealistically idealistic commitment to human rights, he was the senior State Department official who went to the homes of dissenting Chinese artists at a time when human rights in China were simply off the agenda. In 1980, President Chun Doo Hwan of not-very-democratic South Korea crushed a popular uprising in a city called Kwangju, and some leftist critics of Holbrooke have blamed him for the ensuing massacre, in which 144 civilians were killed (along with 26 soldiers and police). The criticism is that Holbrooke gave Chun the green light for the massacre, something that Holbrooke adamantly denied. But whatever his feeling that Chun had to be dealt with for the sake of stability in Korea, Holbrooke also visited Korea's leading political dissenter (and later president) Kim Dae Jung, which was a remarkable gesture at the time. It's hard to think of another assistant secretary of state who did that sort of thing.

Near the end of his term came the invasion of Cambodia by Vietnam, another issue that posed human rights concerns against practical reality. In the view of many people, the Vietnamese, in overthrowing the murderous Khmer Rouge dictatorship, should have been applauded and welcomed as the saviors of Cambodia. But Holbrooke, while entirely aware of Khmer Rouge atrocities, went along with the official American position, which was to denounce the Vietnamese for the invasion and to support the Khmer Rouge as the legitimate Cambodian government.

It was not a comfortable position to be in, but it was another of those instances in which practicality took priority over idealism.

At the same time, Holbrooke used all his considerable skill to press for more help for the new flood of refugees provoked by the invasion. "I remember one moment in particular," Negroponte said. "We were having a huge situation with Congress about getting enough refugee admissions to the U.S., and I was going up for talks with Congress. Dick told me, 'You get no less [than] 12,000 admission numbers per month, and if you don't come back with 144,000 per year, your name is mud, Negroponte.' He was tenacious, and he wasn't going to relent, and we did get 144,000 admissions per year."

In this sense, the Holbrooke who was to emerge as a major public figure later, perhaps the most frequently profiled in major magazines of any of his contemporaries, is already clearly visible in his years in the Carter administration. Certainly his years as assistant secretary were good preparation for many of the things he did later. His work for refugees in Indochina prefigures similar work that he did twenty years later in Bosnia or that propelled him afterward to found and lead the Global Business Council on HIV/AIDS. His negotiations with figures like Marcos or the Vietnamese were good training for his epic negotiation in the mid-1990s that brought an end to the war in the former Yugoslavia. His dealings on the Hill in the late 1970s were a sort of prelude to what some people cite as his greatest overlooked achievement: to get Congress, led in part by the ultraconservative Jesse Helms, to agree to pay over $900 million in back dues to the United Nations.

And always, then and later, there was the man, not yet forty years old when the Carter administration ended, whose larger-than-life quality spawned a thousand anecdotes about his persistence, his irascibility, his boldness, and not infrequently, his generosity. Nick Platt tells one that sums up the Holbrooke persona as well as any other.

"We were in Japan," Platt remembers. It was a state visit by Carter in July 1980. Brzezinski had business to attend to back home, so he had designated Platt as his surrogate.

"I have a fairly modest approach in protocol matters," Platt said. "So when we go to the imperial palace for the audience with the emperor, I plan to sit it out and let them go through the ceremonial part. Holbrooke sees me and says, 'What are you doing here. You come on up. You've got to be part of this.'"

"But my name's not on the list," I said.

"'The hell with that. This is important,' and he pushes me in, and I go forward and I meet the emperor, and Carter introduces me as his national security advisor! Holbrooke just inserted me into the picture. I was very grateful to him for doing that. He wasn't getting anything out of it, but he just thought I should be there."

Escaping the Domino Trap

RICHARD HOLBROOKE
New York Times Magazine, SEPTEMBER 7, 1975

> *Here Holbrooke reflects on the changing dynamics in Asia and the future U.S. role in the region. At the time, the near simultaneous Communist takeovers of Vietnam, Laos, and Cambodia brought renewed concern about the domino theory and American decline. Holbrooke knew better and two years later would be back in government as the Assistant Secretary of State for East Asia working to make sure that Thailand, Indonesia, and other countries did not follow suit.*

In a famous speech in January, 1950, Secretary of State Dean Acheson discussed the American commitment in Asia in light of the triumph of the Chinese Communists only a few months earlier. The purpose of the speech, as he saw it, was to explain where the United States stood in Asia after the final retreat from the Chinese mainland of Chiang Kai-shek's forces.

In it, Acheson seemed to draw a line in Asia, a "defensive perimeter from the Ryukyus to the Philippines." By omission, he seemed to have excluded both Korea and Taiwan from within the perimeter. By excluding Korea did he invite the North Korean assault that took place less than six months later? Some critics think so, although Acheson himself, not surprisingly, later called the charge "specious."

Now, 25 years later, in the aftermath of another great retreat of America and its allies from positions on the Asian mainland, the same questions arise: How do the other nations of Asia adjust to the new situation that they must now face? Where do we draw the line this time?

But there is also another question, which was not asked 25 years ago: Do we draw any line at all? What, finally, should the American role in Asia and the Pacific be?

Once, it all seemed so simple. American policy in Asia was easy enough to be understood by everyone: a mirror image of our containment policies in Europe, based on the idea of a simple battle between the forces of good—the non-Communist countries rimming China—and evil— the 800 million Chinese Reds and their aggressive surrogates and satellites in North Vietnam, North Korea and in the more remote jungles of some of our friends, such as the Philippines.

After 1944, in the aftermath of the collapse of the great colonial empires of Asia—the Japanese, the British, the French, the Dutch— came new and uncertain states, and an obvious power vacuum. It was probably inevitable that as the biggest winner in World War II, the United States, with its vast Pacific fleet, its special status as the occupying power in Japan and its continuing postindependence presence in the Philippines, would play a major role in Asia after the war. The triple threat perceived by Washington in 1950—Mao's triumph in China, North Korea's attack on the south, and the growing success of Ho Chi Minh's guerrilla forces in Indochina—made it inevitable that the United States would try to use its vast influence and power to construct an anti-Communist ring of nations from Korea as far south and west as it could, all the way to a linkup with NATO if possible. For the meaning of these events, and their ultimate source in the worldwide designs of Moscow, seemed clear enough: "We were seeing a pattern in Indochina and Tibet," Harry Truman wrote in his memoirs, "timed to coincide with the attack in Korea and as challenge to the Western world."

Responding to these events, the United States moved into what might be called a "demicolonial" role in Asia. Even while Americans refused to think of their country as a major Asian power, even while politicians refused to admit that our interests and involvement were as deep in Asia as in Europe—or even deeper—the United States entered into a remarkable era, for itself and for Asia. During the 30 years from the end of World War II until April 29, 1975, when Ambassador Graham Martin left the roof of his beleaguered embassy in Saigon, the United States—mostly with the Asians' permission—played the multiple role of a surrogate colonial power throughout Asia. We wrote the constitutions of countries, including the famous one that General MacArthur's command supplied to the Japanese; we underwrote economic development and gave massive technical assistance to nations, usually with a political motive in mind; we participated covertly and even openly in the internal political process of almost every country in the area. In some countries, such as Indonesia, we participated in or had prior knowledge of coups and rebellions; in others, like the Philippines, we helped suppress insurgencies. We put American troops, at one time or another, into Korea, Japan, Taiwan, South Vietnam, Laos, Cambodia, Thailand and the Philippines. American Embassies in Asia were like embassies in no other part of the world: One had the feeling that they really mattered, and leading Asians, having bidden farewell to their British or French masters, looked to our embassies with awe and apprehension, seeking favor or blaming us for all manner of events. An American Ambassador in Saigon once referred to himself half-jokingly as the proconsul; in retrospect, one can see that he was more than half right. In Tokyo, Seoul, Manila, Bangkok, Vientiane and Pnom Penh under Lon Nol, the American Ambassador and the U.S. Government were always the dominant external factor, often the major internal factor as well. In Jakarta, Malaysia, Singapore and Pnom Penh under Sihanouk, while not quite as visible, the American factor was usually the critical one. In India, where the Americans were always an easy target for the intelligentsia and the ruling élite, the American Ambassador, his personality, his wife, his style, were subject to intense scrutiny, almost as though the Indians, having lost the British Viceroy, needed some other Westerner to gossip about, both as person and as symbol; we became, in Daniel Moynihan's apt phrase, a "demi-Raj." Only in Burma, it seems, did the Americans not become the issue; but to achieve this the Burmese virtually disappeared behind a curtain of xenophobia and isolation, refusing all outside aid or assistance.

To countries outside our orbit, the United States also became an easy target, a means of unifying people around a common opposition. Sukarno of Indonesia, as well as virtually every guerrilla movement in the region except those in Burma, found that to raise cries and alarms about American imperialism was a profitable tactic, and often a useful substitute for more direct confrontation of their own problems. American behavior in the area ranged from crude and inappropriate to sympathetic and understanding, but any American behavior at all was inevitably the focus of controversy and contention. What strings were attached to American aid, asked the Indians. What covert C.I.A. activity was hidden within American information programs? What nuclear weapons were placed on our soil without our knowledge or approval, asked the Japanese. And so on.

By our very size we became an issue, but by our great strength and by a shared perception of the Communist threat, we were able to hold the anti-Communist chain together. It took varying degrees of persuasion and coercion, of overt and covert pressure, of bribery and incentive—but it worked for a while. After the civil war of 1965–66 in Indonesia, for example, a country once viewed with great alarm in Washington as the wedge through which China would divide Asia came strongly into the anti-Communist camp, so much so that today Indonesia can be termed the most anti-Chinese nation left in Southeast Asia. And India, despite all its fears and traumas about the Americans, despite its special problems with Pakistan, turned into another strong anti-Chinese pillar after its border wars with the Chinese.

Nineteen-seventy was the high-water mark of the anti-Chinese phase in Asia. The United States stood dominant in the region, the organizer and primary backer of every anti-Communist nation in the region. Within the net at that time, to some degree, was every country from Korea to India, except for Burma. But we were already in very deep trouble in Vietnam, and our new anti-Chinese ally in Cambodia was to prove a hopeless case.

Equally serious, the United States had failed in many countries to use its influence to build anything resembling stable, progressive governments. Our greatest success story was undoubtedly Japan, where Douglas MacArthur and his Supreme Command left behind a truly commendable record; in other parts of Asia, though, our power was used only to obtain military installations on favorable terms, or to promote a sort of ersatz stability depending on strong-man regimes with corrupt power bases.

Then came two historic events, and now as Asia and the United States adjust to them, everything seems changed.

The first was a total surprise to the world, and although secrecy may have been necessary to assure success, it also caused a loss of trust between Asia and Washington. In the summer of 1971, the United States, without any prior warning or hint to any of its Asian friends, leaped over the barriers it had forged and entered the Forbidden City of Peking.

At first, the shock waves overseas were overshadowed by such dramatic sights as Walter Cronkite and Barbara Walters interviewing themselves and Henry Kissinger at the Great Wall during Nixon's 1972 visit, but it was soon apparent that every other country in Asia, having earlier joined in the anti-Chinese front, would now have to work out where it stood in a world in which Washington and Peking, instead of hurling insults at each other across a Bamboo Curtain, exchanged visits of dentists and weight lifters.

The second event was less surprising, but nonetheless shocking, symbolic and dramatic when it came—far more quickly than anyone had expected—in April of this year. The collapse of the American–Lon Nol–Thieu position in Cambodia and Vietnam, with the certain erosion afterwards of our vestigial position in Laos, should not have come as a total surprise to anyone. But many people, in Washington, Saigon, and even in other parts of Asia, had begun to forget about Vietnam, treating it as an issue no longer important. The sudden and dramatic tragedy of April left the American-created chain from Korea south sundered at what was once its most important point, where the Americans had paid the heaviest price over the longest time. In addition, a new power now entered the political equation in Asia in a way that no one had expected—a nearly unified, Communist Vietnam, with more than 40 million people, possessing an army that was one of the best-equipped, best-fed, and certainly the most battle-proven in all of Asia. All this was coupled with the hard-to-measure psychological impact on Asians and Americans alike of those striking images from the last days of the war—American Ambassadors stumbling out of the countries in which they were once so powerful, Vietnamese either abandoned or haphazardly lifted out of beleaguered cities, helicopters pushed over the sides of American carriers into the South China Sea.

If the American reopening of China was the more important of the two events in long-range terms, the end of the war in Indochina was the more symbolic. It was so simple, so dramatic, that everyone could understand it: After 30 years and countless lives, the jungle guerrillas had finally pushed the Westerners right into the South China Sea; there were limits to the power of the world's most powerful nation.

Some of the adjustments that were now taking place seemed in Washington to sound like falling dominoes. Thailand and the Philippines looked to many observers like the first to start tipping; and everyone focused renewed attention on Korea, where many observers expected Kim II Sung to open a new effort to subvert the South Koreans. In Jakarta, a leading weekly news magazine, *Tempo*, ran a cover picture of a delicately balanced stack of dominoes and the caption "Are We a Domino, Brothers?" (They concluded that they were not, so long as the country remained strong internally.)

At first, such perceptions seem logical: After all, if a country moves away from the United States in the post-Vietnam era, isn't that exactly what President Eisenhower had in mind when he first warned of the domino effect that could follow a Communist victory in Indochina? Wasn't any move away from the tight ring that we had once forged a loss of position for us, and thus a gain for "the other side"?

So it seems to many people in the aftermath of Vietnam, and yet in focusing on this more shocking second event, we seem to be ignoring the more important implications of the first. Certainly there is movement—movement of a historic nature—taking place throughout Asia. But what does the movement really prove? Aren't we forgetting that the domino theory was simply one small, rhetorical image from the anti-China containment policy that we ourselves had ended, voluntarily, in 1971? Aren't we forgetting the historical process that had brought us to this new moment, confusing the effects of our Vietnam tragedy with the effects of our China policy? What we are seeing now in Asia is much more the result of our opening the China door than the end of the Vietnam war.

The end of the war was a catalyst, speeding up and giving new and easier justification to the process, but it was bound to come anyway. The most advisable policy for the United States, in these circumstances, would be to show understanding and sympathy and support—and not to wring its hands at the adjustments other nations are now making.

Thailand and the Philippines present good examples. Thailand, pulled from its traditional position of nonalignment into a firm place within the American orbit, in the nineteen-fifties and sixties became a key logistical base for support of American military operations in Laos and Vietnam. We gave the Thais aid and advice on how to defeat the guerrillas operating in three areas of their own country. But now the Thais are part of a chain that no longer exists and the original rationale for the policy is gone, along with the military regime that made those arrangements. What possible reason is there to try to maintain the old policy in the new world?

Philippine President Ferdinand Marcos, who once danced with Lady Bird Johnson, and sent civic-action troops to Vietnam, has now made the trip to Peking and shaken hands, Nixon-style, with Chairman Mao. Is that the end of America's massive military installations at Subic Bay and Clark Air Force Base? Scarcely: Marcos is not about to deliver his country into the hands of the Chinese, who in any case seem content to see us remain in the Philippines as a counterweight to the Soviet Union. But the adjustment process Marcos has started is reasonable, even if his personal behavior and repressive style may be reprehensible to many Americans: diplomatic recognition of one's closest mainland neighbor is hardly the collapse of another domino, as some people have suggested.

In the North Pacific and Northeast Asia, the end of the war had far less impact. But the region faces an even more complicated set of choices than the rest of Asia. Here, an old conflict in Korea keeps memories of the Cold War at its coldest very much alive; but here also, vast changes are no longer impossible to imagine. Extraordinary new possibilities—carrying risks even greater than their opportunities—are coming into view.

By opening up relations with China in 1971 the United States put itself squarely into the middle of the potentially explosive rivalry between Moscow and Peking, and at times our position has probably had real impact on the behavior of the two Communist superpowers toward each other. A misstep could be serious indeed. Henry Kissinger has spent a great deal of time calibrating the American position in this delicate triangle, although we may never know the full nature of his secret manipulations.

That triangular balance is constantly undergoing new tests as the global situation changes. The end of the Indochinese war removes a major ideological and rhetorical obstacle to Peking's Washington connection. Chiang Kai-shek's death, coming as it did before Mao's, removes some of the old personal venom from the continuing issue of Taiwan. The slowly dawning realization that China, if it wishes, may become one of the oil-producing and exporting giants of the world within 15 years will undoubtedly exert a magnetic pull on oil-hungry Japan as time goes by. The age-old rivalry between Japan and China, frozen since 1945 into total hostility, is thawing far faster than anyone expected. The Chinese themselves seem to have embarked on a foreign policy that involves supporting anything in any part of the world that Moscow opposes—hence, their support, for example, of Britain's pro-Common Market vote last June. Peking, which rooted for Richard Nixon's re-election in 1972 (as Moscow did, for different reasons), publicly likens Brezhnev to Hitler and calls for his overthrow. Moscow, in turn, charges secret U.S.-Chinese military collusion aimed at the Soviet Union and leaves a huge number of divisions tied down along its Asia border (while going all-out to make the Apollo Soyuz joint space mission a political, as well as a public-relations, triumph).

Each Communist superpower seeks clearer definition of its relationship to us, at least in part to gain advantage in rivalry with the other. The United States, under Kissinger's adroit manipulations, understandably plays the rivalry for its advantage, but as Kissinger well knows, it is a dangerous game, one that could explode if in less skillful hands.

A President more emotionally or ideologically opposed to the Russians might be tempted to resurrect the old containment policy, only this time, instead of constructing a thin line of Third World states, build it around a new and potentially potent combination, a Washington-Tokyo-Peking axis designed to limit Soviet influence in Asia. The Chinese might be willing to play that game; they certainly are interested in any policy that reduces their vulnerability to the Soviet Union. Japan, too, might like such an arrangement; for although Tokyo always officially describes its relationships as equidistant between Moscow and Peking, there is deep fear of the Russians in Japan.

The great dangers of such a new anti-Soviet alliance should be clear: setbacks to efforts to negotiate any sort of arms limitations, increased tension throughout the world and the risks of a pre-emptive Soviet action against China. But if détente with Moscow seems stalled and domestic disenchantment with détente grows, capitalized on by some politician like Henry Jackson, the temptation to go further—much further—with Peking might prove attractive to some new Administration. It may sound unlikely, but stranger things have happened recently.

If we reject the dangerous possibility of a new anti-Soviet containment policy, however, what can we conclude about the new Asia and our role in it? First, there is the perception. History creates myths, which then take on a momentum of their own. One person's myth becomes another's political reality. In Asia the myth that traps us now is that of dominoes, nations whose internal political tilt and posture have somehow become a reflection of American power and influence. Yet that perception, even if true before 1970, is no longer valid. Yet we find it hard to break out of the old ways of measuring power and influence in Asia.

So first of all, we must understand the true historic significance of the last 30 years. We played a special role in Asia, and the rightness or wrongness of that role will be debated by historians for decades to come. But we must recognize—and then accept, and then welcome—the fact that the demicolonial era in Asia is over.

This should come as a relief to Americans, particularly liberals. It is inconsistent to mourn the "retreat of American power" and then start worrying about events in Bangkok. American power is not in retreat but this time around, one can hope, it will not be necessary to worry about every political event on the mainland of Asia. Acceptance and a degree of detachment will be a major step forward, one that Asians will appreciate.

Second, we should recognize that we remain a Pacific power, if not an Asian power. The distinction has been made for years by some far-sighted people, including Walter Lippman, and by some naval officers who saw the role of seapower as the key to American power (and, not incidentally, saw a larger slice of the defense budget for the Navy). While the Pacific is so vast, and Asia seems far away to most Americans, especially on the East Coast, the simple fact is that we are a two-coast nation; we have two states reaching far into the mid-Pacific; we have territories and trusteeships even deeper into the Pacific; we have treaty commitments and we are still the major external force in the area.

Third, we must accept our role as part of the delicate triangular relationship with China and the Soviet Union, but not overplay it. To prevent a major war between these two Communist superpowers may seem to some like an odd objective for American foreign policy, but that is and should remain one of our objectives; such a war would serve no one's interests, would leave millions of people dead and could easily spread to other countries, including the United States.

Fourth, we must understand the importance of Japan. In a world where many countries claim "special relationships" with us, none except Israel has as strong a claim as Japan. Since the days of the Meiji Restoration more than 100 years ago, the United States has been the primary source of external ideas and technology for Japan; the tragic period of the nineteen-thirties and the Pacific war, strangely, did not remove the special relationship, but turned it instead into one of terrible hate. During the occupation, we developed a unique relationship with Japan even while communication and understanding between the two nations were generally poor.

Today, in part because of a Constitution written by Americans, Japan is without a strong military and defense structure—it is the first great economic power without a military establishment. The United States has been since 1945 the military guarantor of Japan's security. At the same time, the U.S. and Japan remain economic rivals for markets and raw materials in the rest of Asia.

Politically, the Japanese have until now tried to avoid choosing any sides at all, letting the United States show the way internationally. For this reason, they avoided showing any opposition to our Vietnam policy long after they felt privately that our efforts were doomed. But in the wake of the Yom Kippur war, the Japanese, rocked by the effects of the oil embargo and the fourfold jump in oil prices, learned that they would be unable to stay out of political matters. The anti-Japanese rioting in Jakarta in 1974 stunned them too. They had massive investments in Indonesia, and they felt they needed access to the country in order to survive as an economic power; yet they were hated still—not just for the bitter memories of World War II, but for their more recent behavior as an "economic animal." The same was true in Thailand, Korea and elsewhere. The Japanese came to realize that they were almost alone in the world, with no real friends, except one—the United States, which didn't really understand them, but at least was there, and fairly dependable, despite the famous Nixon shocks.

Military partners, with the U.S. carrying the overwhelming portion of the burden; economic rivals, with friction and hostility likely to increase, particularly if worldwide inflation continues to erode markets and profit margins; political allies, with Japan very much the silent partner, at least until recently—are these the ingredients for a special relationship? Amazingly, the answer is yes, and one must add to the complicated mix the shared hostility both feel toward any Soviet ambitions in the Pacific.

That the United States has played this special role in Japan's recent past does not necessarily mean that we must continue to play it. The demicolonial period is over, and we must stop treating the Japanese with the paternalism we developed during the occupation and into which many Americans still fall, lured by the deceptive, painstakingly slow, formalized style with which the Japanese conduct their business. Many Americans, mistaking their peculiar style for weakness or indecision, or simply frustrated by interminable rounds of tea, golf and raw fish, still try to bull their way through Japan, with predictably bad results. In foreign policy, the Japanese have been particularly reluctant until recently to show their hand on most issues, with the exception of the reversion of Okinawa to their nation, and a few other matters directly concerning their territoriality. But the Japanese are emerging from their old ways of reticence, if not abandoning their special style. The new Asia is one in which they understand that they will play a different role. We must be ready to accept that, and, once again, to welcome it.

At the same time, however, we should not abandon our position as the military arm of Japan. Admittedly, the relationship may seem strange, and strained, at times. There will be a growing feeling on both sides that the Japanese must play a greater role in their own self-defense; to a limited degree this has already been proposed privately and hinted at publicly by the director of the Japanese Self-Defense Agency. (When I asked one Japanese defense intellectual why the Japanese were now proposing something they had rejected only a few years ago when it was suggested by Defense Secretary Melvin Laird, he replied with a smile: "Because then you proposed it.")

But even if Japan extends the area in which it patrols its own waters, for example, that is a far cry from remilitarization. The latter, nuclear or nonnuclear, would unsettle Asia in a profound way. Bitter memories that lie close to the surface would re-emerge in every country from Thailand to Korea. The entire delicate balance between the four powers of Asia would be upset by any significant Japanese military capability. It would become far harder for the Chinese and the Japanese to end their differences if Japan were once again a potential military force in the area. The Russians would be tempted to counter a resurgent Japan by more aggressive behavior in the disputed waters and islands lying north of Japan.

So we should continue to act as Japan's military arm. This idea is not much in dispute in the United States, where everyone who has spoken out so far seems to agree on the importance of Japan to the United States, and of our commitment to Japan's security.

In Tokyo and in Washington, strategic thinkers see close connections between what happens in Japan and what happens in Korea; thus the fifth and final conclusion: We must find some way to solve the delicate problem of our presence in Korea. In South Korea, the United States finds itself with a client state on its hands, a regime with a narrow base and a growing reputation for heavy-handed repressive policies. We still keep 42,000 troops in South Korea and recently have taken to issuing warnings that we will use whatever force is required to counter any aggressive behavior from the North.

If that were the whole story, it might be possible to withdraw gradually and risk the creation of "one Korea." But in Tokyo, the argument is made, with great emotion, that what happens on the Korean peninsula can have a direct effect on Japan, and that this must be the governing factor in our policy toward Korea. If we withdraw and the North walks into Seoul, or fights its way in while we do nothing, the argument goes, then Japan's rightists will have a trump card with which to argue for the remilitarization of Japan.

The Japanese do not seem to feel that a unified Communist Korea in and of itself would pose a strategic threat to Japan. The Koreans would never invade us, they say, and we could still do business with them. But the way it might happen—that is on everyone's mind. If the Americans walk out on Korea, turn their backs on their commitments there, if they are pushed into the sea as they were in Vietnam—that would be a different story. On this everyone agrees.

Furthermore, I was told by a number of Japanese earlier this summer, it is true that what happens in Korea will affect Japan directly. "Japanese public opinion can now be said to be divided into three broad groups," said a Japanese professor. "The first group, which remembers the war and believes in Article Nine [the clause in the Constitution prohibiting war-making capability for Japan], will always oppose any militarization. But that group may grow smaller as time goes on. The large middle group, like most people, doesn't care much. Then there is a third group that doesn't remember the shame of the Pacific war, and will think that as a great power we ought to have our own army and navy. If things go badly in Korea they could grow much faster."

If this perception is right, then we run a risk in Korea as great as we did in Vietnam: that we may get trapped in a small and secondary country to which we must remain committed. Can we disengage the two issues—Korea and Japan? Can we build a strategy in which our Japan policy, which seems so strong and reasonable, is not dependent on our Korean policy, which seems so weak and unstable?

The answer is elusive. In the face of widespread fears in the last few months that Kim Il Sung, jealous of the success of his Socialist brothers in Hanoi, would launch another effort to unify Korea by force, it would be impossible to attempt any disengagement right now. (This is true whether or not one accepts the prevailing view that Kim is going to "try something," a view that I do not share.)

The period of time between now and the 1976 election is a period in which we cannot make any significant changes in our Korean policy. We are living in a strange interlude after Vietnam, after Watergate, with a President whom no one except the people of Grand Rapids, Mich., has ever elected—not a likely time for changes in policy.

But it is not too early to look beyond 1976, to the time when we should reconsider our position in Korea. Gaddis Smith recently suggested in these pages that the best outcome for Korea would be the replacement of South Korean President Park Chung Hee with a "moderate, more democratic regime that would encourage renewed discussion with the North."

There is nothing wrong with this suggestion. Indeed, if it had a good chance of happening, it would be worth pursuing. But it seems highly unlikely.

This would leave the United States with the choice of accepting the present situation indefinitely, or until something outside our control happens, for better or worse; or of trying to change our role in Korea in such a way as not to upset the situation in Japan. This question is the sort that should be hotly debated within the U.S. Government, although I am not sure that it has been. When a situation leaves as little room for maneuver as does Korea today, then it is easier, and perhaps wiser at times, to leave things alone, on the chance that someone will die, or something will break, and the new situation can then be exploited.

But in this case, waiting also carries its heavy risks. President Park seems to be on a downgrade, in terms of popularity and effectiveness. His repressiveness is bound to become a growing political issue in the Congress, and, having ended the war in Vietnam and cut off aid to Turkey, Congress might once again gather itself together in its cumbersome way and vote some sort of cutoff or limitation to our involvement in Korea. This might have happened already if it were not for the risks to Japan.

So while there is a chance that things will go on as they have for the 22 years since the ceasefire went into effect along the 38th parallel, there is an equally good chance that the situation will not hold. Will we still have 42,000 men in Korea 22 years from now? Presumably not. The question remains: How do we get them out in a way that is not a betrayal of Korea, that encourages the two Koreas to work things out for themselves, and above all, that does not change the political situation in Japan in a drastic way?

By next year, if Thai Prime Minister Kukrit really means what he says and makes it stick, those troops in Korea will be the last American soldiers on the Asian mainland. Everywhere else, that remarkable era that began as we liberated the Pacific islands from the Japanese Imperial Army will have ended. The United States and China, if not allies, are no longer enemies. Our role as demi-Raj is over. New leaders have come forward, for better or for worse, whom we must treat differently from their predecessors. We remain a great Pacific power, but we no longer need try to dominate events everywhere. As Marina Whitman has said in another context, the hegemonial era is over for America: We are now entering an era in which we can exercise "leadership without hegemony." And that is surely for the better, for Americans and Asians alike.

Conscience and Catastrophe

RICHARD HOLBROOKE
The New Republic, JULY 30, 1984

In this review of William Shawcross's book, The Quality of Mercy,
*Holbrooke reflects on the humanitarian disaster in Cambodia
during the late 1970s and distills the lessons of humanitarian
intervention and the need for UN reform (a subject he would
champion fifteen years later as U.S. Ambassador to the UN). At the
time he wrote this heartfelt recollection of his most recent government service, he was back in the private sector on Wall Street. The
article includes an election-year plug for Walter Mondale, who had
accepted his party's nomination for president two weeks earlier at
the Democratic convention in San Francisco.*

Great human disasters, natural or manmade, put bureaucrats to a
test not only as public officials but as human beings. Normally
insulated from the consequences of their actions by layers of government,
and accustomed to the abstractions of statecraft, they suddenly are
forced to deal with a problem in which every action (or inaction) can
have an immediate effect on whether people will live or die. In an effort
to examine in detail the reaction to catastrophe, William Shawcross
has written *The Quality of Mercy*, a study of the response to the Cambodian food and refugee crisis since 1975. His new book lacks the clear
focus of his ground-breaking *Sideshow: Kissinger, Nixon, and the Destruction of Cambodia*, but it does raise issues of the greatest importance in
a century in which refugees have become a permanent part of our
political landscape.

I must begin by declaring an interest. Having served as Assistant
Secretary of State for East Asian and Pacific Affairs during much of
the period he covers, I cannot pretend to objectivity in thinking about

Shawcross's book. I was deeply involved in the events he discusses and, although Shawcross did not interview me, I am mentioned frequently and generally not unfavorably.

LIKE SHAWCROSS, I HAVE LONG BEEN FASCINATED BY A STRIKING difference between disaster relief and the normal agenda of nations. The routine of government meetings never seems more unreal than when their consequences are so real—literally life or death—for people who have no spokesman present in the room. One such meeting that remains vividly in my mind took place in the White House Situation Room early in 1979. The South China Sea was filled with tens of thousands of Vietnamese refugees, many in ramshackle boats, seeking sanctuary in neighboring countries. Large numbers of them drowned, and others were attacked by pirates. There were ships of the U.S. Seventh Fleet in the Western Pacific, but not where the boat people were in greatest difficulty. At the time, the Navy was following traditional rules of the sea: picking up refugees sighted during regular naval patrols only if they appeared to be in imminent danger. No extraordinary rescue efforts were being made.

The question arose: Should the Seventh Fleet be instructed to make the rescue of refugees fleeing Vietnam, in effect, an additional assigned mission? There was serious division within the U.S. government. The Navy was concerned about the diversion of ships from their primary naval mission. Moreover, some countries in the area, in violation of longstanding rules of the sea, would not let ships unload refugees. What destination, then, for those picked up by the Seventh Fleet? Would the Navy bring them directly to the United States, allowing them to "jump the line" and enter the United States months, or even years, ahead of others already waiting in the swollen camps of Southeast Asia? Some, including at least one staff member of the National Security Council (not Zbigniew Brzezinski), opposed doing anything that might "generate" refugees. They argued that once the news reached Vietnam that the Seventh Fleet was rescuing refugees off the Indochinese coast, many more people would set out to sea in ever more dangerous small boats. This would not only create more refugees, they argued, but would also remove from Vietnam many people who, if forced to remain inside Vietnam, might cause the Communists serious internal problems.

Most of the points raised against the use of the Seventh Fleet had some validity. But as Washington argued, people continued to drown.

Finally the issue made its way to a high-level meeting chaired by Vice President Mondale. Sitting at the head of the long table in the window-less, sterile atmosphere of the Situation Room, as far from the stormy waters of the South China Sea as could be imagined, we debated the issue, at times as though it was just another abstract interagency dispute. Mondale patiently listened to every argument for almost two hours. At the end of it all, he cut through the legalisms and the complications. He could not imagine, he said, being part of an Administration which did not ask its ships to try to rescue innocent people fleeing an oppressive regime. He wanted the orders to the Seventh Fleet amended in order to save lives.

At this time and distance it may be hard to conceive that the decision, so clearly right, was almost not made. There are people who are alive today because of Mondale's decision; of very few actions by a government official can such a thing be said.

I DESCRIBE THIS INCIDENT AT LENGTH BEFORE TURNING TO WILLIAM Shawcross's book because it illustrates several things about the way governments and bureaucrats approach such life and death issues. Many of the people involved in the debate over the use of the Seventh Fleet regarded it as just another bureaucratic problem. Hannah Arendt's memorable idea about the "banality of evil" showed how efficient Nazi bureaucrats could mobilize the German government to carry out a policy of mass slaughter. Perhaps here (on a wholly different scale, to be sure) we were seeing the evil of banality: functionaries engaged in the most routine sort of internal bureaucratic disputes while people in some remote corner of the globe die, or fester in refugee camps.

Shawcross traces the way perceptions of the Cambodia problem evolved in the West. One of his most provocative conclusions concerns the way in which "Cambodia, in the fall of 1979, after long years of disaster, [achieved] critical mass in Western conscience." This happened, he feels, in large part because of "the constant evocation of 'the Holocaust'... [which] was surely crucial to the way in which the disaster assumed such international emotional force." Shawcross agrees, of course, that Cambodia deserved "great attention." But he objects to the comparison with Hitler's war against the Jews as "coarsening" and "unfortunate." He observes correctly the critical historical differences between, say, Auschwitz and Pol Pot's torture chambers at Tuol Sleng, which were reserved primarily for the lapsed cadre of their own fanatical movement. Still, the differences between the Holocaust and Cambodia notwithstanding, the evocation of the memory was important in rallying worldwide support for a relief effort that saved large numbers of lives.

SHAWCROSS MAKES A MORE TELLING POINT WHEN HE OBSERVES THAT the disasters "which do attract our attention are by no means always the most destructive." He cites Jim Grant of UNICEF, who has warned that "loud emergencies [like Cambodia] can drown out the continuous 'quiet emergencies' like the death of at least ten million children every year" from malnutrition. Grant's distinction is valid, but it should not be mis-understood as suggesting that money or one disaster can be reallocated easily to another. If only such a Benthamite calculus could be applied to the vast underclass of desperate peoples throughout the world, and relief funds distributed in strict accordance with need! Unfortunately the world does not work that way. For a variety of reasons, certain catastro-phes will always elicit greater sympathy than others. Some people got more emotional over the killing of baby seals, for example, than the star-vation of children in Angola. And public attention, always inconsistent, is a major factor. From a single memorable photograph, or one reporter in the right place at the right time, vast consequences may proceed. Con-versely, no publicity in the West probably means no relief assistance from the West. Shawcross may lament this unfairness as much as the rest of us, but he offers no solution. As he surely knows, there is none.

At the end of 1978, at almost exactly the same time as the United States normalized diplomatic relations with the People's Republic of China, Vietnam invaded Cambodia, driving Pol Pot's forces into the remote western areas of the country but not destroying them completely (as American intelligence had predicted). This Vietnamese failure to wipe out the forces of their Peking-backed foe was to have enormous consequences.

At about the same time, the world became acquainted with the boat people. As their numbers grew, evidence also mounted that the refugee flood was being cynically encouraged by the Vietnamese as a way of ridding themselves of an undesired element in their own society, par-ticularly the ethnic Chinese, and throwing the burden for their relief onto the West. In June 1979 Jimmy Carter used Presidential authority to allow 168,000 Indochinese refugees (not just boat people but also

Laotians and Cambodians) into the United States annually for an indefinite period of time. Armed with this remarkable act of American generosity, the United States successfully lobbied other nations to join in a worldwide resettlement effort of refugees from the overflowing refugee camps in Southeast Asia. Shawcross barely mentions Carter's courageous decision, and seems either uninterested or unaware of the difficulties and the drama surrounding it. To be sure, the focus of his book is Cambodia, but the Vietnamese refugee problem and the Cambodian relief efforts always had to be dealt with together, and Carter's leadership was vital in mobilizing American and international efforts.

THE NEXT STAGE OF THE CAMBODIAN TRAGEDY THEN ERUPTED. IN THE fall of 1979 the Vietnamese Army pushed the remnants of Pol Pot's forces to and across the Thai border. With the armies came an extraordinary collection of starving refugees, deserters, and wounded. No one will ever know how many people reached the border and how many died trying. At the time Washington received reports that perhaps as many as one million people were on their way to Thailand in desperate need of food and medical help. The Thais, quite understandably, panicked. Cambodia no longer existed as a buffer state between Thailand and Vietnam. The powerful Vietnamese Army was now on the Thai border, only four hours by road from Bangkok.

In *Sideshow*, Shawcross told the story primarily from the point of view of Washington-based policymakers. Here he tries a much more difficult approach, switching vantage point frequently from Geneva to Bangkok to Washington or New York, then taking the reader inside Cambodia for personal reportage. The story is often confusing, filled with the acronyms of the specialized agencies at the U.N., an enormous multinational cast of characters, and an intricate political situation. Shawcross is at his best describing his own trips into Cambodia and the tremendous frustrations that the relief workers faced in trying to help the Cambodian people. He is less successful in explaining the endless battles that took place in Geneva, New York, Bangkok, and Washington. Most seriously, Shawcross has underestimated the role of the U.S. government. In my view, it was the relentless pressure of genuinely concerned American officials that was critical in forcing timid, complacent, and bickering international relief officials to act.

The United States may not have won any popularity contests at the United Nations for its arm-twisting, but the results justified any animosity created.

THE AMERICAN DILEMMA WAS SIMPLE. OUR FINANCIAL CONTRIBUTION to the relief efforts was the largest of any nation. We were resettling by far the largest number of refugees. The requirements of international relief work, however, meant that we had to work primarily through the U.N. specialized agencies and through the voluntary agencies, and to get them to act expeditiously we often pushed very hard. Not surprisingly, many U.N. officials resented this deeply, all the more since they were so dependent on American financial support. The main agent of this pressure was the American who was to play the most important role in the response to the crisis, the brilliant and dedicated ambassador in Thailand, Morton Abramowitz. Shawcross accords Abramowitz grudging admiration; he does not give him the credit he deserves. In my admittedly biased view—Shawcross correctly identifies Abramowitz as a friend of mine, although our friendship was made by working together and did not pre-date our professional association—Abramowitz's relentless harassment of officials in Bangkok, Washington, Geneva, and New York contributed more than any other single factor (with the possible exception of the press coverage) to the ultimate success of the relief operations. Shawcross accurately conveys some of the deep annoyance felt by some officials of the U.N. The reader can judge for himself whether it was worth it.

The first law of disaster relief could well read: every political decision has humanitarian consequences, and every humanitarian program has political implications. For example, the Vietnamese-installed regime in Phnom Penh was ready to let the people of western Cambodia starve rather than permit food to be distributed by truck across the Thai border into areas in which their control was contested. As for food and relief supplies offered by many voluntary agencies to the Phnom Penh regime, the Vietnamese tried to extract political advantage from every offer of humanitarian assistance. In the face of such unrelieved cynicism, it was tempting to give up any effort to get relief supplies into Cambodia, and necessary to remember at all times that the purpose of getting aid inside Cambodia was to help preserve the Cambodian people in spite of the Vietnamese, not in collaboration with them.

Some American officials also contemplated using food to advance political objectives. Deny it to the people under Vietnamese control, one faction suggested, and somehow Hanoi's control over Cambodia would be weakened. Or distribute it only in those refugee areas which also sheltered the Khmer Rouge, and thereby help the anti-Vietnamese resistance continue. Deny it to those same areas, suggested others, and starve out any remnants of the murderous Khmer Rouge. But the use of relief efforts, the use of food, for political ends, would have been tragically wrong. Although Shawcross seems uncertain as to Washington's motives, the fact is that the objective of American policy, constantly reaffirmed at the highest levels, was to save lives on both sides of the Thai-Cambodian border, without regard to politics.

SUCCESS IN THAT OBJECTIVE HAD AN UNINTENDED CONSEQUENCE: the armies on both sides were strengthened by the relief efforts. The effort to save the Cambodian people unavoidably also helped the people who had nearly destroyed Cambodia. This was not the deliberate objective of U.S. policy, but an undesired and unavoidable result. Here is where I believe that Shawcross has gone wrong. While granting that "Vietnam bears the principal, though not the exclusive, responsibility for the continued crisis today," he charges the United States with a "casual acceptance of what was a fundamentally Chinese strategy to rebuild and support the Khmer Rouge [which] exhibited at best a loss of memory and lack of imagination, at worst is cynicism that will have long and disturbing repercussions on international consciousness." This is a misreading of the policy decisions of American officials from President Carter and Secretary Vance on down. Shawcross may have found individual Americans whose attitudes reflected his conclusion, but Abramowitz and his team in Thailand did nothing that was intended to help the Khmer Rouge. The U.S. government was as aware as Shawcross of the murderous nature of Pol Pot's regime. China was of great importance to American foreign policy, but Peking did not decide, or even influence, Washington's approach to food distribution in Cambodia. If it had, Washington would have opposed any aid distribution inside Cambodia, where it was bound to help the pro-Vietnamese side. Instead the United States played a major role in mobilizing relief efforts inside a country whose government it opposed.

RELIEF TO THE PEOPLE ON THE THAI BORDER COULD BE ACCOMPLISHED through a large number of United Nations agencies and private voluntary organizations with the approval of the Thai government. Working inside Cambodia was infinitely more difficult. Since neither the United States nor the U.N. recognized the Vietnamese-installed government in Phnom Penh, all aid within Cambodia had to be channeled through UNICEF, the only U.N. agency that had the authority to operate in the absence of recognition, or through private voluntary agencies like Oxfam.

The division of labor that was finally worked out—UNICEF inside Cambodia, U.N.H.C.R. (United Nations High Commission on Refugees) outside it—made a great deal of sense. But U.N.H.C.R. was terrified of exceeding its mandate and UNICEF was looking for ways to get out of Cambodia and back to its basic worldwide concern for the problems of children. Moreover, camps in Thailand—run by the Thai government and U.N.H.C.R.—were swollen with boat people and refugees from Laos; they were not putting out the welcome mat for Cambodians. Bowing to pressure from Bangkok, the U.N.H.C.R. refused to define the Cambodians who had come to the border as true refugees; the agency took responsibility only for those refugees processed into U.N.H.C.R. camps a few miles away. Thus the most dangerous and desperate area—the strip along the border—became a no man's land between the two major U.N. organizations, neither of which wanted the additional responsibility. Instead, aid and food distribution on the border was left to a motley assortment of uncoordinated organizations and individuals. They did a remarkable job under the circumstances.

BOTH INSIDE AND OUTSIDE CAMBODIA, THE PERFORMANCE OF THE United Nations' specialized agencies was generally disappointing, and would have been more so if not for American pressure. This is a sad conclusion, reluctantly arrived at, especially for those of us who believe the United Nations still has an important contribution to make to the solution of some of the world's problems. To be sure, without the U.N. the relief efforts would have been virtually impossible. But the U.N. agencies were tied up in their own thick web of inefficiency and squabbling. They consistently under-reacted to warnings from the region. Waldheim was reluctant to act; the U.N. Secretary-General behaved as though he was personally offended by the intrusion of the refugees into his long (and fortunately unsuccessful) campaign for reelection, a campaign which required that he not alienate either the Soviet Union or the Third World. What little he did do—such as presiding over the 1979 and 1980 conferences in Geneva—was in large part because of enormous pressure from the United States, Australia, the Western Europeans, and world opinion.

There is special irony in the Nobel Peace Prize awarded to the United Nations High Commission on Refugees in 1980 mainly in recognition of its work in Southeast Asia. Giving this award to the U.N.H.C.R. as a symbolic recognition of the army of dedicated workers, many of them volunteers, who had flocked to the region, made some sense. But the U.N.H.C.R.'s early representatives in Bangkok were incompetent, and failed to recognize the problem. They fought other agencies for primacy, yet they refused to help or accept as refugees hundreds of thousands of Cambodians huddling in the open fields along the border. Giving the Nobel Peace Prize to that group of smug, overpaid, and world-weary Geneva-based functionaries was finally an abuse of that high honor.

I recognize that some, especially among the United Nations international civil servants, will dispute these judgments. They are harsher than, but not inconsistent with, Shawcross's picture of the international relief community, especially in the early period. Defenders of the U.N. agencies will point to the immensely difficult problems in trying to help the people of a country when the government in power has been denied (with American support) representation in the United Nations. Furthermore, the Vietnamese made life almost unbearable for the dedicated relief workers, even holding up barges of perishable food, for example, in an effort to charge heavy "haulage fees"—really payoffs to Hanoi.

Shawcross thinks that the relief agencies and the press exaggerated the size of the Cambodian food crisis. The truth is somewhat more complex than he suggests. No one ever knew exactly how many people were at the border, nor just how serious the threat of starvation was inside Cambodia. There was no time to make a precise determination. Those who cared about the issue needed to mobilize other people and resources, and the best way to do this was to make estimates of disaster which, while credible, were as pessimistic as possible. In the absence of precise information, it was safer to risk overestimating the problem and having too much aid, rather than underestimating it and having too little. As Abramowitz said, "If only 100,000 people die instead of one million, does that mean it is not a crisis?"

Shawcross's book attempts to rescue from dusty archives and fading memories the story of how the world reacted to one particularly grave crisis. His worthy hope is that lessons will be drawn for the next disaster. Too little of this sort of thing has been done; once a disaster has lost its television audience it is quickly forgotten, even if there is still war and there are still refugees along the Thai border today. I would contribute the following conclusions to the discussion:

Despite all the difficulties and inefficiency, the Cambodian relief efforts and the resettlement of Indochinese refugees turned out to be relatively successful. A very large number of lives were saved.

This was due in large part to American leadership, an essential ingredient in such situations. We pay much of the bill, and we have a right to insist on better performance from the international civil servants who carry out the job. We should not shrink from the responsibility. No one else can fill it.

The international agencies of the U.N. and the private voluntary agencies are filled with dedicated people, but they must be pressured constantly. (A personal prejudice: U.N.H.C.R. should not be head-quartered in the unreal beauty of Geneva, but in some sweatier city closer to the world of refugees.)

The press is essential. Without massive coverage—and that means television pictures—little will be done. (In this regard Henry Kamm of *The New York Times* deserves special mention for his reporting from Thailand.)

Relief operations are expensive and inevitably wasteful. But they are an unavoidable obligation of the richer nations. Countries, like Japan, which are slow to recognize this responsibility must be pressured until they too respond.

Politics will always intrude. But the first obligation of the donor nations must be to rescue the victims. Political consequences, even serious ones, must be set aside when lives are at stake.

It is better to overestimate than to underestimate the size of the problem.

There will be other major man-made disasters, and more must be done to anticipate the need for emergency arrangements.

Natural disasters can, of course, occur anywhere on earth. Latin America and especially Africa are more likely candidates for future man-made crises than Asia, and they may receive far less publicity than did disasters that came out of Indochina. Shawcross has done future victims a service by trying to interest people in the complex story of how the world reacts to this kind of disaster. The specifics of each crisis will vary enormously. There will be those who say, for example, that Cambodia teaches us no lessons for African relief. They are wrong. The central lesson, embodied in every detail of Shawcross's story, is that people must care, that extraordinary efforts are required to rouse people from their comfortable good time in order to do something to help those living, in George Steiner's phrase, in the "enveloping folds of inhuman time."

If people do care, miracles can happen. Take the case of Chi Luu, one of the boat people, who came to New York with his family in November 1979, after five months in a refugee camp. Within a year, Mr. Luu had entered City College of New York, studying, working part-time in a can factory, and improving his English. Last month he graduated as valedictorian of his class, with a straight-A average in his major, engineering, and only a single B, in freshman English. He is entering M.I.T. this fall.

Much Too Tough to Be Cute

Richard Holbrooke
Time, March 3, 1997

> *In and out of government, Holbrooke met with Deng Xiaoping*
> *for more than ten years. At the January 29, 1979, state dinner that*
> *he references in this eulogy, Holbrooke sat with Richard Nixon,*
> *who had flown to Washington, D.C., from California at Deng's*
> *insistence—much to the consternation of many Carter officials—*
> *to make his first return to the White House since his 1974 resig-*
> *nation. Less than three weeks later, China invaded Vietnam, a*
> *country that had long enervated the Vice Premier, as Holbrooke*
> *writes here.*

Deng Xiaoping did not have much time for small talk, at least not with outsiders. He was an old man in a hurry; he saw visitors, but only if they could advance the central goal of his life—to make China great again. In the many hours of talks I attended with him, he expressed little personal interest in his foreign visitors except for their technology, which he wanted immediately. Once I brought some books for his beloved grandchildren. Without looking at them, he handed them to an aide and started lecturing me about the need for Washington to lift all export restrictions on modern technologies—not "those of the '70s, but the '80s and '90s," he said fiercely.

His small eyes focused on you with intensity. Then he would look away, far away, perhaps at some distant vision of the China he wanted to build, or possibly at the memory of some past indignity he had survived on his roller-coaster ride between history and oblivion. His hands gestured constantly, and until his family stopped him, he chain-smoked. To those in thrall to the urbane charm of his old ally Zhou Enlai, Deng seemed crude, speaking with a guttural Sichuanese accent and always keeping a spittoon next to his chair. His size—he was truly tiny—did not seem to diminish him, partly because he exuded enormous energy and sharp focus.

His obsession, presumably born in his childhood memories of a prostrate China and his adult humiliation during the Cultural Revolution, was to undo the crimes and stupidities of the Cultural Revolution, break the communist ideological straitjacket and unleash, as he put it, the creative energy of China. His opposition to superstition and ideology, plus his hostility to the Soviet Union, made him seem more liberal than he was. Deng did not believe his nation could be governed democratically—at least not in this century. Sadly, Tiananmen is part of his legacy.

He once offered Shirley MacLaine a glimpse of his wry wit and burning anger. When he sat next to the famously pro-China actress at a White House state dinner in January 1979, she thanked him for the gracious reception she enjoyed in China in the early '70s. Deng, who had been in exile at that time, replied without a moment's pause, "The people who were your hosts then are in jail now."

His grandfatherly appearance made him seem cute. But Deng Xiaoping was not cute; he was far tougher than Americans could possibly imagine. He surely viewed life as a constant struggle, because that's what his own life had been. When visitors talked of injustice in China, he dismissed them with a wave of his hand. What the West would regard as injustice did not concern him much. These were niceties that neither he nor his country could afford. I saw Deng shake with real anger only when he talked about the Vietnamese, whom he saw as impudent. When Deng complained bitterly to Vice President Walter Mondale about the "ungrateful" Vietnamese, Mondale wryly noted, "We have had some experience of our own with the Vietnamese." Deng did not even smile.

The Day the Door to China Opened Wide

RICHARD HOLBROOKE
Washington Post, DECEMBER 15, 2008

Holbrooke writes about a critical moment in the Sino-American relationship—the effort to normalize relations with China during the Carter administration.

The opening with China by Richard Nixon and Henry Kissinger in 1971–72 is justly remembered as a historic breakthrough. Less famous but of equal importance was the next major step: the establishment of full diplomatic relations between China and the United States. Without this action, announced by President Jimmy Carter on Dec. 15, 1978, the relationship could not have moved beyond a small, high-level connection with a very limited agenda.

When they left office in 1977, President Gerald Ford and Kissinger left behind an important but incomplete, and unstable, relationship with China. The United States still recognized the government on Taiwan, which called itself (then as now) the Republic of China, as the legitimate and sole government of all of China. Since 1972, Washington and Beijing had maintained small "liaison offices" in each other's capitals, without recognition. Official communications were limited, and two-way trade was less than $1 billion a year (today, it is a staggering $387 billion annually).

Carter took office hoping to normalize relations with China, which would require switching American recognition from Taiwan to Beijing and ending a sacred defense treaty between the United States and Taiwan. Some saw this as a simple acknowledgment of reality; in fact, it was a momentous step that required diplomatic skill and political courage. A way would have to be found for the United States, while recognizing Beijing, to continue dealing with the authorities on Taiwan without recognizing its claim to represent China; most important, Washington had to retain the right to sell arms to Taipei. The politics were not simple: There was the famed Taiwan Lobby, one of the most powerful in the United States. Led by "Mr. Conservative," Sen. Barry Goldwater, and the leading contender for the 1980 Republican nomination, Ronald Reagan, it was to fight normalization all the way. (Goldwater eventually took the U.S. government to the Supreme Court to challenge, unsuccessfully, Carter's action; Reagan pledged in the 1980 campaign to partially undo normalization—then abandoned that position after he was elected.)

The saga unfolded over the first two years of the Carter administration, out of public sight except for two important trips to China—one by Secretary of State Cyrus Vance, the other by national security advisor Zbigniew Brzezinski (as assistant secretary of state for East Asian and Pacific affairs, I participated in both trips). Incredibly, those involved in the negotiations managed to keep the work secret. The Chinese demanded a complete severing of all official ties between Taiwan and the United States, including arms sales. Knowing that such a move would provoke an enormous domestic backlash, we looked for a formula that would continue official contacts and arms sales with Taiwan even after we had de-recognized it and terminated the mutual security treaty ratified during the Eisenhower years. There was no precedent for this in American or international law. With advice from Eisenhower's attorney general, Herbert Brownell, State Department lawyers drafted the Taiwan Relations Act, a groundbreaking law that allowed the United States to conduct official business on Taiwan, including arms sales, without formal government-to-government relations.

The Chinese wanted trade and other benefits of recognition. When we explained to Beijing why special arrangements with Taiwan were necessary in order to recognize the government on the mainland, it balked. In those Cold War days, recognition would benefit both nations, as Beijing was fiercely hostile to the Soviet Union, with whom it had almost gone to war only a few years earlier. But Taiwan remained a huge obstacle.

The breakthrough came in late 1978, carefully timed to follow the midterm elections. Mao Zedong had died in 1976, and the most important factor was probably the emergence of Deng Xiaoping as China's paramount leader. Deng—who had been forced to wear a dunce cap and denounce himself during the insanity of the Cultural Revolution—had achieved the greatest comeback imaginable; in the fall of 1978, he got enough power to cut a deal with Washington. Beijing would not "agree" to American arms sales or other activities with Taiwan but would proceed with normalization anyway. It was classic Chinese negotiating style: firm on principle, flexible on specifics.

I'm leaving a lot out here, but this was the essence of a very complicated negotiation. In January 1979, Deng made his historic trip to the United States, which began with a private dinner at Brzezinski's house and climaxed with the most sought-after state dinner of the Carter years (also noteworthy for Richard Nixon's first visit to Washington since his resignation; I sat at Nixon's table and retain a menu everyone signed that night). At Zbig's house, Deng spoke of his dreams for a China he knew he would not live to see. He believed China could leapfrog the years in which the world had passed it by, but only with American support. He was ready to cooperate on containing the Soviet Union, even agreeing to the installation of secret American intelligence listening posts along the Chinese border to track Soviet missiles. He accurately foresaw a vast exchange of students, modern technology and trade. More than any American official, he anticipated what the opening to China would accomplish.

But even Deng could not imagine all that was to be unleashed by that announcement on this day 30 years ago—nothing less than the development of the most important bilateral relationship in the world today.

CHAPTER FIVE

Europe in the Clinton Years

Holbrooke in Europe. (Courtesy of Kati Marton)

Holbrooke, a European Power

Roger Cohen

On the eve of the 1999 NATO bombing campaign in Kosovo that would lead to his downfall, Slobodan Milošević pleaded with Richard Holbrooke, "Don't you have anything more to say to me?" Holbrooke thought for a moment and deadpanned, "Hasta la vista, baby."

I don't know of another American diplomat who could put Arnold Schwarzenegger and the vernacular of the *Terminator* movies to work for him in a crisis. But then Holbrooke was an omnivorous iconoclast. He had a strong subversive streak. That was part of his genius. He was impatient with form, at home with improvisation. Action was his medium.

By the time of this last meeting, Holbrooke had known Milošević, the Serbian leader, for four years. An observer at their first encounter in August 1995 commented, "The two egos danced all night." But they danced to a purpose: Holbrooke knew that only Milošević could bring an end to the Bosnian war that had raged for more than three years with the loss of over 100,000 lives. In the American interest, for the stability of post-Communist Europe, he was ready to deal with the thug behind

Yugoslavia's violent unraveling. Holbrooke bullied, cajoled, laughed, threatened, shouted, and raged. But how, I once asked him, did he square the horror he'd witnessed at the outbreak of the Bosnian war with a handshake for the man most responsible for it?

He had been in Banja Luka in August 1992, where, as he put it, he witnessed "an insane asylum with all these half-drunk Serb paramilitaries and middle-aged men going and raping and killing young Muslim women." Later he was given a wooden carving by a Muslim survivor of a Serbian concentration camp. The pose, head bowed in humiliation, captures the terror of the war's first months when hundreds of thousands of Bosnian Muslims were herded from their homes by Serb paramilitary forces equipped and financed by Milošević. So was the carving in his thoughts as he sought to end a European war?

"No," Holbrooke told me, "it's not that linear. I don't sit there looking at these guys and thinking of the piece of wood. You wouldn't, either. But I understand the connection. I'm sure we all do."

Making connections and using them was central to Holbrooke's eclectic repertoire. He liked to compare the diplomat to a jazz musician always looking for some new connective theme. His own connection to Europe was direct. His father, a doctor born of Russian Jewish parents in Warsaw, and his mother, whose Jewish family fled Hamburg in 1933, were refugees from Nazism. They fled the war and genocide that saw power pass from Europe to the United States. Yet Holbrooke was not raised as a Jew; his parents were atheists who took him to Quaker meetings on Sundays because, his mother told me, they "seemed interesting." The eye he brought to bear on Europe was not emotional. It was not freighted with parental trauma or retrospective rancor. It was cool, even detached, and essentially forward looking.

In this bias for the future, as in most things, Holbrooke was an American in full. *Atlanticism*, a term almost quaint these days now that Europe has ceased to be a tinderbox, moved him. The term stood for the network of postwar institutions and relationships that bound the United States to Europe, turned it into a European power, and contained, then vanquished the Soviet threat. For Holbrooke, the fall of the Berlin Wall did not reduce the need for the Atlantic Alliance. It redoubled it.

The opportunity to proceed toward European unification had to be seized. The Bosnian war—he called it the greatest Western security failure since the 1930s—threatened that opening. Untamed, it might compromise the stable Europe built through NATO and the European Union at the very moment when freedom could be pushed eastward into the nations sacrificed to Soviet control at Yalta. So the American interest was clear. But there was also a question of values. Holbrooke could not stand what that little wooden statue made in a European concentration camp in 1992 said about the trampling of the American idea.

It was Holbrooke's juggling of these considerations that thrust him several times into Milošević's presence over a critical five-year period. He once explained the juggling to me this way:

> There's been a long tension in America between a value-based Wilsonian foreign policy and the Realpolitik of a Kissinger. The fact is, America is one of the few countries whose inhabitants came here in pursuit of an idea, and that ideal is part of our values at home and abroad. Often we have not lived up to those ideas but they are our values. I am not a Wilsonian. I think he [Woodrow Wilson] was naïve. I think he was a failure. Those thick red lines he drew at Versailles around imagined ethnic boundaries made a significant contribution to what is going on in the Balkans today. But I also believe Realpolitik for America is self-defeating in its cynicism. We cannot choose between the two—we have to blend the two.

Such blending is rarely smooth. Holbrooke knew you had to swallow the lumps. Perfection and diplomacy make poor bedfellows. The peace concluded at Dayton in November 1995 rewarded Serbian aggression by handing the Serbs almost half of Bosnia under a loose federation and came as the military tide turned in favor of Bosnian Muslims and Croats. There might, hypothetically, have been other more edifying outcomes. But the hypothetical held little appeal for a doer, a realist, a closer. Beautiful ideas do not save a child's life or put food on the table.

All the way to Dayton, in those hectic months of diplomatic shuttling when there seemed to be a magnetic field around Holbrooke, he had been driven by the memory of three colleagues killed on Mount Igman, near Sarajevo, on August 19, 1995. One of the dead, a senior State Department official named Robert Frasure, had commented after an interagency meeting on Bosnia during the years of American diplomatic obfuscation, "Boy, that was like a little-league locker-room rally." Holbrooke was driven to distraction by this prevarication. He ended it, using NATO bombing in the late summer of 1995 to cow Milošević, whose siege of Sarajevo put the U.S. diplomats on that ill-fated road. Then he talked to Milošević. Some might see inconsistency in this course or a hubris blind to evil. I think not. My sense was always of a man fiercely consistent: in his determination to serve the American and European interest by silencing the guns.

The Dayton Accords stopped the war. Not another shot was fired in anger. Countless lives were saved. Europe moved forward to the promise of a continent whole and free.

PARIS WAS HOLBROOKE'S INITIAL LINK TO EUROPE. HE HAD BEEN IN THE French capital in 1968 as a young man, a member of the delegation led by Averell Harriman that conducted the start of what would be five years of intermittent negotiations with the Vietcong. He learned early how to speak to the enemy—and how maddening such talks could be. Starting in 1970, he spent two years as Peace Corps director in Morocco, a further link with the French-speaking world. He was comfortable in French, at home with la vie Parisienne, always comfortable with a table at Hemingway's old haunt, La Closerie des Lilas.

Still, his emotional attachment was to Asia rather than Europe (Holbrooke is the only person to have been assistant secretary of state for both Asia, from 1977 to 1981, and Europe, from 1994 to 1996). He'd gone to Vietnam in 1963 soon after joining the State Department on graduation from Brown University. It was in the midst of this American war that his ideals of public service and settling conflicts were forged. He developed a taste for the passionate puzzles of war. He arrived at the lasting conviction that events could only be understood by seeing them firsthand, even in dangerous situations. Graham Greene once wrote: "What is cowardice in the young is wisdom in the old, but all the same one can be ashamed of wisdom." Holbrooke was ashamed of the "wisdom" that turns people into armchair pontificators or aggregators. He went forth. The new was his adrenalin. He had to slake his thirst on some new frontier.

Asia offered more such frontiers than Europe. It was a vast canvas. It offered an excitement that touched the romantic in Holbrooke; he always spoke about the region in terms of adventure and discovery. Europe, divided through most of Holbrooke's life by the Cold War, was a more sober undertaking with more pinched possibilities, not a setting that put his heart to racing. Rather, it intrigued him, the part of him that studied physics at college, the thinker and strategist. He knew its critical importance even as he kept it at an emotional distance.

American power linked the two regions in his mind. The United States had become the great offsetting force of the postwar world— bringing stability by triangulating old rivalries, be they between China and Japan, or Germany and France. Holbrooke's belief in Pax Americana, in the ultimate beneficence of America's far-flung garrisons, was rooted in on-the-ground observation. By becoming an Asian power, by becoming a European power, the United States diluted old regional poisons.

He joined the State Department in the 1960s at a difficult moment. America's postwar defensive alliances, bent on containment of Communism, were shaken on several fronts: the building of the Berlin Wall in 1961, the Cuban missile crisis of 1962, the rapid escalation of the Vietnam War, and the Soviet invasion of Czechoslovakia in 1968. Holbrooke's belief in what America could achieve had sober grounding. Dag Hammarskjöld, the UN secretary general from 1953 to 1963, once commented, "The United Nations was not created to take mankind to heaven but to save humanity from hell." Holbrooke felt something similar about the United States.

Yet until 1993 he had no deep knowledge of the European country long at the epicenter of America's postwar diplomatic efforts to avert nuclear Armageddon—Germany. When he went there as U.S. ambassador in 1993, it was with some reluctance. He had hoped to become deputy secretary of state and had also vied for the post of ambassador to Japan, a job that Walter Mondale got. He knew no German; and, of course, this would be a return to the nation his mother had fled. But Holbrooke believed in seizing life's possibilities even if they were not altogether the desired ones.

He called his old friend, Fritz Stern, the Columbia professor who is perhaps America's foremost authority on Germany, and asked him to come along as his adviser. Stern had no hesitation, having already seen what "a great and impossible" secretary of state Holbrooke might have made. "His sense of the interconnectedness of political and economic events, and where the national interest fit into that, was quite extra-ordinary," Stern told me. Once they got to Germany, "the speed with which he picked out important people was astounding."

Within the embassy that included Milton Bearden, a veteran CIA station chief with an intimate knowledge of Germany, Holbrooke was solicitous of visiting congressmen and senators. He honed in on the Chancellery, forming a good relationship with Helmut Kohl and his closest advisers. Others encountered the blunt side of hurricane Holbrooke. A rough divide in the embassy was between those viewed as good and those dismissed as brain dead. The supposedly brain dead did not appreciate that. He did not have a huge amount of time for the German foreign ministry either. That ruffled feathers. In short, he cut a swath.

The Germany Holbrooke found was beginning the transition from American Cold War tutelage to some more emancipated state. With that would be birthed a different alliance: Holbrooke's task was to keep it strong. The heavy lifting had been done in a burst of brilliant U.S. diplomacy a few years earlier that achieved German unification within NATO and the West. But there were plenty of loose ends—the move of the capital to Berlin from Bonn; the disposition of U.S. property entailed by that; the departure of American troops from Berlin; the changing relationship between American Jews and a Germany now confronted in Berlin with the charged past from which Bonn had been a mild Rhineland refuge.

Stern was struck by how quickly Holbrooke intuited the issues even as his knowledge of recent historical events seemed sketchy. When the new ambassador went off with Kohl's adviser Joachim Bitterlich to a commemoration of the 180th anniversary of the defeat of Napoleon at the Battle of Leipzig, Stern had to remind him that he could not go to Leipzig and speak only of that faraway battle. He had to salute the brave East Germans of Leipzig who had helped bring down the Berlin Wall just four years earlier. Of course he did so with panache.

Holbrooke dealt lightly with his own family past in Europe. He did not identify himself as coming from a refugee background. But he placed a photograph of his maternal grandfather, Samuel Moos, at the entrance to the U.S. ambassador's residence. It showed him wearing the Prussian spiked helmet and an Iron Cross. Moos, a German Jew, had fought with distinction for the Germans during World War I.

"People would ask me, why this picture?" Holbrooke once told me. "I would say, it is simply a historical truth. My grandfather fought for the Kaiser against the Western Allies and later fled Germany. It is an event so complex you could weave a novel around it. If I was a novelist, which I would have loved to be, I would make that photograph a centerpiece. I used to tell the Germans, 'If it had not been for your history, perhaps I would be Germany's ambassador to the United States today.'"

This was an important layer in Holbrooke's makeup: the writer's eye. He was never so involved in a situation that some part of him was not also observing and recording. His multiplicity often left his interlocutors chasing shadows: He used that to good effect. It also allowed his many friends, often journalists, to live some fantasy through him. He bridged divides: the idealist-realist and the protagonist-writer. Above all, even as he pursued a political life, he believed in the power of ideas. They thrilled him.

One came to him upon the departure of American troops from Berlin on September 9, 1994. The ceremony at the Brandenburg Gate was full of emotional speeches marking the end of a forty-nine-year defense of the city at the perilous pivot of the Cold War. Chancellor Kohl declared: "We will always remember that it was the presence of your soldiers that made it possible to breathe freely in Berlin. They paid for the freedom of Berlin, and thus for the freedom of the whole of Germany. For this, they deserve our lasting gratitude. Today, as you leave Berlin, we can definitely say: Freedom has won." But for Holbrooke, looking forward as ever, more interested in the mission to come than the mission accomplished, the question was: how to fill the void and ensure the bond anchored by American soldiers in Berlin did not fray.

Holbrooke talked a lot to Stern and others about the need for a permanent American institution in Berlin. He imagined a place that would inspire the free flow of ideas from the United States to the new German capital and back. Stern supplied him with a line from Wilhelm von Humboldt who, on founding the Humboldt University in Berlin at the time of the loss of Prussia in the Napoleonic wars, suggested that it might "make up by spiritual means what we have lost physically."

So was born the idea of the American Academy in Berlin. It might have remained just that—an idea. But one thing about Holbrooke, who remained as ambassador for only a year, was that once he focused on a project he would not let go.

By the time Gary Smith, the academy's director, got involved in 1997, Holbrooke had already persuaded the city of Berlin to grant a fifteen-year contract on a magnificent villa overlooking the waters of the Wannsee at a symbolic cost of one mark a year. He had gone to the Arnhold family, German Jews who like his mother fled Nazism to the United States, and persuaded them to fund the renovation of the house in which they had once lived. He had lined up a number of blue-chip German companies to back the project. Four had agreed to give seven-figure donations. In short, he had made a pipe dream viable.

What struck Smith, who had pioneered a scholarly forum in Einstein's former summer house in Potsdam, was that Holbrooke shunned the notion of an institution narrowly focused on policy. He wanted the broadest spectrum of American ideas and creativity brought to Berlin. The pedestrian or traditional was of no interest. It was in this spirit that he hired Smith and in this way that the academy, since its opening in 1998, has brought the likes of Ward Just, C. K. Williams, Jeffrey Eugenides, Maya Lin, Chuck Close, and Jonathan Safran Foer to Berlin. As often with Holbrooke, one suspects he was living out some inner fantasy by allowing these artists to dream in Berlin. He thought Europe, which often frustrated him with its hesitations and divisions, needed bracing through American energy and vitality: The academy was his singular contribution to that endeavor.

Perhaps it's not surprising that the academy should have become, in Holbrooke's later years, an object of his particular affection. The villa had belonged to a German Jewish family and was now reincarnated in the American spirit. It housed writers and artists who, had they been born in the first half of the 20th century and lived in Germany or much of the rest of Europe, would have suffered persecution or annihilation. It overlooked the Wannsee where, in January 1942, senior officials of the Nazi regime gathered to ponder and prepare the Final Solution.

Holbrooke very rarely talked about his family's past. But the academy was a personal statement. It was a way of coming full circle, of reversing the tide, of being an American in full on the European continent. It made up with the spirit for what had been lost physically.

Stern met with Holbrooke at the villa in November 2010, some sixteen years after the idea had first twinkled in their eyes. Holbrooke, laboring in Afghanistan and Pakistan, seemed weary. He gave the impression of a man nearing the end of his tour in the hall of mirrors known as the "AfPak" theater. He was aware that this might be his last government job. Taking Stern aside, he said, "You know, maybe this will be my lasting legacy."

That European legacy in fact has two pillars: the peace in the Balkans around which Europe was able to build its unity and the academy through which America lived in the capital of Europe's biggest and most powerful country. Asia was Holbrooke's passion, but Europe's debt to him is large.

PERHAPS THE MOST GROTESQUE EUROPEAN UTTERANCE AT THE START of the Balkan wars in 1991 came from the former Luxembourg foreign minister, Jacques Poos: "The hour of Europe has come!" That hour turned into years of bloodshed as a divided Europe dithered. The European Union was an economic giant. But even with the Cold War over, it was a diplomatic and strategic pygmy. Diplomacy unsupported by the credible threat of force is often empty. The EU had no army to speak of; the likes of Milošević and the Bosnian Serb commander, General Ratko Mladić, knew that. So they went on calling the Europeans' bluff.

Holbrooke was incensed by this European fecklessness. It was not that he believed the United States had all the answers. But he did believe it had enough of them to be essential to Europe's enduring security. When the Serbs in Bosnia seized United Nations hostages from European nations on May 29, 1995, the day after Holbrooke wed the author Kati Marton in Budapest, the then assistant secretary for Europe exploded: "Give the Serbs forty-eight hours, and if they don't release the hostages, bomb them to hell." It would take another three months for that to happen. Only military force, alongside Holbrooke's diplomacy, could usher in the end game.

Four years separated Poos's grandstanding blather from NATO's bombs. The lesson was clear enough: The United States was still needed. In 1995, in a *Foreign Affairs* article called "America, a European Power," Holbrooke set out his vision of a post–Cold War Europe in which the United States would continue to play a critical role. Its first paragraph said: "In the 21st century, Europe will still need the active American involvement that has been a necessary component of the continental balance for half a century. Conversely, an unstable Europe would still threaten essential national security interests in the United States."

Holbrooke backed up his conviction with several proposals. First, extend to all of Europe the liberal trading and collective security order that have become pillars of the West. Second, expand NATO eastward to make that happen—"Expansion of NATO is a logical and essential consequence of the disappearance of the Iron Curtain and the need to widen European unity based on shared democratic values." Third, accompany NATO expansion with bringing central and Eastern European nations into the European Union—"Expansion of NATO and the EU will not proceed at exactly the same pace. Their memberships will never be identical. But the two organizations are clearly mutually supportive." Fourth, work hard to ensure Russia moves toward democracy and develops a cooperative approach to the West despite its inevitable irritation at NATO expansion. Fifth, preserve the independence of Ukraine—"Its geostrategic position makes its independence and integrity a critical element of European security."

The article quotes Jean Monnet, the great architect of European unity: "Nothing is possible without men, but nothing is lasting without institutions." And it concludes: "The efforts of Monnet, Marshall, and others produced unparalleled peace and prosperity for half a century—but for only half a continent. The task ahead is as daunting as its necessity is evident. To turn away from that challenge would only mean paying a higher price later."

Holbrooke was always looking ahead a decade. He knew details mattered, but his strength was in not getting distracted by them. Where do you want to be a year or five years or ten years from now? These were favorite questions.

Viewed now at a distance of sixteen years, it's remarkable how much of that 1995 vision for Europe has come to fruition: a then sixteen-member NATO alliance is now a twenty-eight-member alliance stretching into the Baltics. The EU has also expanded throughout central and Eastern Europe and now boasts twenty-seven members. Market economies have been established throughout a united Europe. Relations with Russia have sometimes been strained, and the country's transition to democracy is uneven, but renewed confrontation has been avoided. Ukraine's independence has been defended, as has Georgia's, a proud nation for which Holbrooke felt a particular affinity (as he did for Tibet, another nation oppressed by a far bigger neighbor). A war within Europe is unthinkable.

I don't believe Holbrooke could have worked so effectively for such an outcome without a strong sense of European history and past injustice. He was forward-leaning but backward-aware. NATO expansion was vigorously opposed by many. It would needlessly provoke Russia. It would harm European stability. It was impossible. But for Holbrooke, there was a core issue such naysayers overlooked: These nations had been cast into the Soviet totalitarian nightmare at Yalta in 1945, and so the West owed it to them now to ensure their freedom and security. Sometimes it helps to keep issues simple.

Similarly, in that last confrontation with Milošević in 1999 over Kosovo, Holbrooke was very much aware of the history. It was precisely in Kosovo in the late 1980s, as he quashed the region's autonomy and embarked on systematic oppression of its majority ethnic Albanian population, that Milošević had begun the process of whipping the Serbs into a fury of nationalist indignation—one that would lead to the arming of the marauding Serbian militias who hounded Muslim civilians into the packed camps of Bosnia like Omarska.

This Serbian nationalist folly had to end—for the region and Europe as a whole. Holbrooke knew that. The Dayton Accords had settled Bosnia but left Milošević in place and the Kosovo conundrum for another day. Now, despite their years of conversations, Holbrooke had no hesitation. When Milošević balked, NATO bombed—and just over a year later Milošević would be ousted and make his way to the International Criminal Court in The Hague. Today, Croatia is close to joining the European Union and Serbia may not be far behind.

HOLBROOKE KNEW ON WHAT SUFFERING AND BLOODSHED THE NEW Europe was built. In a way, this is what drove him. He never took his eye off ordinary people and their need for a minimum of normality, stability, and decency in their lives. Czesław Miłosz, the great Polish poet, once wrote:

> You who harmed an ordinary man
> Do not feel safe. The poet remembers.
> You may kill him—another will be born.
> Deeds and words shall be recorded.

Holbrooke, the diplomat of the ordinary man, remembered. No act of brutality crossed his hectic path that he did not recall or strive to right. He went out with his boots on because he never wearied of this calling. This is how I recall him: loyal patriot, adventurer with a subversive twinkle to his eye, man of deeds, peacemaker, stoic, author of his own life.

At the end, his personal sense of Europe deepened. His wife, Kati Marton, was also a child of Europe—Jewish Europe, persecuted Europe, the part of Europe lost at Yalta. Americans, they explored this lost and shared past. They went to the synagogue in her hometown of Budapest and were moved. Holbrooke did not have a religious bone in his body. But I have no doubt that the free and stable Europe he worked so tirelessly to build was also his own American retort to the horrors of Auschwitz and Omarska.

America, a European Power

RICHARD HOLBROOKE
Foreign Affairs, MARCH/APRIL 1995

> *When Holbrooke described his vision of abiding American influence*
> *in Europe, he was then serving as Assistant Secretary of State for*
> *European and Canadian Affairs, thus becoming the only person to*
> *hold that position for two different regions. He wrote the piece in*
> *the wake of the 1993 Maastricht Treaty, the formation of the*
> *European Union, and the adoption of the euro, when many felt*
> *that a newly united Europe would challenge American hegemony.*
> *He also was writing at the nadir of the Bosnian war, which he*
> *famously described as the "greatest collective security failure of the*
> *West since the 1930s."*

THE NEW SECURITY ARCHITECTURE

President Clinton made four trips to Europe last year. This commitment of presidential time and attention underlines an inescapable but little-realized fact: the United States has become a European power in a sense that goes beyond traditional assertions of America's "commitment" to Europe. In the 21st century, Europe will still need the active American involvement that has been a necessary component of the continental balance for half a century. Conversely, an unstable Europe would still threaten essential national security interests of the United States. This is as true after as it was during the Cold War.

I do not intend, of course, to suggest that nothing has changed. The end of the Cold War, which can best be dated to that symbolic moment at midnight on December 25, 1991, when the Soviet flag came down over the Kremlin for the last time, began an era of change of historic proportions. Local conflicts, internal political and economic instability, and the return of historical grievances have now replaced Soviet expansionism as the greatest threat to peace in Europe. Western Europe and

America must jointly ensure that tolerant democracies become rooted throughout all of Europe and that the seething, angry, unresolved legacies of the past are contained and solved.

THE FOURTH ARCHITECTURAL MOMENT

Only three times since the French Revolution has Europe peacefully reshaped its basic security architecture. Today, the continent is in the middle of nothing less than the fourth such moment in the last two centuries. The first post-Napoleonic security architecture for Europe, designed in 1815 at the Congress of Vienna, helped prevent all-out continental war for 99 years. The young United States, having fought two wars with England in only 40 years, successfully kept its distance, but for the last time.

In the second period of redesign, at Versailles in 1919, President Woodrow Wilson played a central role, but the United States withdrew almost immediately from the very structures it had helped create, thereby weakening them and thus virtually guaranteeing the tragic resumption of total war 20 years later. When the third opportunity arose in 1945, the great powers initially built a system based on Yalta, Potsdam, and the United Nations. But starting in 1947, when the leaders of the West realized that this system would not suffice to stem Soviet expansion, they created the most successful peacetime collective security system in history, centered around the Truman Doctrine, the Marshall Plan, NATO, Atlantic partnership—and American leadership.

This creative architecture reflected the underlying goals of America's postwar engagement in Europe. Its post-Cold War engagement must focus again on structures, old and new. This time, the United States must lead in the creation of a security architecture that includes and thereby stabilizes all of Europe—the West, the former Soviet satellites of central Europe, and, most critically, Russia and the former republics of the Soviet Union.

All the key participants in the new security equation in Europe—the United States, the West and central European countries, and the other nations of the former Soviet Union—desire a peaceful, stable, and democratic Russia, integrated into the institutions of an undivided Europe. No more important political goal has existed in Europe since a newly democratic West Germany was successfully integrated into the

European political and security structure after World War II. It is for this and other reasons that the crisis in Chechnya, discussed more fully below, has been so disturbing.

Fortunately, most of the great structures of the postwar period offer a usable foundation for building stability. The essential challenge is to maintain their coherence, project their influence, and adapt to new circumstances without diluting their basic functions.

Measured on the post-World War II calendar, the United States is now slightly past the point in the late spring of 1947 when Secretary of State George C. Marshall made his historic speech at Harvard University. The Marshall Plan he outlined that day was not charity. Rather, it was a program of assistance and credits designed to stimulate coopera-tion among the European states. And it is important to remember that Marshall offered the plan not only to Western Europe but to the Soviet Union, which turned it down for itself and its satellites and instead em-barked on a 45-year epoch that condemned an entire region to political and economic ruin.

Today, as after World War II, early euphoria has yielded to a more sober appreciation of the problems, new and old. The tragedy of Bosnia does not diminish the responsibility to build a new comprehensive struc-ture of relationships to form a new security architecture. On the contrary, Bosnia, the greatest collective security failure of the West since the 1930s, only underscores the urgency of that task.

In 1947, Americans learned that those with the ability to preserve the peace have a special responsibility to assist in building stable struc-tures in newly democratic neighbors. Then only the United States was secure and prosperous enough to offer Western Europe the assistance it needed. Today an equally prosperous Western Europe (and Japan, which has a stake in and benefits from a stable Europe) will have to put up the bulk of the actual financial assistance, but the United States must con-tinue to play a leading part. In the words of Secretary of State Warren Christopher, the central goal of the United States is "to help extend to all of Europe the benefits and obligations of the same liberal trading and collective security order that have been pillars of strength for the West."

A final lesson of the Marshall Plan is equally important. Those receiving support must build their own futures. The new democracies must contribute to their own security through both responsible behavior toward neighbors and democracy-building from within. The United

States understands, welcomes, and encourages the desire of new European democracies to join the West through membership in its key institutions. But NATO, the European Union (EU), and the other major institutions of the West are not clubs that one joins simply by filling out membership applications. Over time, each has evolved values and obligations that must be accepted by each new member.

THE CHALLENGE OF CENTRAL EUROPE

Any blueprint for the new security architecture of Europe must focus first on central Europe, the seedbed of more turmoil and tragedy in this century than any other area on the continent. The two most destructive wars in human history began from events on its plains, and the Cold War played itself out in its ancient and storied cities, all within the last 80 years.

Other historic watersheds also have not treated this area well. First the treaties of Versailles and Trianon, then the agreements of Yalta and Potsdam, and finally the collapse of the Soviet empire—those three benchmark events left throughout central Europe a legacy of unresolved and often conflicting historical resentments, ambitions, and, most dangerous, territorial and ethnic disputes. Without democracy, stability, and free-market economies, these lands remain vulnerable to the same problems, often exacerbated by an obsession with righting historical wrongs, real or mythical. If any of these malignancies spread—as they have already in parts of the Balkans and Transcaucasus—general European stability is again at risk. And for Germany and Russia, the two large nations on the flanks of central Europe, insecurity has historically been a major contributor to aggressive behavior.

But if there are great problems there are also great possibilities. For the first time in history, the nations of this region have the chance simultaneously to enjoy stability, freedom, and independence based on another first: the adoption of Western democratic ideals as a common foundation for all of Europe. The emotional but also practical lure of the West can be the strongest unifying force Europe has seen in generations, but only if unnecessary delay does not squander the opportunity.

The West owes much of its success to the great institutions created in the 1940s and 1950s. They serve an important internal function for their members, and they also project a sense of stability and security to others. If those institutions were to remain closed to new members, they would become progressively more isolated from new challenges and less relevant to the problems of the post-Cold War world. It would be a tragedy if, through delay or indecision, the West helped create conditions that brought about the very problems it fears the most. The West must expand to central Europe as fast as possible in fact as well as in spirit, and the United States is ready to lead the way. Stability in central Europe is essential to general European security, and it is still far from assured.

THE BUILDING BLOCKS

The central security pillar of the new architecture is a venerable organization: NATO. To some, the 45-year-old Atlantic alliance may seem irrelevant or poorly designed for the challenges of the new Europe. To others, NATO's extraordinary record of success may suggest that nothing needs to be changed. Both views are equally wrong. Expansion of NATO is a logical and essential consequence of the disappearance of the Iron Curtain and the need to widen European unity based on shared democratic values. But even before NATO expands, its strength and know-how are already playing an important role in building a new sense of security throughout Europe.

Designed decades ago to counter a single, clearly defined threat, NATO is only just beginning a historic transformation. NATO's core purpose of collective defense remains, but new goals and programs have been added. Collective crisis management, out-of-area force projection, and the encouragement of stability to the east through the Partnership for Peace (PFP) and other programs have been undertaken. Command structures have been streamlined. Static forces formerly concentrated to meet a possible Soviet attack across central Europe have been turned into more lightly armed, mobile, and flexible multinational corps designed to respond to a different, less stable world.

Two new structures—the North Atlantic Cooperation Council and the PFP—are specifically designed to reach out to countries that are not NATO members. They deserve closer attention, especially the creative new concept so appropriately named the Partnership for Peace. In just one year, this innovative idea has become an integral part of the European security scene, but it remains somewhat misunderstood and underestimated. Contrary to a fairly widespread impression, PFP is not a single organization; rather, it is a series of individual agreements between NATO and, at last count, 24 other countries ranging from Poland to Armenia, including Russia. Each "partner" country creates an individual program to meet its own needs.

PFP is an invaluable tool that encourages NATO and individual partners to work together. It helps newly democratic states restructure and establish democratic control of their military forces and learn new forms of military doctrine, environmental control, and disaster relief. In the future, it will provide a framework in which NATO and individual partners can cooperate in crisis management or out-of-area peacekeeping.

PFP proved its value immediately. In its first year of existence, allies and partners held joint military exercises in Poland, the Netherlands, and the north Atlantic. Ten partners have already established liaison offices with the NATO military command. Sixteen partners have begun joint activities with NATO, and others will follow. A defense planning and review process has been established within the partnership to advance compatibility and transparency between allies and partners. PFP is also a vehicle for partners to learn about NATO procedures and standards, thus helping each partner make an informed decision as to whether it wishes to be considered for membership in the alliance.

From the alliance perspective, PFP will provide a valuable framework for judging the ability of each partner to assume the obligations and commitments of NATO membership—a testing ground for their capabilities. And for those partners that do not become NATO members the PFP will provide a structure for increasingly close cooperation with NATO—in itself an important building block for European security. If U.S. hopes are realized, and the first year gives every reason to be optimistic, the PFP will be a permanent part of the European security scene even as NATO expands to take in some, but not all, PFP members.

EXPANDING NATO

No issue has been more important, controversial, or misunderstood than whether NATO should remain an alliance of its 16 current members or expand, and if it expands, why, where, when, and how. At the beginning of an important year on this issue, it is useful to clarify where the United States stands, and where it is going.

In essence, 1994 was the year in which, led by the United States, NATO decided it would eventually expand. This decision was reached during the January NATO summit in Brussels and reaffirmed by President Clinton during his return to Europe last June, when he stated that the question was no longer whether NATO would expand but how and when.

Last December, the NATO foreign ministers met again in Brussels, and, again led by the United States, they committed themselves to a two-phase program for 1995. During the first part of this year, NATO will determine through an internal discussion that is already under way the rationale and process for expanding the new, post-Cold War NATO. Then, in the months prior to the December 1995 ministerial meeting, NATO's views on these two issues—"why" and "how"—will be presented individually to PFP members who have expressed an interest in such discussions. This critical step will mark the first time detailed discussions on this subject have taken place outside the alliance. Then the ministers will meet again in Brussels in December and review the results of the discussions with the partners before deciding how to proceed.

This process, which at every stage requires the agreement of all 16 NATO members, is still in its initial stages. It is not yet widely understood. Given the importance of NATO, it is not surprising that some outside observers wish to accelerate the process while others do not want it to commence at all. The Clinton administration and its NATO allies, after some initial disagreements, have chosen a gradual and deliberate middle course—and have begun the process.

Several key points should be stressed:

- First, the goal remains the defense of the alliance's vital interests and the promotion of European stability. NATO expansion must strengthen security in the entire region, including nations that are not members. The goal is to promote security in central Europe by integrating countries that qualify into the stabilizing framework of NATO.
- Second, the rationale and process for NATO's expansion, once decided, will be transparent, not secret. Both Warsaw and Moscow, for example, will have the opportunity to hear exactly the same presentation from NATO later this year, and both should have access to all

aspects of the alliance's thinking in order to understand that NATO should no longer be considered an anti-Russian alliance. As former National Security Advisor Zbigniew Brzezinski, an advocate of rapid expansion, wrote in the January/February 1995 issue of *Foreign Affairs*, "Neither the alliance nor its prospective new members are facing any imminent threat. Talk of a 'new Yalta' or of a Russian military threat is not justified, either by actual circumstances or even by worst-case scenarios for the near future. The expansion of NATO should, therefore, not be driven by whipping up anti-Russian hysteria that could eventually become a self-fulfilling prophecy."

- Third, there is no timetable or list of nations that will be invited to join NATO. The answers to the critical questions of who and when will emerge after completion of this phase of the process.
- Fourth, each nation will be considered individually, not as part of some grouping.
- Fifth, the decisions as to who joins NATO and when will be made exclusively by the alliance. No outside nation will exercise a veto.
- Sixth, although criteria for membership have not been determined, certain fundamental precepts reflected in the original Washington treaty remain as valid as they were in 1949: new members must be democratic, have market economies, be committed to responsible security policies, and be able to contribute to the alliance. As President Clinton has stated, "Countries with repressive political systems, countries with designs on their neighbors, countries with militaries unchecked by civilian control or with closed economic systems need not apply."
- Lastly, it should be remembered that each new NATO member constitutes for the United States the most solemn of all commitments: a bilateral defense treaty that extends the U.S. security umbrella to a new nation. This requires ratification by two-thirds of the U.S. Senate, a point that advocates of immediate expansion often overlook.

A BROAD CONCEPT OF SECURITY

NATO expansion cannot occur in a vacuum. If it did, it would encourage the very imbalances and instabilities it was seeking to avoid. In addition to NATO, a variety of organizations and institutions must contribute to the new structure of peace. The new architecture should involve both such institutions as NATO and the EU, which strive for true integration among members, and others such as the Organization for Security and Cooperation in Europe (OSCE), which provide a wide, inclusive framework for looser forms of cooperation.

Although the EU is primarily a political and economic entity, it also makes an important contribution to European security. The integration of West European nations has virtually transcended the territorial disputes, irredentist claims, social cleavages, and ethnic grievances that tore apart European societies in earlier eras.

The extension of the EU eastward (and southward, if Cyprus and Malta join) will therefore be immensely important. It will integrate and stabilize the two halves of Europe. This process began with the entry of Austria, Finland, and Sweden at the beginning of this year. Europe agreements committed the EU and six central European nations to industrial free trade on January 1, 1995, except in steel and textiles, which will follow in 1996 and 1998. Slovenia and the Baltic states are expected to sign similar agreements soon. In December, the EU heads of state and government agreed on a "pre-accession" strategy for eventual entry, presumably sometime early in the next century, of the central European states, Cyprus, and Malta. For Germany, which, in Chancellor Helmut Kohl's powerful phrase, "cannot remain indefinitely Europe's eastern boundary," the extension of the EU is especially important, which is why Germany led this move during its term in the EU presidency.

Expansion of NATO and the EU will not proceed at exactly the same pace. Their memberships will never be identical. But the two organizations are clearly mutually supportive. Although the relationship between NATO and the EU is complex, particularly as the EU seeks to define its relationship with the WEU to create a European defense identity, it is clearly mutually supportive; the expansion of both is equally necessary for an undivided and stable Europe.

It would be self-defeating for the WEU to create military structures to duplicate the successful European integration already achieved in NATO. But a stronger European pillar of the alliance can be an important contribution to European stability and transatlantic burden-sharing, provided it does not dilute NATO. The WEU establishes a new premise of collective defense: the United States should not be the only NATO member that can protect vital common interests outside Europe.

STRENGTHENING THE OSCE

Neither NATO nor the EU can be everything to everyone, and the other organizations above are focused on narrower issues. There is, therefore, a need in the new European architectural concept for a larger, looser region-wide security organization—smaller, of course, than the United Nations—that offers a framework for dealing with a variety of challenges that neither NATO nor the EU is designed to address, one that includes both NATO members and other countries on an equal basis.

Fortunately, the core for such a structure has existed for some years—the Conference on Security and Cooperation in Europe. Its 53-nation structure of human rights commitments, consultations, and efforts at cooperative or preventive diplomacy was intended to fill a niche in the new Europe. Born out of the 1975 Helsinki Accords, the CSCE unexpectedly provided, through its famous Basket III, a lever on human rights and democratic values that played a major role in undermining communism. But it was clear by the middle of last year that the CSCE, while offering intriguing possibilities, had neither the internal coherence nor the political mandate to meet the challenges facing it.

Moscow and the major NATO allies shared this view. By the fall of last year, all had agreed that as NATO began to look at expansion, the CSCE should be strengthened and upgraded. A significant evolution of this organization, including a name change, began in December 1994 at the Budapest summit attended by President Clinton and Secretary Christopher. The result was a series of steps toward a clearer political and operational mandate, a strengthened consultative apparatus, and a new status. The old "conference" became a full-fledged "organization," and the OSCE was born.

The role of the new OSCE must now be more clearly established. Rather than enforcing behavior through legal or military action, it seeks to improve security by building new forms of cooperation based on consensus. With a membership that literally spans all 24 time zones and a huge array of cultures and nations, OSCE members will often disagree on how its standards are to be implemented. Taking such disagreement as a given, the OSCE must be more aggressive in the search for common ground.

Today security in Europe requires addressing potential conflicts earlier. The OSCE must prove its worth in this area, as the CSCE did in spreading democratic values and legitimizing human rights. The organization has pioneered efforts, however limited, at conflict prevention and crisis management through innovations such as establishing a high commissioner for national minorities and sending resident missions to conflict areas. More must be done.

The United States has taken the lead in pursuing innovations within the OSCE. In the future, the United States will make more vigorous use of the OSCE's consultative and conflict prevention mechanisms. The goal is to establish the OSCE as an integral element of the new security architecture. In a time of great burdens for the United Nations, the OSCE, as a regional organization under Chapter VII of the U.N. Charter, can perform many functions normally expected from the United Nations. The participation of U.N. Secretary General Boutros Boutros-Ghali in the OSCE Budapest summit underlined the importance of such cooperation.

Under no circumstances can the OSCE be a substitute for NATO or the EU. The OSCE can in no way be superior to NATO; the functions of the two organizations are and shall remain entirely different. Conversely, expansion of the role of the OSCE does not conflict with the responsibilities of NATO. Its methods occupy a totally different dimension than those of NATO.

A recent example of this function was the agreement reached at Budapest between Russia and the OSCE to merge negotiating efforts on the difficult issue of Nagorno-Karabakh and provide peacekeeping troops once a political agreement is reached—important steps on the OSCE'S path to becoming a more meaningful organization. More recently, the Russians agreed to an OSCE fact-finding mission on Chechnya. The very fact that Moscow accepted OSCE involvement is significant, but this involvement came far too late and is too limited.

Without question Chechnya is part of the Russian Federation. At the same time, the United States has maintained from the outset that the Russian government should adhere to international standards, enshrined in OSCE resolutions and elsewhere, of respect for human rights. Tragically and unnecessarily, the Russian government prosecuted its military campaign against the city of Grozny in ways certain to cause large numbers of civilian casualties and hinder humanitarian assistance.

The West's overall objective in Russia and the rest of the former Soviet Union remains integration—bringing emerging democracies into the fold of Western political, economic, and security institutions. From the beginning of the battle for Grozny, Chechnya worked in exactly the opposite direction for Russia. Chechnya also has proved a deeply divisive element in Russian political life and has become a serious setback for the cause of reform, democratization, and the evolution of the Russian Federation as a stable, democratic, multiethnic state. The Chechnya conflict, terrible though it is, has not changed the nature of U.S. interests. President Clinton stated in January that, as Russia undergoes a historic transformation, reacting reflexively to each of the ups and downs that it is bound to experience, perhaps for decades to come, would be a terrible mistake. If the forces of reform are embattled, the United States must reinforce, not retreat from, its support for them.

The U.S. objective remains a healthy Russia—a democratic Russia pursuing reform and respecting the rights of its citizens, not fragmenting into ethnic conflict and civil war. America's ability to pursue and develop its partnership with Russia depends on a common pursuit of these values and objectives. The reason Russia has qualified as a friend and partner of the United States is that its people and government have embarked on a path of democratization, development of an open civil society, and respect for basic human rights. That is what the United States continues to support in Russia.

RUSSIA AND UKRAINE

To repeat: if the West is to create an enduring and stable security framework for Europe, it must solve the most enduring strategic problem of Europe and integrate the nations of the former Soviet Union, especially Russia, into a stable European security system. Russia is already involved in most aspects of the emerging architecture. It participates actively in the OSCE and worked closely with the United States in upgrading that organization. Russia has signed an ambitious partnership agreement with the EU. It has joined the Partnership for Peace with NATO. It is a candidate for membership in the Council of Europe. The United States supports deeper Russian participation in the Group of Seven industrialized nations and is sponsoring Russia's membership in the World Trade Organization, successor to the General Agreement on Tariffs and Trade. For the first time since 1945, Russia is participating, as a member of the Contact Group on Bosnia, in a multinational negotiating team presenting a unified position on a difficult security issue.

Enhancement of stability in central Europe is a mutual interest of Russia and the United States. NATO, which poses no threat to Russian security, seeks a direct and open relationship with Russia that both recognizes Russia's special position and stature and reinforces the integrity of the other newly independent states of the former Soviet Union. There have been proposals, including one by Russian President Boris Yeltsin in late 1993, for a special arrangement between NATO and Russia, which could take a number of forms. In urging rapid expansion of NATO, Brzezinski proposed in his *Foreign Affairs* article a "formal treaty of global security cooperation between NATO and the Russian Federation," in conjunction with an upgrade of the OSCE.

Any negotiations between NATO and Russia on this or any other arrangement would be quite complex. They would need to take into account a wide range of factors, including the pace of NATO expansion, the state of other Russian-NATO ties such as the Partnership for Peace, the degree to which the OSCE has been turned into a more useful organization, and the implications of events such as the fighting in Chechnya. Notwithstanding this array of issues, the U.S. government as well as its major allies have supported development of this important new track in the European security framework. Informal discussions of this possibility, while in a highly preliminary phase, began in January when Secretary Christopher met in Geneva with Russian Foreign Minister Andrei Kozyrev.

Any such arrangement must consider the special case of Ukraine. Its geostrategic position makes its independence and integrity a critical element of European security. In Budapest last December, President Clinton and the leaders of Belarus, Kazakhstan, Russia, and Ukraine exchanged documents of ratification for the Strategic Arms Reduction Treaty, formally bringing START 1 into force. At the same time, Ukraine also deposited its instrument of accession to the Nuclear Nonproliferation Treaty, and the United States, Russia, and the United Kingdom provided security assurances to Belarus, Kazakhstan, and Ukraine.

The basic goals of those seeking to take advantage of this moment in history are the expansion of democracy and prosperity, the integration of political and security institutions, and a unity that has always eluded

Europe, even with American involvement. Leaders will have to lead to break through the layers of ambivalence, confusion, complacence, and history that inhibit reforms. As the great architect of European unity, Jean Monnet, observed, "Nothing is possible without men, but nothing is lasting without institutions." The efforts of Monnet, Marshall, and others produced unparalleled peace and prosperity for half a century— but for only half a continent. The task ahead is as daunting as its necessity is evident. To turn away from the challenge would only mean paying a higher price later.

Hungarian History in the Making

RICHARD HOLBROOKE
Travel + Leisure, DECEMBER 1999

*In 1995, Holbrooke had married Kati Marton, the best-selling
Hungarian-American author, in Budapest. Immediately after the
wedding, he gave an address to the Council of Europe. Fifteen years
later, at his Kennedy Center memorial service, Marton recalled that
a group of Bulgarian women approached him after the talk, upon
learning of his marriage: "We did not know you were looking for a
bride in the region! We have so many beautiful ladies in Bulgaria!"
Holbrooke was serving as U.S. Ambassador to the United Nations
when he wrote this article, and five years later, Hungary, as he
predicted, became a part of the European Union.*

Hungary is a normal country now: elections, economic ups and
downs, traffic jams, entrepreneurs, even, unbelievably, membership
in NATO. But just beneath the surface, easily available to a visitor with
a sense of history, lie powerful reminders of the country's turbulent—
and sometimes tragic—recent past.

As Hungarians walk the streets of Budapest, do they remember their
remarkable journey to freedom over the past 12 years? Do they still
see the bullet holes from the 1956 revolution that pockmark many
buildings? Do they hear the ghosts from the 1989 demonstrations in
Heroes' Square—the beginning of the end of Communism in Central
and Eastern Europe? Or do they see only the new, emerging Budapest,
symbolized by a three-floor fast-food joint that proudly claims to be one
of the world's largest Burger Kings?

When my wife, Kati Marton, walks with me through Budapest,
I see the city through her eyes. Kati was born here under Communism.
Her parents, both Hungarian reporters for American wire services, were

jailed by the secret police in 1955 on trumped-up charges that they were spies for the CIA; she and her sister were farmed out to a family that was paid by the Associated Press to take care of political orphans. Kati's Budapest still contains the opening in the fence between her parents' house and that of the American diplomats next door, through which she and her sister would slip to taste Western-style freedom (and food). When we go to the central market, she marvels over the rich variety of goods and recalls the shortages of her childhood. When we visit the ambassador's elegant office in the U.S. Embassy, she sees the very room where Cardinal József Mindszenty stayed during the 15 years he lived there under American protection. Kati's parents were released just before the revolution in 1956, and when the Soviets crushed the uprising, the family also received refuge here. For weeks, the two Marton girls joined the cardinal in his nightly prayers. (It was Kati's father, Endre Marton, who sent the famous "last message" from Budapest, calling, in vain, on the world to help the Freedom Fighters.)

BUDAPEST HOLDS SPECIAL MEMORIES FOR ME NOW, TOO. WE TRY TO VISIT at least once a year, to see Kati's aunt and to check on the changes coming over the country. We were married there, in the garden of the residence of Donald Blinken, then the American ambassador, and his Budapest-born wife, Vera. This was Kati's wish: in her childhood, the building had represented the freedom denied to Hungarians, and the excitement of a distant and then-unattainable land.

Kati, still fluent in her native tongue, walks through the streets like a little girl again, wondering at the once-unimaginable transformation. For me, the walks are an exercise in history—not just a testament to people's capacity to move forward, but a stark reminder of those regions, some only a few miles away, where such progress has yet to occur. Sarajevo, Belgrade, Banja Luka, Pristina, Tetovo, and Tiranë all lie just south and east of Budapest; some of post-World War II's worst moments have taken place in the nearby Balkans, and the drama is not yet over. Many Hungarians live unhappily in neighboring countries—Slovakia, Romania, Yugoslavia—as a result of international boundaries drawn in punishment against the Austro-Hungarian Empire after World War I. Woodrow Wilson is no hero in Budapest.

In good weather, Kati and I like to cross the Danube on the Chain Bridge, completed in 1849 to connect the cities of Buda and Pest.

Knowing the bridge's tortured history over the last 60 years makes the walk more meaningful: it was used to brutally murder Hungarian Jews, who were thrown by the Nazis into the freezing water in the winter of 1944–45; destroyed by the retreating Germans in early 1945; rebuilt after the war by the Soviets, who added the red star of Communism to the Hungarian coats of arms carved into either side (they were only recently removed).

A STROLL DOWN BUDAPEST'S GRANDEST AVENUE, ANDRÁSSY ÚT, GIVES a simultaneous sense of the splendors of Budapest during the Austro-Hungarian Empire, the decay of the Communist period, and the city's latter-day rebirth. Unlike the Champs-Élysées, on which it was modeled, Andrássy has retained its original flavor, with great buildings and mansions along its 1½-mile length. Each time we visit Andrássy, more of the buildings have been repaired, but there are still plenty that continue to deteriorate after decades of neglect or abuse. Nevertheless, the splendid Opera House and many glorious cafés suggest the flavor of the city before World War I, when Hungary was at its most optimistic and sophisticated. Many street signs show crossed-out Communist-era names and their more recent replacements; Andrássy itself regained its original name after having been the Avenue of the People's Republic during the Cold War.

Budapest's cafés and coffeehouses are among its greatest pleasures. Their number declined precipitously in the last century, but those that remain evoke another time, a more leisurely way of life. The once-glorious Café New York, for a while turned into a sporting goods store by the Communists, has closed for two years while foreign investors return it to its former state. Other venerable places, like the pastry shop Gerbeaud and the trendy Centrál in Pest, have already been revived. George Lang, the Budapest-born restaurateur (Café des Artistes is his New York City gem), has restored the *fin de siècle* Gundel's, opened several more excellent establishments, and set a standard that others are now emulating—good places to eat are sprouting up everywhere. Budapest's grandest hotel during the interwar period, the Gellért (in whose baths Kati's family once swam), is coming back to life again after years of neglect. Gresham Palace, a 1906 Art Nouveau masterpiece right on the Danube, is to become a Four Seasons hotel in 2003.

Our friends in Budapest tell us that Hungarians don't think much about ghosts these days. Unlike Kati, they no longer marvel over the extraordinary progress their country has made in little more than a decade, over the peaceful dismantling of a Communist state. They don't talk much about the 1956 revolution. Instead, they complain about the economy and unemployment and prices; they gossip about who's up and who's down politically and socially. Just as in normal countries. In fact—remarkable fact—Hungarians serve with NATO forces in the Balkans, and the country will be one of the first in Central Europe to enter the European Union, probably in 2004 or 2005.

To understand the history of Budapest is to appreciate this great city better. This is, after all, the first time in a thousand years that Hungary is both democratic and free. Budapest is not just another pretty European capital but—like Prague, Warsaw, Dresden, Riga, and other cities that until about a decade ago lived in Moscow's grip—an extraordinary voyage in compressed history.

Hungarians are enormously proud of their capital, which they constantly compare to Paris. Even if you are not fortunate enough to have married a Hungarian (Kati told me to say this), Budapest is a memorable place to visit; visit it before its recent past has all but vanished.

Berlin's Unquiet Ghosts

RICHARD HOLBROOKE
Newsweek, SEPTEMBER 10, 2001

> *After New York, Berlin was one of Holbrooke's favorite cities—*
> *full of history, beauty, tragedy, and possibility. Today, his most*
> *lasting legacy in the city sits on the banks of the Wannsee in the*
> *Hans Arnhold Center, where Holbrooke founded the American*
> *Academy in Berlin.*

Even as a New Yorker, it is hard not to be struck by the raw, often-confusing, always-compelling energy of the new Berlin. Yet exciting as the city's transformation may be, the past is a relentless intruder. A walk through Berlin becomes a living version of a college survey course of 20th-century European history. The parade grounds where Kaiser Wilhelm II, on his horse and hiding his withered arm, reviewed the troops before World War I. Pariser Platz, where Hitler's troops held torchlight parades, the Nazis burned books and Soviet tanks smashed through the Brandenburg Gate in 1945. Hitler's bunker. The ruins of the Gestapo headquarters, saved from the wrecker's ball and turned into a small museum called "The Topography of Terror." The old Jewish quarter, now one of the trendiest parts of East Berlin. The huge air terminal at Tempelhof, once Hitler's pride, then the indispensable landing field through which the Airlift saved the city, now a small commuter airport. Remnants of the Berlin Wall.

No city on earth has gone through such a roller-coaster ride—from villain to victim, from horrors to heroics, all in just the past 70 years. First the decadent (and strangely innocent) pre-Nazi world immortalized in "Cabaret." Then Hitler and the Holocaust: Berlin as the undisputed capital of evil. Yet less than three years after the Battle of Berlin, the city's Soviet liberators, by blockading it, transformed it into the ultimate symbol of the Cold War, a city of heroic freedom-loving survivors. The decades that followed were high theater with Berlin often at center stage: the East German uprising of June 1953, JFK, Checkpoint Charlie, secret spy exchanges, Reagan, the night of November 9, 1989, and, finally, one last photograph for the history books, the Clintons and the Kohls walking side by side through the Brandenburg Gate in 1994 into an ecstatic crowd of more than 100,000 people in East Berlin.

"Berlin is a city that never is, but is always in the process of becoming," the noted German essayist Karl Scheffler once observed. (He added, disapprovingly, that its people are "lured by the promise of Americanism.") He wrote this in 1910. Berlin is now becoming something new: Europe's greatest showcase for modern architecture—although some Berliners, fulfilling their reputation for cynicism, like to say that the world's best architects have come here to build their worst buildings.

But even here, everything seems reflected through the past: Sir Norman Foster's transparent modern dome, for example, sits atop the battle-scarred Reichstag building, enabling the visitor to literally (and symbolically) look down upon the members of the German Parliament. A visit to the Ministry of Finance is especially bizarre: its new home is Goring's indestructible Air Ministry, which survived every Allied attempt to destroy it during the war.

The battle over new and old architecture only underscores the dilemmas of Berlin. Every decision of the planning authority, every new building or monument, triggers an argument based on conflicting views of history. Should more of the Wall be preserved? Should war ruins be paved over? How should the Holocaust be remembered? Is the chancellor's new office too grandiose—that is, too reminiscent of a certain earlier German leader?

The Germans, who gave the world the word *angst*, worry constantly about how to deal with the heavy burden history has placed upon them. One of my friends—a prominent German politician—keeps in his study a painting of his grandfather that clearly shows a Nazi membership badge. "I could easily have had the badge painted over," he told me, "but I felt I had to leave it in, for it is a historical truth. My grandfather thought Hitler would be good for Germany."

"Berlin, Berlin, great city of misery," wrote Heinrich Heine in the 19th century. "In you there is nothing to find but anguish and martyrdom." Heine was prophetic, but I think Berlin's years of excessive drama have finally come to an end. Many Berliners miss the exciting days when they were the center of the world's attention. (Though many still talk of the "Wall in the Head"; that is, the continuing gap between Wessis and Ossis.) But in my view, this is not a time for nostalgia. Having worked closely with many of the new generation of Germans, I have more confidence in them, perhaps, than many of them yet have in themselves.

Still, with its overwhelming history Berlin will never be a "normal" city, even though it is no longer divided, even though American, British, French and Soviet troops no longer face each other across a death zone, even though American presidents no longer fly there to reaffirm our commitment to freedom. The ghosts will remain forever. As they should.

CHAPTER SIX

Bosnia and Dayton

Holbrooke and his Bosnia negotiating team plot their next move after a meeting.
(AP Photo/Jacques Brinon, October 16, 1995)

Ending a War

DEREK CHOLLET

It was an unusual place to celebrate the New Year. Shortly after midnight on January 1, 1993, Richard Holbrooke found himself in one of the few functioning rooms of a bombed-out Holiday Inn in downtown Sarajevo, freezing and writing in his journal. He could hear gunfire outside. Thousands of miles away, in Washington and New York, members of the Democratic foreign policy establishment clinked champagne glasses and buzzed with gossip and anticipation for the inauguration of the first Democratic president in twelve years, Bill Clinton. Yet there was Holbrooke, far away from the jockeying and action he loved so much (and excelled at), alone in Bosnia. He had not played a major role in the 1992 campaign. For the first time in decades, he felt like an outsider. So he decided to pay a private visit to a war few understood, visiting stunned refugees, trading notes with intrepid war correspondents, and meeting with dour foreign officials.

Holbrooke didn't go to Bosnia just to get away, and he certainly didn't spend his time there moping. It was his second trip to the country in six months. He felt compelled to be there, to try to understand the origins of the conflict, and to send the word back to Washington that the U.S. needed to act. "Not since Vietnam had I seen a problem so difficult or compelling," he later reflected.

Few in Washington viewed Bosnia as a priority. But Holbrooke was not one to keep quiet. "If I don't make my views known to the new team," he wrote in his journal, "I will not have done enough to help the desperate people we have just seen; but if I push my views I will appear too aggressive. I feel trapped." Several weeks later, Holbrooke the outsider sent a memo to two prospective Clinton administration insiders—Warren Christopher and Anthony Lake— whom he'd known for decades and who were preparing to become secretary of state and national security advisor. "Bosnia will be the key test of American policy in Europe," Holbrooke wrote, with his usual tone of urgency. "Continued inaction carries long-term risks which could be disruptive to U.S.-European relations [and] weaken NATO." He offered a series of bold moves, including lifting the arms embargo against the Bosnian Muslims.

Holbrooke worried he might seem too pushy, and he was right. He didn't get a response. When he called Lake a few weeks later to ask what he thought of his ideas, Lake replied cautiously that they were "useful." And as the new administration swept into office and filled Washington's high-level jobs, Holbrooke was still in New York watching from afar, his phone strangely silent.

Given where Holbrooke found himself in those early days of 1993—agitating for more attention toward a faraway ethnic conflict, watching the excitement in Washington with his face pressed against the window pane —it was hard for him or anyone else to imagine that in three years he would be nominated for a Nobel Peace Prize for ending the Bosnia war and celebrated as one of the foreign policy heavyweights in the Clinton administration who came within a whisker of becoming secretary of state in 1996 (and again in 2000). The peace agreement at Dayton was the crowning achievement of Holbrooke's career, the effort in which all his considerable skills—as a tireless negotiator, fierce bureaucratic player, showman, impresario, frustrated journalist, and later, a historian—came together in one masterful performance. Bosnia showed that above all else, Holbrooke was a doer. But this story also illustrates a larger point about Holbrooke's career: His achievements were rarely foreordained or easy. Despite his abundant bravado and bluster, he often had to scrap and fight to get his voice heard.

HOLBROOKE'S TWO TRIPS TO BOSNIA IN 1992 FOLLOWED A STANDARD practice throughout his career: to get into the field and see problems first-hand (often paying his own way), gaining expertise, getting a sense of problems and possible solutions, and becoming an advocate. After each visit, Holbrooke would work the media, usually writing op-eds or magazine articles, appearing on television (PBS's *Charlie Rose Show* was a favorite stop since the format permitted him to get beyond sound bites and both expand on his message and engage with a highly knowledgeable, well-prepared interviewer), and, of course, giving speeches, which he did with a combination of seeming spontaneity and a genuine passion. When he was out of government, he always sought to shape the debate. Years later, after the September 11 attacks, Holbrooke followed the same path regarding Afghanistan—making numerous private trips to the country and speaking out, in the media and on the foreign policy version of the rubber-chicken circuit at various think tanks and conferences.

Yugoslavia's unraveling in the early 1990s was the perfect issue for Holbrooke to seize. After the end of the Cold War, there was a sense that America was ready to turn inward; Bill Clinton famously campaigned on "it's the economy, stupid" and criticized George H. W. Bush for caring more about problems abroad than those at home. Holbrooke worried about the consequences of this kind of mood for people in places like Bosnia. "I do not agree with the argument that we cannot afford to deal with these faraway problems when we have difficulties at home," Holbrooke wrote in his journal at the end of his first trip to Bosnia in August 1992. "Such thinking leads to unacceptable global triage. Our society is still rich enough to deal with the outside world, even after the end of the Cold War."

Yet Holbrooke was unable to do little more than agitate. Once the Clinton administration was in office in late January 1993, Holbrooke was still on the sideline, waiting for an offer to join. For months there was none. He was sounded out for the ambassadorship to Japan, a country he had traveled to nearly a hundred times. It would have been one of his dream jobs. After all, at the time he was primarily known as an Asia specialist. But as often happens during the transition period, weeks went by while Holbrooke heard nothing. Then, when the call finally came, to

Holbrooke's complete surprise he was asked to go not to Japan (former Vice President Walter Mondale—who Holbrooke worked with closely during the Carter administration—got that plum), but to Germany.

Although Bosnia rarely came up during his stint as ambassador to Germany, Holbrooke's time in Europe from 1993 to 1994 allowed him to immerse himself deeply in the Continent's post–Cold War challenges and huge potential. He disconnected from the day-to-day events in Bosnia—he said he barely paid attention to the seemingly endless official reports about the war. But as he became more active in debates about Europe's future—such as the enlargement of the NATO Alliance—he understood how a festering war in Bosnia would stand in the way of achieving larger strategic goals, beyond the human costs. If NATO stood aside while an ethnic conflict burned on its doorstep, why was it worth even keeping the alliance, let alone enlarging it?

As Holbrooke turned these questions over in his own mind, he began a running long-distance dialogue with his colleagues in Washington. He was a master at working the phones (at one point later in his life Holbrooke would time his calls—he wanted no single call to run over ten minutes—so he could fit more conversations into his day; despite his best effort at this small step of self-improvement, he failed utterly, and his friends and colleagues were left struggling to devise ways to get him *off* the phone). Given the time change, he would start dialing in the early afternoon, just as Washington was waking up, and the calls would go long into his night. Usually on the receiving end were his tireless friends Strobe Talbott (the deputy secretary of state), Peter Tarnoff (State's number three official and a close ally from Vietnam days), and Tom Donilon (Christopher's chief of staff).

After a while, his colleagues decided to ask him to come back to Washington to become the assistant secretary of state for Europe—the same rank he had held during the Carter administration fifteen years earlier when he had been in charge of the East Asia Bureau—to take charge of two issues: NATO enlargement, and Bosnia. Holbrooke had thrown himself into the Germany job and had come to enjoy it, but he understood that it was more important to be back in the Washington game and leading on two of the administration's priority issues. So he returned to Foggy Bottom in September 1994 (as a going-away gift, his embassy staff presented him with a bronzed beaten-up phone). And after taking his new position, the first meeting he attended was on Bosnia.

Inside the White House Situation Room, Holbrooke briefs President Clinton, Vice President Al Gore, and the national security team. (Official White House Photo, February 20, 1996)

Holbrooke jumped into the job with his usual energy. Soon he was back in the Balkans, this time not as an outside agitator but as the senior American official charged with ending the war. Yet for months it did not go well; Holbrooke found that his efforts were hindered by the limits of what the U.S. was willing to do. There was still a sense that Bosnia was primarily a European problem, and that the U.S. should not become too deeply involved. So after less than a year on the job, the policy appeared mired by indecision, and Holbrooke's frustrations were finding their way into the press.

In the summer of 1995 American policy toward Bosnia threatened to go, as Holbrooke's top deputy, Robert Frasure, described it at the time, "over the waterfall." The war was spinning out of control, and the U.S. seemed to have few options but to either declare defeat or intervene militarily. Then, in July 1995, thousands of Bosnian Muslim men and boys were massacred at the hands of Serb forces in the small valley town of Srebrenica. It was the worst war crime in Europe since World War II, and the U.S. and Europe were compelled to act. The Clinton administration began intense deliberations over what to do, and cooked up a new diplomatic initiative to end the war, with Holbrooke as the lead negotiator.

Choosing Holbrooke to lead the mission was not an easy one for some of President Clinton's senior advisers. As the assistant secretary of state for Europe, Holbrooke was the obvious choice—after all, fixing Bosnia was what he had been brought back from Germany to do. But he was high maintenance, and his maverick style made many officials uneasy.

Moreover, Holbrooke had never hidden his disdain with the direction of the administration's Bosnia policy. Earlier that year he had written in the influential journal *Foreign Affairs* that Bosnia represented "the greatest collective security failure of the West since the 1930's"—a remarkably blunt statement from a sitting official. In an attempt to convince the president to take stronger action, Holbrooke had quietly reached out to Hillary Rodham Clinton, warning her that Bosnia was a "cancer on the presidency." He considered the policy process to be, as he put it, "wheel-spinning," and a "gigantic stalemate machine" that only produced a "watered-down policy." The fact is that despite his considerable bureaucratic skills, Holbrooke was often too impatient with policy processes—he was always more effective in the field than in the Situation Room. And in any event, he doubted whether the administration had the will to implement any tough choices.

But Holbrooke clearly wanted the job. Like an athlete who always wants the last shot when the game is on the line, Holbrooke had long wanted to "test myself against the most difficult negotiations in the world . . . and the toughest seemed to be Bosnia." And he had made clear he would leave the administration if he did not get the assignment. Secretary of State Christopher, with the critical backing of Talbott, Tarnoff, and Donilon—Holbrooke's closest allies who always assumed most of the responsibility for protecting and handling their friend—supported him, and told President Clinton that he had full confidence in Holbrooke.

"I concluded that he was perfect for the task," Christopher recalled. "The very qualities for which he was sometimes criticized—aggressiveness, impolitic interaction with adversaries, a penchant for cultivating the media—were exactly what the situation required." Few could imagine a better match for the motley leaders of the Balkans, who one American official described as the "junkyard dogs"—Serbia's President Slobodan Milošević, Croatia's President Franjo Tuđjman, and Bosnian leader Alija Izetbegović—than Holbrooke. As Christopher put it,

"I knew many who would have paid money from their own pockets for ringside seats." Or, as President Clinton joked while toasting Holbrooke years later: "After all, everyone in the Balkans is crazy and everyone has a giant ego. Who else could you send?"

SO IN AUGUST 1995, HOLBROOKE BEGAN HIS SHUTTLE DIPLOMACY throughout the Balkans, leading a small team of officials from State, Defense, and the White House. On their first trip, Holbrooke's mission almost ended, when three members of his team were tragically killed as their armored personnel carrier rolled off the side of Mt. Igman as they tried to enter into Sarajevo. Holbrooke described their route as the "most dangerous road in Europe," one they had to travel because Milošević could not guarantee their safety through a more direct passage. The loss of these men—Holbrooke's top deputy, Frasure, the Defense Department's Joe Kruzel, and Colonel Nelson Drew of the National Security Council staff—galvanized Holbrooke and propelled him even further. Years later, Holbrooke would still talk about this event with deep emotion, as though it had just happened.

After taking a few days to regroup and memorialize their fallen colleagues, Holbrooke and his team restarted their efforts, not stopping until a peace agreement was signed three months later on the windswept Wright-Patterson Air Force Base in Dayton, Ohio. Holbrooke remarked that he had been preparing for this moment for most of his life; he often reflected on his experiences as the junior member of the U.S. team led by Averell Harriman and Cyrus Vance, two giants of American diplomacy and mentors to Holbrooke, who negotiated with the North Vietnamese in Paris in 1968. He constantly drew upon lessons of that experience in how he conducted the Dayton negotiations—from maintaining cohesion of his team, to how he would interact with Washington. He would not tolerate second-guessing; he insisted on having a long leash, being allowed to negotiate specifics within the broad parameters set by Washington.

The Bosnia negotiation was not a straightforward exercise. It was a highly complex negotiation, involving multiple combatants—Bosnian Muslims, Croats, Serbs, and Bosnian Serbs—as well as the European allies, the Russians, and organizations like NATO and the UN. This played well to Holbrooke's style of diplomacy, which was more like jazz than performing from a score, thus enabling him to improvise and make

A dinner at Dayton: from left, Serb leader Slobodan Milošević, Bosnian Prime Minister Haris Silajdzic, Holbrooke, Sweden's Carl Bildt, Kati. (Courtesy of Kati Marton)

decisions on the fly—whether that meant jetting around Europe at a punishing pace, holding meetings in multiple countries in one day, or convening international meetings in days that would usually take weeks to organize. This also was not a quiet, behind-the-scenes negotiation. It unfolded in the full glare of the global media spotlight, and Holbrooke, a master at diplomatic theater, relished the drama and added to it.

Holbrooke's understanding of how to wield raw power—and his comfort in doing so—proved essential. Military force played a pivotal role in the negotiating process, as for the first time NATO conducted a sustained air campaign against Bosnian Serb forces in response to a brutal attack on innocent civilians (remarkably, Bosnia was NATO's first use of force in its history). Holbrooke worked to use the bombing to his advantage, trying to calibrate his efforts to coincide with the military pressure. The strategy worked: The Serbs clearly reeled from the punishment of weeks of bombing, and Holbrooke used this moment of maximum leverage to broker the end of the Serb siege of Sarajevo—the very siege he had experienced in the carcass of a Holiday Inn on New Year's Day 1993.

The Dayton agreement is reflective of Holbrooke's ambition—and his belief that America's responsibility stretched far beyond simply getting the warring sides to lay down their arms. To be sure, Holbrooke's main objective was to end the war. But for him, a durable cease-fire was not enough. He worked to forge an agreement that would create a unified, democratic, multiethnic, and tolerant Bosnia. Holbrooke described his position as "maximalist," and as such, it elicited doubts within the U.S. government and with the allies, not to mention among the warring parties themselves. Many in Washington and Europe worried that Dayton raised expectations too high, placing too many demands on an international community to be responsible for implementation, and putting at risk thousands of American troops. In the years after Dayton, Holbrooke vigorously defended his approach, arguing that Dayton's shortcomings were mainly due to the fecklessness and half-measures by those responsible for enforcing it.

Looming over all of this was the ghost of Vietnam, which Holbrooke described as always "distant but ever present." Just as Holbrooke drew on the lessons of Munich and the 1930s to argue that the U.S. should never appease aggressors and therefore lead the effort to bring peace to Bosnia, many other political and military leaders recalled Vietnam's lesson that American troops should never again get involved in a civil conflict secondary to U.S. interests. This fundamental tension animated the Clinton administration's policy and the debate about Bosnia, and it shaped the Dayton agreement and its implementation. The 20,000 U.S. troops that went to Bosnia as part of the NATO-led force were the largest deployment since Vietnam, and many feared a similar result. But as Holbrooke often pointed out, the exact opposite happened: When American troops left Bosnia years later and handed over responsibility to a European force, not a single soldier had been killed in combat. And Bosnia, although still imperfect, was at peace.

JUST A FEW MONTHS AFTER THE CLIMAX OF THE DAYTON TALKS IN November 1995, Holbrooke, left the Clinton administration to return to New York and private life. He felt that he had done all he could on the most urgent issue of the day and did not want to return to a third-tier position in the bureaucracy. But by no means did he leave Bosnia behind. Instead, Holbrooke lined up a comfortable Wall Street sinecure largely so that he could remain a player, even if from the sidelines, in the policy debate and process.

Following Dayton, Holbrooke was and would continue to be a global figure—someone well known in Asia and Europe, and now widely celebrated as a peacemaker. He was first nominated for the Nobel Peace Prize in 1996 and appeared to be a favorite to win—he believed he was, and called anyone he could for updates and quiet lobbying—but the prize went that year to Carlos Filipe Ximenes Belo and José Ramos-Horta for their work on East Timor, an issue Holbrooke cared deeply about. Yet Holbrooke's influence did not wane; if anything, it grew. During these years, he would point out that he had access to more high officials than ever before, and that he talked to President Clinton more often now that he was outside government than when he was inside, weighed down by layers of bureaucracy and protocol. Holbrooke was constantly on the phone with his former Washington colleagues and European leaders as they wrestled with the many challenges of Dayton's implementation. And on several occasions, he was enlisted back into duty as a diplomatic trouble-shooter, returning back to the Balkans to iron out some disagreement or send a stern message.

In addition to keeping his hands in the day-to-day action, Holbrooke spent two years after Dayton writing his memoir of the negotiations, *To End a War*. Holbrooke always had a keen sense of history and his place in it, and as he set out to write the book he devoured other histories of major negotiations like Harold Nicolson's memoir of Versailles, *Peacemaking 1919*, and Henry Kissinger's voluminous memoirs. Holbrooke knew that a lasting legacy came not just from the deed itself but from the successful telling of the story—just as it had been for other great diplomats like George Kennan, Dean Acheson, and Kissinger before him. So for days Holbrooke would hole up in his apartment's book-lined study in The Beresford on Central Park West, fielding phone calls and checking in on CNN between writing paragraphs. The only other book Holbrooke had worked on had been Clark Clifford's memoirs, and he drew on the lessons of that experience—including reading the penultimate draft aloud to catch any errors and ensure that the writing was as clear as possible (it took about a week).

But the book was about more than chronicling Holbrooke's exploits. At the time, despite Dayton's success in ending the fighting, many aspects of the agreement remained controversial. With *To End a War*, Holbrooke wanted to defend Dayton while at the same time be candid about the ways it had fallen short. He also believed that the Bosnia story needed to be told urgently, because it offered important lessons for America in the post–Cold War world.

Looking back, Dayton was a turning point for the Clinton administration's foreign policy specifically and America's role in the world generally. After a terrible first few years of American inaction—in which close to 300,000 people had been killed in the former Yugoslavia—Holbrooke helped forge one of President Clinton's first foreign policy successes. In less than six months during 1995, the U.S. had taken charge of the Transatlantic Alliance, pushed NATO to use overwhelming military force, risked America's prestige on a bold diplomatic gamble, and deployed thousands of American troops to help implement the agreement.

That the administration ran such risks successfully gave it confidence going forward. This success also reinforced the logic of the administration's core strategic objective in Europe—to help create a continent "whole and free" by revitalizing and enlarging institutions like NATO. In the wake of Dayton, Clinton seemed to be a more confident foreign policy president. Holbrooke explained that after Dayton, "American foreign policy seemed more assertive, more muscular . . . Washington was now praised for its firm leadership—or even chided by some Europeans for too much leadership."

For Holbrooke, the Bosnia experience taught many lessons, but one was most important: When it comes to solving global problems, American leadership remains indispensable. America's failure to lead during the early 1990s contributed to the international community's inability to stop the crisis, but its bold action in 1995 stopped the war. As Holbrooke wrote in the final passage of *To End a War*: "The world's richest nation, one that presumes to great moral authority, cannot simply make worthy appeals to conscience and call on others to carry the burden. The world will look to Washington for more than rhetoric the next time we face a challenge to peace." It is this fundamental point that propelled Holbrooke's life and career, and it is the legacy his accomplishments and example have left.

Bosnia: The "Cleansing" Goes On

RICHARD HOLBROOKE
Washington Post, AUGUST 16, 1992

> *In early August 1992, Winston Lord, a former diplomat and then Vice Chair of the International Rescue Committee, asked Holbrooke to participate in a fact-finding trip to the Balkans. The Washington Post asked Holbrooke to write about what he saw. This was his grim assessment.*

Banja Luka, Bosnia—A trip through northern Bosnia leaves me grimly pessimistic, convinced that the situation in what was Yugoslavia is far worse than the United States and Western Europe yet realize.

This is no criticism of the many journalists now rummaging through the ruins looking for the latest horrors. Their success in uncovering and reporting the evidence of the unspeakable events that have taken place is the single reason there is still any hope at all.

Our trip—a fact-finding mission for the International Rescue Committee—was a constant struggle to get through checkpoints manned by an assortment of differently uniformed but uniformly ugly-looking police, militia and soldiers. Each checkpoint, except those run by the United Nations peace-keepers, held the constant possibility of detainment or worse. When we failed to reach one checkpoint before it closed for the day, two of our group carrying a large U.N. flag traversed the mines in no man's land to negotiate their temporary removal so we could proceed.

Not even in Vietnam at the height of the war there have I seen so many men carrying weapons and occasionally shooting them either for fun or at some real or imagined target. We passed towns and villages in which every house had been destroyed and—more ominous—some towns in which a few houses were still intact: These were houses occupied by Christian Serbs, while houses of Muslims and Croats had been methodically burned out. We drove through silent and dead towns that had once held as many as 20,000 people—every single building destroyed.

One morning this past week, we saw a relatively mild but chilling form of ethnic cleansing taking place in front of the main hotel in Banja Luka. Moslem families were signing away their homes and property in return for "permission" to leave Bosnia for Croatia or Germany. After paying a local woman—an entrepreneur in the new traffic—a substantial fee to get out of Bosnia safely, they were boarding buses, some tearfully, some with hope that they would finally escape the hell that had overtaken their ancestral homes.

For others, escape will be even more difficult. While the world is focused on the destruction of Sarajevo, the rest of Bosnia is on fire. We drove along the edge of the Bihac pocket, a large area along the Croatian border where 350,000 Moslems are trapped by the Serbs. Their destruction is only a matter of time, say the international relief workers desperately trying to find a way to get help to them.

Three conclusions leap from a brief visit. First, the prison camps and the siege of Sarajevo that have so shocked the world are only the tip of the disaster unfolding here. The real outrage is the totality of the ethnic cleansing, which has been going on for many months with little international attention and is now close to completion.

Second, what the Serbs do not do with guns, winter will do: Ethnic cleansing will become ethnic freezing. Relief efforts will be unable to protect an enormous number of people—perhaps close to 2 million—who now lack heat, shelter and even blankets for the bitter weather ahead.

Finally, the humanitarian effort that has been the focus of the outside world's concern deals with the consequences—not the cause—of this catastrophe. Obscured in the debate over whether the U.N. should authorize force to deliver relief to existing victims is the fact that there is no debate and no plan to prevent more victims from being created.

Every international relief worker here knows this awful truth and grapples with the dilemma it presents. Are they, by helping the victims of ethnic cleansing, inadvertently implementing and sanctioning it?

Beyond that lies the question of whether the world, having increased its humanitarian efforts in the former Yugoslavia, will now begin to turn away? There are so many other desperate problems elsewhere, and this one seems insoluble. Or will the leaders of the great democracies, at this moment of post-Cold War promise, recognize that Yugoslavia—along with Cambodia—poses the first and most critical test of whether the new U.N. system will work?

With Broken Glass

RICHARD HOLBROOKE

New York Times Magazine, APRIL 25, 1993

The New York Times Magazine's *editor in chief, Jack Rosenthal,
asked Holbrooke to write this story after he saw Holbrooke on
"Charlie Rose" with two small statues he had been given during
his trip to Bosnia on New Year's Day 1993 by a Bosnian survivor
of ethnic cleansing. Holbrooke was moved by the gift, a picture of
which ran with this last-page column in the magazine. Later that
summer, President Clinton would nominate Holbrooke to serve as
ambassador to Germany.*

T ell America what is happening to us."
This was in Europe today, not during World War II, in a holding
center for Bosnian Muslim refugees in Karlovac, less than an hour by
car from the Croatian capital of Zagreb, and barely an hour by plane
from the great cities of the new Europe—Rome, Zurich, Vienna, Prague,
Frankfurt, Athens.

The speaker was a young baker from Sanski Most, a town in Serb-
occupied northern Bosnia, the area that has given the world a grotesque
new·euphemism, "ethnic cleansing."

He was 28. He did not give his name, but, with his father and about
a dozen other men surrounding him, he said his mother, who was still
trapped in Bosnia, had been raped in Sanski Most while he was in
prison. The other men interrupted him to tell similar stories.

As they talked the young baker fished a small plastic bag out from
under his mattress and pressed into my hand a wooden figure he had
carefully wrapped in the dirty plastic. "I carved this with a piece of

broken glass while I was at Manjaca prison camp," he said, "to show how we had to stand during the day, with our heads down and our hands tied behind our backs." The small figure seemed to burn in my hand with its pain and intensity. Mumbling something about its power and beauty, I started to hand it back to the young baker. "No," he said, "please take it back to your country, and show it to your people. Show the Americans how we have been treated. Tell America what is happening to us."

Why Are We in Bosnia?

RICHARD HOLBROOKE
The New Yorker, MAY 18, 1998

> *Two years after leaving Washington as assistant secretary of state
> for Europe, Holbrooke was promoting his best-selling book about
> the Dayton negotiations,* To End A War, *from which this article
> is derived. A year after this piece was published, Holbrooke would
> return to the Balkans to present Milošević with an ultimatum on
> Kosovo. The subsequent NATO bombing would lead to the Serb
> president's ouster.*

By 1995, as the crisis in Bosnia approached its climax, America's
armed forces could look back proudly on the skill and courage with
which they had handled a decade of challenges in Kuwait, Panama,
Haiti, and elsewhere. But the memory of Vietnam still shadowed the
Pentagon, which was now led by men who had served as company or
field-grade officers in Southeast Asia. The lesson they drew from that
experience was eloquently summarized by General Colin Powell, who
wrote in his 1995 memoir, "Many of my generation, the career captains,
majors, and lieutenant colonels seasoned in that war, vowed that when
our turn came to call the shots, we would not quietly acquiesce in half-
hearted warfare for half-baked reasons that the American people could
not understand or support."

In addition, three post-Vietnam tragedies haunted the military: the
failed attempt to rescue the American hostages in Teheran in 1980,
which left eight Americans dead; the loss of two hundred and forty-one
marines whose barracks in Beirut were bombed in 1983; and the firefight

of October 3, 1993, when eighteen Americans, serving as part of a United Nations force in Somalia, were killed while trying to capture a clan leader. The wound from that most recent disaster was still fresh, and, together with the ghost of the much greater disaster a generation earlier, had saddled Washington's deliberations on Bosnia with what might be called a "Vietmalia syndrome."

To be sure, there were fundamental differences between Bosnia and "Vietmalia." The Bosnian Serbs were neither the disciplined, ruthless revolutionaries of North Vietnam nor the drunken, ragtag thugs who raced their "technicals" around Mogadishu, guns blazing. But discussion of such distinctions was unwelcome.

American military leaders were generally opposed to involvement in Bosnia. They feared that the mission would be "fuzzy"—imprecise, like the one in Somalia. Of course, General John Shalikashvili, the chairman of the Joint Chiefs of Staff, had made sure that the American military, if it should be ordered into action, would respond quickly and effectively. But the military regarded almost anything beyond self-protection and the carrying out of the military provisions of any peace agreement as constituting "mission creep"—that is, an undesirable broadening of their mission.

The United States, under both Presidents Bush and Clinton, had decided not to commit American soldiers to Bosnia. But there was a critical and little-noticed exception; President Clinton had pledged that American troops would support any massive withdrawal of the United Nations peacekeeping troops already stationed there. As the situation in Bosnia deteriorated dramatically in the spring of 1995, and many countries began talking openly of withdrawing from the peacekeeping force, NATO completed and formally approved a highly classified planning document that covered every aspect—from bridge-building to body bags—of the alliance's projected role in supporting a U.N. pullout. This plan, known as Operations Plan (or OPLAN) 40104, projected the participation of twenty thousand American soldiers.

In June of 1995, in my role as Assistant Secretary of State for European and Canadian Affairs, I asked for a briefing on the plan. After some initial Pentagon resistance, Air Force Lieutenant General Howell Estes III, the Pentagon operations director, came to my office and showed my deputies and me plans that left us stunned. As General Estes told us, it was bold and dangerous. American casualties, he warned, were virtually certain. To take such risks for a withdrawal, when we had not taken them to prevent "ethnic cleansing," seemed inconceivable to me.

As soon as General Estes finished, I rushed to the office of Secretary of State Warren Christopher and urged him to get the same briefing. He did so the next day, and what he heard about OPLAN 40104 left him as worried as I was. But the status of the plan remained less than clear. According to complicated Cold War–era procedures that had never been tested, OPLAN 40104 would become an operational order, adjusted for specific circumstances, if a U.N. withdrawal started. Once that order was given, American troops would be deployed in the Balkans as part of a NATO force under an American commander. But, under our Constitution, only the President of the United States—not the NATO Council or any other international body—can decide to deploy American troops. And, despite the NATO Council's approval of the plan, the President had not approved it, or even been given a formal briefing on it.

U.N. withdrawal would open the way for the greatest disaster yet for the Bosnians. Sending American ground troops to fight the war was out of the question, but something had to be done, or else a Serb victory—and more "ethnic cleansing"—was inevitable. I had long favored NATO air strikes against the Bosnian Serbs, but that proposal had run into fierce opposition from parts of the government, and throughout Europe as well. What if we refused to assist our closest allies in a withdrawal from Bosnia? That, as the British and French told us bluntly, would be a transatlantic catastrophe. It was not an overstatement to say that America's post–Cold War role in Europe was at stake. It was a terrible set of choices, but it was clear that Washington could not avoid direct involvement much longer

AS WE FACED THESE DARK PROSPECTS, JACQUES CHIRAC ARRIVED IN Washington, on June 14, 1995, for his first visit as President of France. It was not for nothing that Chirac had acquired the nickname Le Bulldozer: he was as direct and blunt as his predecessor, François Mitterrand, had been opaque and elegant. He lost no time in threatening to withdraw French troops from Bosnia unless the United States got more deeply involved.

What happened that day has been described, in slightly different form, by Bob Woodward in "The Choice." Late in the morning, we held the "pre-brief," normally a routine session to prepare the President

for an important visitor. It quickly degenerated into an angry, contentious discussion of Bosnia. The initial presentation seemed, in my
view, misleading about the desperate nature of the situation, and
especially about the likely consequences and complications of America's
promise to assist a UN withdrawal. When I began to set forth the
implications of OPLAN 40104, the President, obviously disturbed
that he was receiving contradictory information so soon before his
meeting with Chirac, cut me off. Vice-President Al Gore intervened
with a pithy summation of the situation—the most accurate, in my
view, at the meeting. Then, as people offered differing views, Christopher
and I had to excuse ourselves, in order to go to the French Embassy,
where Chirac was expecting us for lunch. In the car, Christopher and I,
astonished at what had just happened, agreed that we had to talk to the
President again as soon as possible about the true status of the NATO
planning process.

The rest of the day was hectic. The President met alone with Chirac
for well over an hour, instead of the scheduled twenty minutes, while
Gore, Christopher, and half the American Cabinet waited in the Cabinet
Room. The President asked Chirac to visit the Senate Majority Leader,
Bob Dole, and the Speaker of the House, Newt Gingrich, hoping that
the French President would be able to persuade the Republican leaders
to give the Administration greater support on Bosnia. Chirac's meetings
on the Hill, while cordial, changed nothing. He then returned to the
White House for a small "family" dinner, which was spent, for the most
part, in conversation about subjects other than Bosnia.

After Chirac left I stood in the main entrance hall of the White
House, in front of the North Portico, with Christopher, Samuel
(Sandy) Berger, who was then the deputy national security advisor, and
Madeleine Albright, who was then the American Ambassador to the
U.N. The President and the First Lady danced briefly to the music of a
Marine Band ensemble that had played during dinner, and then they
walked over to us. It was a beautiful June evening, and the White House
glowed with its special magic. I looked at Christopher, concerned that
we would lose the moment. He nodded. The President broke the ice.
"What about Bosnia?" he asked suddenly, looking at me.

"I hate to ruin a wonderful dinner, Mr. President," I began, "but
we should clarify something that came up during the day. I'm afraid
that we may not have that much flexibility left. Under existing NATO

plans, the United States is already committed to sending troops to Bosnia if the U.N. decides to withdraw."

"What do you mean?" the President asked me. "I'll decide the troop issue if and when the time comes."

There was silence for a moment. "Mr. President," I said, "NATO has already approved the withdrawal plan. While you can always stop it, it has a high degree of automaticity built into it, especially since we have committed ourselves publicly to assisting the NATO troops if they decide to withdraw."

The President looked at Christopher. "Is this true?" he asked.

"Yes, it appears to be," Christopher said tersely.

"I suggest that we talk about it again tomorrow," the President said, and he walked off without another word, holding Mrs. Clinton's hand.

THE NEXT DAY, AS HE FLEW TO HALIFAX FOR A G-7 SUMMIT, THE President began to press for better options; he understood that sending troops to Bosnia to implement a failure was unacceptable. But events in Bosnia were moving faster than the policy-review process in Washington. While the Administration deliberated, the Bosnian Serbs went on the attack again. This time, their actions would horrify the world.

General Ratko Mladić, the commander of the Bosnian Serb Army, now focused pressure on three isolated Muslim enclaves in eastern Bosnia—Srebrenica, Zepa, and Gorazde—that had been completely surrounded by Serb forces since early in the war. A small number of U.N. peacekeepers had been sent to each enclave, but they had been bottled up, unable to relieve the siege conditions of the three towns. Mladić decided to eliminate the enclaves from the map.

On July 6, 1995, his forces began shelling Srebrenica. What took place over the next ten days was the biggest single mass murder in Europe since the Second World War. The outside world did nothing effective to stop the tragedy. Precise details of the atrocities were not known at the time, but there was no doubt that something truly horrible was going on. By coincidence, I soon had an additional source of information about Srebrenica beyond the official reporting; my younger son, Anthony, who was twenty-five, had gone to Tuzla that week to help interview refugees. Anthony had been working in a refugee camp in Thailand when the president of Refugees International, Lionel Rosenblatt, summoned him to Bosnia. Anthony and Rosenblatt arrived in central Bosnia just as the first, desperate survivors from Srebrenica and Zepa reached the safety of the Muslim-controlled airfield outside Tuzla. They were joined by two key State Department officials: John Shattuck, the Assistant Secretary for Human Rights, and Phyllis Oakley, the Assistant Secretary for Population, Refugees, and Migration.

Together, the four of them interviewed shell-shocked survivors of Srebrenica and heard the stories that would soon horrify the world: how the Serbs, directed by General Mladić, had rounded up all the Muslims in the town and piled them into buses; how most of the men were never seen again; how people were herded onto soccer fields and school grounds and killed in large numbers; how men in the thousands were still trying to escape through the woods toward Tuzla.

On July 13th, as the Serbs were systematically killing Muslims, President Chirac called President Clinton. He said that something had to be done, and proposed that American helicopters carry French troops into Srebrenica to relieve the town. This proposal had already been discussed through official French channels and had run into fierce opposition from the British and the Pentagon and also from Chirac's own generals. It had no chance of being accepted.

No more energy was left in the international system. Everywhere one turned, there was numb confusion in the face of the Bosnian Serbs' brutality. The first line of opposition to any air strike against the Serbs—which I recommended—was the Dutch government, which refused to consider air strikes until all its soldiers were out of Bosnia. Through every channel available, in London, Paris, and NATO headquarters, we pressed for some response, but the Europeans had reached their limits: with their own soldiers at risk, they were not going to agree to any action that endangered the Dutch. The Serbs knew this and held the bulk of the Dutch forces captive in the UN compound at the nearby village of Potocari until their own forces had finished their dirty work at Srebrenica. According to the International Committee of the Red Cross, the toll of Muslims dead or missing and presumed dead in Srebrenica was seven thousand three hundred. Most of the victims had been unarmed, and almost all had died in ambushes and mass executions. Nothing else in the war had matched, or ever would match, Srebrenica. The name would become part of the language of the horrors of modern war, alongside Lidice, Oradour, Babi Yar, and the Katyn Forest.

THE DESTRUCTION OF SREBRENICA WAS AN ENORMOUS SHOCK TO THE Western alliance, and to the conscience of the West. President Clinton pressed his national-security team once again to make an all-out effort to bring peace to Bosnia. As a result, in early August of 1995, after more bureaucratic twists, a last-ditch diplomatic effort was launched, which I was asked to lead. Less than a week into that effort, three of the four members of our negotiating team—Robert Frasure, Joseph Kruzel, and Nelson Drew—were killed when their vehicle, travelling some fifty yards behind mine, slipped off the narrow and dangerous Mt. Igman road as we tried to reach Sarajevo, the besieged capital of Bosnia.

The deaths of these three highly respected and treasured colleagues wrenched the Washington policy discussions into focus. And then—on August 28, 1995, the day our newly reconstituted team resumed the diplomatic shuttle—the Bosnian Serbs killed some thirty-eight people in the Sarajevo marketplace with a single mortar shell. It was, at last, an outrage too far. Within forty-eight hours, under urging from President Clinton and with strong support from our negotiating team, NATO finally did what it should have done years earlier: it launched massive air strikes against Bosnian Serb positions.

Events now accelerated dramatically. We negotiated a lifting of the siege of Sarajevo in mid-September and a general ceasefire in early October. On November 1, 1995, at Wright-Patterson Air Force Base, outside Dayton, Ohio, we convened a risky, all-or-nothing peace conference involving all three Balkan Presidents and senior diplomatic representatives from Russia, Great Britain, France, Germany, and the European Union. For twenty-one days, we cajoled, harassed, and pressured the participants, coming to the very brink of failure on the morning of the last day. Finally, on November 21st, after a last-minute intervention by President Clinton, the three Balkan Presidents initialled the Dayton Peace Agreement.

Dayton marked a turning point in America's post–Cold War role in Europe. It put an end not only to the war in Bosnia but also to several years of widespread concern that the United States was in the process of turning its back on Europe. Even America's harshest critics acknowledged that without the Administration's leadership the war would have ended disastrously—and only after much more carnage.

BUT DAYTON WAS NOT THE END OF THE STORY. ON PAPER, IT WAS A GOOD agreement; it called for a single, multiethnic country and a central government. Countless diplomatic agreements, however, survive only as case studies in failed expectations. Dayton's true place in history would be determined by its implementation.

Dayton's first military deadlines were met easily, and without incident. The first major civilian deadline of the Dayton agreement—and in many ways the most important—was the unification of Sarajevo, which took place on schedule, on March 19, 1996. But on the eve of that achievement the Bosnian Serbs exploited the passivity of the NATO-led Implementation Force, or IFOR, to reassert themselves. Two weeks before Sarajevo's scheduled unification, in a cynically brutal act designed to reinforce ethnic partition, the Bosnian Serb leadership began to order all Serbs in the Sarajevo area—some forty thousand or more—to burn down their own apartments and leave the city. Detailed instructions were broadcast on how to set the fires: pile all the furniture in the middle of the room, douse it with kerosene, turn the gas on, and throw a match into the room as you leave. Often, those Sarajevo Serbs who resisted were beaten by Serb thugs who roamed the streets, while NATO troops stood by. The result was a severe blow to the multiethnic country called for at Dayton, and it would take more than sixteen months to undo the damage.

Even when a President is reelected, his Administration goes through a transition period, although it may be mostly invisible to the public. At the beginning of 1997, the Clinton Administration effected a smooth transition in most areas, and especially at State, where the new Secretary, Madeleine Albright, was familiar with the major issues from her U.N. tour, and on the National Security Council, where Sandy Berger simply moved up to replace Tony Lake as national security advisor. (Although I had left the government in February of 1996 to return to private life in New York, I would continue to work closely with the Administration on Bosnia, returning three times to assist my former colleagues.)

At State, Albright's well-known tough line on Bosnia made her the ideal person to reinvigorate the policy. Nonetheless, by April of 1997 there was a general impression that "Clinton II" was downgrading Bosnia; the emphasis in Europe was almost entirely on a critical summit meeting with Boris Yeltsin, planned for Helsinki, that would determine the future of the Administration's plan to enlarge NATO. Sensing that high-level American interest had declined, Radovan Karadžić, the indicted war criminal who had founded the Bosnian Serb Republic, ventured once more into public view, flagrantly violating a July 18, 1996, agreement he had negotiated with me, in which he had pledged to withdraw "permanently" from public life. His reëmergence went unchallenged by NATO, and suggested, as many journalists noted, that NATO was simply counting the days until its forces left. But as soon as the Helsinki summit ended successfully, with Yeltsin's acceptance of a larger NATO, President Clinton focused again on Bosnia, ordering a full-scale review of American policy.

At about that time, Liz Stevens gave a combined birthday party in honor of her husband, the filmmaker George Stevens, Jr., and my wife, the writer Kati Marton—a party that would have unexpected policy consequences. On arriving early, we found Secret Service agents all over the house. Without telling us, Liz had invited the Clintons, and a few minutes later, ahead of the other guests, they walked in.

To be precise, Hillary walked; the President limped in, on crutches. A month earlier, he had taken a nasty fall outside the home of the golfer Greg Norman. As it happened, I had injured myself at about the same time, tearing ligaments in my ankle, and I, too, was on crutches. We spent a few minutes comparing our rehabilitation programs. As he left, the President pulled me aside for a moment and said, "Come by tomorrow and we can do some therapy and talk."

The next day, I presented myself at the White House and was ushered upstairs to the family quarters, where I found the President pedalling away on a stationary bicycle. We worked out together in silence for a while. Then we adjourned to another room to cool down. Members of the family, including Hillary and her mother, Dorothy Rodham, stopped to chat. Just as I was starting to wonder if we would ever get around to talking about Bosnia, the President said, "Let's go downstairs." With that, we hobbled down to his office in the family quarters.

"What's going on out there?" the President began. It is in the nature of the hierarchical structure of the executive branch that a conversation like the one we then proceeded to have—informal, candid, and alone—would have been next to impossible while I was still in the government; there are simply too many layers between an assistant secretary and the Chief Executive. I had decided, at the enthusiastic urging of Strobe Talbott, to be as frank as I could. I listed the series of reverses and lost opportunities since December.

"While NATO enlargement and your achievement with Yeltsin have been historic, Bosnia has gone nowhere," I said. "These issues are interrelated. People out there are not even sure we still support Dayton, or still care what happens in Bosnia."

I URGED THE PRESIDENT TO GIVE HIS FULL BACKING TO ALBRIGHT AND Robert Gelbard, a career diplomat whom Albright had chosen to be the "czar" for implementation of Dayton. I had first asked Gelbard, a tough, no-nonsense official, to visit Bosnia at the end of 1995. His assumption, in April of 1997, of full-time responsibility for implementing the Dayton agreement would soon produce results, and he and I would make a productive trip to the region together in August of 1997 to accelerate the process.

When the President visited Sarajevo, last December, he said that implementation was running about a year behind schedule—a judgment that coincided with my own. But the situation in Bosnia has greatly improved. There has been no fighting for two years; the three communities have begun rebuilding ties at the local level; Sarajevo, reunified, is rebuilding; large quantities of weapons have been destroyed; four airports have opened for civilian traffic; numerous refugee "open cities" have been created; the odious Bosnian-Serb television transmitters, once Karadžić's greatest asset, have finally been seized by NATO and turned over to broadcasters who are not preaching race hate; Banja Luka, the center of a new, more moderate Serb leadership, has grown in strength. And all this has been done without a single NATO soldier being killed or wounded by hostile action since Dayton.

In January, a new moderate Bosnian Serb, Milorad Dodik, was named Prime Minister of the Serb portion of Bosnia, and pledged full compliance with the Dayton agreement. When the Karadžić forces threatened a coup against him, NATO moved rapidly, in a manner not previously seen, to head off the threat. If such actions continue, the anti-Dayton forces will be progressively weakened, and the chances of creating a viable multiethnic state will improve dramatically.

Still, while the blood lust of 1991–95 has subsided, it is not gone; people on all sides carry deep scars, and many continue to seek revenge instead of reconciliation. Most troubling, the same leaders who started the war are still trying to silence those who call for multiethnic coöperation. The two most dangerous men in the region, the indicted war criminals Karadžić and Mladić, remain at large more than two years after Dayton.

If the United States does not lead, its European allies could falter as they did in the early part of this decade. Indeed, since earlier this year, the old pattern has threatened to repeat itself; in Kosovo, an Albanian Muslim region in Serbia, Serbian police have cracked down on ethnic Albanians. This time, though, the United States immediately condemned the aggressors, and Secretary of State Albright called for fresh sanctions against Belgrade. "We will keep all options open to do what is necessary to prevent another wave of violence from overtaking the Balkans," she said in March. As Kosovo reminded us, there will be other Bosnias in our lives.

Foreword to *The Road to the Dayton Accords*

RICHARD HOLBROOKE
FROM *The Road to the Dayton Accords*, BY DEREK CHOLLET

> *In this foreword, Holbrooke reflects on the Dayton agreement and
> the intense negotiations that led to it with the benefit of ten years of
> hindsight. Holbrooke proves to be a fierce defender of the agreement
> but open about its flaws. The "hypocrisy" he references in the last
> paragraph—with Western officials pledging "never again" while
> two notorious war criminals, Radovan Karadžić and Ratko
> Mladić, remained at large—would be solved when both were
> apprehended and shipped off to The Hague: Karadžić in 2008,
> and Mladić in 2011, after Holbrooke's death.*

There were over thirty ceasefires and agreements in Bosnia prior to
the Dayton Peace Accords. All of them collapsed. Yet what was
agreed upon at Dayton not only survived, it established the basis for a
country that, with all its problems, is moving forward, however painfully,
towards becoming a peaceful participant in twenty-first-century Europe.

In the ten years since Dayton—the name of the city has become not
only a simple shorthand for the entire Bosnian peace process, but an
internationally understood metaphor for taking an aggressive, engaged
approach to conflict resolution—there have been numerous negotiations
in conflict areas around the world which have not been successful, most
notably of course, in the Middle East. Dayton, therefore, has contemporary relevance not because of the inherent drama in the negotiation—
although there was plenty of that—but because it succeeded; in short,
it ended a war.

By the time negotiations began behind a high barbed-wire fence at
the Wright-Patterson Air Force Base on November 1, 1995, the Bosnian

war had become the worst in Europe since 1945, posing a real and present threat to the stability of post–Cold War Europe. Parts of Bosnia were becoming a sanctuary for Islamic terrorists, some of whom belonged to an organization whose name was still unknown in the West, Al-Qaeda. Criminal gangs ran much of the country, sometimes pretending to be nationalist movements. The Bosnian Serbs were openly seeking the destruction of Europe's largest Muslim community in an ancient homeland—a clear case of genocide. And most Bosnian Croats would not have objected if the Serbs had succeeded. A "war within a war" between Croats and Muslims had destroyed most of the once beautiful medieval city of Mostar and its historic bridge. Refugees by the hundreds of thousands had fled to Western Europe, overburdening the resources of countries such as Germany, Switzerland, and Austria.

Yet, for the four preceding years, the European Union and the United States had done little to stop the war. Their mediation efforts were puny and poorly coordinated; NATO was involved only as an accessory to a pathetic UN effort, which the UN's own Secretary General, Boutros Boutros-Ghali, did everything he could to hamper and undermine. Both Washington and Brussels refused to even threaten, let alone use, decisive force against Bosnian Serb aggression. In 1993, when President Clinton briefly considered a more aggressive policy (as he had called for as a candidate the previous year), a majority of Congress, as well as most of the American military, led by a towering Washington figure, the Chairman of the Joint Chiefs of Staff, General Colin Powell, arrayed themselves in opposition. Even after the Dayton Accords ended the fighting almost three years later, an overwhelming majority of the American public still opposed using U.S. troops to help enforce the peace and there were predictions, many from leaders of the foreign policy elite, that Dayton would fail, and that in any case it was not worth its risks and costs.

My generation had been taught in school that Munich and the Holocaust were the benchmark horrors of the 1930s. Leaders of the Atlantic alliance had repeatedly pledged it would never happen again. Yet between 1991 and 1995 it *did* happen again—not only in the Balkans, but also in Rwanda, where an even greater number of people—an estimated 800,000—were killed for purely ethnic reasons in an even shorter period of time.

Bosnia was, as I wrote at the time, "the greatest collective security failure of the West [in Europe] since the 1930s." Rwanda was even worse. How could all this have happened at the end of the twentieth century, in the middle of Europe—and could it happen again?

Bosnia cannot be understood except in its precise historical context: the pre-September 11, 2001, world. In the decade before 9/11, Americans had turned away from the outside world after 60 years of continuous and expensive international involvement, from Pearl Harbor to the disintegration of the Soviet Union at the end of 1991. Americans were proud, of course, that their sacrifices had succeeded in defeating both fascism and communism during that long period, but they were exhausted and ready to turn inward.

Of course, we will never know what America would have done if Bosnia had occurred after September 11, 2001—9/11 made Americans far more willing to support American military interventions in far-away lands, not only in a situation as clear-cut as Afghanistan, but even in Iraq, which had no involvement in the terrorist attacks on New York and Washington. But we are dealing here with pre-9/11 realities. It was not a coincidence that the three greatest disasters of international peacekeeping, disasters that almost brought the United Nations down—Somalia, Rwanda, and Bosnia—all occurred in the decade between the end of the Cold War and 9/11; call it, if you will, "the interwar years."

Sometimes, however, a horrific event can force even the most reluctant people to action. In the summer of 1995, over 7,000 Muslims, including some women and children, were butchered in an isolated town in eastern Bosnia called Srebrenica, while UN peacekeepers from The Netherlands stood by helplessly and NATO refused to intervene. I argued then, and still believe today, that NATO airstrikes would have stopped the Bosnian Serbs, who preferred long-range artillery and short-range murder to anything resembling a real military operation. But London, Paris, and The Hague were fearful for the safety of their own troops, and refused suggestions for military actions until their forces had left the three "safe areas" they had pledged to protect.

President Clinton recognized immediately that, although the American people still would not like it, the United States could no longer avoid involvement. His choice boiled down to this: either assist the UN peacekeeping force in a humiliating withdrawal, or else make an all-out American effort to end the war on terms that protected the beleaguered Muslim community.

So in August 1995, President Clinton launched the diplomatic effort described in vivid detail in this book. It must be stressed that, at the time we began our shuttle diplomacy, no one in Washington imagined that the diplomatic effort would be accompanied by a NATO bombing campaign. That was a result of two events that occurred in the first few days of our travels: the death on Mount Igman on August 19 of three of the five members of my original negotiating team—Bob Frasure, Joe Kruzel, and Nelson Drew—and the Sarajevo marketplace shelling nine days later. These two events rocked the administration (the men who died were extremely popular in Washington, and we paid them emotional farewells at Arlington Cemetery) and changed, in intangible ways, Washington's sense of personal involvement in the war. After the funerals, President Clinton immediately sent me back to the Balkans with a new team, including then Lt. General Wesley Clark, my military adviser and original team member who represented the Joint Chiefs of Staff; Chris Hill, a State Department colleague then on the cusp of a brilliant diplomatic career; Jim Pardew, a tough former Army officer representing the civilian side of the Pentagon; then Brigadier General Donald Kerrick, representing the White House; and Roberts Owen, our wise legal adviser whom we affectionately called "mad dog."

What is remarkable, especially in hindsight, is that strong political opposition to putting American resources, especially troops, into Bosnia continued even after a combination of American airpower and American leadership brought the war to a negotiated conclusion at Dayton. Despite this agreement, which achieved all of the primary objectives of the United States and Europe, there were questions from almost every quarter of the American body politic about President Clinton's decision to send 20,000 American troops to Bosnia as part of the 60,000-strong NATO implementing force. In a national poll taken right after Dayton, only 36 percent of the American public supported sending troops; it was by far the lowest support that President Clinton had on any issue at that time.

Opposition to the deployment was fueled by widespread predictions that Dayton would fail, and that, after the disastrous and bloody experience of the UN peacekeeping force in Bosnia, American casualties would be similarly heavy. "It's not going to work," said America's most respected senior statesman, Henry Kissinger, summarizing a widely held view just after the agreement had been signed. "When you're asking

Americans to die, you have to be able to explain it in terms of the national interest. I see no vital United States interest to support a combat mission there." A month later, Kissinger changed his position, but only slightly. "The only valid purpose for American troops in there," he said, "is to move into a demilitarized zone between the warring parties. We should not risk American lives in nation-building, peacemaking, creating political institutions." His comments were echoed by many on both the liberal and conservative sides of the political spectrum.

The opposition did not let up. In a stunning repudiation of the Administration, the House of Representatives—Newt Gingrich's House, with its Contract for America calling for a strong American national security policy—approved by a lopsided vote of 287 to 141 a bizarre resolution opposing the President's Bosnia policy but "supporting the troops." During the debate, members of Congress waved copies of *Time* magazine, its cover story captioned, "Is Bosnia worth dying for?" In a comment typical of the hostility among most Republicans, Senator Phil Gramm from Texas attacked the Dayton agreement almost as soon as it was signed. "Adding American names to the casualty lists cannot save Bosnia," he said.

There was also trouble in the Pentagon. Secretary of Defense Bill Perry publicly predicted casualties on roughly the same scale as the 1991 war against Iraq, or the failed UN peacekeeping mission in Bosnia. The American military feared Bosnia would be another quagmire. For the older officers, including the Joint Chiefs of Staff themselves, Vietnam was a distant but ever present ghost. (My own three years there, as a Foreign Service Officer working on the pacification effort in the Mekong Delta and Saigon, had marked me deeply, but I felt that the differences between Vietnam and Bosnia were fundamental.) The most notable exceptions were Wesley Clark, who had very close ties to Powell's successor as the Chairman of the Joint Chiefs, General John Shalikashvili, and Donald Kerrick, then on the NSC staff. Clark and Kerrick understood the issues well, and argued courageously with officers senior in rank over the need for very strong "rules of engagement" for NATO.

It therefore took real political courage for President Clinton to send American troops to Bosnia. This was the most important decision in regard to Europe of his presidency, opposed, incidentally, by most of his political advisers. Bill Clinton has not received as much credit as he deserves for this classic Commander-in-Chief decision, which he made alone, without Congressional support, and only reluctant backing from the Pentagon. But it worked; without those 20,000 troops, Bosnia would not have survived, several million refugees would still be wandering the face of Western Europe today, a criminal state would be in power in parts of Bosnia itself—and we would probably have fought Operation Enduring Freedom not only in Afghanistan but also in the deep ravines and dangerous hills of central Bosnia.

Large numbers of body bags—as always, the exact number was a closely guarded military secret—had been prepared for the casualties that the Pentagon believed were certain to come. But in the end, none of the body bags were ever used for combat-related deaths; not one NATO soldier was killed from hostile action in Bosnia. This was due, in large part, to the authority given to NATO in the Dayton agreement: to shoot first and ask questions later—the exact opposite of the sorry rules of engagement under which the UN peacekeeping mission had operated and suffered so many casualties. NATO was thus respected from the very beginning—a vital lesson, I hope, for any future operations involving international peacekeepers.

Seven years ago, I wrote, "On paper, Dayton was a good agreement; it ended the war and established a single multiethnic country. But countless peace agreements have survived only in history books as case studies in failed expectations. The results of the international effort to implement Dayton would determine its true place in history."

Events since support this view. *Vigorous implementation is the key to the success of any ceasefire or peace agreement.* One cannot depend on the voluntary compliance or goodwill of recently warring parties. Force must be used, if necessary (and better early than late) to demonstrate that the agreement must be respected and will be enforced. And while Bosnia is at peace today and moving slowly forward, it would be in much better shape if the initial implementation effort had been more aggressive. "The start," as I wrote at the time, "was rocky."

The international community, including, I regret to say, NATO, did not use its authority enough in the crucial initial phase, the months right after Dayton. NATO was fine in force protection—that is, protecting itself—an important and necessary goal, particularly if compared to the substantial American casualties suffered in Afghanistan and Iraq. But several failures of the NATO command left a permanent mark on the land, inhibiting more rapid progress even today. The first and most important was the failure not to seek the immediate arrest of the two leading Bosnian Serb war criminals, Radovan Karadžić and General Ratko Mladić. These two men, who were still at large ten years later, were most vulnerable right after Dayton, but the opportunity was essentially lost after the NATO commander in Bosnia, U.S. Admiral Leighton Smith, told Bosnian Serb television, "I don't have the authority to arrest anybody." This statement, which was a deliberately incorrect reading of his authority under Dayton, constituted a devastating invitation to Karadžić to resume his political activities, which he did with a vengeance until a subsequent agreement, which I negotiated in the summer of 1996, finally drove him underground. Incredibly, as of the summer of 2005, Karadžić was still moving secretly across the Balkans, supported and hidden by a network of Serb sympathizers that undoubtedly included core members of his political party, the SDS, as well as hard-core monks in the Serb church. His continued freedom, no matter how constrained, was a daily challenge to progress in Bosnia. (After President Clinton left office, he told me that he considered Smith's behavior to have verged on "insubordination.")

The lesson is, I hope, clear: once the United States is committed in such a perilous project, it cannot afford halfway, tentative measures— "in for a dime, in for a dollar," sums it up accurately. To this day, this lesson has not been applied adequately in the Balkans.

In hindsight, there were many other things we could have done better before, during, and after Dayton. I still regret, for example, agreeing to let the Bosnian Serbs keep the name "Republika Srpska" for their entity. Bosnian President Alija Izetbegović was right when he told me it was a "Nazi name"; we should have tried harder to change it, for practical and symbolic reasons. On the other hand, I should not have acceded to a strange Izetbegović request, nine months after Dayton, to allow the SDS (Karadžić's party) to remain a legal party. Instead, we should have disenfranchised it before the first Bosnian elections in September 1996, despite Izetbegović's statement to me that, while he hated the SDS, he "could work with them." Two weeks before he died, lying in a hospital bed in Sarajevo in October 2003, he told me that he thought I was "joking [in 1996] about dismantling the SDS." If that was the real reason for his position against shutting down that criminal party, it was a costly misunderstanding. The SDS has been the main promoter of divisive ethnic politics in Bosnia, while providing the core of the network that has pro-tected Karadžić. If we had banned it and forced it underground, things would be better today, even if parts of it resurfaced under a different name.

A serious mistake was permitting one country to have three armies. It is obvious that such a situation cannot be allowed in a single country. But in 1995, NATO refused to accept responsibility for dismantling the three ethnic armies and creating a single, integrated force, something General Clark and I thought was eminently possible. Yet the NATO high command inaccurately thought it would be dangerous work and refused to allow it in the Dayton agreement. In recent years, NATO be-latedly recognized the necessity of dealing with this problem, and has begun slowly to integrate the army, creating a single defense ministry and an integrated senior staff and command. But under the 2005 reor-ganization, units are still organized on an ethnic basis at the battalion level. This is not a true solution to the problem. The military—and the police, whose reform has been even more difficult—must eventually be organized without regard to ethnicity down to the lowest levels if Bosnia is ever to function without an international security force.

At the end of 2004 that international security presence was trans-formed from a NATO force (SFOR) into a European Union force (EUFOR). This received almost no attention in the United States, and not much in Europe. But it represented a major evolution, not only in Bosnia but in regard to the NATO-EU relationship. I felt at the time that NATO's departure (except for a small NATO "office") should not have taken place until Karadžić and Mladić were in custody. Yet the pres-sure of deployments in Iraq and Afghanistan far larger and longer than anticipated was taking its toll on the American military, and Secretary of Defense Donald Rumsfeld insisted on the change, despite quiet mis-givings expressed by Bosnians. Ironically, the change also suited the long-term French goal of reducing the EU's dependency on NATO, and thus made Rumsfeld and French President Jacques Chirac unlikely bed-fellows on this issue. EUFOR deserves close study to see if it works, but its initial effect was dearly unfortunate: it left the impression that the United States, the only power universally respected in the Balkans, was starting to depart, thus giving encouragement to the obstructionists in Srpska and weakening moderates everywhere.

In the spring of 2005, the new Secretary of State, Condoleezza Rice, placed Balkan policy (including Kosovo) in the hands of her Undersecretary of State, Nicholas Burns, a highly capable professional diplomat who had been at Dayton. This upgrading of the importance of the region—which Rice and Burns confirmed to me in private meetings—was welcome news in a region that respects the United States above all other nations, because without a revitalized American policy, Bosnia and Kosovo will drift aimlessly.

I hope students of conflict resolution will examine the Dayton negotiations carefully, not because they were successful, but to learn what might be applied to other problems. Of course, few other negotiators will have the added leverage that comes with bombing one of the parties, and not all negotiators will be able to lock up the leaders of the contending sides on an American military base. But much can be accomplished without such unusual incentives. To me, the key ingredient is leadership—determined leadership from the world's leading nation, with the clear backing of its allies. Assembling and holding together a coalition of friends is sometimes harder than fighting an enemy, as the current U.S. Administration learned in Iraq. It is often forgotten that it was not easy in Bosnia either; as this book shows, frictions within the Contact Group and the NATO alliance were at times almost unbearable. But the effort has to be made, for the returns are enormous, especially when there is an expectation that other countries will foot the larger part of the reconstruction or nonmilitary bill. This was, of course, the case in Bosnia, as it is in most other parts of the world today, notably including Africa.

It was a huge honor to be part of the team that ended the war in Bosnia. Like the band of brothers Henry V spoke to before the battle of Agincourt, whatever else we do, each of us will remember those amazing days for the rest of our lives.

Ten years after Srebrenica, on July 11, 2005, I found myself back in that valley of evil, as part of the official American delegation appointed by President George W. Bush to represent the nation. It was a moving moment; I walked through muddy hills under a leaden sky as widows and mothers buried almost 700 recently identified remains, their grief undiminished by a decade.

But there had definitely been progress. When I had last visited Srebrenica five years before, ten brave—one might say, recklessly brave—Muslim families had returned, living among 12,000 Serbs who had taken over old Muslim houses. By July 2005, however, over 4,000 Muslims had returned and an equal number of Serbs had left. This was astonishing, and more of the same seemed certain if the international community stayed involved.

It was also a day filled with irony and high drama. From Belgrade and Banja Luka came senior Serb leaders who laid wreaths at the memorial, an appropriate silent acknowledgment of a great war crime. Our route into Srebrenica, and the security itself, was the responsibility of the entity we were in, which happened to be the Republika Srpska. The police—presumably including some who had been involved in the murderous events of 1995—were respectful, if not exactly enthusiastic; they saluted as we passed and, more importantly, treated the endless line of victim families with correct politeness. An event that could have exploded into violence was incident-free (although a large bomb had been found at the site a few days earlier).

Unfortunately, it was also a day for hypocrisy. Senior European, American, and international officials spoke, some apologizing for the past failures, all pledging, as usual, that it must never ever happen again—and that the hunt for Karadžić and Mladić would be pursued with implacable determination. Then they got into their sedans and helicopters and went home.

The Face of Evil

Richard Holbrooke
Washington Post, July 23, 2008

> *Radovan Karadžić, who ordered the massacre at Srebenica, was
> a longtime antagonist for Holbrooke. Two days after Karadžić
> was finally arrested on war crimes charges in Belgrade, Holbrooke
> published this column describing his only meeting with the geno-
> cidaire. Around the same time, Karadžić publicly claimed that
> Holbrooke promised him immunity if he stepped away from Serb
> politics, a claim Holbrooke accurately labeled "a flat-out lie."*

S tanding with Slobodan Milošević on the veranda of a government
hunting lodge outside Belgrade, I saw two men in the distance. They
got out of their twin Mercedeses and, in the fading light, started toward
us. I felt a jolt go through my body; they were unmistakable. Ratko
Mladić in combat fatigues, stocky, walking as though through a muddy
field; and Radovan Karadžić, taller, wearing a suit, with his wild, but
carefully coiffed, shock of white hair.

The capture of Karadžić on Monday took me back to a long night
of confrontation, drama and negotiations almost 13 years ago—the only
time I ever met him. It was 5 p.m. on Sept. 13, 1995, the height of the
war in Bosnia. Finally, after years of weak Western and U.N. response
to Serb aggression and ethnic cleansing of Muslims and Croats in
Bosnia, U.S.-led NATO bombing had put the Serbs on the defensive.
Our small diplomatic negotiating team—which included then-Lt. Gen.
Wesley K. Clark and Christopher Hill (now the senior U.S. envoy to

North Korea)—was in Belgrade for the fifth time, trying to end a war that had already taken the lives of nearly 300,000 people.

These three men—Milošević, Mladić and Karadžić—were the primary reason for that war. Mladić and Karadžić had already been indicted as war criminals by the International Tribunal for the Former Yugoslavia. (Milošević was not to be indicted until 1999.) As leaders of the breakaway Bosnian Serb movement, they had met with many Western luminaries, including Jimmy Carter.

But, in a change of strategy, the negotiating team had decided to marginalize Karadžić and Mladić and to force Milošević, as the senior Serb in the region, to take responsibility for the war and the negotiations we hoped would end it. Now Milošević wanted to bring the two men back into the discussions, probably to take some of the pressure off himself.

We had anticipated this moment and agreed in advance that, while we would never ask to meet with Karadžić and Mladić, if Milošević offered such a meeting, we would accept—but only once, and only under strict guidelines that would require Milošević to be responsible for their behavior.

I had told each member of our negotiating team to decide for himself or herself whether to shake hands with the mass murderers. I hated these men for what they had done. Their crimes included, indirectly, the deaths of three of our colleagues—Bob Frasure, Joe Kruzel and Nelson Drew, who had died when the armored personnel carrier they were in plunged down a ravine as we attempted to reach Sarajevo by the only route available, a dangerous dirt road that went through sniper-filled, Serbian-controlled territory.

I did not shake hands, although both Karadžić and Mladić tried to. Some of our team did; others did not. Mladić, not Karadžić, was the dominant figure that evening. He engaged in staring contests with some of our team as we sat across the table. Karadžić was silent at first. He had a large face with heavy jowls, a soft chin and surprisingly gentle eyes. Then, when he heard our demand that the siege of Sarajevo be lifted immediately, he exploded. Rising from the table, the American-educated Karadžić raged in passable English about the "humiliations" his people were suffering. I reminded Milošević that he had promised that this sort of harangue would not occur. Karadžić responded emotionally that he would call former president Carter, with whom he said he was in touch, and started to leave the table. For the only time that long night,

I addressed Karadžić directly, telling him that we worked only for President Bill Clinton and that he could call President Carter if he wished but that we would leave and that the bombing would intensify. Milošević said something to Karadžić in Serbian; he sat down again, and the meeting got down to business.

After 10 hours, we reached an agreement to lift the siege, after more than three years of war. The next day, we finally were able to fly into the reopened airfield in Sarajevo. The indomitable city was already beginning to come back to life. Two months later the war would end at Dayton, never to resume.

But while the Dayton agreement gave NATO the authority to capture Karadžić and Mladić, an arrest didn't occur for nearly 13 years. Finally, one of these dreadful murderers has begun the trip to The Hague. It is imperative that Mladić follow Karadžić on this one-way journey.

His capture is all the more important because it was accomplished by Serbian authorities. Serbian President Boris Tadić deserves great credit for this action, especially since his good friend Zoran Djindjic, then prime minister of Serbia, was assassinated in 2003 as a direct result of his courage in arresting Milošević and sending him to The Hague in 2001. Karadžić's arrest is no mere historical footnote; it removes from the scene a man who was still undermining peace and progress in the Balkans and whose enthusiastic advocacy of ethnic cleansing merits a special place in history. It also moves Serbia closer to European Union membership.

Karadžić's capture is another reminder of the value of war crimes tribunals. Even though 12 years-plus is an inexcusably long time, the war crimes indictment kept Karadžić on the run and prevented him from resurfacing. In far-away Khartoum, Sudanese President Omar Hassan al-Bashir, who was indicted last week by the International Criminal Court, should be paying close attention.

CHAPTER SEVEN

The United Nations

Seated next to his friend, UN Secretary General Kofi Annan, Holbrooke presides over the UN Security Council in January 2000. (UN/DPI Photo by Evan Schneider, January 10, 2000)

As UN Ambassador, Holbrooke hosted lavish lunches and dinners at his official residence in the Waldorf Astoria—bringing together UN diplomats and world leaders with Washington politicians, journalists, and Hollywood stars. Here, he and President Bill Clinton listen to the great historian Arthur Schlesinger, Jr. make a point., (Courtesy of Kati Marton)

Holbrooke in Turtle Bay

JAMES TRAUB

The U.S. Senate took almost eight months to confirm Richard Holbrooke's nomination as ambassador to the United Nations in the spring and summer of 1999. This meant that the United States had no ambassador during the tumultuous debate over war in Kosovo, nor during the complex discussions of the ensuing peacekeeping mission. Both beyond our borders, and among many American internationalists, this failure was understood as part of a larger, and very dangerous, pattern of disengagement. Far behind on its dues, the U.S. was routinely mocked as a "deadbeat." By the time Holbrooke arrived in New York, in early September, even close allies had grown disgusted with American high-handedness. In one of Holbrooke's first UN meetings, Sir Jeremy Greenstock, the U.K. ambassador, declared that the U.S. "has muffled its voice and stained its reputation." And he made a point of saying it in the new ambassador's presence.

Only a few years earlier, in the Dayton Accords putting an end to the war in Bosnia, Holbrooke had brought off the great diplomatic achievement of his career. In Turtle Bay, as the UN is called after its New

York neighborhood, he found himself enmeshed in a conflict much less morally satisfying—the U.S. was by most accounts the bad guy here—but also much more complicated. The U.S. owed the UN $925 million in back dues by its own reckoning and almost twice that according to UN officials. The arrearage had grown so large that the U.S. was in danger of the unthinkable fate of being suspended from the General Assembly. Such an outcome would only further enrage the conservative Republicans who controlled both houses of Congress and were holding UN dues hostage to their own goals. Senator Jesse Helms of North Carolina had reached a compromise with Democratic Senator Joe Biden that authorized the payment of much—but not all—of the arrearage in exchange for lowering the U.S.'s annual dues payments and imposing a series of onerous "reforms" on the UN, including zero growth in a budget that already had been flat for years. And House Republicans were holding up payment over a wholly unrelated abortion issue.

Here, then, was the task facing Holbrooke that September: He had to persuade congressional Republicans to care about the UN enough not to destroy it in a fit of pique or as a casual by-product of an ideological campaign; to persuade President Bill Clinton and his team to raise the pressure on an issue that won them no votes, and during an election year to boot; and then, once he had brought Washington to heel, to persuade UN officials, his fellow diplomats, and foreign ministers to accept terms that they had every reason to consider extortionate. It was a prospect only someone as fond of risk as Holbrooke could regard with relish. "If we can't afford to lose," he said to me early that fall, "we might as well throw ourselves body and soul into the effort, like a skier in a downhill race just going flat out—you're either going to fall or win." That was the Holbrooke worldview in a nutshell: If it's worth doing, it's worth overdoing.

Holbrooke began the campaign, as was his wont, with a fabulous dinner party. In early October, Holbrooke gave a dinner in the ambassador's residence on the 42nd floor of the Waldorf Astoria for Senator Rod Grams, a Minnesota Republican who sat on the Foreign Relations Committee. In his toast, Holbrooke described Minnesota as "one of my favorite states," which must have placed it in a fifty-way tie. Holbrooke had seated Grams next to his wife, Kati Marton, and a few seats from UN Secretary General Kofi Annan. At his own table, Holbrooke had seated Grams's legislative assistant, Pam Thiessen, whose husband Mark, one of Senator Helms's senior aides, had been invited as well. The U.S.

ambassador toasted the Thiessens on their first wedding anniversary, while a functionary handed Pam a box that appeared to contain a magnum of champagne. The Thiessens were not, it is safe to say, social friends of the Holbrookes. The other guests included Henry Kissinger, Mort Zuckerman, and Michael Bloomberg—one celebrity per table. There would be many more such dinners in the months to come.

Holbrooke was already operating on many levels, only some of them visible to the naked eye. Pique among Western allies had grown so high that the U.S. had been bumped off a seat it held by tradition on the UN's budget committee—a slight that stuck in the craw of ardent patriots like Senator Grams. New Zealand was then occupying the seat instead. Holbrooke cornered European foreign ministers who came to New York for the General Assembly session in September. Peter Burleigh, the career diplomat who had served as interim ambassador, watched the spectacle with awe: "He grabbed them by the throat," Burleigh told me at the time, "and beat the shit out of them. I ran a campaign with the same candidate—the United States—and we were a complete failure. The difference was I was running a campaign with the UN missions here." Kindly and accommodating New Zealand promptly agreed to step aside for the U.S.

Holbrooke now had something he could sell on the Hill, and he began visiting Washington. He would lurk in the House dining room and corner members on the trolley to and from the Capitol. He began with the moderates, hoping they would influence the House leadership. The answer he got, however, was, "It's a leadership decision." The ambassador was making more headway in New York than he was in Washington. I visited Holbrooke in his office at the U.S. mission in late October, and he said that he had been laying siege to Chris Smith, the New Jersey congressman who had been holding up UN funding in order to win passage of a law prohibiting the U.S. from paying for family planning programs abroad that offered abortion counseling or services—even if they used their own money to do so. Holbrooke said, "Smith is like a highwayman in the forest, able to drop down out of the trees and attach his amendment to any bill that's passing by. Nobody I have talked to has been able to explain where and when he will strike again." He knew that he had to get to House Speaker Dennis Hastert, but Hastert was avoiding him.

It wasn't just the conservatives: The State Department and the Clinton administration seemed to have lost the will to fight. Holbrooke said that some administration officials had suggested the U.S. gratify elements on the right by voting against extending a peacekeeping mission in Central African Republic, which cost the U.S. all of $4 million. The sheer nonchalance of it infuriated Holbrooke. "There are," he told me, "two levels of triage being debated in Washington among people who have never gone hungry for a single day in their lives." Level one was: "Africa's hopeless, forget it, let it sink." The more sophisticated argument was "let's reinforce success," and abandon the most pitiful spots, like the CAR. Those UN skeptics might have rejoined that Holbrooke had never gone hungry a day in his life either. But he had chosen to immerse himself in places of suffering, and he had made the cause of people in those places his own cause. He would never be so foolish as to tell a wary congressman that Africa needed the U.S. to take its international responsibilities seriously, but it was certainly what Holbrooke himself thought.

In late October 1999 I went with Holbrooke on one of his flying visits to Capitol Hill. He charged down the halls of Congress with a phalanx of aides handing him cell phones with fresh batteries like so many loaded six-shooters. He had used up most of the Republican moderates, and so he began dropping in on the immoderates. His favorite congressman so far, he said, was the one with the poster that read, "Charlton Heston is my President." All Republicans were fair game. At one point, the team charged out of the Capitol for a meeting in the House, and as they crossed the lawn, Barbara Larkin, the State Department's congressional liaison, whispered to Holbrooke, "That's Steve Largent—go get 'im." Largent was an Oklahoma Republican and former Hall of Fame wide receiver. Holbrooke ambled over to the man and came back laughing—it had turned out to have been Bob Weygand, a Rhode Island Democrat. They talked Brown football. And then Holbrooke instructed an aide to set up an appointment with Largent.

Holbrooke met with something like a hundred members of Congress. In a recent interview, Robert Orr, then the director of the Washington office of the U.S. mission to the UN and Holbrooke's liaison to Congress, said, with what may not be hyperbole, "No cabinet member in any administration since the dawn of time visited as many congressmen as Richard Holbrooke." Many had never before met a UN ambassador and vainly tried to explain that they didn't do foreign policy. "Yes, you do," Holbrooke would say, and would go on to explain how the factory in the congressman's district exporting tractors to the Middle

East would lose business if the place went to hell—which it just might if the UN disappeared.

That was Holbrooke's message everywhere he went: Don't do it for them, do it for us. The UN was crucial to American national security. He had a chart that showed that a grand total of thirty-six American soldiers were serving in peacekeeping missions—one-tenth the number six years earlier—and none of them had been killed in years. The UN was stabilizing places the U.S. couldn't or wouldn't go to. At a hearing of the Senate Foreign Relations Committee, he talked about the peace-keeping mission in East Timor, which had arrived within days of a UN resolution, had put an end to atrocities, and involved no American soldiers and few dollars. "We have learned the lesson of Somalia," Holbrooke testified.

The corollary was: If the U.S. didn't pay up, it would lose the ability to shape UN policy to its own ends. At one point I heard Dave Camp, a Republican from Michigan, ask Holbrooke, "Are you confident we're going to get the reforms we need?" And Holbrooke said, "The main reform is to get the assessment down; and I have no chance to get that done if we don't get our arrears paid." Holbrooke didn't actually think that the U.S., then responsible for 31 percent of world GDP, should pay less than its current 25 percent share of the UN budget, but he had no problem with pretending otherwise if it would tip the balance of opinion inside the House GOP caucus.

At the same time that he was running rampant over Capitol Hill, Holbrooke was tirelessly working the White House. A few years earlier, Representative Smith had attached his amendment to a bill authorizing payment to the International Monetary Fund, and White House officials had persuaded Republican leaders to let go of the IMF—but not the UN. Apparently, the UN could be offered up on the altar of political necessity. Holbrooke's predecessor, Bill Richardson, hadn't gone to the mat on the issue; Holbrooke did. He talked to President Clinton and to anyone else foolish enough to stand in one spot for long. Steven Richetti, the White House deputy chief of staff who had been tasked to work on the issue, said that Holbrooke called him seven times a day. Holbrooke tried to find favors to do; Orr recalls Holbrooke lobbying key legislators on according most-favored-nation trading status to China, an issue then front and center for the administration. He was building up chits on all sides and then cashing them in.

Every week, Orr would call Richetti with a new list of congressmen who had agreed to lift Smith's hold on UN dues. Richetti said at the time, "By virtue of defining national security in a way which included paying our UN dues, the GOP had no choice but to compromise." No less important, once the White House knew that it had the votes, it was prepared to negotiate. As Chris Shays, a moderate Republican, told me then, Smith had always understood that "if the White House made it a high priority, he would have to compromise," Both sides, in short, had moved. In the end, White House negotiators accepted the Smith amendment, and Smith agreed that the president could waive the restriction for sums under $15 million—which would include almost any foreseeable disbursement.

Holbrooke and his team were euphoric. But now he had to face his own disappointed allies. Holbrooke had already tried to deal with UN advocates who despised the Helms-Biden bill and couldn't bear the idea of accepting its strictures. That, he had told them, is the hand they all had been dealt. He had promised Senator Helms he would not publicly disparage the measure, and he had kept his word. But pro-choice forces were now outraged at the White House compromise. Throughout this period, Holbrooke had been talking to every prominent female legislator in Washington, as well as other activists. He had to convince them that he wasn't putting the UN in front of abortion rights. I was in his office when Representative Nancy Pelosi called. Holbrooke covered the mouthpiece, performed a kind of mock recoil, and winked at me; he was never one to hide his stagecraft under a barrel. "OK, I *don't* know what I'm talking about," he said petulantly into the phone. Then he turned soothing, "No, we *beat* Chris Smith. . . . Look, the United Nations is the biggest family-planning agency in the world." Then the teasing, seductive voice: "You know I love you; otherwise I wouldn't scream at you."

The two-month process of winning over Congress had required the Full Holbrooke—a little bullying but a good deal more flattery, a bull-terrier persistence, passionate advocacy, pragmatic scorn for purity, and, at the very back, a sense of ironic delectation of the whole preposterous spectacle reserved for his friends and associates (and a journalist given a privileged position). It had also, of course, required the deep engagement of Secretary of State Madeleine Albright and of key White House officials, as Holbrooke, who knew that he had a way of attracting attention and credit—and then paying a price for it—was quick to point out.

But the game was no more than half won. Holbrooke still had to reconcile the UN to Jesse Helms—and, he hoped, Helms to the UN.

The Clinton administration, which had entered office preaching the doctrine of "assertive multilateralism" and seeking to engage the UN in the post–Cold War work of humanitarian action and nation building, had reacted to reversals by dimming its ardor for the institution. David Malone, a Canadian diplomat and seasoned student of the UN, said to me then that in the aftermath of the calamitous death of eighteen U.S. Rangers in Mogadishu, Albright, then the U.S. ambassador, had concluded that "the path of least resistance"—in Washington—"lay in attacking the UN." The Clinton White House had confirmed this impression three years earlier when it took the unprecedented step of blocking Secretary General Boutros Boutros-Ghali's bid for a second term, though the chief reason was that Boutros-Ghali had become so anathema to Republicans that the administration was getting hammered every time it tried to work with the UN.

Holbrooke had a lot to overcome. And that included his own reputation for wielding a bludgeon. Singaporean ambassador Kishore Mabubhani said in an interview at the time that in one of Holbrooke's first meetings with his new colleagues, the U.S. ambassador said, "I'm sure you're all very critical of me over the arrears; you're right." Diplomats found that Holbrooke was blunt, but not brutal (unless he felt he had to be). He was a schmoozer, a seducer, a confider. And he didn't take cheap shots, at least not in public: Holbrooke made a point of never criticizing Kofi Annan, with whom he forged a relationship of trust. And beyond all that, he *mattered*: After more than a year of having no real interlocutor, Holbrooke's colleagues knew that they now had someone who had the president's ear. And he had proved the point by delivering the arrears.

But UN officials and diplomats felt that they could not accept the Helms-Biden bill. They would have to make cuts in the budget to reach zero growth (though it turned out that unspent funds from the year before would cover the gap). They would have to reapportion dues payments in order to bring the U.S. dues down from 25 percent to 22 (even though countries like Russia and China, permanent members of the Security Council, were assessed next to nothing). And they would have to swallow an American *diktat*. "They hate it," John Rugge, one of Kofi Annan's top advisers, said then. "The choice they're confronted with is: Which do they hate more?" Jeremy Greenstock was quite clear about the answer; he predicted in the fall of 1999 that if the Congress didn't rewrite Helms-Biden, "you'll lose your vote in the General Assembly, because you won't pay the money if the UN doesn't meet your conditions."

But Holbrooke knew that the Congress wasn't about to blink; it had to be the UN. Holbrooke and his team came up with the argument that UN dues payments had not been adjusted for decades; Singapore and Saudi Arabia were still paying the same tiny fraction as when they had been admitted to the body as impoverished nations. Of course, this didn't change the fact that the U.S. had no business reducing its own dues. "It was a fig leaf," Suzanne Nossel, then the U.S. diplomat responsible for management issues, said in a recent interview, "but countries needed a fig leaf so that it didn't seem like they were just capitulating." Just as he sounded the depths of Capitol Hill, visiting congressmen who had never met the U.S. ambassador to the UN, now Holbrooke began roaming the UN missions along First and Second Avenues, equipped with a laminated card indicating how much countries were paying—and should be paying. He met resistance with apocalyptic rhetoric. It was going to be "a train wreck." The future of the UN hung in the balance. It helped that Holbrooke actually thought this way. In the end, the other 185 members of the institution agreed to accept only partial and staged repayment of the arrears, the zero-growth budget, and, ultimately, with much gnashing of teeth, a reallocation of dues payments.

"We took that risk and we took that hit," Greenstock says today, "because we saw that Dick had achieved something fairly amazing on the American side. He forced us all beyond our bottom line. He was a successful bully, but he had also done a huge amount of perspiring homework on this. He held the whole thing together; that was his genius."

This vast, multidimensional campaign constituted, in effect, Holbrooke's negative agenda: That which had to be done in order to make possible that which was worth doing. And what was worth doing was using the UN to solve problems Americans cared about, at least the ones the UN could be helpful with. In January 2000, the U.S., by a happy coincidence, had the rotating presidency of the Security Council. Countries did not, at least at this time, typically advance a program for their presidency. Holbrooke decided that the U.S. needed a theme, and that theme, of course, should be Africa. There could be no better way of proving that the U.S. was back as an active force in the UN than focusing on the region, not of greatest national security importance to Washington, but of greatest need. Holbrooke announced "the month of Africa." And in order to call attention to that neglected continent, he decided to drum up some Big Events involving Major Figures.

Holbrooke persuaded Vice President Al Gore to address the Security Council on the scourge of AIDS in Africa, even though the council had never recognized AIDS or any other public health issue as a threat to international peace and security requiring its attention. Along with Annan, Holbrooke thus elevated the status of AIDS to a global threat worthy of the highest-level attention. He invited Nelson Mandela on the barely plausible pretext that Africa's great man was working to avoid a fresh outbreak of genocidal conflict in Burundi. And he rigged up an extremely complicated piece of diplomacy designed to spur the hopeless process—hopeless to everyone save Holbrooke, that is—of bringing peace to the tormented Democratic Republic of the Congo. Holbrooke called this "Lusaka Plus." It turned out that the peace process could be best advanced in New York: Holbrooke managed to get all seven neighboring heads of state who had signed a prior agreement in Lusaka to come to the UN on January 24.

I came by Holbrooke's office in the middle of "the month of Africa." Mandela himself was on the phone with last-minute suggestions for the dinner party Holbrooke was hosting for him—Denzel Washington, Alfre Woodard. Holbrooke was juggling names for a lunch as well as a dinner. Bryant Gumble, Ted Turner, George Soros, and Bill Cosby were a yes. Katie Couric and Elie Wiesel sent regrets. "Barbara"—that would be Barbara Walters—was hoping to come, but Holbrooke was running out of room. Could he switch some of the dinner guests to lunch?

It was funny, but not to the host. "We're being put to the ultimate test in the Congo," Holbrooke told me solemnly. In the early to mid nineties, UN peacekeeping had failed in Somalia, Rwanda, and Bosnia. Now it was trying to redeem itself in Kosovo, East Timor, Sierra Leone, and—hardest of all—the Congo. "I don't think the world will give the UN a third chance," Holbrooke said to me. This turned out to be only semiprophetic. The UN did prove far more effective in these operations than it had in the calamitous ones immediately following the end of the Cold War. But if Congo was the "ultimate test," few would judge that the UN passed. The seven heads of state never even signed Lusaka Plus, and a Clinton administration official later told me that Holbrooke might have marginally set back the cause of peace by offending some of them.

The UN peacekeeping mission that Holbrooke initiated in the Congo would ultimately grow to vast proportions and suffer grievous setbacks. But Holbrooke was always going to prefer the sin of commission to the sin of omission. "We cannot," he told me, "sit back and say, 'American prestige is hurt if we try and fail.' American prestige is hurt more if we ignore the problem."

But all this dizzying African diplomacy was only a piece of Holbrooke's larger orchestration. Anyone but Holbrooke would have been satisfied with getting the UN and the right-wing Republicans to grudgingly acknowledge one another's existence; Holbrooke wanted them to dance with each other. He knew that the UN had become such a conservative voodoo doll that Bob Dole, a confirmed internationalist running for president in 1996, had mocked the UN secretary general, to great political effect, as "Boutros Boutros Ghali Ghali." This had only emboldened the anti-Americans in and around the UN, which made the place even more of a target. Holbrooke felt that he had to break the pattern. So he invited Jesse Helms to address the Security Council.

This was, to use Holbrooke's skiing metaphor, taking a giant leap off a cliff. Holbrooke could not control what Helms said to the UN permanent representatives, or what they said to him. But he was willing to trust his own instincts. On the appointed morning, the elderly senator hobbled over to the American chair on the council and delivered a speech accusing the institution of undermining the "sanctity" of state sovereignty, of seeking to establish a "new international order," of arrogating to itself the right to grant or withhold legitimacy from American actions. The permanent reps stared at their hands or gazed off into space. And then they showed what diplomacy was all about: Each, in turn, responded with a combination of exquisite politesse and criticism just oblique enough to flummox the old gentleman. Helms went away satisfied. And, of course, Holbrooke then hosted a lunch for his honored visitor to which he invited leading UN officials and diplomats, as well as a few conservative celebrities. Everyone was happy except for the Clinton administration: Holbrooke, I was later told, had neglected to inform officials that he was giving Helms a public forum that would lend unprecedented dignity to the crotchety bomb thrower.

But Holbrooke wasn't quite done yet. He had had the inspired idea of suggesting that the Senate Foreign Relations Committee hold a hearing on the UN in New York. This unprecedented event took place the next day. By now, Helms had sheathed his claws altogether. Over his bald pate, he sported a blue UN cap. Helms was now the host, and this brought out his courtly manners. At the rostrum, he cried, "Let's have the visiting ambassadors stand, if they will." The diplomats among the spectators, utterly bewildered, looked at one another, and then slowly rose to their feet, as if expecting to be cut down by incoming fire. "The General Assembly of the UN will now be in order!" called the organization's new enthusiast. Holbrooke, the chief witness, said, "It's clear that the message has gotten through. And the message is, you're not anti-UN, you have a view of the UN, and you want the UN to succeed on your terms." This was on the order of Minnesota being one of his favorite states—but no matter.

The point is, it worked. Kofi Annan later said to me, "The standoff and taboo has been broken, and we're now engaged." A Helms aide said of his boss, "I think he felt that he was received very respectfully. I would say that he saw the individuals that make up the UN countries and officials in a new way that you can't see from afar. I think this is really a new start." Holbrooke himself concluded, "I think it will be viewed as a significant part of ending a long, bitter period of relations between the U.S. and the UN." He had been in office for all of four months. It is not possible to think of any comparable period in the tenure of any other U.S. ambassador to the UN that had made so striking a difference in America's standing in the institution. With the exception of the Dayton Accords, those four months constitute Holbrooke's greatest diplomatic achievement.

IN ONE OF OUR LAST CONVERSATIONS AT THAT TIME, HOLBROOKE SAID something that I did not much remark upon then, but that turned out to be premonitory. When I asked what he thought he would do next, he said, "If I had my druthers, I would rather be special envoy to a trouble spot in the Balkans or Central Africa or East Timor. What I love more than anything else is going out there, getting down to the lowest possible level, sort of returning to where I began in Vietnam, getting a firsthand assessment of the problems at ground level and then going back up the chain of command to deal with them." He had had his druthers, if in a different place on the planet than he could have imagined then. Richard Holbrooke died doing what he most wanted to do.

The United Nations:
Flawed But Indispensable

Richard Holbrooke
Speech at the National Press Club, Washington, D.C.,
  November 2, 1999

*After a year-long struggle for Senate confirmation, Holbrooke
became U.S. Ambassador to the United Nations in August 1999.
In these excerpts from his first major speech in the post, Holbrooke
outlines his vision for the UN's role in U.S. foreign policy, providing a staunch and clear-eyed assessment of the institution and its
shortcomings. Holbrooke's views of the UN were summed up in
two sentences that he repeated often as Ambassador: "Flawed but
indispensable. Fix it to save it."*

In the past I've talked here about Bosnia and Kosovo and Indochina,
and other parts of the world. One thing they all have in common is
that the United States carries out its foreign policy in part through the
United Nations, and the United Nations is a vital part of our national
security interests.

So today I would like to talk to you about two interrelated issues
which are often treated separately: the future of the UN and American
national security policy.

The future of the UN is not just another issue that can be used as
this month's partisan weapon of choice. To be sure, the UN has been an
easy whipping boy. After all, its effectiveness, its failures, its occasional
bouts of anti-Americanism or anti-Semitism have made it an understandable target.

But we need to approach the question of the UN's value to our
national security with the same sense of foresight and perspective shown
by the leaders in whom all American statesmen and stateswomen

should hope to walk in their shadows—statesmen like Franklin D. Roosevelt and our British colleague and ally Winston Churchill, who conceived and created the United Nations.

In their August 1941 meeting in Placentia Bay off Newfoundland, FDR and Churchill agreed that they would work together toward the establishment of a wider and permanent system of general security. This wasn't some wooly-headed scheme; it was simply in their words "realism," born of the lessons they learned after World War I . . . .

What's needed now is to link this past vision with a new realism. By "new realism" I mean that we need to develop a clearer and more practical vision of what the UN is and what we expect it to be. It means recognizing the many ways the UN serves our national security interests. It means accepting our responsibility to make an organization that we created work. And it means living up to our obligations.

Too often, serious discussion of the United Nations becomes bogged down by false choices: between those who want to see it weakened or altogether eliminated, and those who want its powers unrealistically expanded.

Our discussion should begin therefore by acknowledging that without turning a blind eye to its significant flaws, the UN is, in President Clinton's words, "an indispensable institution, one that serves our national interests."

Let's also be clear about what the United Nations is not. And I speak specifically, not just to the people in this room but to people all over the country and the world who follow some theory that the UN aspires to be a world government—or that some American officials seek to subordinate American sovereignty to the UN.

Prior to my confirmation hearings, I called on many members of Congress who described to me the genuine concern of their constituents over this point. So let me be clear: the UN was never intended to be, nor will it ever be, a world government. It will never make foreign policy decisions for our country; nor will it ever lead our troops in combat. It will never replace the institutions or individuals in this country who in fulfillment of their constitutional obligations to the people make these decisions.

But the UN can be an important instrument for that foreign policy. It should not be an anemic organization like its stillborn predecessor, the League of Nations. Despite its many shortcomings, net-net, as they say in Wall Street, the UN serves American national interests. Eliminating the UN is simply not an option. Weakening it will only undermine our interests.

American leaders of both parties have called the UN vital to our national security for over 50 years. The reason is simple: for all its faults, its inefficiencies, and its shortcomings, if the UN did not exist, we would have to invent it. . . .

We therefore need the UN as a place where nations with common interests can come together; a place, in the words of the UN Charter, to "harmonize the actions of nations towards common ends."

But we have now come to a critical point. In the coming days, our Congress will make one of the most consequential decisions since the end of the Cold War: whether we will pay the United Nations the money we owe.

This question goes to the heart of what kind of power and what kind of leadership Americans aspire to at the end of this century and the beginning of the next. How Congress acts will determine whether the United States will enter the next century alone acting unilaterally, or whether it will seek to lead through partnership. Let me stress our contribution to the United Nations is not for padding the lifestyles of UN bureaucrats living on Park Avenue—or even Fifth Avenue. It's a down payment on America's national security.

But that's not to say that we have a romanticized view of the UN. We must not overlook a basic fact. The U.S. will not always act through the United Nations. We have other vital instruments of national power at our disposal. This was demonstrated quite amply twice in the last four years: in Bosnia, where NATO, led by the United States, bombed and sent in a NATO-led force without UN authority; and in Kosovo, where the bombing again took place without UN authority. . . . I would advocate similar actions again unhesitatingly if it were in the national interest.

But the UN is certainly about more than peacekeeping. Still, peacekeeping is the most controversial aspect of the UN. This is all the more so after Somalia, and the UN's disastrous performance in Bosnia.

Supporting UN peacekeeping abroad does not mean that American troops will be sent to every corner of the world. As of this month, the total number of American military personnel serving as liaison, observers or participants in UN peacekeeping missions is 38—38. In addition, there are about 600 American civilians assisting, supporting or participating in these operations—mostly police.

Compare that to the 260,000 American military personnel deployed around the world. Or compare it to the number of Americans under UN peacekeeping operations in the first year of this administration: it is currently about one percent of the figure it was six years ago.

In fact, there are almost as many American troops in the Bahamas—24—as there are assigned to the whole U.S. peacekeeping operation. And please don't ask me what they're doing there!

As new missions are considered, they must be designed with a clear understanding of peacekeeping's limits. I was an eyewitness to the UN's collapse in Bosnia between 1992 and 1995—a disastrously designed mission that was costing the UN $5 million a day.

And I understand the skepticism and backlash this bred in many Americans. So we must approach peacekeeping skeptically. No more UNPROFORs in Bosnia, no more Somalias. But it is possible to get it right, and that's what we've got to try to do this time around. . . .

In addition to making the world more secure, the United Nations also serves American interests by taking the lead to address problems that know no borders: assisting refugees, tackling starvation and disease, and reversing environmental degradation. I've witnessed firsthand how vital these efforts can be.

Understanding and appreciating both the benefits and limits of what the United Nations can do to advance our political, economic and security interests is the core of the new realism that I'm trying to discuss today. But it's not enough.

The UN must also clean itself up. . . . The UN needs to have structural reform. Secretary General Kofi Annan certainly understands this and has addressed it. And I can assure you that meaningful UN reform will remain my highest sustained priority. I will talk about UN reform in detail later, and I will address it in the context of whether or not the arrears are paid. So let me restrict to three brief bullet points now.

First, the UN must maintain its fiscal discipline, and that begins with keeping its budget constant.

Second, the UN has to reduce its reliance on any single member—and that includes the U.S.—or any handful of members for financial support. This means that we will ask the UN, if we pay our arrears, to reduce our assessment as called for in the legislation, from 25 to 22 percent.

Finally, we need to make the decision-making structure more sensible. And that will require addressing the complicated and elusive issue of Security Council reform.

But all these reforms will require full American support and participation, and by that I mean financial support. Many of the reforms we seek will be impossible if we do not pay our dues. As I stand here today, the United States owes over a billion dollars to the United Nations.

This amount is substantially more than half of all the money owed to the UN. These aren't extra funds that the UN's asking for. It's the money we're legally obligated to provide—and as the president and the secretary of state have said repeatedly, we should pay it.

It's very important for our international critics to acknowledge, however, as we seek to gain this money, that notwithstanding our arrears, we already provide more money to the UN, than other countries. This is a fact which is sometimes obscured. And the irony is that we don't get credit for the money we do contribute, because we're in arrears. So we minimize the effectiveness of our significant contribution.

. . . This cycle cannot go on. It is dangerous and self-destructive. Our ability to influence progress on the UN reform is weakened by our failure to pay our bills, but we can't pay our bills until there is progress on UN reform.

Meanwhile, our ability to advance our vital national interests is weakened because our leverage in New York is undermined by the fact that we continually tell other countries how to behave without putting our money behind our advocacy.

. . . Since I was sworn in nine weeks ago, I've worked hard and directly and personally with members of Congress on this vital issue, and will return to the Hill as soon as this speech is over to continue calling on members of both parties in both houses. I've hosted many Congressional delegations in New York. I'm gratified by the general support the United Nations has gotten from the leaders of both parties and both houses.

As President Clinton recently put it, paying our dues to the United Nations is a legal and moral responsibility. I would add it is a historic duty. More than any other nation, the United States can take credit for the United Nations. It was the work of the men and women of the greatest generation.

Sobered by two terrible world wars and the failure of the League of Nations, they sought a way that future generations would be saved from the horror that they had lived through. It was the insight, the vision, and the tenacity of that generation and its leaders—Presidents Roosevelt and Truman and Eisenhower, Diplomats Sumner Welles and Edward Stettinius, Senators Arthur Vandenberg and Tom Connally—which made the United Nations a reality. Harry Truman once explained that the UN comes from the reality of experience in a world where one generation failed twice to keep the peace. We do not want to be the first generation since that statement to ignore this reality.

With the new era that is dawning, and with signs of hope in New York, mixed by challenges that remain awesome, I ask all of you today—whether in Washington, in New York, or across America—to join our debate about the future role of the United States and its foreign policy, and whether or not the UN remains a vital part of the foreign policy. This means recognizing all that the United Nations does to advance our global security interests. It means expecting the UN to live up to its obligations. It means insisting that the UN make itself more lean and more efficient. It means accepting our unique and our historical role to lead through the UN and all other instruments in pursuit of our national policy, and understanding that without America's political leadership and financial support, the United Nations will not succeed—and America's national security and the interests of all Americans will suffer.

Last Best Hope

RICHARD HOLBROOKE
New York Times Book Review, SEPTEMBER 28, 2003

In this review of Stephen Schlesinger's book, Act of Creation, *Holbrooke reflects on the dramatic history of the UN's founding and draws lessons on how Americans should think about the UN today. This essay contains many of the arguments Holbrooke made about the UN while he served there as U.S. Ambassador, and repeats one of his favorite lines to defend the UN: "Blaming 'the United Nations' for what happens inside the talk palaces on the East River is like blaming Madison Square Garden for the New York Knicks."*

Anyone who has ever watched the History Channel or CNN must be familiar with the grainy black-and-white film of President Harry S. Truman, seated on the stage of the San Francisco Opera House on June 26, 1945, signing the United Nations Charter. That iconic moment links World War II and the Cold War; the great wartime alliance with the Soviet Union still exists as the war enters its final months with Japan, but the tensions that will become the Cold War are already evident to some American and British officials, even as the world celebrates the birth of the United Nations.

Amazingly, the event that led to that ceremony—the San Francisco conference, which once gripped the world—has been almost totally ignored by historians. Stephen Schlesinger, a historian of foreign affairs who runs the World Policy Institute at the New School University, has filled that gap with *Act of Creation*, a superb book that reconstructs this drama with great lucidity, and illuminates its contemporary relevance. With the exception of "FDR and the Creation of the UN," a 1997 study by Townsend Hoopes and Douglas Brinkley that focuses on the Roosevelt era and has only one chapter on San Francisco, little has been published about the founding of the world body. (Schlesinger says that many editors rejected his book proposal the moment he mentioned that it was about the United Nations—the publishing equivalent, he notes wryly, of "biting on a sour lemon.")

The United Nations did not spring full-blown from the minds of Franklin Roosevelt and Winston Churchill (although its name did come from Roosevelt, who burst into Churchill's bathroom at the White House to unveil his inspiration). An obscure but determined State Department official named Leo Pasvolsky had been working in secret on a postwar world organization since the end of 1939, under the direct guidance of Secretary of State Cordell Hull. Pasvolsky, a Russian-born journalist and economist who had covered the failure of the League of Nations first hand, was one of those figures peculiar to Washington—a tenacious bureaucrat who, fixed on a single goal, left behind a huge legacy while virtually disappearing from history.

By 1944 most key elements of the new organization were in place in Pasvolsky's draft, especially an idea that evolved into the United Nations Security Council—a small group of nations that would be empowered to authorize the use of force, in the words of Article 39 of the Charter, "to maintain or restore international peace and security." The most important change in the later drafts was that they accorded to the "Four Policemen"—the United States, the Soviet Union, Great Britain and China—permanent membership on the Security Council and authority to veto its resolutions. At San Francisco, France was also given this special status, with consequences to this day (as Colin Powell can attest).

In the spring of 1945 everybody came to San Francisco, or so it seemed, to draft the final version of the United Nations Charter. The Soviet Union was represented by its rigid foreign minister, Vyacheslav Molotov, and Stalin's young ambassador to the United States, Andrei Gromyko (then at the beginning of an astonishingly long diplomatic career that would not end until Mikhail Gorbachev was already in power). On issue after issue, Moscow took positions that foreshadowed the Cold War. To get around Molotov and Gromyko, Truman used his ambassador in Moscow, Averell Harriman, and Roosevelt's legendary special envoy, Harry Hopkins, who arose from his deathbed to make a final trip to Moscow to persuade Stalin to drop several impossible demands, and, in the view of most observers, including Schlesinger, saved the San Francisco conference.

The American delegation in San Francisco was led by Secretary of State Edward R. Stettinius, a lightly regarded man whom Schlesinger tries to elevate in stature. A handsome former U.S. Steel chairman, Stettinius was described by one delegation member, the future Nobel Prize winner Ralph Bunche, as "a complete dud." He was demeaned by the press (and especially by the most important journalist in San Francisco, James Reston of *The Times*), looked down on by most of his colleagues, and nearly forgotten by history. But it is Schlesinger's surprising conclusion that, in fact, Stettinius presided with skill and patience over a fractious group of prima donnas, and deserves credit for forging a successful outcome from what could have been a chaotic mess.

Stettinius was certainly treated badly by Truman, but he kept his dignity in public, continuing his efforts even after he learned, in the middle of the San Francisco meetings, that he would be replaced as soon as the conference ended by Senator James F. Byrnes of South Carolina. (Stettinius gracefully accepted the position of first American ambassador to the United Nations.) Still, it is not poor Stettinius, but the strong-willed team surrounding him that fascinates today. By any standard it was a remarkable group, containing five men who would seek the presidency (Adlai Stevenson, Nelson Rockefeller, Harriman, Arthur Vandenberg and Harold Stassen), a future Republican secretary of state (John Foster Dulles), the Democratic chairman and the ranking Republican on the Senate Foreign Relations Committee (Senators Tom Connally and Vandenberg), and, as the secretary general of the entire conference, a State Department official named Alger Hiss.

The inclusion of the two senators was Roosevelt's last masterstroke, designed to avoid the risk that the Senate might reject the United Nations as it had the League of Nations in 1920—an event that Roosevelt and Truman were determined at all costs not to repeat. Critical to this strategy was the self-regarding but powerful Vandenberg. Schlesinger shows how his commitment to bipartisan internationalism was locked into place at San Francisco. Vandenberg's vanity made him believe that he was almost singlehandedly responsible for the United Nations. "You could have heard a pin drop all the way through my speech," he wrote in his diary after his Senate speech calling for immediate ratification of the charter. The price of humoring Vandenberg was worth paying; his support ensured easy Senate ratification.

Truman comes across in *Act of Creation* as far more than the executor of Roosevelt's grand design. It was not at all smooth sailing in San Francisco, but through it all Truman steered a steady course. He and Stettinius flattered Vandenberg, co-opted Dulles (who for the rest of his career would respect and support the United Nations), held off Molotov and Gromyko while Hopkins and Harriman worked things out with Stalin, and tried to keep their volatile assistant secretary for Latin America, Nelson Rockefeller, who seemed determined to run a separate foreign policy, under control. Under the guidance of another distinguished assistant secretary of state, Archibald MacLeish (who twice won the Pulitzer Prize for poetry), the administration put together an immensely sophisticated public relations operation—a campaign that involved business groups, labor, church leaders, schoolchildren, women's groups and academia, and created a huge wave of support for the United Nations.

To Truman, the opportunity to preside at the creation of the world organization must have had an almost mystical meaning. Unknown to the public, he had carried folded in his wallet for years several stanzas of his favorite poem, Tennyson's "Locksley Hall," which ended:

> For I dipt into the future, far as human eye could see,
> Saw the Vision of the world, and all the wonders that
>   would be . . .
> Till the war-drum throbbed no longer, and the battle-
>   flags were furl'd
> In the Parliament of Man, the Federation of the World.

Of course, reality would hijack the Parliament of Man: during the Cold War the United Nations was often marginalized, unable to solve, or sometimes even to address, many of the world's most pressing problems. An explosion of new states that almost quadrupled its membership (now 191) changed the very nature of the United Nations. And its inefficient bureaucracy needs more reform, despite some valiant efforts by its current secretary general, Kofi Annan.

For these and many other reasons, it has become easy, even fashionable in some quarters, to criticize the United Nations. But can any serious policy maker actually think that the world—and especially the United States—would be better off without this organization? Its record of achievement—from specialized agencies like UNICEF and WHO to successful peacekeeping operations in such places as Namibia and East Timor—is substantial; without the United Nations the world would be in far worse shape. Despite its flaws, the United Nations still serves American foreign policy interests far more than it hurts them.

Blaming "the United Nations" for what happens inside the talk palaces on the East River is like blaming Madison Square Garden for the New York Knicks. In fact, the United Nations is no more—and no less—than the sum of its member states, and what happens there is determined not in New York but in the world's capitals, which send their ambassadors instructions on major issues. American success at the United Nations therefore requires hard diplomatic work not only in New York but in countries around the world, something that has unfortunately not been a regular ingredient of American foreign relations in recent years; hence such unpleasant surprises as the loss of America's seat on the Human Rights Commission in 2001.

Despite the United Nations' achievements over the years, major improvements are essential. This requires, above all, stronger leadership from the nation that founded the organization, hosts its world headquarters and remains its largest source of funds. But the fault hardly lies solely with the United States. Other nations, especially the so-called nonaligned movement, or NAM, a group of over 120 nations formed as a "third force" during the Cold War, have regularly voted for one-sided General Assembly resolutions concerning Israel and other issues—resolutions full of empty rhetoric and cheap symbolism, but damaging to the organization as well as the Middle East peace process. The United States should work actively to break up or reduce the size of the NAM; this would contribute greatly to advancing the peace process in the Middle East, and strengthen the United Nations. Many will say this is a hopeless quest, but it can be done, as was demonstrated on some key votes during the Clinton administration, when the United States prevented the Sudan from becoming a Security Council member, reformed the entire financial structure of the United Nations, reduced its own dues and repaid most of its huge arrears.

In peacekeeping, still its most important function, the United Nations rises or falls with the actions of the Big Five. Adlai Stevenson, later

President Kennedy's ambassador to the United Nations, saw this with perfect foresight at the very beginning. The charter "is only paper," he said in a speech in Chicago in 1945, "no better and no worse than the will and intentions of its five major members."

No serious policy maker would advocate subordinating American national security interests to the United Nations; for this reason President Clinton twice used force in the Balkans (in Bosnia in 1995 and in Kosovo in 1999) without Security Council authority. But the United Nations provides the United States with an invaluable forum from which to advance parts of its global agenda, fully protected by the Security Council veto in precisely the way that the Truman team foresaw.

Truman correctly called the United Nations "imperfect," but his challenge to future generations was to improve on their creation, not weaken it. This is the deeper meaning of Schlesinger's book. A strong United Nations is in America's national interests; a demeaned, weakened and underfunded United Nations only undermines American diplomacy. With this in mind, it would be a tragedy if 21st-century policy makers continue to fail those who assembled in San Francisco 58 years ago.

CHAPTER EIGHT

Fighting HIV/AIDS

Holbrooke speaking at a Global Business Coalition on HIV/AIDS event. (Courtesy of Kati Marton)

The Global HIV/AIDS Crisis

John Tedstrom

Toward the end of his life, Richard Holbrooke still believed that despite important pockets of progress, we were losing the overall war against AIDS. That belief connected all the other aspects of his work in this area. He pushed for expanded testing; he spoke out on the especially tragic impact of HIV on women and young girls; he supported harm-reduction programs (including needle exchange); and he called for expanding access to affordable treatment *and* prevention programs. He held all of those positions with tremendous urgency, informed by experience in solving other intractable global crises and punctuated by a deep and sincere need to help people who, by no fault of their own, were unable to help themselves.

At the Global Business Coalition on HIV/AIDS, Tuberculosis and Malaria (GBC), which he led as president and CEO from 2001 until he returned to Washington to serve in the Obama administration, he even banned the word *progress*. He argued that to say we were making progress when more people were becoming infected with HIV every day than the number of people who had access to life-saving treatment ignored the key facts and ultimately distorted reality.

As treatment access programs expanded and the ratio of newly infected to those treated gradually declined, Holbrooke eventually, though grudgingly, softened his position. He allowed those of us at GBC to use *progress* in limited and carefully edited contexts. He would always emphasize, however, that progress in this case only meant we were losing the war against AIDS at a slower pace. We were not winning. Were he alive today, Holbrooke would argue that now is the time to redouble our efforts to fight HIV/AIDS. He would have been right.

HOLBROOKE CAME TO THE FIGHT AGAINST AIDS RELATIVELY LATE IN HIS career. He was, of course, aware of the pandemic from its early days. In the 1980s, he was shocked by the way HIV savaged America's greatest cities, like San Francisco and New York. He was appalled by the indifference of our leaders, especially President Reagan, who refused to use the word AIDS until years after the epidemic took root here and after thousands had already succumbed. And he was profoundly saddened and baffled by parents who turned away their own dying children simply because they were sick.

Holbrooke told me more than once that he was also inspired by the courage of America's gay community. He was impressed with how a once self-centered and fractious collection of small and often competitive groups came together locally and nationally to find greater power. He admired the fact that they demanded action from those in power, and he appreciated their argument that health was a human right, even in America.

In 1992, while a private citizen, Holbrooke traveled to Cambodia, a country he had visited often. It was there that he witnessed UN peacekeepers drinking heavily at night and visiting prostitutes. He was convinced that not only were they spreading HIV locally, but they would inevitably take it home. He wrote a letter to the head of UN operations in Cambodia urging him to address the issue—but got no reply. When he became U.S. ambassador to the UN seven years later, this isolated experience in Cambodia—centered on a UN peacekeeping mission— nagged at him and ultimately helped motivate his AIDS activism on a global scale.

At the UN, Holbrooke led a Security Council delegation to sub-Saharan Africa in December 1999. There he first faced the full brunt of the global AIDS crisis. Holbrooke and his delegation visited ten countries and, in each one, met with people living with HIV—young and old, men and women. He began to see the wider social and economic devastation caused by HIV and knew instinctively that this crisis was bigger than the global community generally understood.

During the Africa trip, Holbrooke met with South African President Thabo Mbeki, who argued that AIDS was a result of poverty and denied that the HIV virus was the cause of the disease. A frustrated Holbrooke lectured that while poverty was the crucible in which South Africa's AIDS epidemic was developing, HIV/AIDS was at root a social and public health problem that required a more sophisticated and powerful response.

After returning to New York, Holbrooke decided that the UN Security Council should hold a special session on the global AIDS epidemic. Some resisted, saying that AIDS was not a "security" matter. He had seen with his own eyes, however, how it tore at the fabric of societies and families and threatened the stability of an entire continent. Others argued that the Security Council had never devoted a session to a health matter. But Holbrooke dug in his heels. He found some support among Security Council colleagues. The African countries, naturally, were strongly in favor. The British and French delegations also lent their support. The only major objections came from the Russians. Holbrooke rarely—never?—missed an opportunity to push the Russians on an issue he felt strongly about, and finally they, too, acquiesced. They insisted, however, that they would stay silent during the discussion. That suited Holbrooke just fine.

HOLBROOKE'S ENGINEERING OF THE SECURITY COUNCIL MEETING ON HIV/AIDS and his strong message—public and private—about the importance of the issue to the international community positioned him in a new way among many of his old friends. It also created the basis for him to meet people in the global HIV/AIDS community who he would work with and be close to for the rest of his life. His work in the fight against AIDS bound him to Africa in ways even he didn't expect and gave him an opportunity to master yet another type of job—leader of a start-up international nongovernmental organization with the

*With South African leader Thabo
Mbeki. (Courtesy of Kati Marton)*

audacious (some said crazy) goal of convincing CEOs around the world
that they and their companies had unique assets and should use them
to vigorously fight against AIDS. In 2001, he agreed to become president
and CEO of the Global Business Council on HIV/AIDS (GBC), taking over from MTV's dynamic international president, Bill Roedy. He
would transform the organization and make it into an international
powerhouse in record time. He would even change the name from
"Council" to "Coalition"—to ensure no one had any doubt we were at
war against AIDS, and not just a talk shop.

Four years earlier, in October 1997, ten companies had convened in
Edinburgh, Scotland, to exchange best practices on corporate HIV programs and had agreed to establish the Global Business Council on
HIV/AIDS. Four pharmaceutical companies—whose industry was then
suffering unprecedented, harsh criticism for the high prices charged to
poor Africans for antiretrovirals—spearheaded the meeting.

To the credit of the business leaders assembled in Edinburgh, their
goal was bigger and more honorable than figuring out how to create a
public relations cover for a few pharmaceutical companies. They wanted
to inspire themselves and others to apply the know-how, technology,

infrastructure, and ethos of business to the fight against AIDS. They saw that governments and NGOs were doing their part and felt that businesses ought to take care of their workers, promote health in their host communities around the world, and be active and accountable members of the global debate on HIV/AIDS just as they were on other major issues. They recruited Nelson Mandela to serve as honorary president.

While Holbrooke had no professional credentials in this arena—he wasn't a doctor or scientist or even a social scientist—he had other valuable qualities that led people like Kofi Annan to encourage him to lead GBC and become, overnight, one of the top global leaders in the fight against HIV/AIDS.

First, the way Holbrooke mobilized and convened world leaders at the UN Security Council meeting on AIDS gave him instant and probably unmatched authority in the international AIDS community. Yes, there were people like Peter Piot, who was brilliantly leading the Joint UN Programme on HIV/AIDS (UNAIDS), and the National Institutes of Health's lead HIV scientist Anthony Fauci, not to mention South Africa's Zackie Achmat and other frontline heroes in the fight who were living with HIV/AIDS. All of these leaders were—and are—justifiably important and influential in their own right. But Holbrooke, who would become close to these and many other luminaries, occupied a different place by virtue of his political influence, and he exercised his own brand of authority.

Second, Holbrooke brought to the AIDS fight his passion, commitment, and intellect. As he did with every major challenge, he immersed himself in the data and the research. He asked thousands of questions of hundreds of experts and of people directly affected by HIV/AIDS. He convened. He challenged. He traveled. He tossed out ideas just to hear how the world's best experts would bat them down. It wasn't long before he was shaping the public discussion. The issue of HIV testing would become the most prominent and controversial policy debate Holbrooke would wage during his time as an AIDS activist. And as proved to be the case so many times during his career, he was right (if slightly ahead of his time) on this issue, too.

Third, Holbrooke had a Rolodex—built carefully and maintained for decades—that the most campaign-tested politician or high-priced fund-raiser would envy (and many did). There wasn't anyone on the planet Holbrooke didn't know or couldn't be introduced to by simply asking one friend to make a call. Holbrooke's goals for GBC were ambitious—it needed to grow fast and make a mark if it were to establish itself and survive. While he embraced the underlying belief that businesses really did have a unique and powerful role to play in fighting AIDS, he thought its original organizational aspirations—only fifteen member companies—were much too modest and would ultimately limit the organization's impact. When he took over the job as head of GBC, he set out immediately to take it to the next level. In addition to renaming it the Global Business *Coalition*, he hired key staff, including experts in public health and corporate communications from Africa, and established the organization's number one goal: growth in membership. He believed there was strength in numbers, and he grew the GBC from seventeen companies in 2001 to over two hundred by the time he left and returned to Washington in January 2009.

HOLBROOKE WAS A TIRELESS ADVOCATE FOR HIGH-QUALITY HIV TESTING, recognizing it as one of the most powerful weapons in the fight against AIDS. In a relentless stream of op-eds and speeches, he consistently argued that the lack of emphasis on testing—and the low percentage of individuals being tested—threatened to undermine the entire HIV/AIDS effort. The prevailing guidance from the World Health Organization (WHO) and the Joint United Nations Programme on HIV/AIDS (UNAIDS) encouraged widespread availability of HIV testing but placed the onus for taking the test on individuals who often didn't know they had been exposed or were at risk, or even where testing centers were located. When testing centers were found, they were often in their own buildings, isolated from other health facilities. Walking in the door meant risking a neighbor might see you and suspect you had AIDS. Too many people opted to just keep walking and not go in for a test.

The emphasis Holbrooke placed on testing was grounded in a very compelling body of statistics. It has been shown that upward of 90 percent of those who are HIV-positive worldwide do not know they are infected and can therefore unwittingly spread the virus to their partners and, in the case of infected mothers, to newborn babies. Holbrooke argued that testing would not only allow those who know they are infected to seek treatment and protect their partners from contracting the disease, but also motivate those who know they are HIV-negative to practice safer sex.

Holbrooke was certainly not ignorant of the stigma that testing might trigger. But he argued that the greater good of the public's health outweighs the potential threat to individual autonomy and the corresponding cultural taboos associated with HIV-positive status. He wrote: "When these taboos threaten to destroy the culture itself [of many low- and middle-income countries], they must be defied for the health of the overall public—and to save the culture itself." Holbrooke placed special emphasis on the necessity of testing at three specific moments in life: at marriage, before childbirth, and during any visit to a hospital. "At these moments (and, we hope, others)," he wrote, "public health criteria legitimately take priority over the desire of an individual."

After heated debates, in 2007 UNAIDS and WHO adapted their official recommendations to reflect the growing support for more routine provider-initiated testing. Essentially, health care workers would be encouraged to suggest a test to a patient who would then have to definitively "opt out" if he or she did not wish to take the test.

Holbrooke took on other priority issues in the AIDS fight. He was an early champion of supporting women's health and of focusing on women as a pivotal subgroup in the fight against AIDS. He strongly supported the Global Fund to Fight AIDS, Tuberculosis, and Malaria, and lobbied to ensure that GBC became the focal point for the private-sector delegation to the Global Fund board. While he had his (mostly minor) differences with George W. Bush's President's Emergency Plan for AIDS Relief (PEPFAR), he was proud of it and greatly admired its dynamic young leader, Dr. Mark Dybul. He would often advocate for increasing the budgets of both the Global Fund and PEPFAR in public statements and testimonies.

HOLBROOKE SPENT PERHAPS A DAY OR SO A WEEK ON GBC IN THE EARLY days. That was all the organization needed at the time. Under his leadership, some of the world's largest and most important companies began or scaled up major HIV programs around the world. Holbrooke took personal interest and understood that his access to CEOs and board directors was always useful and often essential to secure the big commitments. He worked personally with the leadership of Coca-Cola, Daimler-Chrysler, AngloAmerican, BD, and others. He relished few things more than helping a GBC staffer convince a multinational company to stretch itself by simply picking up the phone and calling the

CEO to say, "We love you guys so much. You're terrific, but you're about to waste an important opportunity. People will wonder why you didn't fund an expansion of your AIDS program. It won't be good. I can see the headlines now. Time to get this done."

For Holbrooke, the AIDS crisis was so big and the potential of the business community to make a difference was so powerful that he was always ready to consider innovations—even big ones—of the organization in order to make it more effective.

In 2006, when I learned he was looking for a new executive director for GBC, I suggested to a mutual friend that he introduce us. My goal was to propose the merger of GBC with the organization I founded to fight HIV/AIDS in Russia, Ukraine, and other CIS countries, Transatlantic Partners Against AIDS (TPAA). Holbrooke had been struggling to get GBC a toehold in Russia for several years. I was looking for a viable way to go global and share our lessons learned with others who could benefit. In April, I met Holbrooke for lunch in Almaty, Kazakhstan, where he was speaking at a conference on media freedom hosted by none other than President Nazarbayev's daughter. (Later, I would tease him about this; Nazarbayev and media freedom are difficult concepts to merge. As this was our first meeting, I resisted the temptation.) Although we had both served the Clinton administration—working on different issues and geographies and at very different levels of seniority—we had never met. We hit it off immediately and agreed we should join forces. Our next step was to convince our respective boards and staffs that a merger was a unique opportunity (it was), it could be managed quickly and easily (it couldn't), and our teams would naturally fit together (only partially true).

Holbrooke had begun to wonder if GBC needed to add tuberculosis and malaria to its mandate. At my first GBC board meeting in London in spring 2006, Holbrooke, GBC's chairman Sir Mark Moody-Stuart, and other board members agreed to the mandate expansion. I saw at this first meeting that Holbrooke would never let some notion of what had been correct at the moment get in the way of future innovation. At the same time, though, he was cautious and looked at the decision from all angles. He was most concerned that some of GBC's most prominent companies, including, perhaps, some of the founding members, would succumb to AIDS exceptionalism and leave the coalition. He also worried that the global HIV leaders he had come to admire so much—and whose partnership was so important for GBC—would feel we had abandoned ship. That, he felt, would be very damaging to our reputation and limit greatly what we could get done. Once he was convinced that the GBC team understood these concerns and was prepared to deal with them, he advocated for the expansion. As I would learn over and over again during the time we worked together, you have to look at every major decision several times and from every vantage point imaginable before pulling the trigger.

I took this lesson to heart after Holbrooke returned to Washington. In May 2009, and in response to daunting trends in the U.S., GBC launched its first ever domestic initiative focusing on increasing HIV awareness and testing in Washington, D.C. and Oakland, California, both of which rivaled many African countries in terms of HIV prevalence. We found ready partners in the Obama White House, which was eager to forge ties with the business community. The Congressional Black Caucus welcomed us and always tied their support for our work in the U.S. to Holbrooke's leadership on AIDS abroad. The legendary civil rights leader, congressman, and then mayor of Oakland, Ron Dellums, was a strong supporter and partner. Holbrooke himself agreed the time was right to walk the walk at home and was a champion of this work.

It was clear also that after nearly a decade of work on HIV, TB, and malaria, GBC had the capacity to do much more. Indeed, we owed it to the developing world to apply our hard-earned knowledge and skills and our relationships with big business and key governments to other major health challenges. We undertook a major study together with many of our member companies, and by autumn 2010, we had all the support we needed to once again expand GBC's mandate.

But I knew I needed to discuss this change with Holbrooke. It was a huge shift for "his baby," and I owed him an early warning and a chance to dissuade us. Moreover, I wanted his insights and advice. When we met in September 2010 we spent far less time on GBC than I anticipated. I told him, simply, that we wanted to take on a broader public health agenda to help our member companies do more good in poorer regions of the world. I explained that this would mean a total rebranding of GBC, perhaps even changing the name. I was ready for the worst reaction. He had had no warning about this change, and his emotional ties to GBC ran deep. Instead, he simply said, "Very smart. Very smart." He then gave me ten more reasons to make the change.

This was yet another example of Holbrooke not allowing the past to stand in the way of the future.

HOLBROOKE WILL BE REMEMBERED FOR MANY THINGS. IN 2001, HE could have chosen any number of noble and worthy causes to which to devote his time and energy. He also could have simply made tons of money and waited for the next presidential assignment. No one would have questioned that. But he chose to work on HIV and Africa. There was no personal gain in this fight for him. He had to educate himself on a new, complex, and delicate topic and had to embrace a continent and nations he didn't know. He had to add the fight against HIV and a new international NGO to an already overscheduled life. It helped tremendously that his wife, Kati, cared about this issue and was so supportive. But more than anything, his work in this arena speaks to his strong, sometimes overwhelming humanitarian instincts, his intolerance for injustice, and his confidence in good people everywhere to make a positive difference, when given the right opportunity.

AIDS: The Strategy Is Wrong

RICHARD HOLBROOKE
Washington Post, NOVEMBER 29, 2005

> *During the 2000s, Holbrooke frequently spoke out and wrote
> about the global HIV/AIDS crisis, stressing his belief that detection
> and testing should be emphasized—a view that, as these two*
> Washington Post *columns show, sparked controversy.*

Thursday is the 18th annual World AIDS Day, a time for countless statements of concern and commitment from world leaders, thousands of commemorations and remembrances, and reams of statistics. One important article has already appeared on this page, by Jim Yong Kim, the highly respected director of the HIV-AIDS Department of the World Health Organization. After recounting the grim statistics—3 million deaths in the past year alone, 5 million new infections this year, rising infection rates in nearly every part of the world and an admission that "good news is hard to find in the new U.N. report"—Kim wrote that he was nonetheless "optimistic that the epidemic can be stopped."

I respect Kim and admire his commitment, as well as that of every foot soldier in this war. I share that commitment. With respect, then, to my friends and colleagues in the field—most far more qualified than I am—I must nonetheless mark World AIDS Day with a word of pessimism that they will not necessarily welcome. We have to face the truth: We are not winning the war on AIDS, and our current strategies are not working. Every year since the first World AIDS Day, the number of people affected has increased. The very best that can be said is that we are losing at a slightly slower rate.

The huge, and very expensive, international effort has saved the lives of a growing number of people. I have seen some of the beneficiaries of these efforts firsthand in places as remote as rural eastern Uganda—and it is inspiring. The international assistance effort must be continued, indeed increased.

But as Kim acknowledges, "fewer than one in five people at risk of HIV infection has any access to HIV prevention information," and this must be addressed with larger internationally supported programs. (But remember, once a person is on the drugs, it's for life; to stop taking them is to be hit with a mutant of the original virus.) Until a vaccine is found—and that is probably more than a decade away—we must focus on prevention and treatment. Providing treatment is essential, of course, but it is also a bottomless pit as long as the disease continues to spread so fast.

As a strategy, losing more slowly is simply a recipe for an ever-more-expensive, disastrous and deadly failure, which will require more anti-AIDS drugs at ever-greater cost—a modern version of the old story of the boy with his finger in the dike. Moreover, as Kim points out, current policies require "building and strengthening health care systems in the developing world." This is an essential long-term task with or without the AIDS crisis, but one so daunting that linking it so closely to stopping the spread of AIDS only compounds the odds against reaching either goal.

Only effective prevention strategies can stop the spread of AIDS. Yet it is precisely here that current policies have failed most seriously. In the long chain of actions required to stop the spread of AIDS, attack on all fronts is necessary. But on one vital front, the world health community has been shamefully quiet for two decades: testing and detection. Because of legitimate concerns about confidentiality and the risk of stigmatization, testing has always been voluntary, and it has been systematically played down as an important component of the effort.

The results are predictable—and fatal: According to U.N. figures, over 90 percent of all those who are HIV-positive in the world do not know their status. Yet there has never been a serious and sustained campaign to get people to be tested. That means that over 90 percent of the roughly 12,000 people around the world who will be infected today—just today!—will not know it until roughly 2013. That's plenty of time for them to spread it further, infecting others, who will also spread it, and so on. No wonder we are losing the war against AIDS: In no other epidemic in modern history has detection been so downgraded.

When I first suggested, about three years ago, that testing and detection was the weak link in the strategy against AIDS, I was sometimes criticized for ignoring human rights. Having worked in support of human rights for more than three decades, I understand this issue and the passion it arouses. I have met monogamous women who were thrown out of their homes for a disease they got from their husbands, and people who lost jobs and friends once their condition became known.

But the spread of the disease cannot be stopped, and we cannot offer drugs to those who need them, unless people know their status. That knowledge changes people's behavior; many who learn that they are HIV-positive behave more carefully, and they can act on the information to save themselves and their family members. Isn't this the most important human right of all?

Quick and reliable saliva and blood tests, which give results within 20 minutes, are available, increasing the opportunity for confidentiality. Some companies, such as the South African diamond giant DeBeers SA and its affiliated mining company, Anglo-American Corp., have started to strongly encourage testing, using these quick and confidential methods. But governments have been slow to use the tests. In an important breakthrough, three small countries in Africa—Botswana, Malawi and especially Lesotho—recently moved from purely voluntary testing to what is called "opt-out": Testing becomes routine in certain circumstances unless the patient opts out by refusing to be tested.

This seemingly small change has had immediate results. Testing has increased dramatically. And with increased testing has come increased awareness, less stigma, safer sex practices and more people on treatment. Without question, a reduction of the prevalence of HIV-AIDS will follow. Yet the great and influential international organizations fighting AIDS have not yet, for the most part, embraced "opt-out" as part of their core strategies.

On this World AIDS Day, many empty words and promises will be heard. I am gratified that additional money will be pledged and, as a result, more lives saved. But unless the current, failing strategy is changed, we will have to spend even more money later, to treat AIDS victims who might never have been infected had testing been more widespread. Numbers don't lie: Everyone agrees that the number of people infected is still growing sharply, and not just in Africa. Widespread testing is not a single-bullet solution—there is none—but without knowing who is HIV-positive and who is not, there is no chance we can win this war.

Sorry, But AIDS Testing Is Critical

RICHARD HOLBROOKE

Washington Post, JANUARY 4, 2006

> *Never one to back down from an argument, Holbrooke responds to his critics.*

A month ago, on World AIDS Day, I wrote that despite all the public rhetoric about progress, "we are not winning the war on AIDS" and that the "very best that can be said is that we are losing at a slightly lower rate." I thought this was fairly obvious, given the fact that on each World AIDS Day since the first one 18 years ago, the number of people who are HIV-positive has increased. I thought it was even more obvious from just one stunning fact: that of the 12,000 people who will be infected in the *next 24 hours* around the world, over 90 percent will not learn they are sick until roughly 2013, when they develop full-blown AIDS. Meanwhile, not knowing their status, they will unintentionally spread it to other people over the next eight years, and these people will spread it to still more, and so on.

Given this situation, I suggested that current strategies are clearly not working, especially on prevention. While continuing to support increased funding for treatment of those who already have AIDS, I argued that far more emphasis should be put on detection and testing so that people learn their status and then, with counseling, change their behavior if they are HIV-positive, thus reducing the spread of the HIV virus.

This may sound simple, even self-evident, to those not involved with the issue on a regular basis, but no column I have written for this newspaper provoked a greater reaction. To listen to some of the criticism you would think I had called for mandatory testing and quarantining of people with AIDS. "This man is out of control," wrote one prominent AIDS activist under the headline. "Someone stop this man." I was accused of "championing a conservative, traditionalist public health approach, which is simply looking to identify the infected and contain them."

Such criticism ignored my strong public advocacy over the past six years of much more funding for treatment. But far more distressing were the assertions of "progress" from world leaders and editorial pages. Originally designed to put pressure on public officials, World AIDS Day has turned into an empty rhetorical ritual in which world leaders issue high-minded statements, after which they let another year of living ever more dangerously pass.

Although there were plenty of calls for more funding for treatment, so far as I am aware no one suggested new prevention strategies or even admitted that today's approaches are not working. Current policies on prevention are simple enough: Conservatives emphasize promoting abstinence (which is why a minimum of 30 percent of the American contribution to the effort is earmarked for that purpose), while liberals stress the use of condoms and the need to avoid needle-sharing. Of course, any of these practices, if followed rigorously, will prevent the spread of AIDS, but none is ever going to be used by enough people to reverse the spread of the disease. It is a classic case of American "red state–blue state" politics and ideology trumping the brutal reality on the ground, or, more accurately, in a bedroom or alleyway.

I have been told repeatedly, for more than four years, that the case for testing is not proven. But isn't it obvious that AIDS will continue to spread more rapidly as long as 90 percent of those affected do not know their status? Wouldn't greater knowledge of one's status—held in the strictest confidence (an essential part of any testing program)—greatly modify behavior, both for those who are HIV-positive and for the large majority who, even in the worst-hit areas, are not infected? And wouldn't the greatest beneficiaries of widespread testing be women, who are all too often helpless victims but who do not know either their own status or that of any man in their life—and who have no way of getting their men to be tested?

Yet the dedicated and committed professional community engaged in this desperate struggle, including UNAIDS and the World Health Organization, still refuses to make testing a top priority. (One commendable exception is Randall Tobias, the Bush administration's special envoy on AIDS, who makes it a practice to be publicly tested—if possible with a local official—in every country he visits; he well may be the most tested person on Earth.)

Why, in general, is the issue played down? I believe it is partly a case of a mind-set that was locked in 20 years ago, at the dawn of the AIDS crisis. Stigmatization was a huge problem then, even in the United States, and antiretroviral drugs were not yet available.

But times have changed, and so has the nature of the disease and the way it is spreading. (The greatest step forward in prevention would be the development of an effective microbicide that women could self-administer, but that goal is still eluding researchers.)

Recently there has been encouraging action in three small African nations—Lesotho, Botswana and Malawi—which have started making testing routine and officially encouraged (but not mandatory). Lesotho's new policy, creatively called KYS, or "Know Your Status," is especially worth watching because it is a formal, widespread national effort. If it works, perhaps the high priests of the worldwide effort on AIDS will stop listening to their own echoes and unexamined assumptions—and take action. If ever there were a place where an ounce of prevention was worth a ton of cure, this is it.

CHAPTER NINE

Afghanistan and Pakistan

With President Obama at the State Department in January 2009, on the day Holbrooke was announced as the President's Special Representative for Afghanistan and Pakistan. (White House Photo)

The Last Mission

David Rohde

For four days in March 2006, Richard Holbrooke crisscrossed Afghanistan as a private citizen. The country's resilient people and rugged landscape fascinated him. He was enthralled during a two-hour conversation with an imprisoned young Taliban militant, appalled by the American police training and counternarcotics effort, and welcomed by Afghan President Hamid Karzai. At a farewell dinner attended by American generals and Afghan ministers, he held forth in classic Holbrooke fashion. For thirty minutes, he laid out his vision of a sweeping new American effort in the region.

Two years later, the Obama administration named Holbrooke its special representative for Afghanistan and Pakistan. In theory, Holbrooke should have been at the zenith of his diplomatic skills and career. Decades of work in Washington and war zones had prepared him for what he called his last mission. The then sixty-seven-year-old diplomat was determined and captivated, and carried personal ties to the region. In 1971, Holbrooke had briefly visited Afghanistan while working as a Peace Corps official.

"I saw this romantic, exotic, harmonious, multi-ethnic society," he later told a journalist, "just a few years before it was destroyed."

But it was not an easy task for the man famed for nearly singlehandedly bringing peace to the Balkans. His bluntness and bluster initially alienated Afghan and Pakistani officials. His perceived competitiveness with his peers compounded suspicions in Washington. And a multidimensional conflict, combined with nagging questions about the extent of American influence and patience, proved far less susceptible to Holbrooke's or America's will than the war in the former Yugoslavia.

As a journalist who covered the conflicts in Bosnia, Afghanistan, and Pakistan, I saw Holbrooke soar and stumble. And in a deeply personal way, I experienced his goodwill and his determination. The legendary American diplomat helped save my life—twice.

Instead of simply giving up in Afghanistan and Pakistan, Holbrooke waited, narrowed his focus, and played what he called "the long game." While much has been written of Holbrooke's struggles, he achieved a great deal in the region. In his final year, he revitalized his relationship with Afghan and Pakistani leaders, enjoyed policy victories in Washington, and achieved diplomatic breakthroughs in the region. A man stereotyped as a publicity-seeking egotist kept many of those successes secret.

Sadly, just as his labors began to bear fruit, on December 11, 2011, he collapsed in a meeting with Secretary of State Hillary Clinton in her ornate office on the State Department's seventh floor. Two days later, he passed away before his strategy could be put to the test.

Four lessons emerge from Holbrooke's effort in Afghanistan and Pakistan. First, the period represents the culmination of Holbrooke's approach to diplomacy. The techniques he used, open internal debate he encouraged, and team he assembled are a model for aspiring diplomats.

Second, Afghanistan reaffirmed Holbrooke's lifelong belief that American foreign aid programs must empower local governments and officials. When impatient American aid workers or troops do the work of local officials, it creates a destructive dependency, he argued, that delegitimizes local governments and draws the United States into quagmires.

Third, Holbrooke's fervent work in Pakistan showed the indispensable value of sophisticated, respectful, and passionate diplomacy in the field. By repeatedly journeying to Pakistan, candidly engaging officials and the Pakistani public, and responding pragmatically to a traumatic natural disaster, Holbrooke did more than any other American official since 2001 to ease long-running Pakistani mistrust of the United States.

And fourth, Holbrooke lived the ultimate life of service. After joining the State Department at twenty-one and serving every Democratic president since John F. Kennedy, he accepted a virtually impossible assignment in Afghanistan and Pakistan. Holbrooke died, literally, while serving his nation and showed all Americans the value, dignity, and worth of public service.

PERSONAL AND PROFESSIONAL PASSIONS DROVE HOLBROOKE'S DECISION to return to Afghanistan in 2006, according to family and friends. A successful New York investment banker, he did not need to survey a war overshadowed by the spiraling conflict in Iraq. On a personal level, though, Holbrooke wanted to see what had become of the Afghanistan he visited as a young man. And on a professional level, he made the trip in his capacity as chairman of the Asia Society, an organization he believed needed to focus more on South Asia.

When he arrived in Kabul, Holbrooke despaired over the physical destruction of the country, and expressed shock at the ongoing suffering of the Afghan people—particularly once-independent urban women now clad in burqas.

Throughout his life, Holbrooke's diplomacy often centered on the sufferings of individuals. A refugee he met in Bosnia inspired his work there. HIV-positive women he met in Namibia fueled his AIDS activism. In one of his first press conferences in Kabul, he told Afghan journalists that he hoped to help re-create the peaceful Afghanistan he drove across over three decades earlier.

After his 2006 trip, he devoured books and reports on the country and found any excuse to consult with regional experts. He also employed one of his favorite habits: mining journalists for what they knew. Holbrooke invited me to lunch in December 2006 to discuss my experience covering Afghanistan and Pakistan for the *New York Times* since 2001. He listened as I described the need for a larger American effort in the region—and then interrupted me.

"We can't force Pakistan to accept democracy," I remember him saying. "It will never work."

Holbrooke was eager for the United States to avoid the slow escalations that entangled it in Vietnam. For him, one of the central lessons of Vietnam was the danger of not deeply studying a complex foreign policy problem before acting. In March 2008, Holbrooke returned to Afghanistan, again as a private citizen, and embedded with American troops in the eastern province of Khost. Impressed by the local governor, the commanding American military officer, and the American diplomat serving there, he hailed them in a monthly column he wrote for the *Washington Post*.

He also tried to lower expectations and talked about the importance—and dangers—of American intervention. One of his largest fears was that a sweeping American presence in Afghanistan would create dependence and inadvertently undermine the local government, as he had seen in Vietnam. American good intentions, he warned, could prolong the conflict in Afghanistan.

"With each tactical achievement, Afghanistan will become more dependent on international support," Holbrooke wrote. "Will short-term success create a long-term trap for the United States and its allies, as the war becomes the longest in American history?"

NINE MONTHS LATER, HOLBROOKE DID NOT HESITATE WHEN THEN president-elect Obama and Hillary Clinton offered him the position of special representative for Afghanistan and Pakistan. Despite warnings from numerous friends that he was doomed to fail, Holbrooke embraced a seemingly hopeless undertaking. His decision to accept was driven both by his desire for the limelight *and*, critically, by the same call to public service that had caused him to join the foreign service after graduating from Brown.

Holbrooke, who had always argued that people were the difference between good and bad policy, immediately began assembling what he described as an all-star team of advisers and aides. As he had throughout his career, he hired people with little government experience and broke bureaucratic protocol.

On the night before his appointment was announced, he reached out to Vali Nasr, an Iranian-American academic known for his knowledge of Pakistan. Three months later, on a shuttle flight from Washington to New York, he made an impromptu job offer to Rina Amiri, an Afghan-American expert on Afghan politics and former UN official.

He was equally creative inside the government. After Steve Berk, an obscure U.S. Department of Agriculture official who had briefly

*With President Obama and Vice President Biden in the Oval Office.
(Official White House Photo/Pete Souza)*

served in Afghanistan, sent Holbrooke an unsolicited e-mail detailing his thoughts on agriculture in Afghanistan, Holbrooke made him a job offer. When Vikram Singh, a young aide to Under Secretary of Defense for Policy Michele Flournoy, impressed Holbrooke during a trip, he hired him as well.

While the offers may have seemed spontaneous, Holbrooke was acting strategically. When it was complete, his thirty-member team had ties to every government organization vital to the office's success. Treasury, Defense, Agriculture, Homeland Security, and Justice as well as USAID, the FBI, the Joint Staff, and the British and German governments were all represented.

Holbrooke exhibited little of his famed imperiousness and constantly encouraged, challenged, and supported his staff, according to former aides on his Afghanistan-Pakistan team. Over the years, his abrasiveness appeared to have mellowed. He worked grueling hours and pushed his staff hard, but his advisers said they relished the experience. Comparing his office to an Internet start-up, they praised the veteran diplomat for keeping the organization as flat as possible. All staff members had access to Holbrooke, they said, and he encouraged frank and honest policy discussions.

Amiri, the expert on Afghan politics, said Holbrooke insisted that she typically present the local perspective on what was occurring in

Kabul, not the Washington view. "He looked at me to give the Afghan lens, not simply the objective lens," Amiri said. "How Afghans would see things on the ground."

In a September 2009 *New Yorker* profile, Holbrooke described his method as "a form of democratic centralism."

"You want open airing of views and opinions and suggestions upward," he said. "But once the policy's decided you want rigorous, disciplined implementation of it."

His exhaustive travel reflected another abiding belief that dated to Vietnam. For Holbrooke, intricate foreign policy problems could only be understood in the field. Impatient with what he considered Washington's glacial pace and myopic bureaucratic views, he traveled to the region once every two months.

Vietnam had also taught him to be skeptical of the American government's ability to produce cohesive efforts in foreign countries. Whatever challenges lay inside Afghanistan, he believed that getting the White House, military, intelligence community, State Department, and Congress to unite behind—and implement—a multifaceted plan was extraordinarily difficult.

"One thing he definitely understood was the daunting complexity of Washington," said Nasr, the Pakistan expert on Holbrooke's staff. "He knew what the strength of the United States was. And he knew its weaknesses."

In his 1970 *Foreign Policy* essay "The Machine That Fails" (see chapter one), Holbrooke—then a young foreign service officer who had been in government for just eight years—warned of the cumbersome nature of Washington's foreign policy apparatus. Despite repeated efforts to rein them in, multiple government agencies—as well as multiple bureaus within the State Department—pursued their own bureaucratic interests and projects.

"Over time, each agency has acquired certain 'pet projects' which its senior officials promote," Holbrooke wrote. "These are often carried out by one agency despite concern and even mid-level opposition from others."

Lastly, Holbrooke was wary of the tendency of American diplomats and aid workers to bypass slow-moving or corrupt foreign officials and do things themselves. Too large an American effort created passivity, he believed, and undermined the local government in the long term.

"That creates a dependency culture," Holbrooke said in a 2009 *Charlie Rose* interview. "I saw that when I was a young diplomat in Vietnam. I've seen that in other parts of the world."

And in a final nuance often misunderstood by many American liberals, Holbrooke believed in the use of military force in certain circumstances. His mind—and his thinking—was supple. Holbrooke, according to his aides, saw the use of force as an instrument that might lead to a negotiated settlement. He viewed diplomacy and military force as tools that complement one another, not as stark alternatives.

"It was never black and white," said a former aide. "In Holbrooke's mind, military pressure was the key to any political effort."

WHEN HOLBROOKE TRIED TO APPLY THESE LESSONS TO SOUTH ASIA after taking office in 2009, he struggled. India was not part of his diplomatic brief, putting the central dynamic that destabilized the region—India-Pakistan tensions—out of his reach. Pakistani leaders despised the term "AfPak"—an expression Holbrooke had championed—because they felt it equated their nuclear-armed nation with its far poorer and smaller neighbor, Afghanistan.

Like all of us, Holbrooke made mistakes as well. His blunt manner and habit of talking to the press initially alienated Afghan and Pakistani leaders. Before an April 2009 trip to Islamabad, Holbrooke and Admiral Mike Mullen, the then chairman of the Joint Chiefs of Staff, publicly alluded to ties between Pakistani intelligence and the Afghan Taliban.

For years, American and Pakistan analysts had accused Pakistani military intelligence of supporting the Afghan Taliban as a proxy force to prevent India from gaining influence in Afghanistan. This public airing of the issue, though, infuriated military officials in Pakistan.

Holbrooke's initial relations with Karzai were even more contentious. Before taking office, Holbrooke publicly criticized the Afghan president in his March 2008 *Washington Post* column. He disparaged Karzai for failing to arrest an infamous Afghan warlord, Abdul Rashid Dostum, after he attacked, brutalized, and nearly killed a rival commander in Kabul.

"The effect on Karzai's standing and reputation has been enormous," Holbrooke wrote. "Excuses were made, but none justified his open disregard for justice."

Holbrooke and Afghanistan President Hamid Karzai. (©OMAR SOBHANI/Reuters/Corbis)

In his first meeting with Karzai as special representative in February 2009, Holbrooke reportedly lectured the Afghan leader. Six months later, their relationship unraveled after Karzai supporters committed widespread fraud in the 2009 Afghan presidential elections.

According to media accounts, Holbrooke and Karl Eikenberry, then the American ambassador in Kabul, met with Karzai to discuss the race the day after the balloting. The Afghan president and Holbrooke clashed when the American diplomat asked Karzai if he would accept a runoff election. Karzai insisted he had won the required 50 percent of votes and there was no need for a runoff. Holbrooke, though, refused to drop the issue.

"Holbrooke was extremely blunt with Karzai," said a former aide. "You cannot behave this way in Afghanistan. This is not the Balkans."

Within days, the BBC reported that Holbrooke's meeting with Karzai had been "explosive" and a "dramatic bust up." Holbrooke insisted the meeting had not been confrontational, but the story went viral. Across Afghanistan and the Web, Holbrooke was portrayed as Karzai's American taskmaster.

In Washington, Holbrooke struggled as well. Fairly or unfairly, his prominence made his job more difficult. Holbrooke could be exhausting, even to his staunchest allies and defenders. His rivals in Washington looked for the slightest indication of his famed ego or misbehavior. His friend Hillary Clinton repeatedly had to defend him. Stories of his difficulties inevitably found their way into the press.

It was widely reported, for instance, that officials at the U.S. Agency for International Development deeply resented a push by Holbrooke to funnel more aid through Afghan ministries and reduce the role of American contractors. Holbrooke's goal was to lessen Afghan dependency, but many reportedly believed the Karzai government was too weak and corrupt to handle additional aid. According to media reports, tensions between some agency officials and Holbrooke soared.

To Holbrooke's surprise, the press—traditionally his ally—complicated his efforts. The rise of partisan cable news channels intensified Washington's demand for instant winners and losers. Reports of waste, incompetence, and failure in Afghanistan and Pakistan overshadowed calls for patience, diplomacy, and nuance. Books and news coverage about the new administration described the clichéd Holbrooke of the 1990s—the abrasive, egocentric "bulldozer." The public heard little of the deeply committed public servant who unleashed tremendous energy and creativity into Afghanistan and Pakistan policy discussions that for years lacked such high-level attention and care.

As 2009 came to a close, Holbrooke faced disappointment on multiple fronts. Friends advised him to resign, return to New York, and stop wasting his time on a mission impossible.

INSTEAD, HOLBROOKE WAITED. IN 2010, HE LEARNED FROM HIS MISTAKES, narrowed his focus, and quietly achieved successes in Afghanistan, Pakistan, and Washington. One of the most important was a historic July 2010 transit agreement between Afghanistan and Pakistan that allowed Afghan trucks to cross Pakistani territory to deliver goods to India. The agreement lessened the stranglehold India-Pakistan tensions had put on trade in the region for decades.

In Afghanistan, he hampered the illicit flow of ammonium nitrate fertilizer—which insurgents used to make roadside bombs—from Pakistan to Afghanistan. He focused so intently on agriculture—the country's traditional economic engine—that Clinton dubbed him "farmer Holbrooke." And he reversed the Bush administration policy of demanding the eradication of opium crops in southern Afghanistan, a practice he and American military commanders believed increased support for the Taliban.

After months of intensive effort, Holbrooke salvaged his relationship with Karzai, according to Amiri, his adviser on Afghanistan. He met with the Afghan leader six times between January and April 2010, with the final meeting lasting over two hours. Holbrooke then used a Karzai visit to Washington in May to laud the Afghan leader with pomp, circumstance, and attention. Most importantly, he fought for Karzai's request that the Afghan leader be allowed to carry out negotiations with the Taliban.

"He worked very hard at repairing that relationship," Amiri said. "I think Karzai realized this was the man who could deliver reconciliation from the administration."

In Pakistan, Holbrooke learned from his mistakes as well. He worked furiously at courting Pakistani leaders and public opinion.

"He did have a grand strategy," said Nasr, Holbrooke's senior adviser on Pakistan. "He believed that we needed to stabilize the government and we needed to close the gap in trust that had developed for decades."

After mishandling his April 2009 trip to Islamabad with Mullen, Holbrooke played a central role in Hillary Clinton's successful October 2009 trip to Pakistan. After years of American diplomats taking few questions in brief, tightly scripted press conferences, Clinton held a series of well-received public forums where she tried to address the concerns of average Pakistanis. He also encouraged American military officials to focus on developing a long-term relationship with the Pakistani military.

Holbrooke's efforts bore the most fruit in the summer of 2010. That July, epic floods engulfed nearly 20 percent of Pakistan, unleashing the worst natural disaster in the country's history and wiping out roads, bridges, power lines, schools, and health clinics built over decades.

Holbrooke flew to Islamabad to coordinate American relief efforts. In his element in the field, he brought decades of experience to bear. Holbrooke drove the American government bureaucracy, demanding that U.S. military helicopters be shifted from Afghanistan to Pakistan to deliver aid. He met with Pakistani officials and listened to their needs. And he carefully managed the media.

Pakistani television showed images of American helicopters delivering aid to desperate flood victims. American newspapers printed photos of Holbrooke consoling Pakistani refugees. On blazingly hot days, Holbrooke reached camps for the displaced before Pakistani officials did.

To his admirers, the floods were Holbrooke at his best. On a governmental level, he fiercely pursued pragmatic policies that delivered concrete results. On a diplomatic level, he developed respectful relationships with Pakistani officials. And on a public relations level, he presented dramatic proof of American caring. Most importantly, his core human empathy suffused—and drove—the effort.

In speeches, interviews, and private conversations, Holbrooke called for a more respectful long-term relationship between the United States and Pakistan. He expressed interest in the long-term welfare of the Pakistani people. After years in which the "global war on terror" had defined the U.S.-Pakistani relationship, Holbrooke deemphasized that aspect of a relationship that he insisted must be permanent and multidimensional.

"This cannot be a transactional relationship," he told me several months before he died. "We have to create a long-term relationship."

Holbrooke's diplomacy played out in unexpected ways as well. After the Obama administration worked with Congress to triple annual American civilian aid to Pakistan to $1.5 billion, Holbrooke helped convince Islamabad to issue more visas to American civilians. Some of the Americans implemented aid programs. Others were dispatched to Pakistan to track terrorists like Osama bin Laden. Holbrooke did not live to see it, but one could argue his diplomacy played a small but important role in the May 2011 death of al-Qaeda's leader.

And after nearly a year of quiet, persistent effort, Holbrooke won approval for the first meeting between American government officials and Taliban representatives since 2001. As has been widely reported in the spring of 2010, German and Qatari officials offered to set up a meeting between the two sides. Holbrooke and his staff then tirelessly worked in Washington to gain support for it. In an example of Holbrooke's deep belief in diplomacy's central role in ending conflicts, American government and Taliban representatives met on November 28, 2010, near Munich. Two weeks later, Holbrooke died.

In the end, the American strategy in the region adopted many of the pragmatic policies that were Holbrooke's hallmark. Two months after Holbrooke's death, Hillary Clinton spoke at the inaugural Richard C. Holbrooke Memorial Lecture at the Asia Society in New York. She

Holbrooke sharing a moment with Kati and his close friend and ally, Secretary of State Hillary Rodham Clinton. (Courtesy of Kati Marton)

praised Holbrooke for helping the administration mount military, civilian, and diplomatic surges in the region. She also outlined the terms and approach for the Taliban reconciliation process that Holbrooke had helped initiate in the weeks before his death.

"He had a flair for the dramatic, to be sure, but it was for more than theatrics," Clinton said. "He understood in every cell of his body that bold action and big ideas can and will change history. After all, he did it himself, again and again."

If the post-2001 effort in Afghanistan and Pakistan falters, it will be primarily due to continuing tensions between India and Pakistan and the limits of the international community's influence in the region. If anyone could have succeeded in South Asia, it would have been Holbrooke, but the challenge might have proven too great even for him.

I ALSO HAVE A DEEPLY PERSONAL UNDERSTANDING OF THE FEROCIOUS energy and empathy that Holbrooke brought to his diplomacy. During the war in Bosnia, Serb forces arrested me in 1995 after I discovered a mass grave near the town of Srebrenica, site of the massacre of 8,000 Bosnian Muslims. At the time, Holbrooke was at the peak of his diplomatic power. He had convened peace talks in Dayton, Ohio, to end the three-year conflict.

As my family and editors watched, Holbrooke and his wife, journalist Kati Marton, pressured Serb officials to free me. To their amazement, Holbrooke deftly rattled the Serbs. In one meeting, he picked up the Bosnian Serb vice president's plaid wool fedora and intimidated him. "Maybe I can hold your hat hostage," Holbrooke said. Finally, he told Serbian President Slobodan Milošević that the peace talks would be halted until my release. Days later, I was freed.

For years, Holbrooke ribbed me for complicating his already-difficult Balkan peace talks. I promised him and my family it would not happen again. In November 2008, a Taliban commander proved me wrong. After inviting me to an interview outside Kabul, he kidnapped two Afghan colleagues and me and ferried us to the tribal areas of Pakistan.

Again, Holbrooke flew into action. He raised my case in meetings with senior officials in Islamabad. He forced senior Pakistani officials to meet with my wife and family in Washington. Yet Holbrooke's pressure produced few results. At first, Pakistani generals falsely insisted that I was being held captive in Afghanistan, not Pakistan. Then they failed to act.

In an indirect way, though, Holbrooke might have saved my life. My captors scoured the web for information about me and discovered our history in Bosnia. They gleefully announced that Holbrooke was my "best friend" and that I was a "big fish." Perhaps that made me worth more to them alive than dead.

In June 2009, we escaped from captivity, bringing a sudden resolution of a captivity that seemed destined to drag on for years. After being flown to the American military base in Bagram, Afghanistan, I was told that Holbrooke was demanding to speak with me by phone. It was a conversation I dreaded. For the second time, I had complicated a hugely complex diplomatic task Holbrooke faced. Expecting to be lambasted, I picked up the phone and said: "I apologize." Holbrooke's response surprised me.

"God," he declared, his voice booming with genuine warmth and affection. "It is so good to hear your voice."

That day, a conversation began that continued in the United States over the next several months that showed how Holbrooke had changed. Instead of chastising me, he tried to use my time with the Taliban as a means to better understand them.

"Who are they? Why are they fighting? What do they want?" Holbrooke asked, rapid-fire. A man known for his impatience then quietly listened to my long explanations. He even set up meetings with senior American officials who he thought should hear my story.

In the larger scale of events, of course, Holbrooke's handling of my captivities is trivial. The Dayton agreement saved the lives of countless Bosnians. His work in Vietnam, China, Germany, Africa, and at the United Nations saved many others. The diplomatic groundwork he laid in Afghanistan and Pakistan may yet bring peace to tens of millions of civilians there who have endured thirty years of brutal conflict.

In the Balkans, Holbrooke had the threat of seemingly omnipotent American-led NATO air strikes to force the Serbs to make peace. In South Asia, he labored to get Pakistani generals to stop seeing the Taliban as friendly proxies they could use to thwart Indian influence in Afghanistan. It was a different conflict; in many ways, a different world.

For me, Holbrooke will always be a source of inspiration. He devoted his life to public service, a notion that is now derided in many quarters. Some say his death marks the end of a Kennedy-inspired generation—and an America—that believed it could be a virtuous force in the world. I fervently disagree. All of us have the chance to follow his example.

Rebuilding Nations

RICHARD HOLBROOKE
Washington Post, APRIL 1, 2002

> *After 9/11, Holbrooke continued to serve as vice chairman of*
> *the private equity firm Perseus LLC, but kept a close eye on*
> *Afghanistan, a country he had first visited in 1971 when he was*
> *backpacking while on leave from the Peace Corps. In this article,*
> *he draws on his experiences with peacekeeping in the Balkans*
> *and Vietnam to assess the challenges ahead in Afghanistan.*

In Afghanistan American strength and skill will win every military engagement. But those victories will be worth little in the long run if they are not followed up by a successful nation-building effort. This will undoubtedly be lengthy, costly and difficult, but given the stakes in Afghanistan, we must succeed in this larger mission or face what could ultimately be a failure, no matter how well the military campaign goes.

It's not surprising that the Pentagon is wary of supporting such an effort. Peacekeeping—a necessity for successful nation building—is not a traditional military assignment. When peacekeeping begins to look like police work, it is especially distasteful. But police work is not what American troops have been doing in Kosovo and Bosnia. The role of NATO has been to provide a stabilizing security presence so that these war-ravaged areas can be nursed back to political stability and economic health—and our forces withdrawn or reduced in numbers.

This is precisely what happened in Bosnia. After bombing the Bosnian Serbs and forcing the parties to agree to a peace settlement at Dayton,

Ohio, in November 1995, the Clinton administration sent 20,000 American troops to Bosnia as part of a 60,000-soldier, NATO-led force. This force changed the facts on the ground instantly. While more than a thousand U.N. peacekeepers were killed or wounded in the four bloody years of war before Dayton, there have been, in the six years since, no—repeat, no—U.S. or NATO casualties from hostile action. This is because NATO went in "heavy": The Dayton peace agreement gave it the authority to shoot first and ask questions later. The war ended and will not resume.

With a security blanket in place, a separate international civilian structure—not the military—was given the responsibility for nation building. Many problems were encountered, and in my view, the international community has often been too passive in imposing its will on the die-hard rejectionists in all three ethnic communities who have sought to thwart a single, multiethnic state. But although progress has been too slow, it has been steady, allowing for the withdrawal of three-fourths of the original outside forces and an even higher percentage of the Americans, who now constitute only about 15 percent of the residual force of just more than 15,000 troops.

Despite this clear progress, there are, within the current administration, senior officials who refer to Bosnia and Kosovo as failures. If this is failure—two wars ended, the majority of the peacekeepers already withdrawn without casualties and inexorable (if painful) progress toward stability—then we can only wish for such a "failure" in Afghanistan. In fact, my greatest regret is not that we have done too much but that we have done too little.

So as Washington confronts the challenge in Afghanistan, the question must be asked: What's wrong with nation building anyway? Somewhere along the road from Vietnam—where it was once the proudly proclaimed mission of the United States, including its military—to Somalia, this once important part of our national security policy became a dirty word. By the mid-1990s everyone in Washington was proclaiming that we were not nation building, and this trend only accelerated after the argument about it during the second presidential debate in 2000.

Euphemisms were substituted; I'm on a nongovernmental task force studying "post-conflict reconstruction." But whatever we call it, nation building is an essential part of our policies in the Balkans and Afghanistan—and when we move against Saddam Hussein, it will be essential in Iraq as well.

Despite Vietnam and Somalia, there are important examples of success at nation building, most notably during the Cold War in countries from Greece and Japan to Korea. No country seemed more hopeless than South Korea after the end of the war in 1953: Annual per capita income was less than $100; there were millions of refugees and no industry; the South faced a heavily armed and dangerous Communist foe. But because the United States accepted the long-term obligation of providing security and also offered a huge aid program, South Korea rose from the ashes to the front ranks of stable, economically viable democracies. Nonetheless, we still have 40,000 troops protecting Korea 49 years after the war ended. No one objects to this very expensive deployment.

If it is in our vital national security interests to remain in Korea, why are much smaller deployments in the heart of Europe so controversial? Why is the Pentagon's leadership so opposed to expanding and contributing to the international peacekeeping force in Afghanistan, something that Afghanistan's interim leader, Hamid Karzai, U.N. Secretary-General Kofi Annan, Pakistan's beleaguered President Pervez Musharraf and top State Department officials are all urgently requesting?

When the United States turned its back on Afghanistan after Soviet forces were driven out in 1989, it proved to be a grievous, costly mistake that led to Sept. 11. But no one could show a strategic stake there in 1989. Today there can be no such miscalculation: Afghanistan may be as important now as Korea was a half-century ago. If we restrict ourselves to a military campaign, it will, no matter how successful, be insufficient. After we have finished scouring the caves, the terrorists will return to them to plot against the West and the indispensable Musharraf. Meanwhile, if the present trend continues, the rest of Afghanistan will fall back into the hands of warlords and drug lords (often the same people). Iran, part of the "axis of evil," will dominate western Afghanistan.

Having worked on both successful and unsuccessful nation-building efforts over 40 years on three continents, I'm under no illusion as to the immense difficulty of such a task in a country as remote, ethnically diverse and historically xenophobic as Afghanistan. I am not speaking of creating a modern free market democracy in Afghanistan, but of putting the country on a path toward stability and reconstruction. Nor am I remotely suggesting that the United States bear the burden alone. But it must take the lead. If it doesn't, others will not follow.

Let us therefore talk no longer of exit strategies or firm timetables (a mistake we made in Bosnia). As a retired four-star general replied recently when asked in a private meeting how long we should stay in Afghanistan: "As long as necessary, until we have finished the job."

It may be long and costly, but if Afghanistan is important enough to wage war over—and it is—it is equally important to stabilize and re-build, not only as a humanitarian goal but in our own vital national interest, as an integral part of the war on terror.

Afghanistan: The Long Road Ahead

RICHARD HOLBROOKE
Washington Post, APRIL 2, 2006

> *Another of Holbrooke's dispatches from Afghanistan, which*
> *focuses on what would later be called the "AfPak" problem. At the*
> *time, NATO troops were taking over the fight, and the Taliban,*
> *whose leadership was largely untouched in Pakistan, was resurgent.*
> *Holbrooke notes the particularly egregious failure of U.S. anti-*
> *narcotics efforts, and decries the lack of funds for Afghanistan's*
> *reconstruction—something he would fight for three years later*
> *inside government.*

Kabul, Afghanistan—In a region of Pakistan almost unknown to most Americans, a sort of failed ministate offering sanctuary to our greatest enemies has arisen. It is a smaller version of what Afghanistan was before Sept. 11, 2001, and it poses a direct threat to vital American national security interests.

Waziristan and North-West Frontier Province, where Osama bin Laden and the Taliban leader Mullah Omar are hiding, have become a major sanctuary in which the Taliban and al-Qaeda train, recruit, rest and prepare for the next attacks on U.S., NATO and Afghan forces inside Afghanistan. The most recent, on March 29, resulted in the deaths of one American and one Canadian soldier. More attacks must be expected.

For the United States, the dilemma is huge. There is no chance that the training of the Afghan army and police will produce a force able to defend itself as long as the Taliban has sanctuary in Pakistan. Other than "hot pursuit," which is already permitted, the United States cannot invade Waziristan; such an operation would have little chance of success and would create an enormous crisis in U.S. relations with Pakistan. Leave Afghanistan, and the Taliban will return, along with bin Laden and al-Qaeda. The only viable choice is to stay, in order to deny most of the country to the enemy. That means an indefinite U.S. and NATO military presence in Afghanistan. No U.S. official will say it publicly, but the conclusion is clear: We will be in Afghanistan for a very long time, much longer than we will remain in Iraq.

The Afghans have a simple solution to the sanctuary problem: Washington should tell Pakistan's president, Pervez Musharraf, that he must clean out the border areas—or else. The Pakistanis have an equally simple response: They are doing the best they can in a historically lawless tribal area and, in cooperation with the Americans, have already arrested or killed hundreds of terrorists. The Afghans, who deeply distrust Musharraf, do not believe this; while grateful to the United States for freeing them from the hated Taliban, they think Washington is too easy on Pakistan, in part to make up for Pakistan's anger at the recent nuclear deal with India.   .

The biggest program of Washington and the European Union is the drug eradication effort. Almost 90 percent of the world's heroin comes from Afghanistan. Official U.S. and U.N. reports claim that last year's programs reduced poppy production by 4 percent—at a cost of close to $1 billion. That means the United States spent more than the entire national budget of Afghanistan to accomplish essentially nothing! Yet the failed drug policy is continuing without significant change.

If the drug program is the biggest failure, American-inspired efforts to give the women of Afghanistan a chance for a better life have the greatest potential. First lady Laura Bush deserves credit for making this a signature issue. Insisting that more than 25 percent of the seats in the National Assembly be reserved for women was risky but inspired. I met with 10 female legislators; they were more animated and more excited about their country than any of the men. If they form a women's caucus, a process that has started with encouragement from the National Democratic Institute for International Affairs, they will become a powerful force for progress.

But let no one confuse progress for women at the higher levels (there is even one female provincial governor) with a significant change for the average girl or woman. Each time Afghanistan tried to advance the status of women, the men reacted with a strong backlash. They will do so again. Progress is distant and virtually meaningless to rural women. That striking symbol of Afghanistan, the head-to-toe covering of women that is known as the burqa, remains widely used everywhere. One vivacious legislator on the provincial council in Herat told me that while she did not like the burqa, she dared not let her "beautiful" 15-year-old daughter out without it. "The burqa," she said, "is my weapon." And self-immolation, forced on women by their families if they violate strict codes of conduct, is actually on the rise.

Herat, the only major city in the west, highlights the complexities of Afghanistan. Less than 100 miles from the Iranian border, it is enjoying an economic boom and almost no Taliban threat. But the economy is fueled in large part by Iran, which is visibly gaining economic and political influence in the region. So here is the ultimate irony of a situation filled with irony: Our "strategic ally" (in President Bush's phrase) in Pakistan is giving sanctuary to the Taliban and al-Qaeda in the east, while an "axis of evil" country is playing a stabilizing role in the west. In fact, of course, Iran is pursuing the same long-term strategic goal there as it does everywhere: to create a Shiite region stretching from Lebanon as far east as possible. Iran's growing strength in Herat can only heighten Tehran's sense that events are going its way these days.

With so much at stake, it is surprising that the administration asked for a pittance (about $40 million) for Afghan reconstruction in its recent supplemental, after the State Department and the U.S. Embassy requested about 10 times as much. Still worse, Congress compounded the lowered funding request by cutting the appropriation to $4 million.

Let us hope that these cuts were simply an aberration caused by Hurricane Katrina and bureaucratic confusion. Afghanistan will be difficult, and we must do a much better job on the ground. There is always a risk that our presence will, over time, create an Iraq-like anti-American xenophobia (in a country with a famously xenophobic history). But Afghanistan is not Iraq. Denying the country to our enemies is not a long-term strategy, but it is essential in the current phase of history, especially as Iraq stumbles toward an increasingly bleak future.

Still Wrong in Afghanistan

RICHARD HOLBROOKE
Washington Post, JANUARY 23, 2008

> *Holbrooke had not been particularly outspoken against interdiction
> programs until he assessed their disastrous cost in Afghanistan.
> Then actively campaigning for Senator Hillary Clinton for presi-
> dent, Holbrooke would later help Secretary of State Clinton lead
> a change in U.S. policy on the matter as the Special Representative
> for Afghanistan and Pakistan.*

I'm a spray man myself," President Bush told government leaders and
American counter-narcotics officials during his 2006 trip to
Afghanistan. He said it again when President Hamid Karzai visited
Camp David in August. Bush meant, of course, that he favors aerial
eradication of poppy fields in Afghanistan, which supplies over 90 percent of the world's heroin. His remarks—which, despite their flippant
nature, were definitely not meant as a joke—are part of the story behind
the spectacularly unsuccessful U.S. counter-narcotics program in
Afghanistan. Karzai and much of the international community in Kabul
have warned Bush that aerial spraying would create a backlash against
the government and the Americans, and serve as a recruitment device
for the Taliban while doing nothing to reduce the drug trade. This is no
side issue: If the program continues to fail, success in Afghanistan will
be impossible.

Fortunately, Bush has not been able to convince other nations or
Karzai that aerial spraying should be conducted, although he is vigorously

supported by the American ambassador, William Wood, who was an enthusiastic proponent of aerial spraying in his previous assignment, in Colombia. Wood, often called "Chemical Bill" in Kabul, has even threatened senior Afghan officials with cuts in reconstruction funds if his policies are not carried out, according to two sources.

But even without aerial eradication, the program, which costs around $1 billion a year, may be the single most ineffective program in the history of American foreign policy. It's not just a waste of money. It actually strengthens the Taliban and al-Qaeda, as well as criminal elements within Afghanistan.

According to the U.N. Office on Drugs and Crime, the area under opium cultivation increased to 193,000 hectares in 2007 from 165,000 in 2006. The harvest also grew, to 8,200 tons from 6,100. Could any program be more unsuccessful?

The program destroys crops in insecure areas, especially in the south, where the Taliban is strongest. This policy pushes farmers with no other source of livelihood into the arms of the Taliban without reducing the total amount of opium being produced. Meanwhile, there is far too little effort made against the drug lords and high-ranking government officials who are at the heart of the huge drug trade in Afghanistan—probably the largest single-country drug production since 19th-century China—whose dollar value equals about 50 percent of the country's official gross domestic product. There is a direct correlation between opium production and security. In relatively secure areas, production has dropped, but along the Pakistan border in the insecure south, production is increasing and amounts to about 80 percent of the overall crop.

Everyone talks about "alternative livelihoods" and alternative crops as the solution to the drug problem. This is true in theory—but this theory has been tried elsewhere with almost no success. Poppies are an easy crop to grow and are far more valuable than any other product that can be grown in the rocky, remote soil of most of Afghanistan. Without roads, it is hard to get heavier (and less valuable) crops to market—and what market is there, anyway? It will take years to create the networks of roads, markets and lucrative crops that would induce farmers to switch, especially when government officials, including some with close ties to the presidency, are protecting the drug trade and profiting from it. (Any Kabul resident can point out where drug lords live—they have the largest and fanciest houses in town.)

Barnett Rubin, a leading expert on Afghanistan and a fellow at the Asia Society in New York and New York University's Center on International Cooperation, writes in a forthcoming study that "the location of narcotics cultivation is the result—not the cause—of insecurity." He adds, "Escalating forced eradication"—as the U.S. Embassy wants to do—"will only make the effort fail more quickly because it actually builds the insurgency it is trying to eliminate."

To be sure, breaking the narco-state in Afghanistan is essential, or all else will fail. But it will take years, and American policies today are working against their own objective. Couple that with the other most critical fact about the war in Afghanistan—it cannot be won as long as the border areas in Pakistan are havens for the Taliban and al-Qaeda— and you have the ingredients for a war that will last far longer than the war in Iraq, even if NATO sends more troops and the appalling National Police training program is finally fixed. Solving this problem requires bold, creative thinking. Consideration should be given to a temporary suspension of eradication in insecure areas, accompanied by an intensified effort to improve security, build small market-access roads and offer farmers free agricultural support.

When I offered these thoughts on this page almost two years ago ["Afghanistan: The Long Road Ahead," op-ed, April 2, 2006], I was told by several high-ranking U.S. government officials that I was too pessimistic. I hope they do not still think so. Even more, I hope they will reexamine the disastrous drug policies that are spending American tax dollars to strengthen America's enemies.

Hope in Pakistan; The Problems Are Real, But So Is the Progress

Richard Holbrooke
Washington Post, March 21, 2008

> *Writing after the historic Pakistani election of February 18, 2008,*
> *which ended the seven-year rule of Pervez Musharraf, Holbrooke*
> *expressed hope that Pakistan was on the road to stability, despite*
> *the December 27, 2007, assassination of Benazir Bhutto.*
> *Holbrooke would become very close with Bhutto's husband,*
> *Asif Ali Zardari, who, in January 2011, as President of Pakistan,*
> *would attend Holbrooke's memorial service at the Kennedy Center*
> *in Washington, D.C.*

P eshawar, Pakistan—Pakistan has had a such run of bad news in
recent years that it may seem delusional to describe the current
mood here as hopeful. Yet that is the impression this country—often
called by the American media the most dangerous on Earth—is offering
a visitor.

The main reason for the new mood is the return of a vibrant democratic process and what is widely believed to be the end of a decade of
military rule. Less than two months after Benazir Bhutto's murder, her
Pakistan People's Party and the party of her chief rival, former prime
minister Nawaz Sharif, swept parliamentary elections that were widely
accepted as honest. They have formed a Pakistani version of a grand
coalition, with Bhutto's PPP on top.

The victory of these parties—broadly based political organizations
with widespread popular appeal—is only half the story. The other half is
equally important: The military seems to have pulled out of the political
arena, at least temporarily, after President Pervez Musharraf's party won

less than 20 percent of the seats in the newly elected National Assembly. Since Musharraf's real power base was as military commander, when he "took off his uniform" last year, it turned out that his residual power as president was largely ceremonial—"like the queen of England," as one enthusiastic new parliamentarian put it. The new military chief, Gen. Ashfaq Kiyani, has said emphatically that the military should stay out of politics. In a country where the military has stepped into the political process with unfortunate regularity since the birth of the nation in 1947, this could be the biggest news of all—if Kiyani and his colleagues mean it. The military has a central role to play in Pakistan's security, but not in the political arena.

Another positive straw in the wind is the poor showing of the overtly religious parties in February's elections—they got only 4 percent of the total vote. In the volatile tribal areas near the Afghan border, where the Taliban and al-Qaeda have had a sanctuary from NATO operations in Afghanistan, the Muslim parties were shut out.

This does not mean, of course, that the border region is free of terrorists; sheltered deep in the valleys and villages of western Pakistan, they pose a serious threat to American and NATO troops fighting in Afghanistan. Dealing with them will require a massive program of security and development that goes far beyond the current plan, which is about $150 million in U.S. assistance per year. After visiting the border areas this week, I believe that the place to start is with a vastly improved, better-equipped, better-trained and better-paid Frontier Corps. This ancient force, created by the British in the 19th century, has only 50,000 troops; incredibly, it faces a better-armed Taliban and local rebel groups. Put another way, the eastern front of the American war in Afghanistan is surely worth more than $150 million a year—money that, I should note, has not yet arrived in any significant amount.

Huge mistakes were made by the Musharraf regime in the tribal areas. Even Musharraf admits that his government's 2006 peace deal with the Taliban was a disaster that gave the Taliban a huge advantage in the Pakistani tribal areas and greatly weakened the NATO effort in Afghanistan. (Inexplicably, the United States publicly endorsed the deal, perhaps as part of its generally pro-Musharraf policies.)

But it seems a large overstatement to see the militants in the tribal areas as a threat to the rest of Pakistan. Pakistan's problems—including terrorism—are monumental, and its future is uncertain. (A bright spot in recent years has been a quietly improving relationship with India.) But Pakistan, the world's second-largest Muslim nation, is too big and its civil society—with its deeply established political parties, its free press, its vibrant and very visible lawyers, its thousands of nongovernmental organizations, its huge business community, and its own moderate Muslim leaders—too extensive to in fact become "the world's most dangerous nation."

For their part, educated Pakistanis are following the American presidential campaign carefully. Whoever is elected, they will continue to pay close attention to Washington. (An example: Asif Ali Zardari, Bhutto's widower and co-chairman of the PPP, told me that in choosing a woman to be speaker of the National Assembly, he was deeply influenced by his wife's friendship with Nancy Pelosi.)

Over decades, Washington has usually sent mixed signals to Pakistan. This time the message should be clear and consistent: democracy, reconciliation, the military out of politics, a new policy for the tribal areas—and more democracy.

CHAPTER TEN

Mentor and Friend

Holbrooke at work in his New York office. (© Andrew Holbrooke/Corbis)

All That's Left

SAMANTHA POWER

Richard Holbrooke will not go away.

And he might approve of that opening. "Every book chapter and article should begin with either a summary of what follows or a provocation," he told me one morning in the kitchen of his New York apartment. It was 7:30 on a Thursday morning in 2007, his wife Kati was reading the newspaper at the kitchen counter, and he sat next to her, holding a draft book chapter of mine that looked more like a U.S. government document declassified through a Freedom of Information Act request—bearing more of his black marker than my computer's black font. He was barefoot, wearing an untucked pink oxford shirt and khaki shorts. He peeled tangerines, and looked back and forth between my mangled chapter and *Morning Joe*, which he muted during the commercials. "At the start of every chapter, the first sentence should make the reader want more." He read out loud the sentence that led my chapter and laughed giddily. "Wordy, wordy, wordy, too many words," he said. "Anyway," he continued, not at all self-conscious that he might be stating the obvious or bruising a fragile ego, "you are just lucky you have me as an editor."

At the next commercial he made me follow him into his study. He pulled a large Clark Clifford volume off the shelf. "Now this is somebody who knew how it was done," he said, failing to remind me that he had ghost-written the book he was praising. As I eyed the clock and reminded him of his 9 a.m. meeting in mid-town, he told me he would not leave until I too knew what I was doing. With that, he patiently read every first sentence of every one of the 35 chapters in the 736-page book. And he paused for me to marvel each time. "I get it, I get it," I said, wanting the tutorial to end. "If there were any evidence you got it," he said firmly, "I would already be driving downtown to my meeting."

This encounter, and so many like it, rattle around in my head whenever I start an article, a government memo, or even an email. And there are dozens, if not hundreds, of people out there who have endured—and benefited from—similar schooling. The members of Holbrooke's Afghanistan/Pakistan team at the State Department got almost as many writing and editing lessons as they got strategic policy guidance. "Cut this down by 40 percent and bring it back to me," he would say. To supplement his own lesson plan, he printed two dozen copies of George Orwell's splendid 1946 essay, "Politics of the English Language," and demanded instant improvement in the clarity of their prose. "Don't write like a bureaucrat," he would say, "write like a real person. You can't forget that there are real people on the other end of your memos who are going to read what you write."

Every one of us who ever enjoyed Richard Holbrooke's unique "quality of attention" was incredulous when he zoomed in on us. "Why the hell is Richard Holbrooke making time for *me?*" we asked ourselves. After all, this was a man who had a reputation for looking over the shoulder of an American president to see if there might be someone more useful behind him. Yet, again and again, no matter his assignment, he picked up mentees in much the same way that other ambassadors picked up exotic carpets and statuettes. Holbrooke flattered, disappointed, interrupted, teased, interrogated, lectured, embraced, and above all, *taught* us all. The famed power seeker surrounded himself with younger people who had nothing but earnestness to offer him. It was never clear how he found the time, how he always found the time.

WHAT RICHARD HOLBROOKE TAUGHT WAS NOT ALWAYS THE SAME AS what the rest of us learned. We listened to what he said, of course. But we also watched him, which exposed some of his legendary contradictions.

Mentoring for him was not a sign-up sheet exercise where young staff stopped by for fifteen minutes of career advice; it was a commitment that had no expiration date. His teachings aren't the kind that the Foreign Service Institute passes along to future diplomats. But perhaps from now on they should be.

For starters, Richard Holbrooke taught us that rank and status are bunk; knowledge is what matters. In the summer of 1995, nearly two years into my stay as a rookie reporter in the former Yugoslavia, I got a call from Holbrooke out of the blue. "This is Richard Holbrooke speaking," he said, pausing for effect. My heart stopped at the sound of a voice I had heard only on television. "I heard you are thinking about going to law school." Although he had never before spoken to me, he had strong views about my future. "Why the hell would you do that, when you've been in the Balkans long enough to actually know something about something?" He demanded I come to meet him on his next visit to the region. I did as I was told, but when I arrived there was no small talk, none of the guidance counseling I hoped I might receive. "You've lived here a couple years," he said, after a cursory greeting. "You know things we can't know from Washington. What are we doing right? What are we doing wrong? What should we do differently?" These were Holbrooke questions. The essence of what he was always asking was, *How do we help better?* Impact on the ground was everything. He could not have cared less that his source was a twenty-four-year-old freelance correspondent who had never set foot in the State Department or White House.

My memory of this incident is so vivid, but—in its way—so far-fetched that I didn't quite trust my recollection. However, the many tributes to Richard since his death confirm that this was his common practice. When Holbrooke was ambassador to the UN, Jordan Dey earned a job interview with him and traveled to New York from a tiny town in Kosovo where he was running an NGO. Expecting to be grilled on what he would do if he got the job, Dey was instead asked for a grand strategy. "What is the solution for Kosovo?" Holbrooke asked. "What should we be doing differently?" He treated job interviews as fact-finding missions. He didn't have time for snobbery or hierarchy—he just wanted ideas and answers.

And he assumed others operated the same way, seeking out the doers, irrespective of their level in a hierarchy. Mary Ellen Glynn, his press spokesman at the U.S. Mission to the UN, said he once ordered her to pry a decision loose from the Pentagon. "Call Bill Perry and get this done!" Holbrooke shouted, forgetting that the U.S. secretary of defense might be disinclined to take a call from an unknown aide to the U.S. ambassador.

Holbrooke placed a premium on "knowing something about something." He prized knowledge that came from experience in the field, but equally that from books and articles, which he devoured. He knew an enormous amount about American politics and American and European history, and he loved sharing what he knew. He delighted in adventures from times past and reflexively drew connections to the present. As is widely known, he cultivated ties with journalists for what they could do for him and his agenda; but he also was drawn to them because he admired their craft, and because they had stories to tell and fresh facts to share. Because they knew something about something, he simply found them good company.

In the rare instances when he saw that his enthusiasm alone wasn't changing the reading habits of those around him, he would give strict instructions. "You cannot speak with such confidence on this subject and not have read this book," he would say. He viewed facts and preparation as his lifeblood, not least because such knowledge gave him a tactical advantage in his negotiations. In pursuit of a deal in which the U.S. would pay back its overdue dues to the UN, for example, he had to convince other countries to raise their assessments while the U.S. lowered its own. Holbrooke insisted that his negotiators track down minute details on each of the other countries' spending history in the UN. As Suzanne Nossel, a Holbrooke aide, recalled, "We knew more about what they paid than they did." Holbrooke used this information, sealing a grand bargain for repaying U.S. dues, while slashing the U.S. share going forward—a deal most had thought could not be done.

A second lesson Richard Holbrooke taught was, get the hell out of Washington if you want to learn, but do come back to Washington if you want to have an impact. In his own life he had inhabited both worlds. When Dean Rusk, the father of his best friend and John F. Kennedy's future secretary of state, spoke about the U.S. Foreign Service to Holbrooke's Scarsdale High School senior class in 1958, Holbrooke was intrigued. He graduated from Brown University in 1962, not long after President Kennedy's summons to public service, which had motivated others in his generation to join the new Peace Corps or ride freedom buses to fight segregation in the South. His first choice was a job at the *New York Times*, but, turned down by Scotty Reston, he joined the Foreign Service instead. Within a year of his graduation from Brown, the young Holbrooke had completed language training and area studies and earned himself a posting to Saigon. The undersecretary of state for political affairs, U. Alexis Johnson, selected him to be part of a new program that would give a select group of foreign service officers field experience, away from embassies. Holbrooke joined a division of the U.S. foreign aid mission called the Office of Rural Affairs and was sent to the Mekong Delta, where he was responsible for distributing American funds and supplies to assist the local authorities. He developed two tastes early: first, to be at the center of the largest foreign policy crisis of his time (Bosnia and Afghanistan would follow Vietnam); and second, to get close to the people whose lives were affected by U.S. government decisions. For the rest of his life, notwithstanding his omnipresence in the halls of power, he always held the windowless Situation Room and the sterility of Washington policy discussions in less esteem than he did a trip to a refugee camp.

Amid it all, of course, Richard Holbrooke needed Washington. The town enthralled him just as it consumed him. It picked him up as often as it ground him down. "There is simply nothing like the power of the United States of America to do good in the world," he would tell journalists, academics, and college students, as he tried to lure them into public service. But if he ever sensed that those he mentored were taking themselves or the U.S. government too seriously, he would remind them of the absurdity of their existence, and the shortcomings of a town of migrants with lousy sports teams, insufficient culture, and a steady diet of political casualties on which to fixate. When he met colleagues for drinks after work, he grew visibly irritated if they kept their government badges on. "You know something is wrong in a place where it is considered normal for people to wear pictures of themselves around their necks," he would say.

The destinations most likely to meet with Holbrooke's approval were overseas diplomatic or journalistic postings, where one could experience history firsthand, learn languages, meet people, and be changed by a new place. Short of that, he counseled, you should live in New York.

Third, he taught us to be direct except when it was better not to be. Richard Holbrooke could be crushingly blunt. When he came over for dinner, he would take up the whole meal venting about the inanities of the bureaucracy he served, but then yawn ostentatiously when it took his dinner companions longer than a couple of sentences to get to the point. When one protested his impatience, he would say, "What do you think this is? The Council on Foreign Relations?" Sometimes, when he told me a story I had heard before, I'd complain, and he'd say, "Well, I've seen nothing in your actions that indicates that you have retained it, so I'm trying again." When we sought his advice on how to manage a particular work challenge, he would often cut us off in mid-sentence with, "You know what your problem is?" and then—on a good day—he might say, "You care too much about substance," or "You tell the truth." (On a bad day, he could say, "You don't know the first thing about politics," or "You haven't read enough.") One of his favorite retorts, designed to stop both journalists and junior colleagues in their tracks, was, "I have no idea what that means." Just as Barney Rubin, a senior adviser on Afghanistan and Pakistan, was preparing to speak with Secretary Clinton about the region for the first time, Holbrooke told Rubin, "I've noticed that you have a tendency to be somewhat arrogant and condescending when speaking to nonspecialists." Rubin assured him that he took the point but added, "Funny. I've heard the same thing about you." Holbrooke quickly flashed, "See? That's exactly what I'm talking about." Chris Hill, his senior aide during the Kosovo crisis, and good friend, referred to Holbrooke as "my mentor and my tormentor."

A principle of natural selection undergirded his habitat. In the company of the famously thin-skinned Holbrooke, only the thick-skinned survived. And the truth is, those around him unwittingly promoted this principle of natural selection, as they often fell in love with one another and reproduced. He saw himself as responsible for five weddings in a single year while he was ambassador to the UN ("You were inspired by my relationship with Kati," he told his staff). And as difficult as he was—and as complicated as it was to work for him—his former staff were more often than not repeat offenders, those who signed up to serve with him multiple times. Why? As Paul Jones, his deputy working on

Afghanistan and Pakistan, put it: "When you were in the presence of Richard Holbrooke, you knew you were alive."

Fourth, Holbrooke, the famed self-promoter, sought to elevate those around him, arguably with even more enthusiasm. A young Holbrooke had sought out older statesmen—Clifford, Harriman, Kissinger—and studied their every move. By the time he had built up personal authority in the world, he instinctively sprinkled it like fairy dust on others. "You have just said something truly significant," he would say to a junior aide unexpectedly, and they would quickly rewind the tape to remember what it might have been. He was "Richard Holbrooke," capital R, capital H. He had built that brand name from scratch, he knew it had come to mean something, and he doled out his anointings liberally, knowing the attention he could generate for others. Our ideas, books, plays, movies, government memos. He actually said things like: "Not since the Long Telegram have I seen a more important memo." This complete conviction—combined with his remarkable social network (before Facebook, there was Holbrooke)—meant that a Holbrooke endorsement became a foreign policy wonk's version of an Oprah seal of approval. When he bragged about his AfPak team, he evoked the ten-year-old Holbrooke running through the glories of the Yankee lineup. He conjured up excuses for his team members to meet—and preferably brief—Secretary Clinton; he hustled journalists so as to get a staff member's name in the newspaper; he fought for them to be included in his White House meetings and, if unsuccessful, he regaled them after the fact with two-hour recaps of the personalities and atmospherics, as well as the policy outcomes; and he dramatically inflated their achievements when he introduced them around town, giving them job titles they never held and crediting them with headline-grabbing policy achievements ("Meet Rina Amiri, she wrote the Afghan Constitution"). He especially admired those with qualities he knew he did not have in abundance.

And his loyalty and enthusiasm did not abate when his staff moved on. When Mary Ellen Glynn, his former spokesman, got married and moved from Washington to Portland, Oregon, he volunteered to write introduction letters for the two people he knew there. These two people were the CEO of Nike and the former governor of Oregon. He also never forgot those with whom he had worked successfully. For Glynn, this meant that when he took the job of special representative for Afghanistan and Pakistan, he wanted her back. When she sat down with

Secretary Clinton, the secretary told her, "Richard Holbrooke has been asking me about you *every day*." Because he believed people were the key to sound policy, his staffing choices were as important to him as the substantive content of his meetings with Afghan president Hamid Karzai. And the care he took finding, educating, and promoting the right people did not simply gratify his desire to be surrounded by the best team possible. It had its own payoff. If he lifted people up, they would be in a better position to lift up what he deemed worthy policy ambitions.

Fifth and above all, Richard Holbrooke became a model for how to love and delight in those around him. He had lots of targets for his love—his family above all, of course—Kati, Anthony and David, Lizzie and Chris, his grandchildren, the individual members of the teams he built around him. He raved about each of them and their feats, to all who would listen. He was surprisingly sentimental, keeping in his wallet for seventeen years the small scrap of paper on which he had first written Kati's telephone number. And he applied this same capacity for love and delight to an insightful column, a bad movie (he talked about *Something About Mary* like it was *Citizen Kane*), a briefing by an aid worker in Kandahar. When he liked something or someone, he was all in.

And he had a deep interest in who and what other people loved as well. He imbibed gossip, and nothing interested him more than other people's love lives—the one topic for which he had endless patience. Though it was often late at night when he did so, he frequently told staff that they should get home to their families to "avoid making the same mistakes" he had made by being away so much when he was raising his sons. To single friends and staff, he offered advice in love that was prescriptive and sometimes dogmatic, especially when he was advising ending a relationship that he believed wasn't going anywhere. Never were his listening skills more evident—or his work schedule more accommodating—than for a broken heart. He had found in Kati a beloved partner with whom he could read, argue, explore, and laugh uproariously, and he wanted that for the rest of us. When I first started dating my husband, Cass, he was one of the first people I called to tell. Indeed, on one of our first dates, I rudely answered a call from Holbrooke and passed the phone to Cass. Holbrooke was as warm as could be in saying, "If you hurt her, Mort [Abramowitz] and I will break your kneecaps."

As he was rushed to the hospital—unsure of his fate, but certain things weren't good—he said again and again, as if to reason with the gods, "But there are so many people I love, there are so many people I love." To the very end, Richard Holbrooke thought first of those he loved.

ON THE AWFUL NIGHT WHEN RICHARD HOLBROOKE'S HEART GAVE OUT, his friends and mentees staggered in disbelief to the lobby of George Washington University Hospital. There were colleagues from his days in Vietnam, from Wall Street, Bosnia, Kosovo, Democratic political circles, the UN, Afghanistan, and every country and obsession in between. They were the people he had taught, but also the second family he had created. And every person in that hospital lobby—no matter how high they had risen in life—seemed profoundly lost and unmoored.

After Holbrooke's passing, David Brooks, the *New York Times* columnist, spoke for many when he said, "it is like driving through Colorado and looking up and seeing the Rockies are no longer there."

The legacy of Richard Holbrooke shows up all over the world—the American Academy in Berlin, the carefree patrons of open-air cafes in Sarajevo, the HIV-positive workers at companies that now provide treatment, the Taliban fighters who have laid down their weapons. But his greatest imprint—invisible to the naked eye—may be in the hearts and heads of those of us who have had the privilege of learning from him, laughing with him, and loving all of him.

A Sense of Drift, a Time for Calm

RICHARD HOLBROOKE
Foreign Policy, No. 23, SUMMER 1976

> *Holbrooke published this piece as one of his last at the helm of*
> Foreign Policy, *which he left in July 1976 to become a full-time*
> *foreign policy adviser to Jimmy Carter's presidential campaign.*
> *With an eye to the election, Holbrooke strikes a moderate tone,*
> *seeking middle ground between guilt-ridden liberals and*
> *neoconservatives, a then-nascent movement.*

For 12 years, until one year ago, one issue—Vietnam—provided a relatively simple litmus test for everyone. People were placed with relative ease on a single-band spectrum from hawk to dove; and individuals moved along it, invariably from right to left, as the war ran into increasing difficulties and growing opposition at home.

Many thought that the battle lines shaped during those years of hard and divisive national debate would continue in the post-Vietnam era. Had they survived intact, the debate would have been relatively clear-cut, easier to understand and follow, than has in fact been the case. But that did not happen.

The sides are no longer clearly drawn. Indeed, the confusion is often so great that one cannot even tell which side of certain debates some of our highest leaders favor. One week the president seems to side with those fearful that America has become militarily inferior to the Soviet Union. The next week, he asserts that America remains "second to none." His uncertain trumpet is matched by others, including his secretary of state, whose private gloom over the decline of the West is exhibited only rarely in public, where he sticks for the most part to statements that if America will only regain its national consensus and follow its commander in chief, it will again be the most powerful nation on earth. Critics argue that we are getting weaker and must take decisive action to regain clear-cut supremacy. Others assail us for continuing the arrogance of power, of insensitivity to the new realities.

That these are the most difficult questions our nation must face is obvious. But the answers are neither obvious nor, ultimately, empirically derivable. They must come, in fact, out of the confusion of the national debate, and we must understand in advance that the answers will not be definitive.

There is among some observers a feeling that the very casualness of our process argues against hope, presents a case for despair and a pessimistic outcome. Thus we hear James Reston, for example, constantly lament the fact that "Washington" is dealing with "the politics of the problem," not with the problem itself. Yet the distinction is largely misguided; politics is the problem but also the opportunity, indeed, the essence of the nation's strength as a democracy.

ODD CONVERGENCE

As America enters its third century, we find an odd conjunction in American political life—a convergence of two different critiques of America: the Vietnam-based, guilt-ridden anguish of the left, and the striking emergence, in the last year, of a new pessimism within what is often called the neoconservatives. Each group inadvertently reinforces the other, and adds to our national sense of drift and uncertainty.

Vast differences, of course, exist between the two groups here described, and it is for this reason that one must assume, and hope, that their present conjunction is inadvertent and temporary. Increasingly, the left has looked on the state as an enemy, a force that must be weakened since it cannot be captured. The conservatives on the other hand now see strong state power as their potential ally, and view what they regard as its erosion as a grave threat. These are not straw men; they are the focus of the debate. Both approaches are equally misguided.

Liberals, predictably, will find themselves in the middle of this overly simplified spectrum. Their present anguish is by now well documented.

It stems primarily from Vietnam, but many other issues merged over recent years to reinforce the lessons of that ugly war. The roll call of policies which liberals advocated and which turned out to be corrupt is almost too long to list.

A few key elements of this view of America as a corrupting influence in the world should be mentioned, however, if only to remind us of just how sad our recent string of revelations has been. Beyond Vietnam they include: Cambodia, Chile, Bangladesh, Burundi, Angola, Cyprus, FBI and CIA abuses and excesses, Watergate, Lockheed and other improper business practices overseas, ITT, and assassination attempts. Each revelation was an essential part of the process of redefining our past and rethinking our future; those who argue that the revelations themselves are wrong are missing the deeper significance of what they call an "orgy of self-destruction." It is essential to understand our past in order to reshape our future.

But the left's critique of America's role in the world has taken on some ominous overtones. There are those who now accept the proposition that because America has done some evil things, America itself is an evil force in the world. The theological overtones are disturbing, of course, but so is the ease with which some people can now embrace extreme extrapolations.

But even more fundamental is the abuse of reason which is involved in such black-and-white views of foreign policy. At its best, foreign policy is often a choice between the lesser of two evils. And many policy issues come down to a choice between conflicting positive principles—when, for example, the principle of nonintervention in the internal affairs of another country conflicts with a concern for human rights.

These conflicts must be resolved in ways that do not seem immoral or unreasonable to most people. That this so often has not always been the case does not mean that our nation is itself evil or incapable of finding a better foreign policy. It does mean that we have been badly led. Thus, in their sweeping horror at the consequences of the use of power, in their willingness to assume the worst about their own country, in their disillusionment with the bright, liberal rhetoric of the Kennedy years, the left critique—at least at its anguished worst—is a cul-de-sac, a dead end, which could lead to isolation from the rest of the nation.

This potential isolation is by no means a sure thing. Relatively few people want to cut themselves off entirely. What looks like a group is in fact a spectrum, a range of opinions. While some people are falling off the end, many are climbing back on. It seems likely, for example, that if the Democrats regain the White House in November, what some now treat as a left-liberal grouping will split into two broad segments—those who continue to view the government with suspicion and hostility primarily because it is the government, and those who seek reinvolvement with public policy.

THE NEW PESSIMISTS

The left has recently been met more than halfway by some people who are not even perceived of as a group. Some of them have been called neoconservatives, but they have now become, in fact, "the new pessimists"—although they would presumably resist the description.

The new pessimists tend to see their worst fears about the decline of American power coming true. Many of them predicted that if the United States abandoned its commitments to the South Vietnamese government of Nguyen Van Thieu, it would mark the end of American leadership in the world. In the congressional votes on such issues as Turkish aid and Angola, they find grim evidence that they were right. In the assaults and revelations of the press—including for some even Watergate—they see signs of the collapse of essential authority. In the growth of Soviet military power, they see the greatest imaginable threat to America's survival.

A remarkable example of this sort of thinking was Norman Podhoretz' lead article in the April issue of *Commentary*, which he edits, dramatically titled, "Making the World Safe for Communism." But other examples abound; the verbal similarities between the left and right pessimists symbolize the strange convergence that is taking place. Bruce Russett, an opponent of the war, and Henry Brandon, reflecting in part the outlook of Henry Kissinger, write of "The Retreat of American Power." Henry Steele Commager calls his latest collection of essays, simply: "The Defeat of America." Commentary runs an entire issue under the theme, "A Failure of Nerve?" Richard Rosecrance edits a collection of essays by leading American and European observers with the odd and wholly inaccurate title, "America as an Ordinary Country."

C. L. Sulzberger, writing in *The New York Times* from London, describes a decline in American prestige overseas exceeding "by far what most Americans imagine to be the case." Many Americans, wrote Stanley Karnow in *Newsweek International*, were reluctantly conceding General de Gaulle's cruel description of the United States as a nation that had gone from "infancy to decadence without attaining maturity." Daniel Patrick Moynihan, having lately left his bully pulpit at the United Nations, has described democracy as a "recessive form of government, like monarchies used to be, something the world is moving from, rather than to." James Schlesinger has written that "The West is clearly in disarray, and within a few years could actually be at bay." And *U.S. News and World Report* ran a special cover story asking, "Is Democracy Dying?" Their "upbeat" answer, in effect: "Not Yet."

The message of the new pessimists varies, and sooner or later they usually make some rhetorical bow in the direction of traditional American pride. Politics requires even pessimists to express some faith in their country, but there is an underlying gloom which can be summarized as follows:

- The presidency is so important as an institution that we must be ready even to accept specific errors of presidents, such as Vietnam or Watergate, in the national interest.
- Public debate and congressional involvement in foreign policy are dangerous, if not downright immoral. Congress, in particular, is a body whose involvement in foreign policy is by and large an unwarranted interference.
- The true measure of a nation's strength is its international reach and influence. Domestic issues may come and go, but the nation is measured primarily by its international standing.
- That standing is in turn measured by the amount of disposable power—military power—that a country can apply.
- The hard give-and-take of the democratic process, at least when it intrudes into foreign policy, is somewhat distasteful. The press in particular is an adversary, increasingly seen as a threat to democracy rather than one of its main attributes.

Every one of the arguments cited above has, in my opinion, some validity; none comes solely from thin air or overheated imagination. Congress is a mess, often shallow and ineffectual. The press is a mixed bag, ranging from outstanding through irrelevant to just plain awful and irresponsible. Public debate on foreign policy issues does make implementation of policy more constrained, more chaotic, and more difficult. And military power is, without question, a vital ingredient of our policy.

Furthermore, the nation is clearly drifting. Its leaders have failed us far too often in recent years, the bright promises of their television rhetoric dimmed by poor performance and shallow deceits. Public relations has replaced policies: imagery has succeeded where imagination has failed. This failure of leadership goes far beyond weakness in the Oval Office, and encompasses Congress and the press, business and labor. It is not surprising that every survey of the people shows that confidence in institutions—virtually all institutions with the possible exception of the Supreme Court—is at an all-time low.

WHO ARE THE NEW PESSIMISTS?

What are we to make of this extraordinary conjunction of the new pessimism of the conservatives with the older, Vietnam-based, guilt-ridden pessimism of the liberals? Is it temporary, an accidental meeting of different groups with different objectives, momentarily joined in common dismay with the situation we confront? Or is it rather, in Winston Churchill's phrase from another time, the "end of the beginning" of our magnificent history? Daniel Bell, for one, is not sure. After writing that "The American century lasted scarcely 30 years, [and] foundered on the shoals of Vietnam," he concludes on a hopeful note: "Of all the gifts bestowed on this country at its founding, the one that alone remains as the element of American exceptionalism is the constitutional system...." If that remains, says Bell—referring to the "common respect for the framework of law, and the acceptance of outcomes under due process"—then the United States may remain "humanized among nations." It is a thoughtful and sober yet hopeful conclusion, one that I share. Unfortunately, it is not shared by many of the new pessimists, or the left, still confused by the recent past.

Recently I talked with a distinguished American political scientist, now spending a year in Paris. "What are you doing?" I asked. "Oh," he replied, "I spend most of my time explaining to French editors and professors that America is not finished in the world." "But why do they think that?" I asked. "Because Kissinger keeps telling it to them in private," he replied.

What an extraordinary thought. Kissinger would deny it, of course, but think of it a moment: The U.S. secretary of state as a leading spokesman for the theory that America is in retreat.

Is it true?

Lately, Kissinger's sensitive antennae have begun to tell him that too many people have heard him lament the future of civilization, that he has been too gloomy, and that his message is not consistent with the demands of the presidential campaign. Accordingly, he has begun to swing around again, and in his public statements he has begun to extol our virtues and our strengths.* But his recent repositioning seems more tactical than thoughtful; for a long time it has been no secret that Kissinger is desperately concerned about the fate of this country, and that his own personal political difficulties have heightened his gloom.

So, despite recent public adjustments, Kissinger must be understood as a key to the new pessimism. Normally, no single person could have such a pivotal role, but Kissinger remains unique, a man with continuing influence among academicians and intellectuals, journalists and foreign leaders. Even in his decline, Kissinger's voice is by far the most powerful and important in this country today on foreign policy; raised now in private frustration against his own country's recent course and his own growing troubles, it is being listened to overseas.

Kissinger's behavior is, to my mind, strange for a secretary of state. He has confused his own troubles with those of the republic. But even if his assessments were true, which I do not believe to be the case, Kissinger should not make the kinds of statements that he has recently been making in private. If Kissinger believes that the American era is over, crushed beneath the weight of our unwieldy processes that he does not believe in, he is hardly the best man to represent our nation internationally, no matter how skilled he is as a negotiator.

But Kissinger stays on, convinced that if our decline is under way, then he is the man best equipped to get the best deal for us before it is too late. One may be pardoned, I hope, for questioning both assumptions.

Kissinger is not alone in his views. But curiously, the two men in public life who have taken positions most close to his, in overall, historic

---

* In Phoenix, Arizona, for example, on April 16, Kissinger sounded oddly like the man he was attacking, Ronald Reagan. But rhetoric makes strange bedfellows.

terms, have been such bitter personal rivals for power and attention that the unlikely trio has gone so far unremarked. I refer, of course, to Daniel Patrick Moynihan and James Schlesinger. While in the government, both men were thorns in Kissinger's bureaucratic side. Each sought access to the president, and a role in the formulation of American policy which exceeded Kissinger's desires. What Kissinger wanted, as we all know, was maximum control over the processes and policies of the executive branch, and minimum interference from Congress. Neither Moynihan nor Schlesinger was willing to concede the game to Kissinger, and thus, while each was still in service, Kissinger fought them regularly, raged against them behind their backs, and intrigued against them at every opportunity. In the case of Schlesinger, Kissinger succeeded too well, and now finds himself facing a new secretary of defense who is less knowledgeable about technical defense issues, yet more potent politically—that is, a man who knows less and can get more. In Moynihan's case, Kissinger helped make Moynihan a minor folk hero.

But my point does not concern their differences, which were often overadvertised by the press and are, in any case, no longer a factor in the formulation of policy. The critical conjunction does not concern their disagreement on the Soviet Backfire bomber, or what Kissinger and Moynihan say about each other.

Rather, it is the common conviction all three seem to share that America's strength has been shattered by the erosion of unity at the center, by the excessive interference of Congress, by the attacks of the press, by our weakness in standing up to our critics overseas, and by an unchecked growth of Soviet power.

To all three men, and to others who share their views, the fault seems to lie in a lessening of central authority, in a weakening of the strength of the institutions, far more than a weakness in our leaders. Listening to them, I fear that I hear them saying, between the lines, "The fault is in the people, who, egged on by Congress and the press, are losing faith in their institutions." They don't say, as I would, "Perhaps the fault is in the quality of leadership."

The quality of leadership—no wonder people shy away from the issue. After all, it is hard enough to judge such matters generations later, even for historians who can argue heatedly over the nature and quality of, say, Franklin Roosevelt's leadership. Impossible, then, to deal with a comparison between today's pygmies and the giants of our mythic memory.

Yet it is hard to believe that they, or their subordinates, will measure up to the men of earlier times.

I do not mean to sound nostalgic, but I fear we are in the hands of a pygmy generation, and that instinctively people know it. The last of the great figures of World War II and the Cold War have departed the active scene, replaced by their staff aides, special assistants, and cautious bureaucrats. In business, faceless organization men have taken over huge, self-perpetuating corporations. In journalism, a more confusing picture, worthy of more detailed analysis, has emerged, for the press can no longer hide behind its traditional shield as a mere observer—it has become a participant, and to some a very special object of hate and blame. Its dominant force now is television, its guiding lights a new set of values; success is show biz. In Congress, the collapse of the rigid old baronies was necessary, but nothing coherent has come forward to replace them yet; instead, chaos under decent and ineffectual leaders has been the trend. And in labor, the dinosaurs hang on, immensely powerful, but without vision.

EASY ANSWERS

To some, the answers to America's present malaise are simple. They call for more unity behind the president—simply because he is president, right or wrong; increased defense spending, to counter the growth of the Soviet military; and ways to restrain the press, that unruly and sensation-seeking adolescent who keeps printing the wrong thing at the wrong time.

In particular, lately, a growing number of critics of the so-called "neoconservative" school are concentrating their fire on the "media," blaming it for, or crediting it with—take your pick—far more than it really deserves. If the news is bad, the press is increasingly blamed for bringing it to us, for twisting it into a negative mold.

No matter what the excesses and errors of the press, this argument strikes me as a refuge for people who are no longer willing to present their case openly, to let it ride or fall on how it is judged by the people. The role of the press and television is critical in America today, but it is not the villain some have made it out to be.

What is really going on? Our internal debates have been so bitter that it is hard to look at the real strength of the nation.

Not that this task is easy. Disputes rage these days over almost every measurement of our national strength, especially in comparison to that of the Soviet Union. Who is spending more on defense? Who has the greater strategic weapons capability? Who has more natural resources? Who produces more steel? Food? Doctors? Who gained and who lost in Angola? In the Middle East?

I do not propose to address each one of these difficult questions here. But it is important never to lose sight of some basic facts about our nation's real strengths—strengths so immense that they have carried us through the traumas of the last decade; strengths which are still there, waiting to be rekindled by new and better leaders.

First, to start with Schlesinger's own definition of power, we remain, by a considerable margin, the most powerful nation on earth militarily. While Schlesinger would admit this, he would maintain that the trend is disturbing. But our strategic nuclear striking power is more than enough to deter an attack by any rational decision maker, and no amount of power can deter an attack by an irrational leader.

But I would question the very measurement of power as partially outmoded. America must remain a strong power militarily, but what we have learned in recent years is that other kinds of power are growing rapidly in importance—economic power, resource and energy power, food power. To maintain enough strength to influence events as we need to, we need all these kinds of power—and fortunately we do, to a degree that is still unmatched in the history of the world, except by our own recent past.

Economically, the United States enters its third century still in a clear world leadership role. At the end of a world war in which everyone else paid devastating costs, we were totally dominant, and that hegemonial era, of course, has ended. America's importance in the world economy has declined in relative terms, but we remain first. Our share of world GNP, 39 percent in 1950, is down to 27 percent now—still a huge percentage. The dollar has grown in importance, and there is every likelihood that it will remain the dominant currency for at least the next decade.* In short, if we no longer make all the rules in the economic world, we remain the unquestioned leader.

---

* See Richard N. Cooper, "The Future of the Dollar," *Foreign Policy* 11.

Is this a bad thing, a sign of decline? Hardly. The nearly absolute position of dominance that followed the 1944 Bretton Woods agreements had to end, and indeed our own enlightened policies of foreign aid to Europe and Japan encouraged and hastened the process. The problems we now deal with in the economic sphere are to a considerable extent problems of success. That does not lessen their importance—but it should at least put the situation in perspective.

What the present situation requires has been expressed by Marina v.N. Whitman as follows: " . . . to find the political will to modify our own short-term economic interests to the requirements of an international economic order which we no longer control."We must use our natural strengths, she concludes, to replace "leadership based on hegemony with leadership based on persuasion and compromise."While the task will be difficult, it is within reach; Whitman points out, "there is no acceptable alternative."*

As for energy and natural resources, the emphasis has been, rightly, on our growing dependence on foreign sources. But we should, once again, not forget that solutions or at least reductions in the size of our problems are within our reach, and that the United States has been hurt less than any other importing country by the fivefold increase in the price of oil since 1973. Our comparative advantage, ironically, increased in many ways during this period.

Then there is food. It is by now well known that we have become the breadbasket of the world. The United States and Canada will probably export, for example, a total of 94 million metric tons of grain in 1976. Of the seven major regions of the world, only one other, Australia–New Zealand, will be a wheat exporter. The rest of the world will be net importers, and the second biggest importer of all will probably be the Soviet Union.

This is a relatively new development. Prior to World War II all geographic regions except Western Europe were net exporters. The two worst performances in this area have been in Asia and the Soviet Union. In fact, the Russian performance in agriculture is appalling, and must be taken into account when trying to measure how the two powers compare. And as for the rest of the world, the worldwide movement outside

---

* See Marina v. N. Whitman, "Leadership without Hegemony," *Foreign Policy* 20, p. 160.

North America from export to import status has been a one-way street: no country has gone against this trend in the last two decades. Here, surely, is an area where we must take the lead internationally, demanding certain performance levels and reserve systems, while still dealing with farmers' concerns at home.

If we remain the strongest nation militarily, economically, and in terms of resources and food, why do some Americans fear that history now favors the Russians?

The answer, of course, takes us right back to where we started, not with our strengths but our divisions. Kissinger and many others feel that such sights as the congressional rejection of aid to Angola are an invitation to the Soviet Union to begin knocking on the next door, perhaps Rhodesia or Zambia. Or that Castro, emboldened by Angola, will try his hand again. Or that the Israelis will conclude that we would no longer stand by them in a showdown. In short, that our word is no longer good; that, in Podhoretz' prophecy, we are witnessing the beginning of "Finlandization from within."

There is a serious conceptual trap which is implicit in these theories of America's decline. They are derived in large part from the concept that perceptions of power and national will are just as important as actual national strength itself—and that the world perceives our resolve and will as eroded.

But from what evidence would one deduce the erosion of American will or strength? In fact, the people who profess the greatest concern with that erosion are the same people who most regularly proclaim it; they are the heralds of the very thing they most lament.

This approach is difficult to deal with because it confuses objectives and values. Was Angola, for example, of real importance to the United States? Not really—and anyway, we could have sought relations with the MPLA. Yet the Russians were there, and we were caught again in the old and cruel trap—if Moscow is on one side, we must be on the other, as indeed we have been for many years. The result, in this case, was accentuated by Kissinger's public behavior. Knowing in advance that the Congress would reject any request for aid in Angola, Kissinger nonetheless made major public statements that the vote was critical, and if it failed, then we would be seen around the world as having measurably weakened. How unskillful to draw attention to a certain impending defeat! What priorities and values lie behind such odd action? I confess to some uncertainty as to whether or not Kissinger did it because he wanted to emphasize the importance of the vote and perhaps turn it around, or because he and the president wanted to lay responsibility for the inevitable MPLA triumph in Angola at Congress' feet. In either case, it is not the sort of thing that a person seeking to maximize his strength would do— to choose a losing battle and then raise the ante just before defeat. Angola, however, followed a recurring pattern.

HISTORY DOES NOT FAVOR MOSCOW

In any case, history does not favor the Russians. In a dreadful decade for America, they have made few inroads internationally—and have been set back themselves in some areas. They have seen their side gain for the first time in Africa just now, but they have lost in the Arab world since 1972, when Sadat kicked them out of Egypt. They have made gains in South Asia, in India, but have not turned Communist Vietnam or half-crazed Cambodia into part of their orbit. Their bitter conflict with China continues. In Western Europe, they have watched Rumania follow Yugoslavia into nearly independent status, and have been unable to keep control over the Communist parties of Italy and France. In Portugal, the situation, once so bright, has dimmed. Their leadership is old and uninspired, their system destructively rigid. "A process of degeneration has set in," says Zbigniew Brzezinski, although "it has not yet reached critical proportions."

Some scholars viewing the twin difficulties of the two greatest powers have concluded that there is something systemically wrong with the way governments and institutions deal with the problems of the modern world. But I suspect that the differences between the two systems are so vast that they will respond differently to future challenges.

We are living in a peculiar moment, almost suspended between Vietnam and Watergate on the one hand, and the election of a president on the other. For the first time we have an appointed president. We have been going through a relentless and grueling reexamination of ourselves, a period of self-revelation and public exposure that might have caused a revolution in a country less strong than ours. But to sweep the problems away, or to deny them, or to punish those who draw attention to them, would be unwise and still more divisive. What is vitally important is that we learn from our mistakes and our past, but not give up our dreams and values as a nation.

That we have fallen far short of those dreams and values we all know. But they are worthy goals, and worth pursuing still. The nation is still strong, far stronger than its critics of either liberal or conservative persuasion realize. It can survive everything but its own defeatism. We must take counsel of our fears, but not be governed by them.

We still possess, in addition to the sheer measurable elements of power already mentioned, an enormous force that we cannot use these days, but that I hope will once again, someday, be part of our "arsenal"— the basic moral force that exists in the principles of our system of government—a force eroded in recent years under leaders who apparently did not really believe in them.

Implicit in the beliefs and attitudes of some of our recent leaders is the feeling that we can only be strong by not being ourselves; that surely is the domestic equivalent of one of the most unfortunate phrases from the Vietnam war, that "We had to destroy the town in order to save it."

I end, then, not with a prediction—for the world is too uncertain for that—but with an expression of personal hope: that this slum of a decade we have lived through will end, and that we will regain our self-confidence and self-esteem; that we will recognize that we do not need to dominate the world in order to live safely in it, still the most powerful nation on earth. And above all, we must retain our belief in the exceptional nature of our system of democracy. That is our ultimate source of strength.

The Next President: Mastering a Daunting Agenda

RICHARD HOLBROOKE
Foreign Affairs, SEPTEMBER/OCTOBER 2008

Thirty-two years after Holbrooke surveyed the foreign policy scene on the eve of the 1976 election, he turns to the 2008 campaign and the global challenges facing the next president. Holbrooke asserts that the United States can and must right itself from the drift of the George W. Bush years. He acknowledges, however, that the international challenges facing the incoming president will be more daunting than those faced by any American leader since Truman. This would be one of Holbrooke's last major published articles.

The next president will inherit leadership of a nation that is still the most powerful in the world—a nation rich with the continued promise of its dynamic and increasingly diverse population, a nation that could, and must, again inspire, mobilize, and lead the world. At the same time, the next president will inherit a more difficult opening-day set of international problems than any of his predecessors have since at least the end of World War II. In such circumstances, his core challenge will be nothing less than to recreate a sense of national purpose and strength, after a period of drift, decline, and disastrous mistakes.

He will have to reshape policies on the widest imaginable range of challenges, domestic and international. He will need to rebuild productive working relationships with friends and allies. He must revitalize a flagging economy; tame a budget awash in red ink; reduce energy dependence and turn the corner on the truly existential issue of climate change; tackle the growing danger of nuclear proliferation; improve the defense of the homeland against global terrorists while putting more pressure on al-Qaeda, especially in Pakistan; and, of course, manage two wars simultaneously.

To make progress on this daunting agenda, the president must master and control a sprawling, unwieldy federal bureaucracy that is always resistant to change and sometimes dysfunctional. He will also need to change the relationship between the executive and the legislative branches after years of partisan political battle; in almost all areas, congressional support is essential for success. So is public support, which will require that the next president, more effectively than his predecessor, enlist help from the private sector, academia, nongovernmental organizations, and the citizenry as a whole.

The presidency of the United States is the most extraordinary job ever devised, and it has become an object of the hopes and dreams— and, at times, the fears, frustration, and anger—of people around the world. Expectations that the president can solve every problem are obviously unrealistic—and yet such expectations are a reality that he will have to confront. A successful president must identify meaningful yet achievable goals, lay them out clearly before the nation and the world, and then achieve them through leadership skills that will be tested by pressures unimaginable to anyone who has not held the job. A reactive and passive presidency will not succeed, nor will one in which a president promises solutions but does not deliver—or acts with consistent disregard for what the Declaration of Independence called "a decent respect to the opinions of mankind."

Although not every issue the new president inherits requires change, every major one requires careful reexamination. In many cases, new policies and new people—loyal to the president and capable of mobilizing the support of the permanent bureaucracy—will be necessary. But a comprehensive national security policy is more than a collection of individual positions. A coherent vision for the United States' role in the world must be based on its enduring national interests, its values, and a realistic assessment of its capabilities and priorities; not even the most powerful nation can shape every event and issue according to its own preferences. The days when a single word, such as "containment," could define U.S. foreign policy will not return in this world of many players and many, many issues. Still, there is a need to define a broad overarching concept of the United States' national interests. (The Bush era's focus on the "global war on terror" was simultaneously too limited and too broad.)

To restore the United States to its proper world leadership role, two areas of weakness must be repaired: the domestic economy and the United States' reputation in the world. Although the economy is usually treated as a domestic issue, reviving it is as important to the nation's long-term security as is keeping U.S. military strength unchallengeable. This will require more than a cyclical upturn; to repair the economy in the long term, a new national policy on energy and climate change will be essential. And restoring respect for American values and leadership is essential—not because it is nice to be popular but because respect is a precondition for legitimate leadership and enduring influence.

The president should address both issues as early as possible in order to strengthen his hand as he tackles pressing strategic issues, including the five neighboring countries at the center of the arc of crisis that directly threatens the United States' national security—Turkey, Iraq, Iran, Afghanistan, and Pakistan. A few early actions that lie wholly within his authority can make an immediate impact. The most compelling such actions would be issuing a clear official ban on torture and closing the detention facility at Guantanamo Bay, Cuba, which now holds only 260 prisoners. Because the Bush administration limited itself to punishing only those at the very bottom of the chain of command at Abu Ghraib, the damage to the United States' image has been immense and continuing—the gift that keeps on giving to the United States' enemies. Presidential directives making clear that the U.S. government does not tolerate or condone torture are necessary in order to separate the new administration from that costly legacy. As for Guantanamo, closing it is complicated, as Bush administration apologists (and many lawyers) say. Well, a lot of things in life are complicated. Guantanamo must not become the next president's albatross, too; closing it, no matter how difficult, is not just desirable but imperative.

A NEW FACTOR

History is not immutable. But there is one pattern that comes very close to being a law of history: in the long run, the rise and fall of great nations is driven primarily by their economic strength. Rome, imperial China, Venice, France, the Netherlands, Portugal, the United Kingdom—all had their day, and their international decline followed inexorably from their economic decline.

Starting in the late nineteenth century, nothing was as important to the emergence of the United States as its spectacular economic growth. That growth was fueled, literally, by cheap domestic oil. The United States always overcame its periodic economic downturns, even the Great Depression. It is therefore reasonable for Americans, who are optimistic by nature, to assume that the nation's current economic difficulties are just another temporary cyclical setback. But a new factor has emerged, unlike any the United States has previously faced. With the price of oil quadruple what it was four years ago, Americans are witnessing—or, more to the point, contributing to—the greatest transfer of wealth from one set of nations to another in history. Politicians and the press understandably focus attention on the domestic pressures caused by the high price of oil—the "pain at the pump." But the huge long-term geostrategic implications of this wealth transfer, so far virtually neglected, also require the next president's attention.

Consider the following, from the noted oil expert Daniel Yergin: the United States consumes more than 20 million barrels of oil a day, about 12 million of which are imported. Based on prices from the first half of 2008, that means the United States is transferring about $1.3 billion to the oil-producing countries every day—$475 billion a year. (At the more recent price, $140 for a barrel of crude, the amount is far greater.) The other major consumers, including China, the European Union, India, and Japan, are sending even greater portions of their wealth to the producing countries, for a total annual transfer of well over $2.2 trillion. These figures are climbing.

Suppose high oil prices continue for, say, another decade—a gloomy but not unreasonable scenario given the long lead time required to wean the consuming nations off their expensive habit. The wealth now accumulating in the producing nations will lead over time not only to even greater economic muscle but also to greater political power. Some of these producing nations have very different political agendas from those of the United States, Europe, and Japan. Groupings of oil-rich nations with goals opposed to those of the United States and its European allies will become more common and act more boldly. More money will be available to fund dangerous nonstate actors who seek to destroy Israel or destabilize parts of Africa or Latin America—or attack the United States. There is a well-known example of this, although the West seems not to have learned any lessons from it: Saudi Arabia, which, although it has long worked with Washington to bolster world oil output and keep prices within an acceptable range, has simultaneously allowed billions of (ostensibly nongovernmental) dollars to go toward building extremist madrasahs and funding terrorist organizations, including al-Qaeda. There will be more such complicated double-dealing in the future: Does anyone doubt that the current assertiveness on the international stage of, for example, Iran, Russia, and Venezuela comes from the economic muscle that accompanies their growing petrodollar reserves? (Venezuela now spends five times as much as the United States on foreign aid to the rest of Latin America.)

At the same time, the problem of climate change has reached a level that, in the view of many scientists, threatens the planet; many believe that there is only a decade to act to avoid a catastrophic tipping point, which would otherwise come somewhere around the middle of the century. Even as former Vice President Al Gore crossed the globe raising the alarm, the Bush administration wasted seven and a half irreplaceable years, refusing to address the issue. There was little sense of urgency in this administration or among its congressional allies; they opposed almost anything other than voluntary conservation measures—until the prices at the pump hit $4 a gallon. It was only at the end of 2007, under immense political pressure, that the Bush administration finally agreed to the first increase in fuel-efficiency standards in 32 years. (By that time, fittingly, Gore had won the Nobel Prize.) Then, at the 2008 G-8 summit in Japan, George W. Bush agreed to a vaguely worded and essentially meaningless "aspirational" goal on the reduction of carbon emissions.

Over time, stronger conservation measures, together with investments in new technologies, will undoubtedly be put into effect. But if oil and gas prices fall from their current bubble-like levels, consumption will rise again. On the other hand, if prices stay high, consumption may fall, but the United States and its closest allies will continue to hemorrhage petrodollars. Either way, absent an effective energy and climate-change policy, the planet will suffer from continued warming. Drought and famine will increase in some of the poorest places on earth, food prices will continue to rise, and people will abandon areas that are no longer arable. Glaciers and icecaps will melt faster, ocean levels will rise, and more species of plants and animals will become extinct. The Bush administration's neglect of these issues is beyond astonishing—it is as shocking, in its own way, as the administration's performance in Afghanistan and Iraq.

The two major presidential candidates, Senator Barack Obama (D-Ill.) and Senator John McCain (R-Ariz.), both say that they take climate change seriously. But an examination of their positions on the issue shows important differences. Obama has a far more comprehensive plan, with an ambitious goal for emissions reduction, a market-based mechanism that has broad support among economists on the left and the right, and substantially greater investments than McCain's plan in technologies that will help achieve these goals. McCain stresses removing environmental restraints on domestic and offshore drilling. This is hardly a serious long-term solution to anything; even if major new fields were found, they would have no effect on supply for at least a decade, and they would do nothing for climate change or conservation.

The search for effective energy and climate-change policies will require a national consensus on the seriousness of the situation and an action plan entailing compromises and sacrifices on everyone's part, sacrifices normally associated with war—all without undermining economic growth. As a cautionary tale, it is worth recalling President Jimmy Carter's fervent but unsuccessful attempt to rally the nation in a prime-time televised speech in April 1977. Wearing a much-mocked cardigan sweater, he said that his energy-independence project would be the "moral equivalent of war." When someone pointed out that the initials of that phrase spelled "meow," the press had a field day, ignoring the substance of Carter's proposals. A true national debate was deferred for 30 years. One of Ronald Reagan's first acts as president was to remove from the White House roof the solar panels Carter had had installed.

The twin challenges of energy dependence and climate change offer an opportunity for a breakthrough between the two most important nations in the world today, which also happen to be the world's top two polluters. Together, China and the United States produce almost 50 percent of the world's carbon emissions. In the last year, China has passed the United States as the world's largest polluter. In 2007, two-thirds of the worldwide growth in global greenhouse gas emissions came from China, according to the Netherlands Environmental Association, which estimates that China now emits 14 percent more climate-warming gases than the United States does. On a per capita basis, however, it is still not even close—as every Chinese points out. The United States produces

19.4 tons of carbon dioxide per person per year; China (5.1 tons) trails not only the United States but also Russia (11.8 tons) and the countries of western Europe (8.6 tons). India checks in at only 1.8 tons per capita.

The effort to produce a new international climate-change treaty to supplant the Kyoto Protocol, which expires in 2012, is getting nowhere fast. A new agreement is supposed to be finished and ready to be signed in Copenhagen at the end of 2009. Do not count on it. With neither China nor the United States playing a leading role in the negotiations, many members of Congress are warning that there is no greater possibility of Senate ratification for the Copenhagen agreement next year than there was for the Kyoto Protocol in the 1990s (in other words, none)—unless at least Brazil, China, India, and Indonesia agree to limits on their carbon emissions. And without China and the United States, the value of the treaty, although still real, would be limited.

Here is a seemingly insoluble Catch-22: the major emerging economies will not agree to any treaty containing meaningful limits on their emissions, and the U.S. Senate will not ratify an agreement that does not include them. There is, however, another approach that should be considered, without abandoning the Copenhagen process: multiple agreements in which various combinations of nations address specific parts of the larger problem. In such a collection of agreements, there would be a greater opportunity for genuine U.S.-Chinese cooperation. In particular, the two nations could reach bilateral agreements for joint projects on energy-saving, climate-change-friendly technology. The mutually beneficial goal would be an increase in energy efficiency and a reduction in carbon emissions in both countries. (Japan, the world's most efficient energy consumer—and an indispensable ally of the United States—could participate in such arrangements; it has much to teach both nations, and it already has bilateral technology-exchange agreements with China.) From carbon capture to clean coal to solar and wind energy, there is vast untapped potential in joint projects and technology sharing—but no institutionalized U.S.-Chinese framework to encourage them.

On a recent trip to China, I raised the possibility of such bilateral agreements with senior Chinese officials, who showed interest and a willingness to explore the idea unofficially through nongovernmental channels. Their concern, freely expressed, was that any energy plan the West proposed would be just another device to slow down China's economic growth. Whether true or not, this deeply felt view, shared by India and other major emerging markets in regard to their economic growth, must be understood and taken into account in order to make progress. Perhaps the window is already opening slightly: Wang Qishan, the powerful vice premier in charge of trade and finance, recently called publicly for joint research laboratories for renewable energy and pollution-reducing technologies. "Stronger cooperation between the two countries in energy and the environment," he wrote in the *Financial Times* on June 16, "will enable China to respond better to energy and environmental issues and also bring about tremendous business opportunities and handsome returns for American investors." In the careful language of one of China's top officials, this is an unexpected and welcome signal. The next administration should not ignore it. Vigorous follow-up would not only address one of the world's most pressing problems; it would also open up a new door for cooperation in the world's most important bilateral relationship.

AGREEMENTS AND DISAGREEMENTS

Given the dissatisfaction of Americans with the nation's present condition, it is hardly surprising that both Obama and McCain have sought to emphasize the changes they would bring. Both have said that they would put more emphasis on Afghanistan—an early Bush administration success that has deteriorated dramatically as a result of neglect, miscalculation, and mismanagement. Both candidates have promised to strengthen U.S. relations with NATO allies. Both have expressed concern—although in very different language—over the recent behavior of Russia, especially in Georgia. (McCain has gone overboard, however, speaking in a highly confrontational manner and calling for the expulsion of Russia from the G-8, the group of highly industrialized states—something that he surely knows would never be agreed to by the other six G-8 members and a bad idea in its own right.) Both have promised to rebuild the armed forces and take better care of the wounded from Afghanistan and Iraq. Both are committed to the support and defense of Israel. (Although both have said they would close down the detention facility at Guantanamo and ban torture, a significant difference emerged in a recent Senate vote: Obama supported, and McCain opposed, an important statutory requirement to hold the CIA to the same standards for interrogation as the military, as mandated in the U.S. Army Field Manual.)

It is the differences between Obama and McCain that are truly revealing, and they offer important insights into the values and styles of the two men, their profoundly divergent attitudes toward the role of diplomacy, and their contrasting visions for the United States. Obama's policy proposals—whether on climate change, energy, Africa, Cuba, or Iran—are forward-leaning; he proposes adjusting old and static policies to new and evolving realities. He emphasizes the need for diplomacy as the best way of enhancing U.S. power and influence. On trade, although McCain accuses Obama of neoprotectionism, in fact Obama argues for improving trade agreements to take into account elements such as labor and environmental standards—improvements that would give them more domestic support.

In contrast, McCain's boldest proposals are neither new nor original: his vague "League of Democracies," for example, sounds like an expansion of an organization, the Community of Democracies, created by former Secretary of State Madeleine Albright that still exists but is virtually ignored by the current administration. Although McCain says his league "would not supplant the United Nations," he explicitly proposes that it take collective action when the UN does not. "The new League of Democracies," he said last year, ". . . could act where the UN fails to act, to relieve human suffering in places like Darfur [and] bring concerted pressure to bear on tyrants in Burma or Zimbabwe, with or without Moscow's and Beijing's approval." McCain calls this "the truest kind of realism." Whatever McCain says, his "League," unlike the forum created by Albright, would be viewed by everyone as an attempt to create a rival to the UN. Recent conversations I have had with senior officials in many of the world's leading democracies confirm that not even the United States' closest allies—let alone the world's largest democracy, India— would support a new organization with such a mandate.

The UN has been undermined and underfunded for the last eight years, often making it weaker and more vulnerable to anti-American positions. The UN is, to be sure, a flawed institution. But it plays an important role in U.S. foreign policy, and if correctly used, it can advance U.S. national interests and play a more effective role in peacekeeping in such difficult areas as Sudan. Yet the UN can only be as strong as its largest contributor (which is also a founding member), the United States, wants it to be. Obama would improve and reform the organization in ways that would serve the United States' interests, starting by asking Congress to pay the arrears that have grown once again, under Bush, to over $1 billion (an American debt of similar size was paid down after an arrangement made in the last year of the Clinton administration). Creating a new organization, instead of making a renewed effort at serious UN reform, would work against the very objectives McCain says he supports.

In his speech on nuclear proliferation delivered at the University of Denver on May 27, McCain said he would reconsider his long-standing opposition to the Comprehensive Nuclear Test Ban Treaty if a renegotiation could "overcome the shortcomings that prevented it from coming into force"—a vague and elusive conditionality. Obama, in contrast, flatly favors this important treaty. Similarly, Obama has endorsed the goal of eliminating all nuclear weapons, as outlined in the now-famous article by former Secretary of State George Shultz, former Secretary of Defense William Perry, former Secretary of State Henry Kissinger, and former Senator Sam Nunn. McCain has pointedly refused to do so.

Looking at these and other differences, it is clear that the U.S. electorate is being offered two different visions of the United States' role in the world and two different attitudes toward diplomacy. On most issues, with the important exception of climate change, McCain supports or takes harder-line positions than the Bush administration. (For example, he expressed deep skepticism about the partial agreement President Bush announced in late June on the halting of North Korea's nuclear weapons development.) Although McCain prefers to describe himself as a "realist" or, more recently, a "realistic idealist," looking broadly at his positions, it is impossible to ignore the many striking parallels between him and the so-called neoconservatives (many of whom are vocal and visible supporters of his candidacy).

IRAQ AND IRAN

Of course, no disagreement between Obama and McCain reaches the level of importance of their disagreements over Iraq and Iran. Policy toward these two countries will shape perceptions of the new president more than policy on any other issue; in some ways, the election is a referendum on Iraq. When McCain says that the United States is in Iraq to win, he means it—no matter what the costs or the duration of the war might be. No other issue engages him as deeply or as emotionally, and his feelings derive not from political calculation but from profound personal conviction. He believes that recent reductions in American and Iraqi casualty rates are proof that the United States is winning the war. As of this writing, however, he has not said that this highly welcome improvement in the situation would lead to significant troop withdrawals in 2009 beyond the removal of the "surge" troops whose departure has already been announced. He has repeatedly made clear that he is ready to leave troops in Iraq indefinitely rather than take the risks that he believes would accompany major reductions. He never acknowledges the risks and costs associated with continued deployments.

Obama, on the other hand, believes that military victory, as defined by Bush and McCain, is not possible—a judgment shared by the U.S. commanders in Iraq. He finds unacceptable the costs to the United States of an open-ended commitment to continue a war that should never have been started. Obama concludes that in the overall interest of the United States, it is necessary to start withdrawing U.S. ground combat troops at a steady but, he emphasizes, "careful" pace. This will, he predicts, put far more pressure on Iraqi politicians to reach the compromises necessary to stabilize the country than leaving the troops there. Emphasizing diplomacy as an indispensable component of U.S. power, Obama has also called for an all-out effort to involve all of Iraq's neighbors in a regional diplomatic and political effort to stabilize the country.

McCain charges that his opponent's position (which he and his supporters often misrepresent as "precipitous withdrawal") would snatch defeat from the jaws of victory, encourage the United States' enemies, and weaken the nation. But he offers no exit strategy, no clear definition of achievable victory, and no plan for promoting political reconciliation within Iraq. His policy amounts to little more than a call for continuing the war because of the risks associated with trying to end it. Such a negative goal is not a sufficient rationale for putting still more American lives at risk.

Some of McCain's opponents have misstated, at times, his position on a key point: he never said that the United States might have to fight in Iraq for a hundred years. But what he did say was equally unrealistic and highly revealing of his mind-set. Using as his model South Korea, where 28,500 American forces remain 55 years after the armistice agreement, McCain said that he was ready to station U.S. troops in Iraq for at least that long, if not longer, even a hundred years. Such a multi-decade commitment, even under peaceful conditions, is inconceivable in the xenophobic and violent atmosphere of the Middle East. In the end, McCain defines every other issue in terms of Iraq. "Its outcome," he wrote in these pages late last year, "will touch every one of our citizens for years to come." That may be true, but perhaps not in the way that he intends.

Obama stands McCain's core argument on its head. "The morass in Iraq," he wrote, also in these pages, "has made it immeasurably harder to confront and work through the many other problems in the region—and it has made many of those problems considerably more dangerous." Like McCain, who favored the war even before it began, Obama has been consistent: he opposed the war from its outset. He is well known, of course, for his intention to start withdrawing combat troops as soon as possible. But because he recognizes the complexities of withdrawal, he has also emphasized (to little press attention) the need to be extremely careful at every step of that process. Obama has said that he would maintain flexibility in regard to whether to leave a residual force and follow an exact timetable. "This redeployment," he wrote in these pages, "could be temporarily suspended if the Iraqi government meets the security, political, and economic benchmarks to which it has committed. But we must recognize that, in the end, only Iraqi leaders can bring real peace and stability to their country." He added, "The best chance we have to leave Iraq a better place is to pressure these warring parties [the Sunnis and the Shiites] to find a lasting political solution. And the only effective way to apply this pressure is to begin a phased withdrawal of U.S. forces."

The dispute between the Iraqi government and the Bush administration over a "status-of-forces agreement" highlights this issue. When the Iraqi prime minister insisted on a timetable for U.S. withdrawal (suggesting a three- to five-year adjustable schedule), why did both the current administration and McCain demure? Bush had often said that the United States would leave when it was not wanted; now he objects to a reasonable request from a sovereign state, seeming to prove the charge that the United States seeks a permanent presence in Iraq. Obama, on the other hand, calls it "an enormous opportunity . . . to begin the phased redeployment of combat troops." In July, reports surfaced that the administration might withdraw one to three combat brigades still in Iraq after the departure of the surge troops. If true, both candidates could claim they were right; Obama could plausibly say that this was what he had called for all along, and McCain could say that it justified his support for the surge.

At the heart of the United States' geostrategic challenge lie five countries with linked borders: the United States' NATO ally Turkey, Iraq, Iran, Afghanistan, and Pakistan. In this arc of crisis, incoherence has marked U.S. policy since 2003. This five-nation area falls into three different regional bureaus in the State Department. Washington preaches different policies on democracy in neighboring countries, confusing everyone—pressuring Israel and the Palestinians, for example, into letting Hamas, the terrorist organization, run in the 2006 Palestinian elections, with disastrous results, while backing away from democracy promotion in Egypt. There is little coordination or integration of policies toward Afghanistan and Pakistan, although the two countries now constitute a single theater of war. No single concept beyond the vague "global war on terror"—defined in any way that suits the short-term needs of the administration—has guided U.S. strategy. Relations with all five countries have deteriorated.

Any serious policy will require dealing with all the countries in this region, as well as Israel and the Palestinian Authority, Lebanon, Syria, and Saudi Arabia. This unfortunately includes the very unpleasant reality at the center of this region, Iran. Both Obama and McCain agree that preventing Iran from becoming a nuclear weapons state must be a major priority. Both would tighten sanctions. Neither would remove the threat of the use of force from the table. But from that point on, their emphasis and language differ significantly. Obama has said repeatedly that he is ready to have direct contacts with Iran at whatever level he thinks would be productive, not only on nuclear issues but also on Afghanistan, Iraq, and Iran's support for terrorist organizations, including Hamas and Hezbollah (which Iran has equipped with tens of thousands of rockets aimed directly at Israel's heartland). McCain not only opposes such direct talks but also has famously said that the only thing worse than a war with Iran would be a nuclear Iran. Obama's forthright approach has been met with cries of alarm from McCain and his supporters, as though the very thought of talking to one's adversaries were in and of itself a sign of weakness, foreshadowing another Munich. This position is contradicted by decades of U.S. diplomacy with adversaries, through which U.S. leaders, backed by strength and power, reached agreements without weakening U.S. national security. Diplomacy is not appeasement. Winston Churchill knew this, Dwight Eisenhower knew it, and so did John F. Kennedy, Ronald Reagan, and George H. W. Bush.

This singular difference between Obama, on the one hand, and George W. Bush and McCain, on the other, offers an important insight into the underlying philosophies and values of the two candidates. Although McCain and his advisers have sometimes looked for ways to distance him from Bush, his position on Iran (as with Iraq) is tougher than that of the Bush administration. This is, one can safely assume, McCain's real view, which he sometimes expresses in pungent and humorous language ("Bomb, bomb, bomb, bomb, bomb Iran," he once sang at a public rally). Coupled with his criticism of the Bush administration's deal with North Korea and his call to throw Russia out of the G-8, his position suggests a deep, visceral aversion to talking to one's adversaries, perhaps stemming from a concern that such dialogue might be viewed as weakness. It also shows an innate skepticism of diplomacy as a frontline weapon in the United States' national security arsenal. Although both Bush and McCain attack Obama as weak, Obama's position is in fact closer to the traditional default position of almost everyone who has ever practiced or studied diplomacy or foreign policy. Even loyal pro-McCain Republicans, such as James Baker, Robert Gates (before he became secretary of defense), Henry Kissinger, and Brent Scowcroft, have disagreed with the McCain position on Iran and Russia.

Of course, there is no certainty that serious talks are possible with the real power center of Iran: Supreme Leader Ayatollah Ali Khamenei and his inner circle. It is therefore important, before starting down the diplomatic track, to have a clear idea as to what should be done if talks either are refused or make no progress. Contacts should begin through private and highly confidential channels to determine if there is a basis on which to proceed. The ongoing low-level communication through the U.S. and Iranian embassies in Baghdad, although limited in scope and unproductive so far, could allow for initial probing with little risk of compromise, and there are several ongoing private "track-two" efforts that could also be useful. The model that comes to mind, not surprisingly, is the one that President Richard Nixon and his national security advisor,

Kissinger, used to open a dialogue with China in 1971, after 22 years of noncontact. Nixon's decision to talk to one of the most repressive regimes in the world, at the height of the insanity of the Cultural Revolution, came at a time when Beijing's treatment of its own population was certainly worse than that of Tehran today. China was also supporting guerrillas fighting U.S. troops in Southeast Asia. Yet Nixon and Kissinger talked to Mao Zedong—and changed the world. (The way not to proceed is to emulate Reagan's move in 1987, at the height of the Iran-contra drama, when he secretly dispatched his national security advisor, Robert McFarlane, to Tehran carrying a chocolate cake decorated with icing in the shape of a key.)

Would an effort at dialogue with Iran produce results? Could it reduce the overt anti-Israel activities of the Iranian government, which poses an existential threat to the Jewish state? Could it stop the Iranian nuclear program? Is there enough common ground to enlist Iran in a regional project to stabilize Iraq and Afghanistan? None of these questions can be answered in advance, but most scholars and experts believe that there are sufficient parallel interests to make the option worth exploring, just as Obama (and all the other candidates for the Democratic nomination) has suggested. Combined with the threat of tougher sanctions—and with the use of force remaining on the table—this carrot-and-stick approach would not threaten the security of either Israel or the United States, and it would strengthen the United States' position elsewhere in the world, especially with other Muslim states, regardless of its outcome.

If Tehran rebuffs an opportunity to have meaningful talks with Washington, it will increase its own isolation and put itself under greater international pressure, while the United States will improve its own standing. Of course, this journey, once begun, will require adjustments along the way. Diplomacy is like jazz—an improvisation on a theme. Let it begin next year, as part of a new foreign policy in which diplomacy, conducted with firmness and enhanced by U.S. power, and consistent with American values, returns to its traditional place in the United States' national security policy.

Such an approach toward Iran, coupled with the drawdown of U.S. combat units in Iraq, would have an important additional benefit: it would enhance the value of a return by the United States to its role as a serious, active peacemaker between the Israelis and the Palestinians. As with so many other issues, the Bush administration wasted most of its eight years not attending to this one, only finally engaging with it in 2007, with the "Annapolis process" launched by Secretary of State Condoleezza Rice. That effort will not lead to anything more than, at best, a loose framework agreement before the administration's time runs out. The next president must engage personally with this issue, as every president from Nixon to Bill Clinton has in the past.

THE OTHER WAR

Although both Obama and McCain agree on the importance of the "other war"—that in Afghanistan—this alone is not sufficient. Current U.S. policy in Afghanistan is a failure. American voters should hear in more detail what each candidate would do about it. For McCain, the question arises as to where the additional resources needed would come from if he continues the war in Iraq. Obama has already pledged at least 10,000 more troops.

Since the U.S.-led coalition's initial success in driving the Taliban from the cities, the basic U.S. plan and timetable in Afghanistan have been upended time and again by events that were not foreseen and policies that were inept. This past year, disaster was staved off only with the dispatch of additional British, Canadian, French, and U.S. troops. The right course now does not lie in a huge increase in NATO forces, although additional forces will be required for the southern and eastern parts of the country. The Taliban cannot win in Afghanistan; their terror tactics and memories of the "black years" repel most Afghans. But by not losing, by staying alive and causing continual trouble, the Taliban are achieving a major objective—preventing success by the central government, tying down large numbers of NATO troops, rallying "jihadists" from around the world to a remote but oddly romantic front. Faced with this challenge, the central government has shown that it is simply not up to the job. Meanwhile, the international community, a vast and uncoordinated collection of nongovernmental organizations, international agencies, and bilateral organizations, does enormous good but, paradoxically, sometimes undercuts its own goals by creating an ever-deeper dependency on foreigners for services that Kabul cannot deliver.

The situation in Afghanistan is far from hopeless. But as the war enters its eighth year, Americans should be told the truth: it will last a long time—longer than the United States' longest war to date, the 14-year conflict (1961–75) in Vietnam. Success will require new policies with regard to four major problem areas: the tribal areas in Pakistan, the drug lords who dominate the Afghan system, the national police, and the incompetence and corruption of the Afghan government. All present immensely difficult challenges, but the toughest is the insurgent sanctuaries in the tribal areas of western Pakistan. Afghanistan's future cannot be secured by a counterinsurgency effort alone; it will also require regional agreements that give Afghanistan's neighbors a stake in the settlement. That includes Iran—as well as China, India, and Russia. But the most important neighbor is, of course, Pakistan, which can destabilize Afghanistan at will—and has. Getting policy toward Islamabad right will be absolutely critical for the next administration—and very difficult. The continued deterioration of the tribal areas poses a threat not only to Afghanistan but also to Pakistan's new secular democracy, and it presents the next president with an extraordinary challenge. As a recent *New York Times* article stated, "It is increasingly clear that the Bush administration will leave office with al-Qaeda having successfully relocated its base from Afghanistan to Pakistan's tribal areas, where it has rebuilt much of its ability to attack from the region and broadcast its messages to militants across the world." Nothing—not even Iraq—represents a greater policy failure for the outgoing administration.

AN OVERFLOWING AGENDA

The focus here on a few major issues does not mean that others can be ignored. If history is any guide, issues that are neglected too long often emerge at the top of the policy agenda—Somalia, Bosnia, Cambodia, Darfur, Myanmar (also known as Burma), Tibet, and Zimbabwe are only a few recent examples. So even as a new administration starts to deal with the arc of crisis, it must also pay close attention to issues that could easily overwhelm it, in much the way Rwanda did Clinton's administration in 1994, when the president's focus was on Bosnia. A good example is Sudan, where, in addition to there being a deepening crisis in Darfur, the North-South agreement, once hailed as a genuine Bush-era success, is now in danger of collapse. It is likely that its key provision (national elections followed by a referendum on independence in the South) will be ignored or repudiated. By 2010, the odds are that Sudan will once again explode into a major North-South conflict, with the perennial risk of involvement by its neighbors. Preventing such a scenario will take intense efforts, led by the United States and the Africa Union and requiring the active involvement and support of China.

U.S. relations with the Muslim world will require special attention; efforts so far to encourage moderate Muslims to deal with extremists have not worked. A new, creative approach to public diplomacy must be developed. Then there is the odd problem posed by the "democracy agenda" of the last six years. The Bush administration's inept advocacy of a fundamental human right has contaminated one of the nation's most sacred concepts. Bush did the dream of democracy a huge disservice by linking it to the assertion of U.S. military power. Pressuring other countries to adopt the superficial aspects of a complex and subtle system of governance is simply not the route to follow in promoting American values or security interests. Yet the goal is correct and should not be abandoned—only presented in a style and a tone far more sensitive to how it is perceived in other lands. The next administration should focus more on human rights (a phrase curiously absent from the Bush lexicon) and basic human needs while still encouraging the development of democratic forms of government, accompanied by the evolution of a pluralist political culture, the rule of law, and improvements in material conditions, especially through job creation. If there is progress in these areas, democracy will follow, in ways that countries will determine for themselves—with U.S. encouragement. That is the lesson of Chile, Indonesia, the Philippines, South Korea, Taiwan, and several promising young democracies in Africa.

It was in Africa that President Bush produced his greatest success—his anti-AIDS program, one of the few bipartisan policies of the last eight years. The United States has spent over $13 billion on the program since 2003. It has saved well over one million lives so far and incentivized other nations to do more. But the Bush administration's Africa policy has been notably deficient in addressing the strategic, economic, and environmental dimensions of Africa's plight. It has failed to deploy the instruments of statecraft in addressing Africa's debilitating cycle of violence—in the Democratic Republic of the Congo, Sudan, Zimbabwe, and the obscure but explosive Horn of Africa. The world needs a strategy to address Africa's endless conflicts, and that strategy must include a political approach to conflict resolution. The next administration must attend to the crises and mobilize support from its allies and from the African Union. The Bush administration played a useful role during the postelection crisis in Kenya (as did Obama, who gave interviews to Kenyan media and the Voice of America), but nowhere else on the continent has the United States been particularly effective. The UN is a key player, but the United States must lead the effort to get more resources for UN peacekeeping in Africa, or else such efforts will have no chance of success. In Obama's extraordinary trip to Africa in 2006, he gave early hints of the promise of his candidacy. When I visited Kenya a few months later, I felt the excitement that his visit, including his undergoing a public HIV test in Nairobi, had generated. The conventional wisdom on Africa is that it is a hopeless case. This view—which amounts to triage by continent—is neither true nor acceptable morally, politically, or strategically.

In Latin America, the United States must begin to redress the widespread skepticism toward U.S. leadership—but not by making implausible promises to eradicate poverty and inequality or to stop drug trafficking and rampant crime. The greatest boost the next president can give to the realization of the long-elusive consolidation of a social contract in Latin America starts with recovering the social contract at home. Immigration reform and policies to alleviate economic anxiety, from introducing universal health care to making major investments in education and infrastructure, will create the surest path to rebuilding U.S. public support for what is now de facto integration with Latin America, whether through capital or language, commerce or culture.

To advance U.S. interests, Washington needs a different relationship with Mexico and strategic ties with Brazil. In Mexico's case, thriving trade along a 2,000-mile border, vast population networks, and shared vulnerability to increasingly pervasive organized-crime syndicates require sustained presidential attention, as Bush promised but was unable to deliver. In Brazil—the world's ninth-largest economy, a leading global producer of food and ethanol, an emerging petroleum giant, a potential nuclear power, and a major emitter of greenhouse gases—the next president can find a partner to advance key global initiatives, help define the shape of multilateral institutions, and act as a diplomatic ally in confronting the toughest regional challenges.

LEADING IN A MULTIPOLAR WORLD

The United States is not a helpless giant tossed on the seas of history. It is still the most powerful nation on earth, and within certain limits, it can still shape its own destiny and play the leading role in a multipolar world. It can still take the helm in addressing the world's most pressing problems (as President Bush did effectively on only one issue, AIDS). There are many issues waiting for inspired and, yes, noble U.S. leadership, backed up by enlightened U.S. generosity that is also in the United States' own interest. The United States is still great. It deserves leadership worthy of its people, leadership that will restore the nation's pride and sense of purpose. That task must begin at home, but the world will be watching and waiting.

ONCE IN OFFICE ...

It is a well-established historical fact that what candidates say about foreign policy is not always an exact guide to what they will do if elected. Historians point to a myriad of examples: Franklin Roosevelt's 1940 promise to not send "your boys ... into any foreign wars," Lyndon Johnson's statements in 1964 that he would not send ground troops to Vietnam, Richard Nixon's 1968 references to a nonexistent "secret plan" to get out of Vietnam, Ronald Reagan's 1980 pledge to upgrade U.S. relations with Taiwan to "official" status, Bill Clinton's 1992 promises to take a strong stand on Bosnia and stand up to the "butchers of Beijing," George W. Bush's 2000 call for a "more humble" foreign policy that would never again have the United States involved in "nation building." If a candidate takes a position that, on reaching the White House, he concludes is wrong, it obviously would be irresponsible to stick with that position; national interest must take precedence over statements made in the heat of a campaign. However, reversals of campaign positions, no matter how necessary, are painful for any politician and certain to be used against him by his opponents regardless of the circumstances. (A memorable experience for me involved Jimmy Carter's 1976 campaign pledge to withdraw all U.S. ground troops from South Korea, a pledge he reaffirmed publicly shortly after the election. I had argued against it, but as Carter's assistant secretary of state for East Asian and Pacific affairs, I then had to defend it publicly while, under the direction of Secretary of State Cyrus Vance and Secretary of Defense Harold Brown, working to reverse it as quietly as possible—which was finally done, after two difficult years, in the summer of 1979.) Whatever their ultimate fate, however, campaign positions are key indicators of the priorities and thinking of each candidate as he approaches the most powerful and difficult job in the world. It is therefore valuable to examine them carefully.

Notes

TWO – REPORTING TRUTH TO POWER, BY E. BENJAMIN SKINNER

1. Richard Holbrooke, "Potomac Scenario" (letter to editor), *New York Times*, December 16, 1973.

2. Richard Holbrooke, "Apple of the Times," *Washington Post*, October 6, 2006, p. A23.

3. Simmi Aujla, "Q&A with Holbrooke," *Brown Daily Herald*, September 18, 2007, p. 1.

4. Matthew Arnold, "The Buried Life," in *The Poems of Matthew Arnold 1940 to 1967*, (Whitefish, MT: Kessinger, 1952), p. 168.

5. Richard Holbrooke, "A Visit with the Former Leader of Democratic Russia," *Brown Daily Herald Supplement*, October 5, 1959, p. 6.

6. Richard Holbrooke, "Mailer Directs Group Tour of Mailer World," *Brown Daily Herald*, November 18, 1960, p. 1.

7. Jack Roth, "Norman Mailer Sent to Bellevue over His Protest in Wife Knifing," *New York Times*, November 23, 1960, p. 26.

8. Richard Holbrooke, "Network Radio in Providence: An Abnegation of Responsibility," *Brown Daily Herald Supplement*, September 22, 1960, p. 7.

9. Richard Holbrooke, "King Praises Stand of New President on Human Rights," *Brown Daily Herald*, November 14, 1960, p. 1.

10. Editorial, "Herald Reporters Cover the Nation and the World," *Brown Daily Herald Supplement*, October 9, 1960, p. 2.

11. Richard Holbrooke, "Khrushchev's Drive Forces Summit," *Brown Daily Herald*, May 9, 1960, p. 1.

12. Richard Holbrooke, "A Wedding Also: Britain Sets Hopes on Summit Conference," *Brown Daily Herald*, May 10, 1960, p. 1.

13. Richard Holbrooke, "British Hesitant on Unified Berlin," *Brown Daily Herald*, May 11, 1960, p. 1.

14. Richard Holbrooke, "How the *New York Times* Covered the Paris Summit," *Brown Daily Herald Supplement*, October 9, 1960, p. 3.

15. David Halberstam, *War in a Time of Peace: Bush, Clinton, and the Generals* (New York: Scribner, 2001), p. 187; and Editorial, "Herald Reporters Cover the Nation and the World," *Brown Daily Herald Supplement*, October 9, 1960, p. 2.

16. "Statement by N.S. Khrushchev, Chairman of the U.S.S.R.," in *Foreign Relations of the United States, 1958-1960*, Volume IX, Berlin Crisis 1959–1960; Germany; Austria, Document 168: Memorandum of Conversation (Office of the Historian, United States Department of State, Washington, D.C.).

17. Richard Holbrooke, "How the *New York Times* Covered the Paris Summit," *Brown Daily Herald Supplement*, October 9, 1960, p. 3.

18. Ibid.

19. William Taubman, *Khrushchev: The Man and His Era* (New York: W.W. Norton & Company, 2003), p. 465.

20. Richard Holbrooke, "How the *New York Times* Covered the Paris Summit," *Brown Daily Herald Supplement*, October 9, 1960, p. 3.

21. "Topics: The Writing on the Wall," *New York Times*, July 27, 1961, p. 30.

22. Richard Sale, *Clinton's Secret Wars: The Evolution of a Commander In Chief* (New York: Thomas Dunne Books, 2009), p. 95; and Halberstam, *War in a Time of Peace*, p. 187.

23. Halberstam, *War in a Time of Peace*, p. 187.

24. Richard Holbrooke, "Front Man," *New Republic*, October 24, 1988.

25. Christopher Hitchens, *The Trial of Henry Kissinger* (London: Verso, 2001), p. 15.

26. Richard Holbrooke, "A Sense of Drift, a Time for Calm," *Foreign Policy*, Summer 1976, p. 106.

27. Ibid., p. 107.

28. Ibid.

29. Remarks by Richard Holbrooke, *Foreign Policy*'s 40th Anniversary, Corcoran Gallery of Art, Washington, DC, November 30, 2010.

30. Aaron Latham, "Carter's Little Kissingers," *New York Magazine*, December 13, 1976, p. 96.

31. Michael J. Berland and Douglas E. Schoen, *What Makes You Tick? How Successful People Do It—And How You Can Learn from Them* (New York: HarperCollins, 2009), p. 167.

32. Richard Holbrooke, "Eulogy: Kurt Schork," *Time*, June 5, 2000.

THREE – RICHARD HOLBROOKE AND THE VIETNAM WAR: PAST AND PROLOGUE, BY GORDON M. GOLDSTEIN

1. Richard Holbrooke, Unpublished Memorandum, November 12, 1969.

2. Ibid.

3. Ibid.

4. Ibid.

5. Ibid.

6. Ibid.

7. Ibid.

8. Ibid.

9. Memorandum from Holbrooke to George Melvin, November 29, 1963.

10. Memorandum drafted by David E. Bell, Director of the Agency of International Development, to Secretary of State Dean Rusk, May 13, 1964.
11. Author's Interview with Rufus Phillips, May 24, 2011.
12. Richard Holbrooke, Weekly Province Report, Ba Xuyen, June 1964.
13. All quotes drawn from a letter written by Richard Holbrooke, November 2, 1963.
14. Richard Holbrooke, Letter to Litty Holbrooke, March 16, 1965.
15. Ibid.
16. Author's Interview with Peter Tarnoff, May 26, 2011.
17. Richard Holbrooke, "The Doves Were Right," *New York Times Book Review*, November 30, 2008.
18. Author Interviews with Peter Tarnoff and John Negroponte, May 26 and 27, 2011.
19. Richard Holbrooke, Unpublished Memorandum, November 12, 1969.
20. Richard Holbrooke, "An Unimportant Incident," Undated and Unpublished Memorandum.
21. Ibid.
22. Author's Interview with Peter Rosenblatt, May 25, 2011.
23. "Memorandum from Richard Holbrooke of the White House Staff to the President's Special Assistant (Komer)," Document 321 in Foreign Relations of the United States, 1964–1968, Vol. IV, Vietnam, 1966.
24. Uncredited Holbrooke analysis, "Re-Emphasis on Pacification: 1965–1967," *The Pentagon Papers*, Senator Gravel Edition, Vol. II (Boston: Beacon Press), p. 515.
25. Uncredited Holbrooke analysis, "Re-Emphasis on Pacification: 1965–1967," p. 516.
26. Ibid., p. 529.
27. Ibid., p. 578.
28. Richard Holbrooke, Undated Letter to Litty Holbrooke, 1968.
29. Ibid.
30. Richard Holbrooke to Ethel Kennedy, June 7, 1968.
31. Richard Holbrooke, Unpublished Memorandum, November 12, 1969.
32. Richard Holbrooke, "The New Vietnam Myth," *Washington Post*, April 20, 1975.
33. Richard Holbrooke, "Relentless Patterns to Our Vietnam Nightmare," *Washington Post*, May 15, 1972.

FOUR – HOLBROOKE: THE CARTER YEARS, BY RICHARD BERNSTEIN
1. *New York Times*, June 5, 1980.
2. *New York Times*, March 27, 1978.
3. Patrick Tyler, *A Great Wall: Six Presidents and China* (New York: PublicAffairs, 1999), p. 253.
4. Ibid., p. 256.

"I believe in history. I think history is continuous," Holbrooke said in one of his last public speeches. *"You need to take counsel of history but never be imprisoned by it."* (© Don Pollard Photography)

About the Contributors

Richard C. Holbrooke was the U.S. Special Representative for Afghanistan and Pakistan from January 2009 until December 2010. He served as the U.S. Ambassador to the United Nations, where he was also a member of President Clinton's cabinet (1999–2001). As Assistant Secretary of State for Europe (1994–1996), he was the chief architect of the 1995 Dayton Peace Agreement that ended the war in Bosnia. He later served as President Clinton's Special Envoy to Bosnia and Kosovo and Special Envoy to Cyprus on a pro bono basis while a private citizen. From 1993 to 1994, he was the U.S. Ambassador to Germany.

During the Carter Administration (1977–1981), he served as the Assistant Secretary of State for East Asian and Pacific Affairs and was in charge of U.S. relations with China at the time Sino-American relations were normalized in December 1978.

After joining the Foreign Service in 1962, he served in Vietnam (1963–1966), including a tour of duty in the Mekong Delta for AID. He worked on Vietnam issues at the Johnson White House (1966–1968); wrote one volume of the Pentagon Papers; and was a member of the American delegation to the Vietnam Peace Talks in Paris (1968–1969).

He was Peace Corps Director in Morocco (1970–1972), was Managing Editor of *Foreign Policy* (1972–1977), and held senior positions at two leading Wall Street firms, Credit Suisse First Boston (Vice Chairman) and Lehman Brothers (Managing Director). He wrote numerous articles and two bestselling books: *To End a War*, a memoir of the Dayton negotiations, and (as coauthor) *Counsel to the President*, Clark Clifford's memoir. He previously wrote a monthly column for the *Washington Post*.

He received over twenty honorary degrees and numerous awards, including several Nobel Peace Prize nominations. He was the Founding Chairman of the American Academy in Berlin, a center for U.S.-German cultural exchange; formerly President and CEO of the Global Business Coalition, the business alliance against HIV/AIDS; and former Chairman of the Asia Society. He was a board member of the American Museum of Natural History, the National Endowment for Democracy, the Citizens Committee for New York City, the

Council on Foreign Relations, and Refugees International, all NGOs. He was Director Emeritus of the Africa-America Institute, was on the Advisory Board of MEMRI, was a Fellow of the American Academy of Arts and Sciences, and was formerly a member of the U.S. Board of Governors of Interpeace and a former Professor-at-Large, Brown University.

Jonathan Alter is a columnist for *Bloomberg View*, an analyst for NBC News and MSNBC, and the author of *The Defining Moment: FDR's Hundred Days and the Triumph of Hope, Between the Lines: A View Inside American Politics, Media and Culture*, and *The Promise: President Obama, Year One.*

Richard Bernstein was a correspondent in Asia and Europe for both *Time* magazine and the *New York Times*. In 1980, he opened the *Time* bureau in Beijing where he and Richard Holbrooke, who went there on frequent official visits, used to exchange views on early post-Maoist China. Bernstein's books include *From the Center of the Earth: The Search for the Truth About China* and *Ultimate Journey: Retracing the Path of an Ancient Buddhist Monk Who Crossed Asia in Search of Enlightenment.*

Derek Chollet is the author of *The Road to the Dayton Accords: A Study of American Statecraft* and coauthor of *America Between the Wars: From 11/9 to 9/11*. His writing has also appeared in the *Washington Post, Financial Times, Politico,* and numerous other publications. He assisted Richard Holbrooke with the research and writing of his book *To End a War* and served as Holbrooke's chief speechwriter while he was U.S. Ambassador to the United Nations.

Roger Cohen is a columnist for the *New York Times* and the *International Herald Tribune*. Born in London and educated at Oxford, he is a naturalized American. He covered the wars of Yugoslavia's breakup and wrote a book about that experience, *Hearts Grown Brutal: Sagas of Sarajevo*. At a time in 1995 when ending the conflict looked hopeless, he met Richard Holbrooke in Sarajevo and chronicled his hectic peacemaking shuttle. He has taught journalism at Princeton and lectured at Harvard.

Gordon M. Goldstein is the author of *Lessons in Disaster: McGeorge Bundy and the Path to War in Vietnam*, a strategic and historical analysis of the American intervention in Southeast Asia based on his collaboration with the former national security advisor to President Kennedy and President Johnson. Goldstein is a former Senior Adviser to the Strategic Planning Unit of the Executive Office of the UN Secretary General and a former Project Director at the Council on Foreign Relations and the Brookings Institution. His articles have appeared in the *New York Times, Washington Post, Newsweek*, and other publications. He is a graduate of Columbia University, where he was an International Fellow and was awarded a B.A., M.I.A., M. Phil, and Ph.D.

Kati Marton has combined a career as a reporter and writer with human rights advocacy. Born in Budapest, Hungary, and a former ABC News and National Public Radio correspondent, Marton is the author of seven books and has contributed to *The New Yorker*, the *Washington Post*, and the *New York Times*. Her most recent book, *Enemies of the People: My Family's Journey to America*, was a 2010 finalist for the National Book Critics Circle Prize. She is the former chair of the International Women's Health Coalition and a former Human Rights Watch board member. She is former chair and current director of the Committee to Protect Journalists. Marton is a board member of Central European University and the New America Foundation. She has been honored for her writing, reporting, and human rights advocacy with a George Foster Peabody Award and, most recently, the 2010 United Nations Association Leo Nevas Human Rights Award.

Samantha Power is the Pulitzer Prize–winning author of *"A Problem from Hell": America and the Age of Genocide* and *Sergio: One Man's Fight to Save the World*. A contributor to *The New Yorker* and *The New Republic*, and a professor of the practice of global leadership at the Harvard Kennedy School, she was the founding executive director of Harvard's Carr Center for Human Rights Policy. From 1993 to 1996 she reported on the wars in the former Yugoslavia, where she first met Richard Holbrooke in 1995.

David Rohde is a two-time Pulitzer Prize–winning journalist and a foreign affairs columnist for Reuters. Previously, he reported for the *New York Times* for fifteen years. He won his first Pulitzer in 1996 for uncovering the Srebrenica massacre in Bosnia for the *Christian Science Monitor* and his second in 2009 as part of a team of *New York Times* reporters covering Afghanistan and Pakistan. He is the author of *A Rope and a Prayer: The Story of a Kidnapping* and *Endgame: The Betrayal and Fall of Srebrenica*. He covered Richard Holbrooke's work in Bosnia, Afghanistan, and Pakistan.

E. Benjamin Skinner is a Senior Fellow at the Schuster Institute for Investigative Journalism of Brandeis University. His first book, *A Crime So Monstrous: Face-to-Face with Modern-Day Slavery*, was awarded the 2009 Dayton Literary Peace Prize for nonfiction and a citation from the Overseas Press Club in its book category for 2008. Previously he served as Special Assistant to Richard Holbrooke. His articles have appeared in *Time, Travel + Leisure*, the *Los Angeles Times*, the *Miami Herald, Foreign Affairs, Foreign Policy*, and other publications.

Strobe Talbott knew Richard Holbrooke since the early 1970s, when both were journalists: Talbott a reporter for *Time*, and Holbrooke editor of *Foreign Policy*. Talbott served in the Clinton administration as deputy secretary of state, working closely with Holbrooke on a range of issues, including the Balkans, the enlargement of NATO, the United Nations, and Africa. Since 2002 Talbott has been the president of the Brookings Institution, where Holbrooke participated in numerous events and projects.

John Tedstrom is President and CEO of GBCHealth, the successor to the Global Business Coalition on HIV/AIDS, Tuberculosis, and Malaria (GBC), which Richard Holbrooke established in 2001 and led until January 2009. In 2003 Tedstrom founded Transatlantic Partners Against AIDS (TPAA) as a joint U.S.-Russian NGO to fight AIDS in Russia, Ukraine, and other CIS countries. In 2006, he and Holbrooke merged TPAA with GBC and Tedstrom served as Executive Director. Tedstrom served as Director for Russia, Ukraine, and Eurasian Affairs at the National Security Council in 2000–2001 and prior to that was a senior economist at RAND.

James Traub is a contributing writer for the *New York Times Magazine* and a weekly columnist for foreignpolicy.com. In recent years he has reported from Afghanistan, Pakistan, Iraq, Turkey, Egypt, and from across West and sub-Saharan Africa. His most recent books are *The Freedom Agenda*, on democracy promotion, and *The Best Intentions*, on the UN under Kofi Annan. He is currently writing a biography of John Quincy Adams. He also teaches a class on U.S. foreign policy at a New York University program in Abu Dhabi. In 2000 he wrote a cover story on Richard Holbrooke in the *New York Times Magazine*.

Index

9/11 and U.S. foreign policy, 227
60 Minutes, 118

abortion issue, 241–242, 245
Abramowitz, Morton, 117, 122, 124,
    126, 151–152, 155, 317
Abu Ghraib, 335
Acheson, Secretary of State Dean, 24,
    40, 132, 207
Achmat, Zachie, 268
Act of Creation, 257–262
aerial eradication of poppy fields,
    303–305
Afghanistan
    9/11 and, 227
    ammonium nitrate fertilizer in, 290
    Bush administration and, 338
    dependency culture in, 285, 287–288,
        290
    Holbrooke as representative to (*See*
        Afghanistan, Holbrooke as spe-
        cial representative for)
    interdiction programs in, 303–305
    Iraq vs., 302
    McCain vs. Obama on, 340
    opium crops in, 290–291, 300–305
    as "other war," 348–349
    Pakistan border with, 307
    Phillips in, 109
    private visits to, 200
    Provincial Reconstruction Teams in,
        112
    rebuilding, 296–302
    recommendations for, 345, 348–349
    Vietnam and, 94–95
    women in, 301–302
Afghanistan, Holbrooke as special
    representative for
    appointment as, 281–282, 285

blunders, 288–290
building team to serve, 286–287
challenges facing, 283
on dangers of American interven-
    tion, 285, 287–288
drug-eradication efforts, 290–291,
    300–305
field diplomacy and, 282–287
frustrations of, 20
lessons from, 283–284
military pressure and, 288
press and, 290
studying issues, 284–285
successes, 290–293
Taliban and, 288
transit agreement and, 290
Washington and, 289–290
Africa, 156, 266, 273, 350–351
Africa Union, 350
African Americans, 5
Agency for International Development
    (AID), 25, 81
agenda setting, 349–351
AIDS. *See* HIV/AIDS
al-Qaeda, 95, 174, 292, 303–305, 337,
    349
    in Bosnia, 226
    military force vs. diplomacy against,
        20
    in Pakistan, 300–302, 306
Albanians, 174
Albright, Secretary of State
    Madeleine, 10, 16, 217, 221,
    223–224, 245–246
Alter, Jonathan, 1, 58, 360
Amanpour, Christiane, 43, 60
"America as an Ordinary Country,"
    322
American Academy, 170–172, 194

American Nazi Party, 47
Amiri, Rina, 285–287, 291, 316
ammonium nitrate fertilizer, 290
Andrássy Út, 192
Anglo-American Corp., 276
Angola, 149, 330–331
Annan, UN Secretary General Kofi
    on aid for Afghanistan, 298
    on AIDS, 248
    on GBC leadership, 268
    on Helms's visit to UN, 250
    Holbrooke and, 10, 246
    on reforming UN, 254, 260
    at Security Council meeting, 239
    at Waldorf Astoria meetings, 241
Annapolis process, 348
Aquino, Benigno, 125–126
Arendt, Hannah, 148
Arlington Cemetery, 228
Armacost, Michael, 124
Armstrong-Jones, Anthony, 48–49
Arnhold family, 170–171, 194
Arnold, Matthew, 46
Asia
    American demicolonialism in,
        133–135
    Chinese-American relations open-
        ing and, 135–136
    containment policy in, 132–133
    domino theory in, 136–145
    Holbrooke's sympathy with, 167–168
    Vietnamese Communism influenc-
        ing, 135–136
Asia, Carter administration and
    Chinese-American relations stabiliz-
        ing, 120–121, 126–128, 159–161
    Holbrooke's preparation to serve,
        119–120
    Japanese-American relations, 121,
        130–131
    Korea, withdrawing troops from,
        123–124
    new-boy network influencing,
        122–125
    Philippines, human rights in,
        125–126
    refugee relief in, 116–119
    restoring American prestige in,
        120–121
    South Korea, massacre in, 129
    Vietnam invading Cambodia, 129–
        130
Asia Society, 284, 292, 305
Asian Wall Street Journal, 55

Aspin, Les, 110
Associated Press, 191
Atatürk, Kemal, 37
Atlantic partnership, 177
Atlanticism, 165
Auschwitz, 148, 175
Australia, 329
Austro-Hungarian empire, 191
"axis of evil," 298, 302

Ba Xuyen province, 81–82
Babi Yar, 219
Babyak, Blythe, 123
Baker, James, 346
Balkans
    Afghanistan vs., 289
    Albright on, 224
    Clinton's use of force in, 262
    danger of halfway measures in, 231
    ending war in, 18, 94, 202–206
    ethnic cleansing in, 226
    fact-finding trip to, 209–211
    George H. W. Bush's passivity
        toward, 12
    humanitarian intervention in, 19
    implementing Dayton Peace
        Accords in, 207
    Kennan on, 41
    nation building in, 297
    NATO forces in, 216
    U.S. acting without UN Security
        Council, 262
    World War I impact on, 36–37
    Yugoslavia's creation in, 37, 166
Bangkok, 140. See also Thailand
Banja Luka, 165, 209–210, 223
Basket III, 185
BBC, 289
Bearden, Milton, 169
Beijing, 126–128, 160–161. See also
    China
Beirut, 214
Belarus, 188
Bell, Daniel, 324
Bell, David, 81
Belo, Carlos Filipe Ximenes, 207
Berger, Samuel, 217, 221
Bergsten, C. Fred, 69–70
Berk, Steve, 285–286
Berlin, 48–49, 96, 170–171, 194–196.
    See also Germany
Berlin Wall, 96–97, 165–169, 194
Bernstein, Richard, 116, 360
Bhutto, Benazir, 306

Biden, Vice President Joseph, 10, 240
Bihac pocket refugees, 210
bilateral defense treaty, NATO, 183
Bildt, Carl, 205
bin Laden, Osama, 95, 292, 300–301
Bitterlich, Joachim, 169
Blinken, Donald, 191
Bloomberg, Michael, 242
"the blowtorch," 88
bluntness, 315
boat people, 147–156
Bonn, 21, 169
Bonner, Ray, 60
Bosnia
    9/11 and, 227
    Clinton sending troops to, 229–230
    Contact Group on, 188
    Croats in, 210, 226
    Dayton Peace Accords and (*See*
        Dayton Peace Accords)
    ethnic cleansing in, 202, 209–211,
        219–220
    historical context of war in, 225–227
    Holbrooke as ambassador to Ger-
        many and, 201
    Holbrooke as assistant secretary of
        state for European affairs and,
        201–203
    Holbrooke's private visits to,
        198–200
    implementing Dayton agreements
        in, 228–229
    Islamic terrorists in, 226
    legacy of, in Afghanistan, 296–299
    Muslims in (*See* Muslims in Bosnia)
    negotiating to end war in, 202–203
    Nobel Peace Prize and, 60
    OPLAN 40104 for, 215–218
    prison camps in, 210
    reluctance to commit to, 214–215
    Sarajevo in (*See* Sarajevo)
    Serbs in (*See* Bosnian Serbs)
    UN failing in, 248, 253–254
    war in, 164–165, 176
    World War I impact on, 37
Bosnian Serb Republic, 222
Bosnian Serbs
    arresting Rohde, 293–294
    attacking Muslims, 165, 174,
        218–219, 226
    Dayton Peace Accords and, 204–205
    Dodik leading, 223
    Republika Srpska and, 231
    rewarded at Dayton, 166–167

seizing UN hostages, 172
    unification of Sarajevo and, 221
Botswana, 276, 280
Boutros-Ghali, UN Secretary General
    Boutros, 186, 226, 246–249
Boynton, Ralph, 78–79
Brandenburg Gate, 170, 194, 195
Brazil, 351
Bretton Woods agreement, 329
Brezhnev, Leonid, 70–71, 139
Briggs, Ellis, 33
Brinkley, Douglas, 258
British leadership, 48–49, 220, 258
Brooks, David, 318
Brown Daily Herald, 45–49, 58
Brown, Secretary of Defense Harold,
    353
Brown University, 45–47, 77, 167, 314,
    360
Brownell, Herbert, 160
Brussels, 182
Brzezinski, Zbigniew, 55, 119, 126–127,
    160–161, 183, 188, 331
Budapest, 96–97, 185–186, 188,
    190–191
Bunche, Ralph, 259
Bundy, McGeorge, 84–85
Burleigh, Peter, 242
Burma, 134–135, 341, 349
Burns, Nicholas, 233
Burt, Richard, 58
Bush administration. *See also* Bush,
    President George W.
    on Afghanistan, 340, 348–349
    on AIDS, 280, 352
    "democracy agenda" of, 350–351
    on environmental crisis, 337–339
    on Iraq and Iran, 343–348
    Iraqi government disputes with, 344
    on nation building, 352
    overcoming failures of, 333–337,
        340–342, 352
Bush, First Lady Laura, 301
Bush, President George H. W., 12,
    107, 200, 346
Bush, President George W.
    as appointed president, 331
    campaign promises vs. postelection
        priorities of, 352
    on carbon emissions, 337
    declaring "war on terror," 20, 334,
        345
    President's Emergency Plan for
        AIDS Relief and, 270

Bush, President George W. *(continued)*
  recovering from administration of,
    333
  sending delegation to Srebrenica,
    233
  on Vietnam's legacy, 107
  visiting Afghanistan, 303
Byrnes, Senator James F., 259

Cambodia, 116–117, 129–130,
    135–136, 146–156, 265, 331
Camp, Dave, 244
Camp David, 303
campaign promises vs. postelection
    priorities, 352–353
Campbell, John, 54
Can Tho, 82–83
Canada, 329
Cao, General, 83
Cape Sunion, 62
carbon emissions, 337–339
Carter administration. *See also* Carter,
    President Jimmy
  Holbrooke's preparation to serve in,
    119–120
  human rights in Philippines during,
    125–126
  Japanese-American relations during,
    121, 130–131
  massacre in South Korea during, 129
  new-boy network in, 122–125
  refugee relief during, 116–119
  restoring American prestige,
    120–121
  stabilizing Chinese-American rela-
    tions, 120–121, 126–128, 159–161
  Vietnam invading Cambodia
    during, 129–130
  withdrawing troops from Korea,
    123–124
Carter, First Lady Rosalynn, 117–118
Carter, President Jimmy
  admitting Indochinese refugees to
    U.S., 149–150
  on Cambodian refugees, 152
  campaign promises vs. postelection
    priorities of, 352
  energy-independence project of, 338
  Holbrooke as assistant secretary of
    state for East Asia for, 16
  Holbrooke campaigning for, 54–55,
    119, 319
  on withdrawing troops from Korea,
    123–125

Castro, Fidel, 64, 330
Central African Republic (CAR),
    243
central Europe, 179–180, 182
Central Intelligence Agency (CIA),
    24–25, 31, 91, 124, 340–341
Chain Bridge, 191–192
Charlie Rose Show, 200, 212, 288
Chechnya, 177, 186–187
Cheney, Vice President Dick, 107
Chiang Kai-shek, 132, 138
Chieu, Colonel, 83
China
  Acheson on, 132
  Cambodia and, 135
  carbon emissions of, 338–339
  Carter administration and, 121, 149,
    159–161
  energy agreements with, 339–340
  India and, 135
  Indonesia and, 135
  Japan and, 138–139
  Nixon opening relations with,
    120–121, 135–137, 346–347
  Shantung peninsula and, 36–37
  Soviet Union and, 138–140, 331
  Sudan and, 350
  on UN Security Council, 258
  Vietnam and, 137–138, 157–158
Chirac, President Jacques, 216–219,
    232
"The Choice," 216
Chollet, Derek, 198, 225, 360
Christian Science Monitor, 56
Christian Serbs, 210
Christopher, Secretary of State
    Warren, 21, 178, 185, 188, 198,
    203–204, 215–218
Chun Doo Hwan, President, 129
Churchill, Prime Minister Winston,
    252, 258, 324, 346
CIA (Central Intelligence Agency).
    See Central Intelligence Agency
    (CIA)
Civil Operations and Revolutionary
    Development Support, 87–88
civil rights movement, 47
Clark Air Force Base, 125–126, 138
Clark, Lt. General Wesley, 228–229,
    232
Clemenceau, Georges, 37
Clifford, Secretary of Defense Clark
  memoir of, 207, 311
  mentoring Holbrooke, 316

opposing escalation of Vietnam war, 91, 93
on U.S. recognition of Israel, 59
climate change, 337–339
Clinton administration. *See also* Clinton, President William
Bosnia as turning point for, 208
Dayton Peace Accords and, 206
on repaying debt to UN, 241–249
Rwanda and, 349
UN votes during, 261
Clinton, President William
after Dayton Peace Accords, 208
appointing Albright Secretary of State, 16
appointing Holbrooke as ambassador to Germany, 212
Balkans, acting without UN Security Council, 261–262
Bosnia, inaction on, 226
Bosnia, informal discussions with Holbrooke on, 222–223
Bosnia, ordering bombing strikes on, 220
Bosnia, ordering review of policy on, 222
Bosnia, sending troops to, 215–217, 229–230, 296–297
at Brandenburg Gate, 195
at Budapest summit, 185
campaign promises vs. postelection priorities of, 352
Dayton Peace Accords and, 220
domestic vs. foreign policies of, 200
Europe during administration of. *See* Europe in Clinton years
on Holbrooke, 14
Holbrooke's ongoing relationship with, 207
inauguration of, 198–199
at memorial service for Holbrooke, 10
on NATO expansion, 41, 182–183
OPLAN 40104 and, 216–218
on repaying U.S. debt to UN, 255
on Russian reforms, 187
Srebrenica and, 219, 227
toasting Holbrooke, 204
on UN's indispensability, 252
Vietnam and, 107
visiting Europe, 176
at Waldorf Astoria meetings, 239
Clinton, Secretary of State Hillary
Bosnia, appealing for action on, 203

defending Holbrooke, 290
giving Richard C. Holbrooke Memorial Lecture, 292–293
Glynn and, 316–317
Holbrooke as representative to Afghanistan and Pakistan for, 8, 282–285, 303
Holbrooke collapsing in office of, 11, 283
on Jones vs. Holbrooke, 22
at Marton's birthday party, 222
at memorial service for Holbrooke, 10
Pakistan, visiting, 57, 291
Close, Chuck, 171
CNN, 257
Cohen, Roger, 164, 360
Cold War. *See also* post-Cold War era
Berlin as symbol of, 195
dividing Europe, 168
Europe after, 176–177
Germany after, 169
nation building during, 298
origins of, 178
signing of UN charter and, 257
UN during, 260
Columbia University, 40–41
Commager, Henry Steele, 322
Commentary, 322
Committee to Protect Journalists, 56
Communism
after World War II, 132–136
in Asia, containing, 132–135
balancing superpowers of, 138–140
domino effect of, 136–145
ending in Hungary, 190
in Vietnam, 136
Comprehensive Nuclear Test Ban Treaty, 342
Conference on Security and Cooperation in Europe (CSCE), 185
Congo, 248–249
Congress of U.S. *See* U.S. Congress
Congress of Vienna, 177
Congressional Black Caucus, 272
Connally, Senator Tom, 256, 259
Contact Group on Bosnia, 188
containment policy, 132–135, 168
Contract for America, 229
Copenhagen agreement, 339
corruption
of Afghan government, 349
American foreign policy and, 321
American influence seen as, 321

corruption *(continued)*
  bypassing, 287–288
  of Karzai government, 290
  liberals and, 321
  stability vs., 135
  in Vietnam, 78, 95, 112
Cosby, Bill, 248
Council on Foreign Relations, 93
Counsel to the President, 93
counterculture, 52
counterinsurgency strategies, 79–81,
    86–87, 95, 111
Couric, Katie, 248
Croatia, 37, 174, 204
Croats in Bosnia, 210, 226
Cronkite, Walter, 136
Cuban missile crisis, 96–97, 111, 168
Cultural Revolution, 158, 347
Cyprus, 184
Czechoslovakia, 33, 168

Da Nang, 85–86, 103–104
Dalai Lama, 128
Daniel, Clifton, 49–50, 52
Darfur, 341, 349–350
Dayton Peace Accords
  as achievement of Holbrooke's
    career, 240
  aftermath of, 206–208
  American leadership in, 220
  at Dayton, Ohio, 37–38
  failures of, 231–232
  historical context of, 204, 225–228
  implementation of, 207, 220–225,
    228–234
  lives saved by, 295
  negotiations for, 204–206
  news stories at time of, 61
  Nobel Peace Prize and, 59
  peacekeepers in Bosnia after,
    296–297
  prelude to, 225
  results of, 166–167, 174
  scope of, 206
de Gaulle, President Charles, 48–50,
    63, 323
debt bondage, 57
Declaration of Independence, 334
"The Defeat of America," 322
Dellums, Mayor Ron, 272
demicolonialism of United States,
    120–121, 133–135, 140
democracy
  belief in future of, 332

  Bush administration on, 350
  human rights as foundation for, 350
  in NATO expansion, 183
  OSCE and, 186–187
  in Russia, 187
  in U.S. foreign policy goals, 178
democratic centralism, 287
Democratic Republic of the Congo,
    248–249
Deng Xiaoping, 127, 157–158, 161
Department of Agriculture, 68
dependency cultures, 285, 287–288,
    290
Derian, Patricia, 125–126
detente with Soviet Union, 65–66, 71,
    139
Dey, Jordan, 312
DeYoung, Karen, 60–61
Diem, Ngo Dinh, 78, 83, 112
diplomacy
  Afghanistan and Pakistan as culmi-
    nation of, 283, 292
  appeasement vs., 346
  Clinton on, 14
  compromise and, 166
  field, 167, 282–287, 313–315
  German unification and, 169
  Holbrooke's style of, 1–2, 17, 204
  importance of, 345–346
  jazz and, 19, 204, 347
  learning from failures in, 34
  military power and, 20, 172, 288
  Obama vs. McCain on, 341–343
  preventive, 185
  shuttle, 204, 228
  in UN debt repayment, 248–249
Dodik, Milorad, 223
Dole, Senator Bob, 217, 249
domino theory, 121, 136–145
Donaldson, William H., 68
Donilon, Tom, 201
Dostum, Abdul Rashid, 288
Drew, Colonel Nelson, 204, 220, 228
Duc, Thich Quang, 78–79
Dulles, Secretary of State John Foster,
    259–260
Dybul, Dr. Mark, 270
Dylan, Bob, 51–52

Eagleburger, Larry, 68
East Timor, 207, 244, 261
economic factors, 68–70, 328–329,
    335–338
Edinburgh, 267–268

Egypt, 331, 345
Eikenberry, Karl, 60, 289
Eisenhower, President Dwight, 24, 48–50, 137, 256, 346
Ellsberg, Daniel, 53, 99
Élysée Palace, 50
environmental issues, 337–339
Estes III, Lieutenant General Howell, 215–216
Eugenides, Jeffrey, 171
Europe in Clinton years
  Atlantic Alliance in, 165–166
  Berlin, 194–196
  Bosnian war, ending, 164–165, 167, 174–175
  Germany, 168–171
  Holbrooke's proposals for, 173–174
  Hungary, 190–193
  legacy of, 172
  See also specific countries.
European Union (EU)
  Bosnia, inaction on, 226
  drug-eradication effort in Afghanistan, 301
  expansion of, 184–185
  Hungary and, 193
  responsibilities of membership in, 179
  Russian agreement with, 187
  security force of, 232
  stabilizing effect of, 166, 172–173
European Union security force (EUFOR), 232

"A Failure of Nerve," 322
Fauci, Anthony, 268
"FDR and the Creation of the UN," 257–258
Ferdinand, Archduke Franz, 51
Financial Times, 340
Finlandization, 330
Fitzhugh Report, 30
Fleming, Renée, 9
Flourney, Michele, 286
Foer, Jonathan Safran, 171
food, 68–69, 151–152, 329, 337
Food for Peace Program, 27–28
Ford, President Gerald, 159
Foreign Affairs
  founding of, 54
  Holbrooke on Bosnia in, 203
  on NATO expansion, 183
  "X" article in, 39
Foreign Policy

founding of, 54
  Glasser editing, 61
  Holbrooke editing, 11, 59
  Kennan in, 40
foreign policy of U.S.
  9/11 and, 321
  on Afghanistan (*See* Afghanistan)
  after Dayton Peace Accords, 208, 226
  on Bosnia (*See* Bosnia)
  bureaucracy of, 23–33
  Carter and (*See* Carter, President Jimmy)
  on China (*See* China)
  compromise and, 321
  Congress influencing, 243–244
  corruption and, 321
  democracy in, 178
  economic issues in, 69
  Holbrooke passionate about, 12–18
  human rights in (*See* human rights)
  influencing post-Vietnam era of, 93, 99
  Kennan in, 39–41
  Kissinger in (*See* Kissinger, Secretary of State Henry)
  McCain on, 340–342
  new-boy network influencing, 122–125
  new pessimists on, 323–324
  Nixon on, 23
  Obama on, during campaign, 340–342
  studying issues in, 285
  superpowers in, 140
  UN and, 251–256, 261–262
  on Vietnam (*See* Vietnam)
  Wilsonian, 35–36, 166
  world leadership and, 334–335, 351–352
Foreign Relations Committee of the U.S. Senate. *See* U.S. Foreign Relations Committee
Foreign Service. *See* U.S. Foreign Service
Foreign Service Journal, 56
Foster, Sir Norman, 195
Four Power Summit, 48–51
Fourteen Points, 36
France, 94, 109, 167, 258, 331
Frasure, Robert, 204, 220, 228
Freedom Fighters, 191
Fritchey, Polly, 53
Frontier Corps, 306

Fukuda, Prime Minister Takeo, 123
Fulbright, Senator J. William, 70

G7 summit, 118, 218
G8 summit, 337, 340, 346
Gates, Robert, 346
Gelb, Leslie
  on Brzezinski and China normal-
    ization, 127
  career of, 58, 93
  in Carter years, 122
  on Holbrooke's relations with Asian
    leaders, 129
  on Holbrooke's style, 123
  on human rights in Carter years, 125
  at memorial service for Holbrooke,
    10
  Pentagon papers and, 89
Gelbard, Robert, 223
Gellért, 192
gender barriers, 46–47
Geneva, 154–155
George Washington University
    Hospital, 11, 318
Georgia, 173, 340
Germany. See also Berlin
  1918 surrender of, 35
  after World War II, 177–178
  brokering U.S.-Taliban talks, 292
  on EU expansion, 184
  Four Power Summit and, 48–49
  Holbrooke as ambassador to, 21,
    168–169
  instability and aggression of, 179
  invading Poland, 34
  mass slaughter in, 148
Gingrich, Newt, 217, 229
Glasser, Susan, 61
Gleysteen, William, 122, 124–125,
    127
Global Business Coalition on
    HIV/AIDS (GBC)
  businesses in, 267, 270–271
  expanding mandate of, 271–273
  formation of, 267–268
  high-quality HIV testing and,
    269–270
  Holbrooke as president and CEO
    of, 264
  Holbrooke's qualifications to lead,
    268–269
  Mandela as president of, 268
Global Business Council on
    HIV/AIDS, 130

Global Fund to Fight AIDS, Tubercu-
    losis and Malaria, 270
global war on terror. See war on terror
Glynn, Mary Ellen, 313, 316–317
Goldstein, Gordon M., 76, 360–361
Goldwater, Senator Barry, 160
Gorazde, 218
Gorbachev, Mikhail, 12, 258
Gore, Vice President Al, 217, 248, 337
government service, orientation to,
    96–100
graffiti, 52, 62–64
Gramm, Senator Phil, 229
Grams, Senator Rod, 241–242
Grant, Jim, 149
Great Depression, 336
Great Man theory, 13
A Great Wall, 127
Great Wall, 136
Great War, 36
Greece, 298
Greene, Graham, 116, 167
greenhouse gases, 338–339
Greenstock, Sir Jeremy, 240, 246–247
Gresham Palace, 192
Gromyko, Andrei, 258, 260
Grozny, 186–187
Guadalcanal, 103
Guantanamo Bay, 335, 340
Gumble, Bryant, 248

Habib, Philip, 92
Hagerty, James, 50
The Hague, 174
Halberstam, David, 84
Hamas, 345
Hammarskjöld, UN Secretary General
    Dag, 168
Hanoi, 94
Hans Arnhold Center, 194
Haqqani, Husain, 57
Harriman, Averell, 16, 40, 92, 119, 167,
    204, 258, 260
Harriman, Pamela, 40
Hastert, House Speaker Dennis, 242
Heine, Heinrich, 196
Helms-Biden bill, 241–247
Helms, Senator Jesse, 3, 35, 130,
    241–250
Helsinki Accords, 185, 221–222
Hemingway, Ernest, 167
Herat, 302
Heroes' Square, 190
heroin, 303

Heston, Charlton, 243
Hezbollah, 345
Hill, Chris, 228, 315
Hiss, Alger, 259
history
    of campaign promises vs. postelection priorities, 352
    Holbrooke as student of, 45–46
    importance of, 13–14, 95, 358
    laws of, 335–336
History Channel, 257
Hitchens, Christopher, 54
Hitler, Adolf, 35, 96, 194–195
HIV/AIDS
    in American cities, 265, 272
    Bush on, 350, 352
    in Cambodia, 265
    detection by testing for, 269–270, 274–280
    Global Business Coalition on, 267–269
    Gore addressing, 248
    Holbrooke electing to fight, 273, 284
    losing battle against, 264–265, 274–275, 277–278
    preventing, 279
    stigmatization and, 280
    treatment access programs for, 265
    UN Security Council and, 3, 266–268
Ho Chi Minh, 34–35, 94, 101, 133
Hoi An, 103
Holbrooke, Anthony, 10, 218–219
Holbrooke, David, 10
Holbrooke, Richard
    accomplishments of, 295
    ambitions of, 12–14, 16–17
    aversion to grand strategies of, 19
    aversion to ideology of, 18
    biographical summary of, 359–360
    Blythe Babyak and, 123
    Carter campaign and, 54–55, 352–353
    Dayton Peace Accords and. See Dayton Peace Accords
    death of, 8–11, 292
    as doer, 14–16
    failing health of, 22
    family of, 45, 71, 165
    at Foreign Policy, 53–54
    on Four Power Summit, 48–51
    on history's importance, 13–14, 95, 358
    as journalist, 45–52, 58–61

Kati Marton and (See Marton, Kati)
    "last mission" of, 282
    legacy of, 318
    Larrine Sullivan and, 47, 82–85
    as mentor (See mentoring)
    Milošević and, 164–166
    as networker, 129
    on OPLAN 40104, 215–218
    as Peace Corps director in Morocco (See Peace Corps director in Morocco, Holbrooke as)
    playfulness of, 11–12
    pride of, 21–22
    psychology, interest in, 17
    Rohde kidnappings and, 294–295
    as talking head, 56
    as team builder, 128
    in Vietnam, 76–87
    in Vietnam coordination effort, White House, 88–91
    at Vietnam peace talks, Paris, 92
    on Vietnam's legacy, 76–77, 92–95
    on war correspondents, 56
Holocaust, 226. See also Nazis
Hoopes, Townsend, 258
Hoover, President Herbert, 30, 35
Hopkins, Harry, 258–259, 260
Hosseini, Khaled, 22
Huey, Talbott, 82–83
Hull, Secretary of State Cordell, 258
human rights
    in Cambodia, 129–130
    in Carter years, 125–126
    in Chechnya, 186
    in China, 128–129
    in democracy building, 350
    HIV/AIDS treatment as, 265
    Kennan on, 41
    in Korea, 129
    in Russia, 70
    in Tibet, 128
Human Rights Commission, 261
humanitarian efforts
    in Cambodia, 146, 148–156
    Clinton administration on, 246
    Holbrooke oriented to, 128
    political decisions and, 151
    in Vietnam, 147–156
Humboldt University, 170
Hungary, 37, 96–97, 190–193. See also Budapest
Huntington, Samuel, 53–54
Hurricane Katrina, 302
Hussein, Saddam, 297

Ignatieff, Michael, 19
Implementation Force (IFOR), 221
India, 134–135, 288, 293, 308, 339–341
Indonesia, 134–135, 141, 339
International Committee of the Red
    Cross, 219
International Criminal Court, 174
International Monetary Fund (IMF),
    244
International Rescue Committee, 61,
    209
Iran, 298, 302, 337, 342–348
Iran-contra scheme, 347
Iraq, 36, 108, 227, 297, 302, 338,
    342–348
"Is Democracy Dying?," 323
Islamabad, 291–292. See also Pakistan
isolationism, 321–322
Israel, 261, 340, 345, 347
Italy, 331
Iwo Jima, 103
Izetbegović, President Alija, 203, 231

Jackson Amendment, 70
Jackson, Senator Henry, 70–71, 139
Jakarta, 141
Janklow, Mort, 59
Japan
    in Carter years, 120, 130–131
    China and, 36–37, 138–139
    energy consumption leadership of,
        339
    Korean impact on, 143–145
    MacArthur in, 135
    nation building in, 298
    U.S. as military arm of, 140–142
    U.S. occupation of, 133, 135
Japanese Self-Defense Agency, 142
Javits, Senator Jacob, 89
Jennings, Lizzie, 10
Jewish people, 66, 70, 165, 192
Johnson, Jim, 10
Johnson, Lady Bird, 6, 138
Johnson, President Lyndon, 20, 25, 85,
    87–88, 90–92, 352
Johnson, U. Alexis, 314
Joint Chiefs of Staff, 10, 91
Joint UN Programme on HIV/AIDS
    (UNAIDS), 268–270, 280
Jones, General Jim, 22
Jones, Paul, 315–316
journalism, Holbrooke studying, 45–53
journalists
    blaming, 327

briefing Holbrooke on Afghanistan
    and Pakistan, 284
covering refugee problem in East
    Asia, 118
Holbrooke's relationship to, 59–61,
    200
Kissinger wooing, 67
pessimism of, 327
in Vietnam, 84
Just, Ward, 171

Kabul, 284–289, 304. See also
    Afghanistan
Kalb, Bernard, 76
Kalb, Marvin, 76
Kamm, Henry, 155
Kant, Immanuel, 18
Karadžić, Radovan, 221–225, 231–234
Karlovac, 212
Karnow, Stanley, 55, 84, 323
Karzai, President Hamid, 288–291,
    298, 303–305
Katyn Forest, 219
Katzenbach, Undersecretary of State
    Nicholas, 4, 89–91
Kazakhstan, 188
Kennan, George F.
    in Foreign Policy, 54
    Kissinger and, 70
    memoir of, 207
    paradox of, 39–41
    on President Wilson, 35
Kennedy Center, 10, 306
Kennedy, President John F., 92, 96–97,
    111, 284, 295, 314, 346
Kennedy, Senator Robert F., 92
Kenya, 351
Kerensky, Alexander, 46
Kerrick, Brigadier General, 228, 229
Kerry, Senator John, 106–108
Khamenei, Ayatollah Ali, 346
Kharlamov, Mikhail, 50
Khmer Rouge, 116, 129–130, 152
Khost province, 285
Khrushchev, Nikita, 48–51
"Kilroy was here," 63
Kim Dae Jung, 129
Kim Il Sung, 137, 144
Kim, Jim Yong, 274
King, Jr., Martin Luther, 47
Kissinger, Secretary of State Henry
    career of, 93
    Chinese-American relations and,
        120, 136, 159

Communist superpowers and, 138–139
on Dayton Peace Accords, 228–229
diplomatic model of, 346–347
in *Foreign Policy*, 54
grand design of, 102
on Holbrooke, 14
Holbrooke on, 65–71
McCain vs., 346
memoir of, 207
on nuclear arms, 342
pessimism of, 324–326
on President Wilson, 35
Realpolitik of, 166
on rejection of aid to Angola, 330–331
in Vietnam, 76
at Waldorf Astoria meetings, 242
The Kite Runner, 22
Kiyani, General Ashfaq, 307
"Know Your Status" (KYS), 280
Kohl, Chancellor Helmut, 169–170, 184
Komer, Robert W., 87–88
Koppel, Ted, 61
Korea, 120–121, 124, 132–133, 137, 142–145, 342. *See also* South Korea
Kosovo
after Dayton Peace Accords, 224
Dey in, 312
NATO bombing of, 164, 173–174
peacekeeping forces in, 297
World War I impact on, 37
Kozyrev, Foreign Minister Andrei, 188
Kruzel, Joe, 204, 220, 228
Kukrit, Prime Minister, 145
Kurdistan, 36
Kwangju, 129
Kyoto Protocol, 339

La Closerie des Lilas, 167
Laird, Defense Secretary Melvin, 142
Lake, National Security Advisor Anthony, 78, 82–86, 110, 122, 198
Lang, George, 192
Lang Ha, 112
Lansdale, Major General Edward, 80, 109–112
Lansing, Secretary of State Robert, 36
Laos, 117, 153
Largent, Steve, 243
Larkin, Barbara, 243

Latin America, 156, 351
Lattimore, Owen, 98
Lawrence of Arabia, 35
le Carré, John, 13
League of Democracies, 341
League of Nations, 252, 256, 258–259
Lehovich, Vladimir, 78, 83, 110–111
Leipzig, 169
Lenin, 46
Lesotho, 276, 280
liberals
on AIDS prevention, 279
Jackson Amendment and, 70
on military force, 288
on NATO enlargement, 41
post-Vietnam pessimism of, 320–327
Lidice, 219
life of service, 284
Lin, Maya, 171
Lippman, Walter, 140
"Locksley Hall," 260
Lodge, Senator Henry Cabot, 35, 90
Lon Nol–Thieu position, 136
London, 48–49
Lord, Winston, 68, 209
Lumumba, Patrice, 47
Lusaka Plus, 248
Luu, Chi, 156

Maastricht Treaty, 176
Mabubhani, Kishore, 246
MacArthur, General Douglas, 133–135
MacLaine, Shirley, 158
MacLeish, Archibald, 260
MacMillan, Margaret, 34–35, 37, 38
Macmillan, Prime Minister Harold, 48–50
Madison Square Garden, 21, 257, 261
Mailer, Norman, 46
Majanca prison camp, 213
"Making the World Safe for Communism," 322
malaria, 271
Malawi, 276, 280
Malaysia, 117
Malcolm X, 47
Malloch-Brown, Mark, 9
malnutrition, 149
Malone, David, 246
Malta, 184
Mandela, Nelson, 248
Manhattan, 72–74
Manshell, Warren, 53
Mao Zedong, 128, 133, 161, 347

Marcos, President Ferdinand, 125–126, 138
Marines, 86–87, 103–104
Marshall Plan, 96, 177–178
Marshall, Secretary of State George C., 178
Martin, Ambassador Graham, 133
Marton, Endre, 191
Marton, Kati
  about, 361
  background of, 175
  birthday party for, 222
  on HIV/AIDS, 273
  Hungarian childhood of, 190–191
  introduction by, 1–6
  at memorial service for Holbrooke, 10
  Powers with, 310
  pressuring Serbs to free Rohde, 294
  at Waldorf Astoria meetings, 241
  wedding of, 172
Maugham, Somerset, 116
Mbeki, President Thabo, 266–267
McCain, Senator John, 107, 338, 340–349
McCarthy, Senator Joseph, 96–97
McCloskey, Robert, 67
McFarlane, Robert, 346–347
McNamara, Robert S., 35, 89
McPherson, Harry, 76
Meiji Restoration, 140
Mekong Delta, 80–81, 111
Melville, Herman, 7
Melvin, George, 79–80
memorial service, 9–10
mentoring
  on directness, 315
  elevating others in, 316–317
  on field work vs. Washington's influence, 313–315
  on importance of knowledge vs. status, 312–313
  legacy of, 318
  love and delight in, 317–318
  loyalty and, 316–317
  making time for, 21, 311
  natural selection in, 315–316
  on reading habits, 313
Mexico, 351
Middle East, 71, 225, 261
military power vs. diplomacy, 20, 172, 288, 323–324
Milošević, Slobodan
  calling Europeans' bluff, 172

Holbrooke and, 164–167, 174
  as "junkyard dog," 203
  Marton on, 3
  psychology of, 17
  releasing Rohde, 56, 294
  ultimatum given to, 214
  unable to guarantee safe passage of diplomats, 204
Milosz, Czeslaw, 174
Mindszenty, Cardinal József, 191
Mitterrand, François, 216
Mladić, General Ratko
  after Dayton Peace Accords, 224
  apprehending, 225, 234
  attacking Muslim enclaves in Bosnia, 218–219
  calling Europeans' bluff, 172
  failure to seek arrest of, 231–232
Moby Dick, 7
Mogadishu, 215, 246
Molotov, Vyacheslav, 258, 260
Mondale, Vice President Walter, 125–126, 146, 148, 158, 168, 201
monks, self-immolation of, 78
Monnet, Jean, 173, 189
Montenegro, 38
Moody-Stuart, Sir Mark, 271
Moos, Samuel, 169
Moose, Richard, 122
Moralpolitik, 19
Morgenthau, Professor, 71
Morning Joe, 310
Morocco, 53, 99, 167
Moscow. See Soviet Union
Mount Igman, 228
Moynihan, Daniel Patrick, 134, 323, 326
MPLA (People's Movement for the Liberation of Angola), 330–331
MSNBC, 59
Mullen, Admiral Mike, 10, 288, 291
multipolar world, 352
Munich, 292
Musharraf, President Pervez, 298, 301, 306–307
Muslim world, 350
Muslims in Bosnia
  1995 massacre of, 202
  Dayton Peace Accords and, 204
  ethnic cleansing of, 210
  Mladić attacking, 218–219
  returning to Srebrenica, 233–234
  Rohde discovering mass grave of, 293–294

Serbs violating, 165, 174
Srebrenica massacre of, 227
Muslims in Pakistan, 306
Mutombo, Dikembe, 10
Myanmar, 349. *See also* Burma

Nagy, Imre, 98
Namibia, 261, 284
Napoleon, 169
Nasr, Vali, 285, 287, 291
nation building, 110, 229, 246, 296–299
National Association of Manufac-
    turers, 70
National Democratic Institute for
    International Affairs, 301
National Institutes of Health, 268
National Press Club, 251–256
National Public Radio (NPR), 56
National Security Council (NSC), 25,
    32, 67–68, 147–148
NATO
    acting without UN approval, 220,
        253
    in Afghanistan, 301, 308, 348
    American leadership in, 208
    Bosnia, peacekeepers in, 296–299
    Bosnia, spurring to act in, 201,
        205–206
    Bosnian armies, integration of, 232
    Bosnian war and, 164–167, 172–174,
        228
    containing Communism, 133
    Dayton Peace Accords, aftermath of,
        223
    Dayton Peace Accords, implement-
        ing, 229–234
    Dayton Peace Accords, role in,
        204–205
    enlarging, 41, 181–184, 201
    EUFOR and, 232
    in European security architecture,
        177–183
    German unification and, 169
    Holbrooke briefing by leaders of, 49
    Hungary and, 193
    Implementation Force and, 221
    Karadžić and, 222
    OPLAN 40104 and, 215–218
    OSCE and, 184–187
    Russian Partnership for Peace with,
        187–188
    Srebrenica and, 227
    Turkey and, 345
    Yeltsin on enlargement of, 221–223

Navy, 107, 147–148
Nazarbayev, President, 271
Nazis, 148, 165, 171, 192, 194–196
Negroponte, John, 77, 85–86, 93, 110,
    122, 128, 130
neoconservatives, 54, 319, 320–327, 342
Netherlands, 181, 219, 227
Netherlands Environmental Associa-
    tion, 338
Neustadt, Richard, 25
new-boy network, 122–123
new pessimists, 322–327
The New Republic, 101–105, 146–156
New School University, 257
New York City, 62–64, 315
New York Knicks, 21, 257, 261
New York Times
    best-sellers, 45
    on Bosnia, 229
    Brooks eulogizing Holbrooke in, 318
    on Cambodian food crisis, 155
    on Four Power Summit, 49–51
    Holbrooke clerking at, 51–52
    on new-boy network, 122
    rejecting Holbrooke, 56, 58, 314
    Reston and Rosenthal at, 46
    Rohde at, 284
    Sulzberger in, 322–323
New York Times Magazine, 120–121,
    123–124
New York University's Center on
    International Cooperation, 305
The New Yorker, 214–224, 287
New Zealand, 242, 329
Newfoundland, 252
Newsweek, 61, 194–196
Newsweek International, 55, 323
Nicolson, Harold, 37, 207
Nightline, 61
Ninth Marine Regiment, 103
Nitze, Paul, 54
Nixon, President Richard
    campaign promises vs. postelection
        priorities of, 352
    Chinese-American relations and,
        120, 159
    Deng Xiaoping and, 157–158, 161
    diplomatic model of, 346–348
    election of, 92
    Holbrooke on, 23
    Japan and, 141
    on President Wilson, 35
    signing peace agreement, 71
    visiting China, 136

Nobel Peace Prize
  Belo and Ramos-Horta winning,
    207
  Bonner on Holbrooke earning, 60
  Bunche winning, 259
  Gore winning, 337
  Holbrooke's Bosnian work nomi-
    nated for, 199
  UN High Commission on Refugees,
    154
nonaligned movement (NAM), 261
nongovernmental agencies (NGOs),
    266–268
Norman, Greg, 222
North Atlantic Cooperation Council,
    180
North Korea, 124, 132–133, 342. See
    also Korea
North Vietnam, 94, 132–133. See also
    Vietnam
North-West Frontier Province, 300
Nossel, Suzanne, 247, 313
nuclear arms, 64, 188, 288, 342
Nuclear Nonproliferation Treaty, 188
Nunn, Senator Sam, 342

Oakley, Phyllis, 219
Oakley, Robert, 122
Obama administration. See also
    Obama, President Barak
  challenges facing, 333–339
  Global Business Coalition on
    HIV/AIDS and, 272
  Holbrooke in, 20, 285
  increasing aid to Pakistan, 292
Obama, President Barak
  on Afghanistan during campaign,
    340, 348–349
  challenges facing, 349–353
  on climate change during campaign,
    338–339
  on foreign policy during campaign,
    340–342
  HIV testing of, 351
  Holbrooke as special representative
    to Afghanistan and Pakistan for,
    8, 127, 281
  Holbrooke on election of, 5
  on Iraq and Iran during campaign,
    342–348
  on Jones vs. Holbrooke, 22
  on Kenya, 351
  at memorial service for Holbrooke, 9
Oberdorfer, Don, 124

Office of Civilian Operations, 87–88
Office of Rural Affairs, 109–114, 314
oil, 71, 86–87, 138, 141, 336–338
Okinawa, 142
Omarska, 174–175
Operation Enduring Freedom, 230
Operations Plan (OPLAN) 40104,
    215–218
opium crops, 290–291
Oradour, 219
Organization for Security and Coop-
    eration in Europe (OSCE),
    184–187
Orr, Robert, 3, 243–245
Orwell, George, 59, 311
Our Kind of Traitor, 13
Owen, Roberts, 228

Pacem in Terris conference, 68–69
Pacific Ocean, 140
pacification strategies, 86–91, 109–114
Paine, Thomas, 9
Pakistan
  ammonium nitrate fertilizer in, 290
  debt bondage in, 57
  democracy in, 284
  dependency culture in, 287–288
  destabilizing Afghanistan, 349
  flood relief in, 291–292
  as geostrategic challenge, 345
  Holbrooke as representative to (See
    Pakistan, Holbrooke as special
    representative for)
  India and, 288, 293, 308
  progress in, 306–308
  refugee camps in, 61
  as sanctuary for al-Qaeda and bin
    Laden, 300–301
Pakistan, Holbrooke as special
    representative for
  appointment, 281–282, 285
  blunders, 288–289
  building team to serve, 286–287
  field diplomacy, 283–284, 287
  lessons from, 283–284
  press and, 290
  Rohde kidnappings and, 294–295
  studying issues, 284–285
  successes in, 290–293
  Taliban and, 288
  transit agreement and, 290
  Washington and, 289–290
Pakistan People's Party, 306
Palais de Chaillot, 49–51

Palestine, 345
Pardew, Jim, 228
Paris, Four Power Summit in, 48–51
Paris Peace Talks on Vietnam, 11, 92, 167, 204
The Paris Review, 44
Pariser Platz, 194
Park Chung Hee, 124–125, 144
Parker, Maynard, 61
Parkinson's Law, 27, 29
Partnership for Peace (PFP), 180–182, 187–188
Pasvolsky, Leo, 258
Patterson, Anne, 57
Pax Americana, 168
PBS, 200
Peace Corps director in Morocco, Holbrooke as
    Afghanistan visit as, 282–283
    assignment as, 11
    Ellsberg visiting, 53
    French language and, 167
    writings of, 99–100
Peacemaking 1919, 37, 207
Peking, 135–136. *See also* China
Pelosi, Representative Nancy, 245, 308
Pentagon Papers, 45, 53, 58–59, 89–90
Pentagon reforms, 30–31
Perry, Secretary of Defense William, 229, 313, 342
Perseus LLC, 296
Peshawar, 306
pessimists, 322–327
Peterson, Peter, 68–69
Peterson Report, 30
Petraeus, General David, 111
pharmaceutical companies, 267
Philippines, 117, 125–126, 132–134, 137–138
Phillips, Rufus, 76, 80–83, 86
    counterinsurgency and, 80
    Diem's overthrow and, 83
    Holbrooke reporting to, 81–82
    in Vietnam, 76, 86
phone calls, usefulness of, 201
Pierce, Kitty, 47
Piot, Peter, 268
pirates attacking refugees, 118, 147–148
Placentia Bay, 252
Platt, Nicholas, 122, 125, 130–131
Pnom Penh, 102, 134, 151
Podhoretz, Norman, 322, 330
Pol Pot, 148–149, 152
Poland, 34, 181, 182

"Politics and the English Language," 59, 311
polyvalent approach, 117
Pompeii, 62
Poos, Jacques, 172
Porter, Deputy Ambassador William J., 84
Portland, Oregon, 316
Portugal, 331
post-Cold War era
    assertive multilateralism in, 246
    Bosnia providing lessons for, 207, 216, 226
    central Europe in, 179–180
    Dayton Peace Accords and, 220
    on European Continent, 201
    European security architecture in, 177–179
    peacekeeping disasters in, 227
    U.S. isolationism in, 200
Potomac fever, 16
Potsdam, 179
Powell, General Colin, 214, 226, 258
Power, Samantha, 4, 10, 312, 361
Powers, Francis Gary, 48
presidency of U.S., 29–32, 333–339.
    See also specific presidents.
President's Emergency Plan for AIDS Relief (PEPFAR), 270
Princeton University, 96
Princip, Gavrilo, 51
Provincial Reconstruction Teams, 112
public service, 92–98, 284, 295, 314
Pulitzer Prize, 260
pygmy generation, 326–327

Qatar, 292
Qishan, Wang, 340
Quakers, 165
The Quality of Mercy, 146, 148–156

Ramos-Horta, José, 207
Ramsey, Doug, 110
Randal, Jonathan, 59
Reagan, President Ronald, 160, 265, 338, 346–347, 352
Realpolitik, 19, 166
refugees
    in Bosnia, 226
    in Cambodia, 128–129
    Holbrooke on, 21
    in Indochina, 116–119
Refugees International, 14–15, 218–219
Reichstag building, 195

Republic of China, 126–127. *See also* Taiwan

Republican Party, 241. *See also* neoconservatives

Republika Srpska, 231, 234

Reston, James (Scotty), 46, 48, 50, 52, 259, 314, 320

"The Retreat of American Power," 322

Rice, Secretary of State Condoleezza, 232, 348

Richard C. Holbrooke Memorial Lecture, 292

Richardson, Bill, 244

Richetti, Steven, 244–245

The Road to the Dayton Accords foreword, 225–235

Rockefeller, Nelson, 260

Rockwell, George Lincoln, 47

Rocky Mountains, 318

Rodham, Dorothy, 222

Roedy, Bill, 267

Rogers, William, 67

Rohde, David, 56, 282–283, 293–294, 361

Roosevelt, President Franklin D., 252–260, 326, 352

Roosevelt, President Theodore, 18

Rosecrance, Richard, 322

Rosenblatt, Lionel, 116–118, 218–219

Rosenblatt, Peter, 88

Rosenthal, Abe, 46, 49, 56

Rosenthal, Jack, 212

Rubenstein, David, 10

Rubin, Barnett, 305, 315

Rugge, John, 246

Rumania, 331

Rumsfeld, Secretary of Defense Donald, 232

Rusk, David, 45, 77

Rusk, Secretary of State Dean, 27, 47, 52, 77, 81, 119, 313

Russett, Bruce, 322

Russia. *See also* Soviet Union
AIDS effort, resisting, 266
carbon emissions of, 339
Chechnya and, 186–187
Dayton Peace Accords and, 204
in European security architecture, 177
Global Business Coalition on HIV/AIDS and, 271
Holbrooke's father from, 165
instability and aggression of, 179
Kerensky in, 46
McCain on, 340, 346
NATO and, 182–183, 188
OSCE and, 186–187
petrodollar spending of, 337
in post-Cold War era, 173–174
in security architecture, European, 187–189

Russian Revolution, 32

Rwanda, 226–227, 248, 349

Safer, Morley, 76, 84

Safire, William, 122

Saigon. *See also* Vietnam
Diem's overthrow and, 83
Holbrooke arriving in, 78–79
Holbrooke's assignment to, 84–87, 314

Sainteny, Jean, 94

Sakharov, Andrei, 65, 70

San Francisco, 257–262

Sanski Most, 212

Sarajevo. *See also* Bosnia
after Dayton Peace Accords, 223
bombing of marketplace in, 220, 228
diplomatic team killed en route to, 204
Holbrooke in, 51, 198
siege of, 167, 205
as tip of Bosnian disaster, 210
unification of, 221

Saudi Arabia, 336–337

Sawyer, Diane, 56, 59

Scarsdale High School, 313

Scheffler, Karl, 195

Schlesinger, James, 323, 326, 328

Schlesinger, Jr., Arthur, 26, 71, 239

Schlesinger, Stephen, 257–262

schools, building, 80–81, 104

Schork, Kurt, 56

Schwarzenegger, Arnold, 164

Scowcroft, Brent, 346

second civil war, 106–108

security architecture, European, 176–189

Security Council. *See* UN Security Council

self-determination, 36

self-immolation by monks in Vietnam, 78

self-immolation by women in Afghanistan, 302

Senate of U.S. *See* U.S. Senate

Senior Interdepartmental Group (SIG), 25

Serbia, 37, 174
Serbs. *See* Bosnian Serbs
SFOR (NATO security force), 232
Shalikashvili, General John, 215, 229
Shantung peninsula, 36–37
Sharif, Prime Minister Nawaz, 306
Shattuck, John, 219
Shawcross, William, 146, 148–156
Shays, Chris, 244–245
Sheehan, Neil, 84
Shiites, 302
Shriver, Sargent, 119
Shultz, Secretary of State George, 342
Shura, 21
Sideshow: Kissinger, Nixon, and the
     Destruction of Cambodia, 146
Silajdzic, Prime Minister Haris, 205
Sindh province, 57
Singh, Vikram, 286
Skinner, E. Benjamin, 44, 361–362
Smiley, George, 13
Smith, Admiral Leighton, 231
Smith, Congressman Chris, 242,
     244–245
Smith, Edie, 110
Smith, Gaddis, 144
Smith, Gary, 171
Soc Trang airport, 82
Solarz, Stephen J., 117–118
Somalia, 215, 227, 244, 248, 253–254,
     298, 349
Soros, George, 248
South Asia, 287, 293
South China Sea, 136, 147–150
South Korea. *See also* Korea
     1980 massacre in, 129
     Carter and, 123–124, 143–145
     Carter's campaign promises on,
          352–353
     as model for U.S. involvement in
          Iraq, 343–344
     nation building in, 298
South Vietnam, 102, 322. *See also*
     Vietnam
Soviet Backfire bomber, 326
Soviet Union. *See also* Russia
     Africa and, 330–331
     Budapest's Chain Bridge and, 192
     China and, 126–127, 137–140, 161
     detente with, 65–66
     dissolution of, 176–177
     Four Power Summit and, 48–50
     history not favoring, 331
     importing food, 329–330

     invading Czechoslovakia, 168
     rejecting Marshall Plan, 178
     in UN Security Council, 258
Srebrenica. *See also* Bosnia
     massacre in, 202, 227
     Mladić attacking, 218–220
     Rohde discovering mass grave in,
          293–294
     ten years after massacre in, 233–234
Stalin, 40, 258–259, 260
State Department
     Brzezinski vs., 127
     criticisms of, 25–26
     death of delegates to Bosnia from,
          166, 204
     death of Holbrooke at, 8, 61, 283
     formation of UN and, 258–259
     Historian's Office of, 76
     Holbrooke at, 20–21, 359
     Holbrooke joining, 168, 284
     Holbrooke succeeding at, 58, 91, 119
     human rights and, 129
     ideal role of, 32
     Kissinger wooing, 67–71
     Obama at, 281
     reforming, 31
     on repaying U.S. debt to UN,
          242–243
     Srebrenica and, 219
     Taiwan Relations Act by, 160
Steiner, George, 156
Stern, Fritz, 13, 168–172
Stern, Larry, 70
Stettinius, Secretary of State
     Edward R., 256, 259–260
Stevens, Jr., George, 10, 222
Stevens, Liz, 54, 222
Stevenson, Adlai, 259, 261–262
Strategic Arms Reduction Treaty
     (START), 188
Subic Bay Naval Base, 125–126, 138
Sudan, 261, 349–350
Sukarno, 134
Sullivan, Larrine, 47, 82–85
Sulzberger, C. L., 322–323
Summers, Larry, 9, 22
Swift Boat Veterans for Truth, 106

Taipei, 126–127
Taiwan, 121, 126–128, 132, 138,
     159–161
Taiwan Relations Act, 160
Talbott, Strobe, 8, 10, 40–41, 201, 222,
     362

Talese, Gay, 44, 52
Taliban
drug-eradication effort strengthening, 303–305
evicting from Kabul, 20
Karzai negotiating with, 291
kidnapping Rohde, 294–295
liberating Afghanistan from, 301
Musharraf's peace deal with, 308
objectives of, 348
opium crops and, 290–291
in Pakistan, 288, 300–302
Pakistani elections and, 306
U.S. officials negotiating with, 292
Tarnoff, Peter, 85–86, 93, 110, 122–124, 201
Taylor, General Maxwell, 80
Tedstrom, John, 264, 362
Tehran, 214. See also Iran
Tempo, 137
Tennyson, Lord Alfred, 260
Terminator, 164
terror, war on. See war on terror
Tet Offensive, 91, 94
Thailand, 116–117, 137, 145, 150–151
Thiessen, Pam, 241–242
Thieu, Nguyen Van, 322
A Thousand Days, 26
Tiananmen, 158
Tibet, 128, 173–174
Time magazine, 157–158
Tinker, Tailor, Soldier, Spy, 13
Tito, Marshal, 37
To End a War, 59, 207–208, 214
Tobias, Randall, 280
Tokyo, 118. See also Japan
Tolstoy, Leo, 13
"The Topography of Terror," 194
Transatlantic Partners Against AIDS (TPAA), 271
Traub, James, 3, 240, 362
Travel + Leisure, 45, 190–193
Treaty at Versailles, 34–35, 177
Truman Doctrine, 177
Truman, President Harry S., 24, 133, 256, 257–262
tuberculosis, 271
Tudjman, President Franjo, 203
Tuol Sleng, 148
Turkey, 345
Turner, Ted, 248
Turtle Bay. See UN, Holbrooke as U.S. ambassador to UN

Tuzla, 218–219
Tyler, Patrick, 127

U-2 spy plane downing, 48–50
The Ugly American, 109
Ukraine, 173, 187–189
UN, Holbrooke as U.S. ambassador to. See also United Nations (UN)
African diplomacy under, 243, 247–249
campaigning for debt repayment, 241
China's trade status and, 244
conclusions about, 250
first major speech as, 251–256
reputation of U.S. and, 240, 250
Senate Foreign Relations Committee and, 244, 249–250
weddings while, 315
UN Security Council
in Africa, 266
on AIDS, 3, 266–268
Annan at, 239
in Balkans, acting without, 261–262
Helms at, 249–250
Pasvolsky and, 258
UN (United Nations). See United Nations (UN)
UNAIDS (Joint UN Programme on HIV/AIDS), 268–270
UNICEF, 149, 153–154, 261
United Nations High Commission on Refugees (U.N.H.C.R.), 153–155
United Nations (UN)
in Africa, 351
on AIDS, 248
American leadership in, 341–342
Bosnia, failing in, 227, 248, 253–254
Bosnia, inaction on, 210–211, 226
Cambodian refugee relief effort of, 150–151, 153–155
Charter of, 143, 258
Dayton Peace Accords and, 204
Holbrooke as ambassador to (See UN, Holbrooke as U.S. ambassador to)
Kissinger at, 68
Last Best Hope on, 257–262
League of Democracies vs., 341
on opium crops in Afghanistan, 301
OPLAN 40104 and, 215–218
OSCE under, 186
peacekeepers spreading HIV/AIDS, 265

peacekeeping missions of, 209, 253–254
reforming, 254–255
repaying U.S. debt to, 130, 313, 342
Security Council of (*See* UN Security Council)
Srebrenica and, 227
Truman signing charter of, 257–262
U.S. acting independently of, 253
U.S. national security and, 251–256
United States Information Agency (USIA), 24–25, 30
United States Operation Mission (USOM), 78–79
United States (U.S.)
Bosnia, inaction on, 226
carbon emissions of, 338–339
Congress of (*See* U.S. Congress)
foreign policy of (*See* foreign policy of U.S.)
Foreign Service of (*See* U.S. Foreign Service)
at Four Power Summit, 48–51
governmental seat of (*See* Washington, D.C.)
leadership of (*See* U.S. leadership)
presidency of (*See* presidency of U.S.)
Senate of (*See* U.S. Senate)
State Department of (*See* State Department)
UN leadership of, 261–262, 341–342
U.S. Agency for International Development (USAID), 109, 290
U.S. Congress
administration loyalists vs., 102
after Dayton Peace Accords, 226–229
aid to Afghanistan, 292, 302
aid to Angola, 330–331
Black Caucus, 272
essential support of, 334
Indochinese refugees and, 117–118, 129–130
Jackson Amendment and, 70
new pessimists on, 323–324
repaying debt to UN, 130, 241–250, 253–255
State Department and, 32
Vietnam War and, 102
U.S. Foreign Relations Committee, 66–70, 244, 249–250, 259–260
U.S. Foreign Service
criticisms of, 26
Holbrooke in, 19, 52–53, 110

Holbrooke joining, 313–314
Institute, 312
Kennan in, 39–41
Kissinger and, 67
reforming, 31
training program for, 78
U.S. leadership
after World War II, 177
in Bosnia, 228
in Cambodian refugee crisis, 155
Dayton Peace Accords and, 208, 220
immediate tests of, 12–13
new pessimists on demise of, 322
U.S. Mission to the UN, 313
U.S. News and World Report, 323
U.S. Rangers, 246
U.S. Senate
on CIA, 340–341
confirming Holbrooke as UN ambassador, 240
Copenhagen agreement and, 339
Foreign Relations Committee of (*See* U.S. Foreign Relations Committee)
formation of UN and, 259–260
NATO membership and, 183
Wilsonian foreign policy vs., 35–36
U.S. Seventh Fleet, 147–148

Vance, Secretary of State Cyrus, 16, 21, 55, 92, 126–127, 152, 160, 353
Vandenberg, Senator Arthur, 256, 259–260
Vann, Lieutenant Colonel John Paul, 53
Venezuela, 337
Versailles, 34–35
Vest, George, 68
Vietnam
Afghanistan and, 94–95, 287–288
Americanization of war in, 84–87
Bosnia and, 229
Cambodia invasion by, 129–130, 149
China invading, 157–158
containment policy and, 168
counterinsurgency strategies in, 79–82
Dayton Peace Accords and, 206
Diem's overthrow in, 83
escalation of involvement in, 284–285
Holbrooke assigned to, 52–53, 79–80, 314
Holbrooke's writings on, 45

Vietnam *(continued)*
  legacy of, 76–77, 92–98, 104–105
  as longest war, 349
  lying vs. self-deceit of U.S. about,
    99–100
  nation-building failure in, 298
  North (*See* North Vietnam)
  pacification strategies in, 87–91,
    101–105
  Paris Peace Talks on (*See* Paris Peace
    Talks on Vietnam)
  Pentagon affected by, 214–215
  political climate in U.S. after, 65
  as political litmus test, 319–320
  precedent of, 19–20
  press and, 59
  refugees in, 147–148, 149–150
  as second U.S. civil war, 106–108
  South (*See* South Vietnam)
  Soviet Union and, 331
  unification of, 136
  why it matters, 109–114
Vietnamese News Agency (VNA), 55
Voice of America, 351
von Humboldt, Wilhelm, 170

Waldheim, UN Secretary-General,
    153–154
Waldorf Astoria, 239, 241
Wallace, Mike, 118
Walt, General Lewis, 87, 101–105
Walters, Barbara, 136, 248
Wang Keping, 128
Wannsee River, 171, 194
war on terror
  Afghanistan's role in, 299
  Bush declaring, 20, 334
  Pakistan and, 292
Washington, D.C. *See also* United
    States (U.S.)
  9/11 in, 227
  Chirac in, 216
  Congress in (*See* U.S. Congress)
  George Washington University
    Hospital in, 11, 318
  HIV/AIDS in, 272
  Holbrooke as assistant secretary of
    state for European affairs in, 201
  Holbrooke as UN ambassador in,
    242–250
  Holbrooke criticizing, 16–17, 287
  Holbrooke on impact of, 313–314
  Holbrooke's residence in, 53
  Karzai in, 291

Kennedy Center in, 306
  machine of, 22–33, 287
  National Press Club in, 251
  Nixon returning to, 161
  orthodox thinking in, 41
  power to do good of, 314
  Senate in (*See* U.S. Senate)
  Vietnam War Memorial in, 77
Washington, Denzel, 248
Washington Post
  on Afghanistan, 20
  on Carter's withdrawal of troops
    from Korea, 124
  Holbrooke's column in, 55, 59
  on Karzai, 288
  on Khost province, 285
Watergate, 321–322, 331
Waziristan, 300–301
wealth transfer, 336–337
Weisman, Steven, 60
Welles, Sumner, 256
Westmoreland, General William, 85,
    90–91
Weston, Kael, 112
Weygand, Bob, 243
White House. *See administrations of
    specific presidents.*
Whitman, Marina, 145, 329
WHO (World Health Organization),
    261, 269–270, 274, 280
Wiesel, Elie, 248
Wilhelm II, Kaiser, 194
Williams, C. K., 171
Wilson, President Woodrow, 18, 35,
    166, 177, 191
wiretapping, 66
Wisner, Jr., Frank, 10, 85–86, 88, 93,
    110, 118–119, 127
Wisner, Paul, 53
women's issues
  in Afghanistan, 284, 301–302
  health, 270, 279–280
  in Pakistan, 308
Wood, William, 304
Woodard, Alfre, 248
Woodcock, Leonard, 127
Woodrow Wilson School, 96
Woodward, Bob, 40, 216
World AIDS Day, 274, 276,
    278–279
World Policy Institute, 257
World Trade Organization, 187
World War I, 36, 191–192. *See also*
    Wilson, President Woodrow

World War II
    Asia after, 132–133
    Asian-American relations after,
        120–121
    European security architecture after,
        177–178
    Moos in, 169–170
    signing of UN charter and, 257
    today's challenges vs., 333
wounded veterans, 340
Wright-Patterson Air Force Base, 204,
    220, 225
writing, Holbrooke's appreciation for,
    170, 310–311

"X" article, 39–40
Xa Loi Pagoda, 79

Yalta, 179
"Yankee Go Home," 63

Yeltsin, President Boris, 188,
    221–223
Yergin, Daniel, 336
Yom Kippur war, 141
Yugoslavia
    dissolution of, 208
    ethnic cleansing in aftermath of,
        209–211
    Kennan on, 41
    Soviet Union and, 331
    unraveling of, 200
    World War I impact on, 37

Zagreb, 212
Zardari, President Asif Ali, 306, 308
Zepa, 218–219
Zhou Enlai, 157
Zimbabwe, 341
Zorthian, Barry, 84
Zuckerman, Mort, 242

PublicAffairs is a publishing house founded in 1997. It is a tribute to the standards, values, and flair of three persons who have served as mentors to countless reporters, writers, editors, and book people of all kinds, including me.

I. F. STONE, proprietor of *I. F. Stone's Weekly*, combined a commitment to the First Amendment with entrepreneurial zeal and reporting skill and became one of the great independent journalists in American history. At the age of eighty, Izzy published *The Trial of Socrates*, which was a national bestseller. He wrote the book after he taught himself ancient Greek.

BENJAMIN C. BRADLEE was for nearly thirty years the charismatic editorial leader of *The Washington Post*. It was Ben who gave the *Post* the range and courage to pursue such historic issues as Watergate. He supported his reporters with a tenacity that made them fearless and it is no accident that so many became authors of influential, best-selling books.

ROBERT L. BERNSTEIN, the chief executive of Random House for more than a quarter century, guided one of the nation's premier publishing houses. Bob was personally responsible for many books of political dissent and argument that challenged tyranny around the globe. He is also the founder and longtime chair of Human Rights Watch, one of the most respected human rights organizations in the world.

•　　•　　•

For fifty years, the banner of Public Affairs Press was carried by its owner Morris B. Schnapper, who published Gandhi, Nasser, Toynbee, Truman, and about 1,500 other authors. In 1983, Schnapper was described by *The Washington Post* as "a redoubtable gadfly." His legacy will endure in the books to come.

Peter Osnos, Founder and Editor-at-Large